Psychology of Emotion

Since the turn of the twenty-first century, the psychology of emotion has grown to become its own field of study. Because the study of emotion draws inspiration from areas of science outside of psychology, including neuroscience, psychiatry, biology, genetics, computer science, zoology, and behavioral economics, the field is now often called emotion science or affective science. A subfield of affective science is affective neuroscience, the study of the emotional brain.

This revised second edition of *Psychology of Emotion* reviews both theory and methods in emotion science, discussing findings about the brain; the function, expression, and regulation of emotion; similarities and differences due to gender and culture; the relationship between emotion and cognition; and emotion processes in groups.

Comprehensive in its scope yet eminently readable, *Psychology of Emotion* serves as an ideal introduction for undergraduate students to the scientific study of emotion. It features effective learning devices such as bolded key terms, developmental details boxes, learning links, tables, graphs, and illustrations. In addition, a robust companion website offers instructor resources.

Paula M. Niedenthal is Professor of Psychology and director of the Niedenthal Emotions Lab at the University of Wisconsin-Madison. Her research crosses the areas of the psychology of emotion and the affective neurosciences, and focuses on the ways by which individuals represent and process emotional information.

François Ric is Professor of Psychology and laboratory director at the Université de Bordeaux. His research focuses on the underlying processes of social behaviors, with a special interest in the role of emotions, and in implicit processes.

Psychology of Emotion

Second Edition

**Paula M. Niedenthal
and François Ric**

Routledge
Taylor & Francis Group

NEW YORK AND LONDON

Second edition published 2017
by Routledge
711 Third Avenue, New York, NY 10017

and by Routledge
2 Park Square, Milton Park, Abingdon, Oxon, OX14 4RN

Routledge is an imprint of the Taylor & Francis Group, an informa business

[First edition published by Routledge 2006]

Library of Congress Cataloging in Publication Data
Names: Niedenthal, Paula M., author. | Ric, François, author.
Title: Psychology of emotion : interpersonal, experiential, and cognitive approaches / by
    Paula M. Niedenthal and François Ric.
Description: Second Edition. | New York : Routledge, 2017. | "First edition published by
    Routledge 2006". | Includes bibliographical references and index.
Identifiers: LCCN 2016033789 | ISBN 9781848725119 (hb : alk. paper) |
    ISBN 9781848725126 (pb : alk. paper) | ISBN 9781315276229 (e)
Subjects: LCSH: Emotions.
Classification: LCC BF511 .N534 2017 | DDC 152.4—dc23
LC record available at https://lccn.loc.gov/2016033789

ISBN: 978-1-84872-511-9 (hbk)
ISBN: 978-1-84872-512-6 (pbk)
ISBN: 978-1-315-27622-9 (ebk)

Typeset in Times
by Apex CoVantage, LLC
Printed and bound by CPI Group (UK) Ltd, Croydon, CR0 4YY

Visit the companion website: www.routledge.com/cw/Niedenthal

Contents

Acknowledgements

The first edition of the *Psychology of Human Emotion* was a textbook written for doctoral students of social psychology in European countries. The task of revising the book for a second edition, this time targeted at undergraduate psychology majors in North America, was a monumental undertaking. Not only did the textbook require stronger organization and far greater accessibility, but research findings that had been published since 2006 also had to be incorporated.

We could never have accomplished the feat of revising (or, more accurately, writing anew) this textbook without, first, the tireless help of Crystal Hanson. Crystal performed the herculean tasks of referencing; creating tables and figures; proofreading; managing information, communication, and personnel involved in the project; and basically being a production manager. Thank you, Crystal, and don't move too far away.

In the middle of the revision project, we lost the involvement of one of the former co-authors. In order to pick up the slack, we signed on (for pay!) Evie Rosset, who helped with detailed outlines of the Happiness chapter; Mathias Hibbard, who did the same for the Brain chapter; Sebastian Korb, who took Mathias's outline and wrote the entire first draft of that Brain chapter; and Adrienne Wood, who researched and largely revised the Emotional Expression chapter. Stephanie Carpenter read and commented on multiple chapters and suggested additions of missing concepts and findings to the Emotion Regulation chapter. Jared Martin helped us write and refine discussions of the physiology of emotion. All but one of these people are (or were) students, graduate students, or postdocs at the University of Wisconsin-Madison, and they are all amazing. We are indebted to you.

Throughout the revisions, we also received considerable help from the undergraduate research assistants in the Niedenthal Emotions Lab. These wonderful students include Jay Graiziger, Sarah Hevrdejs, George Perrett, Emma Phillips, Adam Sitter, and Olivia (Fangyun) Zhao.

Colleagues and scientists in the field read individual chapters and provided invaluable feedback. These include Janet Hyde, Yuri Miyamoto, James Russell, Magdalena Rychlowska, and Eliot Smith. Thank you so much for that help.

In order to improve the readability of the textbook, we hired two exceptional editors who live and work in Madison, Wisconsin. Ann Schaffer and Timothy Storm pointed out, commented, nudged, encouraged, suggested, and even rewrote. Ann and Tim, we are forever grateful.

Our families suffered through our grumpy and sometimes absent moments with great humor and resourcefulness. We love you.

Finally, one of our mothers Corrine Niedenthal, became ill during the revision of the textbook. She passed away during its production, and was the best mother in the world, and we dedicate the book to her.

How to Use This Book

The *Psychology of Emotion*, Second Edition, is intended to introduce undergraduate students to the scientific study of emotion. Since the turn of the twenty-first century, this endeavor has become its own field of study. Because the study of emotion draws inspiration from areas of science outside of psychology, including neuroscience, psychiatry, biology, genetics, computer science, zoology, and behavioral economics, the field is now often called **emotion science** or **affective science** (terms we use interchangeably). A subfield of affective science is affective neuroscience, the study of the emotional brain.

The explosion of ideas and research findings in emotion science created a quandary for the present authors. We had to decide what the book was going to include and not include. Because of our combined expertise in social psychology, cognitive science, and social cognition, we decided to focus the textbook on emotion in the typically developing individual. In other words, our textbook does not include chapters on emotion and mental health (e.g., affective disorders). Also, we focus largely on processes basic to emotion. We chose to omit historical and philosophical analyses in favor of summarizing and interpreting contemporary scientific methods and discoveries. We do believe it is important to provide students with that intellectual groundwork. However, as university professors who teach courses on the psychology of emotion, we find we prefer to present such material in lecture.

Lest the reader wonder what remains: a lot. Our chapters review theory and methods in emotion science; we discuss findings about the brain and the function, expression, and regulation of emotion; we delve into similarities and differences due to gender and culture; we examine the relationship between emotion and cognition; and we account for emotion processes in groups. We have made every effort to organize, prioritize, and interpret the meaning of the research findings featured in each chapter. We have also added some effective learning and teaching devices. In particular, each chapter includes:

- Bolded key terms, which flag concepts students should master.
- Developmental Details boxes, which zoom in on chapter topics as they relate to a point in the life cycle, most often infancy or childhood.
- Learning Links, which are suggested Internet sites that provide illustrations of or enrichment ideas about topics addressed in each chapter. (The links were active as of 2016. Should they become inactive, please use the information provided to locate the same material on a new site.)
- Tables, graphs, illustrations, and comics designed to expand on the chapter discussions.

Enjoy.

1   Theories of Emotion

Contents at a Glance

Imagine what your life would be like if you could not experience emotion. What if you felt no joy at seeing a newborn baby and no pride upon receiving a long worked-for diploma? What if you felt no anger and no fear when you heard that a terrorist attack had occurred in your country? What if you felt no jealousy at seeing a boyfriend or girlfriend flirt with someone else at a party, and you felt no awe when standing on the rim of the Grand Canyon? What would your life be like then? Would we even call it human life? And could human life indeed exist if we felt no emotion?

Perhaps life without emotion would still seem human if you believed that emotions were undesirable states, reflecting animalistic vestiges of our evolutionary past. A theme in philosophy for many hundreds of years was that emotions, or passions as they were sometimes called, were at odds with the more desirable and lofty processes of reason (Solomon, 1976, 1993). A wide range of philosophers, including Plato, the Stoics (Zeno de Citium, Epictetus, and Marcus Aurelius, among others), and Descartes, argued that reasoning and having emotions were antithetical to each other. They viewed reason as a uniquely human achievement and a virtue. In contrast, they viewed emotions as the province of animals (and sometimes women and children!), as primitive drives that interfered with reason. Even in today's world, people in some cultures consider displays of emotion, particularly in public places, as undesirable and as casting doubt on the psychological health of the person expressing emotions. Of course, in other cultures, public expression of emotion is so commonplace it attracts no attention at all.

These days most emotion scientists believe that emotions are absolutely essential to human life and we could not survive without them (Barrett & Salovey, 2002; Damasio, 1999; Fredrickson, 2001; Keltner & Haidt, 2001; Mehu & Dunbar, 2008; Niedenthal & Brauer, 2012). As you will see throughout this book, emotions hold people together in relationships and social groups; help to determine priorities within relationships; signal to the person experiencing the emotion the state of her relation to the environment; and are an important part of the functional evolution of our nervous systems, attentional processes, decision making, communication, and behavioral regulation.

This textbook introduces you to the psychology of emotion. Because our aim is to show you how hypotheses and predictions about emotion are tested with the tools of science, we will also refer to the science of emotion. In the present chapter you will learn how emotion scientists define emotions as well as the principles of the major theoretical approaches to the topic of emotion. Chapter 2 introduces you to the tools of the science of emotion. You will learn how to induce emotions and measure their occurrence. Part of having emotion involves events that take place in the brain. After learning about methods for imaging the brain, Chapter 3 then introduces you to the main neural circuitry and chemistry that support our emotional responding. We have already noted that emotion scientists believe that emotions are functional, and Chapter 4 shows you how that is so. One of the functions of emotions is to communicate to others, and Chapter 5 discusses the expression of emotion on the face as well as through the body and voice. In Chapters 6 and 7 you will learn about the more complex self-conscious emotions and the very popular emotion of happiness, respectively. Chapter 8 details the many relationships between emotion and other mental processes such as attention, memory, and decision making. Some of the relationships are related to the strategies that people use to control or regulate their emotions, which are summarized in Chapter 9. Lest you think that emotions are a personal affair, Chapter 10 reviews research on how people share emotions in groups and have emotions due to the fact that they are members of groups. And speaking of groups, there is variation in how people express and to some degree experience their emotions as a function of gender (Chapter 11) and culture (Chapter 12) as well.

Because most everyone has emotions, you might feel that you are already an expert on emotion. But scientific findings have a way of surprising you. When it comes to something as important and weighty as emotion, it helps to look at the findings of basic research; you might just learn something about yourself! In order to begin this discovery, though, we need to begin with a definition of our topic.

Definitions of Emotion

In psychology, we find it useful to distinguish between different types of mental states and their associated behaviors. For instance, some scientists study learning, or memory, or perception, or the focus of this book, emotions. In reality, all of these processes are occurring simultaneously and influencing one another so that it can be quite difficult to determine, for instance, where perception "ends" and cognition "begins," or what behavior is driven by emotion versus some other mental state. It is impossible to truly isolate a single mental process, and most processes, from scratching your nose to falling in love, involve complex neural systems working in synchrony. Similarly, feeling an emotion like fear depends on the ability to *perceive* something in the world, *remember* it as a threat, and *act* to escape it. In turn, an emotion such as fear has powerful influences on the content and structure of other cognitive and behavioral processes.

Given how intertwined emotions are with other mental and behavioral states, how do scientists even begin to define them?

A simple way to distinguish between emotions and other mental processes is to consider their function (see Chapter 4). We have big, wrinkly brains that allow us to compose sonnets, raise children, tell jokes, and invent wheels; but none of these cognitively complex tasks would be accomplished if we were not motivated—motivated to survive, have fun, explore, avoid danger, connect with one another, and all the other things we want in life. Emotions are the fire that fuels human behavior and the driving motivational forces in life.

The first step in the science of emotion is settling on a more specific definition of the term. Keltner and Gross define emotions as "episodic, relatively short-term, biologically-based patterns of perception, experience, physiology, action, and communication that occur in response to specific physical and social challenges and opportunities" (Keltner & Gross, 1999, p. 468). This definition is not simple, nor is it accepted by all scientists or interpreted by all scientists in the same way. It does, however, narrow our focus to relatively brief states that arise in response to an object or event. The important thing is that emotions are responses to things, people, and events we encounter in the world and to our own thoughts. They are not affective disorders, personality temperaments, or moods. In addition, this definition acknowledges that emotions can be functional. That is, emotions help people attract the right things and protect themselves from the wrong things. Put in another way, "Emotions are a kind of radar and rapid response system, constructing and carrying meaning across the flow of experience. Emotions are the tools by which we appraise experience and prepare to act on situations" (Cole, Martin, & Dennis, 2004, p. 319).

Theories of Emotion

Before you can evaluate the scientific study of emotion and understand why researchers have conducted research as they have, you need to be familiar with the major theories of emotion. Theories of emotion are testable statements about exactly how emotions come about. To understand what we mean by this, let's examine a theory that was famously proposed by Schachter and Singer (1962): the **Two-Factor Theory** of emotion. Schachter and Singer claimed that emotions come about through the combination of 1) autonomic arousal—caused by almost anything; and 2) a label that describes the experience in terms of the current situation. The theory is depicted in Figure 1.1.

As an example of how this theory explains emotions, imagine you and your friend both drink a highly caffeinated beverage that makes you both very aroused, causing your heart rate to increase and your palms to sweat. Now imagine that you are teleported to a wedding in a fun location. Meanwhile, your friend is teleported to the edge of a cliff. The Two-Factor Theory predicts that you would label yourself "happy" and enjoy the full experience of joy, whereas your friend would label herself as "afraid" and experience fear. Your arousal would get labeled by the nature of the circumstances you found yourself in, and an emotion would result. According to the Two-Factor Theory, this is all we need to know about emotions.

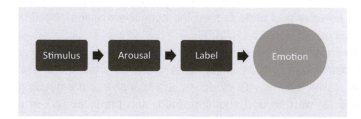

Figure 1.1 A schematic diagram of Schachter and Singer's (1962) Two-Factor Theory of emotion.

Contemporary emotion scientists believe that there is more to emotions than arousal and labels, and we will discuss three other ways to explain how emotions happen. The theories we consider in this chapter are evolutionary theories, appraisal theories, and psychological constructionist theories. To compare the specific ideas and preoccupations of the distinct groups of theories, we need to understand each one's claim about:

1)   The **antecedents** of an emotion (what causes them)
2)   The **biological givens** (innate emotional capacities)
3)   The **integration** of emotional experience (how components of emotion fit together)

As we investigate theories of emotion in this chapter, keep in mind that the various theories are not equally concerned about addressing each claim. In an oversimplification we could say that, that traditional appraisal theories are most focused on antecedents, evolutionary theories on biological givens, and psychological constructionists on how learning and experience cause the integration of emotional experience. Nonetheless, we will attempt to explain what roles emotion antecedents, biological givens, and integration play in each theory.

Developmental Detail

What Is a Developmental Theory of Emotion?

Developmental theories of emotion both acknowledge that emotional development is partly preprogrammed in the organism and recognize that all aspects of emotion are responsive to the context in which the child is developing. That is, our emotions incorporate social experience, including cultural rules and norms (Saarni et al., 2008). In developmental theories, then, both **nature** (genes) and **nurture** (experience) make possible the full differentiation and elaboration of emotional life (Pollak, 2013).

A developmental perspective on emotion involves more than documenting the ages at which the components of emotion are first observed in infants and children and charting their course over the life cycle. A complete developmental theory associates the unfolding of the components of emotion with that of many other skills and capacities (Saarni, 2008). These include maturation of the visual and motor systems and the acquisition of complex cognitive capacities, such as the ability to represent the self as an object of thought. For example, the behavioral and physiological components of fear rely on having a body with response systems that are mature enough to detect danger and run away. Similarly, as we discover in Chapter 5, emotions such as envy and pride require the cognitive abilities of self-reflection and social comparison (Lewis, 2007).

An important social context for the development of emotion and emotional competencies (such as empathy) is the initial attachment relationship with a caretaker. If an infant's caregiver is responsive to her needs (including the needs for warmth and soothing, food, and predictability), she learns that the world is a safe place and that other people can be trusted. From this relational base, future emotional relationships can be launched. The experience of having needs met also supports the healthy development of neural and endocrine systems for emotion (Pollak, 2012).

Now that you are oriented to the challenges of investigating emotion over the life cycle, pay attention to the Developmental Detail box in every chapter of this book. Each one illustrates how an understanding of the subject of the chapter (e.g., brain, emotional expression) benefits from a developmental perspective.

Evolutionary Theories

Evolutionary theories of emotion are based in the writings of Charles Darwin (Darwin, 1872/1998). Darwin was interested in using facial expression of emotion to support his general theory of evolution by natural selection. Facial expression was particularly useful for developing his theory because the continuity of expression across species of animals was relatively easy for him to document. Darwin examined the emotional displays of animals and compared them to humans. He also solicited information from missionaries living outside of his native England to examine the possibility that the same facial expressions of emotion were found all over the world. Darwin believed that the results of his studies demonstrated cross-species continuity and universality of a number of facial expressions of emotions. Based on these types of observations, he developed hypotheses about the causes of emotional expressions.

Darwin thought that facial expressions came about because they were **serviceable habits**, or gestures that solved whatever problem elicited in the first place. For example, exposure to contamination (e.g., poison, decaying food) is a problem of survival because contamination can kill you. Fortunately, such exposure causes disgust, which serves to shut you off from further contact with potentially harmful substances; it is designed to expel things from the mouth and to prevent the intake of odors through the nose (e.g., Susskind et al., 2008). These days, individuals do not have to worry too much about ingesting a food or drink that is dangerous. However, because in our evolutionary past the facial gesture associated with expulsion was serviceable, we still make this grimace when we encounter things, such as dog feces, that generate feelings of disgust.

Darwin also proposed a communicative function of facial expression. Specifically, he suggested that facial expressions tell members of the same species how the expresser is feeling. Such communication is useful because the feelings of another person provide important information about the current situation and about what actions might be required to deal with it. If you see that someone looks happy, you typically want to begin doing what she is doing. Darwin did not conduct scientific studies of the communicative function of facial expression, but many scientists subsequently did (Buck, 1983; Buck et al., 1992; Ekman & Friesen, 1971, 1975; Horstmann, 2003; Keltner & Kring, 1998; Marsh & Ambady, 2007).

Causes of Emotion: Adaptive Challenges and Opportunities

In evolutionary theory, **adaptive problems**—challenges to survival and opportunities for reproduction—emotions that result in actions designed by evolution to solve the problem (Cosmides & Tooby, 2000; Tooby & Cosmidis, 1990). High cliffs and wild predators, for example, have repeatedly threatened survival (Öhman, 1986). Because they signal that a problem

Table 1.1 Plutchik's theory of actions (behaviors) that respond successfully to fundamental life challenges and opportunities and the emotions that motivate the actions

Emotions and Adaptive Problems			
Adaptive Problem	*Emotion*	*Behavior*	*Outcome*
Threat	Fear, terror	Running away or flying away	Protection
Obstacle	Anger, rage	Biting, hitting	Destruction
Potential mate	Joy, ecstasy	Courting, mating	Reproduction
Loss of valued person	Sadness, grief	Crying for help	Reintegration
Group member	Acceptance, trust	Grooming, sharing	Affiliation
Gruesome object	Disgust, loathing	Vomiting, pushing away	Rejection
New territory	Anticipation	Examining, mapping	Exploration
Sudden novel object	Surprise	Stopping, alerting	Orientation

for survival is being experienced cause, these signs of danger are called **signal stimuli** (and sometimes **biologically prepared** stimuli). A potential mate is also a signal stimulus. Signal in theory have the same survival meaning for all people, and they reliably cause a particular emotion because that emotion confers an adaptive benefit (Öhman & Mineka, 2001). The benefit goes beyond the function of facial expression. In theory, emotions are associated with **action tendencies**, which make the person ready to perform specific behaviors to successfully address challenges and take advantage of opportunities (Frijda, 1986). The term "action tendency," rather than "action," is intended to suggest that the action is not inevitable. It could be adapted to best fit the specific situation, or even prevented from occurring if necessary.

Researchers have defined adaptive problems for humans by looking at animal behavior. What do animals face in their environment, and what actions do they take to survive? Drawing on Scott's (1958) analysis, Plutchik (1980, 1984) enumerated the actions that reflect stereotypical responses to problems of adaptation. He then tried to show how specific emotions motivate the actions that respond successfully to the problems. The actions and their corresponding emotions are listed in Table 1.1. You can see that signal stimuli that represent the possibility for mating and bonding cause positive emotions such as joy and acceptance (or love). These emotions then generate a set of responses that make the mating and bonding actually happen. When threats occur, fear and anger occur, and those two emotions motivate appropriate action for the threat conditions, either withdrawing or attacking, respectively.

Many of the behaviors described by Plutchik involve responding to opportunities and threats to reproduction. However, it is a mistake to classify adaptive problems in terms of short-term survival of the individual. The concern of evolution, according to most current theories, is the survival of the gene. That means a particular feature of a species' neural architecture will spread over generations because it enhances the possibility of dealing successfully with recurring reproductive opportunities (such as the appearance of a potential mate) or, alternatively, threats to reproduction (such as the appearance of a sexual rival).

Also, these opportunities and threats are not limited to a small number of behaviors such as sex, violence, and eating. Rather, an evolutionary approach to emotion requires an ongoing, meticulous, give-and-take mapping of different adaptive problems to the structure and function of the emotions.

Biological Givens: Basic Emotions

Silvan Tomkins (1962, 1963), and subsequently Carroll Izard (1977, 2007) and Paul Ekman (1992), theorized about the biological bases of emotions from the perspective of evolutionary theory. They endorsed the existence of a small set of emotions, which they called **basic**

emotions. Basic emotions are innate neural and bodily states that are elicited rapidly and unintentionally—automatically—by the signal stimuli we just learned about (cf. Buck, 1999; Ekman, 1994; Izard, 1977; Johnson-Laird & Oatley, 1992; MacLean, 1993; Öhman & Mineka, 2001; Panksepp, 1998). Because no one has ever opened the body and head and found something like a basic emotion inside, theorists have had to propose testable criteria for classifying an emotion as basic. Such criteria now include:

- Universal expressions, which may involve more than just the face (e.g., the voice)
- Discrete physiology
- Presence in other primates
- Automatic appraisals or evaluations of the environment

This list means that if you take everything you ever considered to be an emotion (joy, sadness, jealousy, guilt), only those that are identifiable by a bodily and facial response, have a specific signature in the body's physiology, appear in nonhuman primates, and involve predictable assessments of the environment get to be called basic emotions. Because scientists have not yet tested these features for all emotions, there is not yet a definitive set of basic emotions. Based on existing research, however, the emotions of fear, disgust, anger, surprise, joy, and sadness have been called basic. Those six are represented by the distinct facial expressions shown in Figure 1.2. The emotion of contempt has been included as a seventh basic emotion (Ekman, 1999). More recently, researchers have also found evidence at least for the universal expression of other emotions such as shame and pride (Chapter 5; Tracy & Robins, 2004), whereas others argue that disgust and surprise should not count as emotions (Ortony & Turner, 1990; Panksepp, 2007). As you can see, the list of so-called basic emotions changes as science moves forward.

The evidence used to support the existence of six or seven basic emotions comes from tests of the first two criteria in the previous list, namely on the universality of facial expression and the differentiation of patterning in the automatic nervous system.

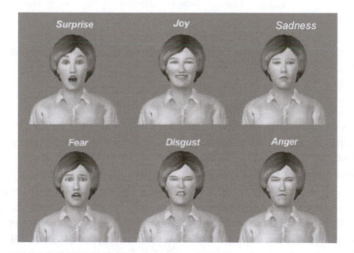

Figure 1.2 The expressions of the six basic emotions.

In Chapter 5 you'll read about evidence suggesting that facial expressions corresponding to the six basic emotions are recognized and produced cross-culturally (Ekman, 1999; Ekman & Rosenberg, 2005; Ekman et al., 1969; Keltner & Ekman, 2000; Keltner et al., 2003). These expressions appear to constitute a universal repertoire of human communication. The expressions

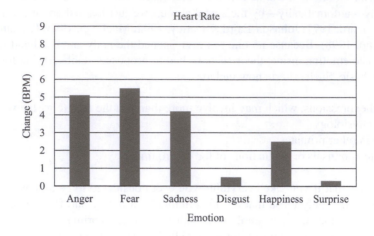

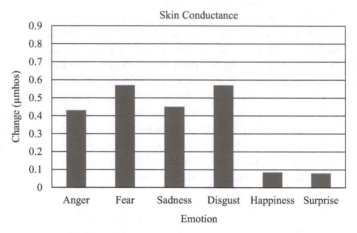

Figure 1.3 Heart rate and skin conductance during six emotional configurations. Adapted from Levenson, Ekman, and Friesen (1990).

also exist in the communicative displays of primates (e.g., Parr et al., 2007; Waller & Dunbar, 2005). This occurs despite variation in details of the facial anatomy across species and even across individuals.

The **autonomic nervous system** (ANS) is a control system that regulates the workings of bodily organs—such as the heart, lungs, and stomach—that are responsible for making us feel aroused and active. It controls heart rate, digestion, and breathing, among other things. William James (1890) proposed that the ANS could make us feel discrete emotions, arguing that the combined working of these organs could create different types of arousal that make up the feelings we call anger, fear, disgust, sadness, and joy. This **peripheralist** position—so called because it held that emotions were composed largely of specific activity in the peripheral nervous system—was attacked for over a century, both by scientists who believed that arousal was nonspecific, and thus could not possibly cause the experience of qualitatively different emotions, and by those who believed that the ANS responds too slowly to support discrete emotional states.

The question of whether different emotions have different ANS profiles has since been studied systematically by emotion scientists. Levenson et al. (1990), for instance, induced emotions in participants with the use of a method called the Directed Facial Action task. In this task, the experimenter points at muscles on an experimental participant's face and asks her to contract them. By choosing specific muscles, the experimenter can get the participant to form each of the six basic facial expressions without mentioning the facial expression at all. While participants held each facial expression, Levenson and colleagues measured, among other things, heart rate, finger temperature, and skin conductance—activity of the ANS. As you can see in Figure 1.3, the six emotions seemed to have different ANS patterns. For instance, anger showed more pronounced finger temperature changes than all the other emotions studied. By the same token, anger, fear, sadness, and disgust were all associated with greater changes in skin conductance (more sweating, that is) than were surprise and happiness. These same results were also obtained in a study in which the participants were men in West Sumatra (Indonesia) who lived in isolation from Western cultures (Levenson et al., 1992).

Subsequent studies also suggest that discrete emotions like fear, anger, and sadness have distinct physiological profiles (Friedman, 2010; Kreibig, 2010; Rainville et al, 2006). Still, despite demonstrations of ANS differentiation of emotion, sufficient confusion exists in the literature to lead some researchers to conclude that there is no distinct ANS patterns for any single emotion (Barrett, Ochsner, & Gross, 2007). This ambiguity may be due to the fact that experiments all vary in context, emotional intensity levels, or motivational states (Larsen et al., 2008; Stemmler et al., 2001; Stemmler & Wacker, 2010 for discussion).

The Integration of Experience: Affect Programs

According to the definition of emotion given earlier in the chapter, emotions are composed of many components, more than the arousal and labels that make up the Two-Factor Theory of Schachter and Singer. Theories of emotion specify whether the components of emotion all occur every time an emotion occurs and, if so, in what order (e.g., Lazarus, 1991; Roseman, 1984, 1991; Scherer, 1984). Evolutionary theories say that the components of emotion occur in concert every time you have an emotion. All of the components of an emotion happen together (or "cohere") because they are integrated in an **affect program**, a term attributed to Tomkins (Tomkins & McCarter, 1964). Affect programs are innate brain systems that are preset to tell the body what to do when faced with a particular event (i.e., the adaptive tasks just discussed). In this view, there is a distinct program for each of the basic emotions. This does not mean that everyone's anger looks and feels exactly the same. Although affect programs develop similarly for all people (they are innate), they can change to include knowledge gained through individual experience (Ekman & Cordaro, 2011).

There is some evidence that the components of emotion do cohere. The strongest evidence in favor of coherence usually comes from studies linking facial expression to self-reported feeling (Bonanno & Keltner, 2004; Fridlund, Ekman, & Oster, 1987). Mauss et al. (2005) also found evidence of some coherence for amusement and for sadness, using films to induce those emotions. Feelings of amusement and facial expressions were positively related and also positively related to activity of the autonomic nervous system. Sad experiences and facial behaviors were positively related to one another and negatively related to activity in the autonomic nervous system. However, as reviewed later, many other studies show little coherence in the components of emotion. For example, having strong feelings of disgust does not mean that a facial expression or change in autonomic activity is guaranteed to co-occur.

In sum, an emotion from the perspective of evolutionary theories is illustrated in Figure 1.4. Biologically prepared signal stimuli reliably elicit affect programs designed to respond adaptively.

Figure 1.4 A schematic diagram of evolutionary theory.

Appraisal Theories

Whereas evolutionary theories link emotions to biological adaptation in the distant past, appraisal theories link emotions to people's immediate evaluation of their circumstances. Appraisal theorists believe that very few objects or events inevitably cause the same emotion in all people (Arnold, 1960; Frijda, 1986; Lazarus, 1966; Roseman & Smith, 2001). That is, they do not recognize the existence of signal stimuli. Rather, they note that failing an exam, losing a favorite hat, or accidentally missing a meeting with a friend might cause sadness in one person, but shame or anger in another person. Appraisal theories are designed to explain the variation, not the sameness, of emotional life.

The claim of these theories, therefore, is that emotions are determined by how an individual appraises his or her circumstances. **Appraisal** is the mental process that allows you to detect objects and events in your environment and evaluate their significance for your immediate well-being (Ellsworth & Scherer, 2003; Frijda, 1986; Lazarus, Averill, & Opton, 1970; Parkinson & Manstead, 1992; Reisenzein, 2001; Roseman, 1984; Smith, 1989; Smith & Lazarus, 1990). Appraisals are not as simple as judgments of "good" or "bad" for your well-being, though. Circumstances can be appraised in many ways, and it is the pattern of appraisals across those ways that is so important for understanding and predicting emotions. For example, many appraisal theories state that individuals evaluate their surrounding circumstances in terms of how positive, novel, relevant to current goals, and congruent with norms their circumstances are, as well as whether the self or someone else was the initial cause of the circumstances.

Possible formations of appraisals are given in Table 1.2 (from Ellsworth & Scherer, 2003). In theory, if you knew how people appraised a given circumstance, such as giving a public speech, you would be able to figure out if they were happy or afraid to give the speech. We will see how this works in the next section. For now, note that appraisals are not on and off; they are a matter of degree. That is, things that you encounter and experience are not just good or bad, or just controllable or not. Circumstances might be a little, somewhat, or very novel and a little, somewhat, or very positive. In other words, appraisals are experienced on a continuum (like a scale from 1 to 10). In appraisal theory, this type of continuum is known as a **dimension**. Importantly, theorists do not assume that people making appraisals are doing so consciously and intentionally. Individuals assign values (a little, somewhat, and so forth) to appraisals rapidly, and they usually do so unconsciously and unintentionally.

The claim that people can experience different emotions in response to the same event as a function of their appraisal of the circumstances was demonstrated in a delightful study conducted in the Geneva, Switzerland, airport (Scherer & Ceschi, 1997). The investigators videotaped travelers as they reported that their luggage was lost to an agent at the baggage

Table 1.2 Comparative overview of major appraisal dimensions as postulated by different theorists. From Ellsworth & Scherer (2003).

	Frijda (1986)	*Roseman (1984)*	*Scherer (1984)*	*Smith/Ellsworth (1985)*
Novelty	Change Familiarity		Novelty Suddenness Familiarity	Attentional activity
Valence	Valence		Intrinsic pleasantness	Pleasantness
Goals/needs	Focality	Appetitive/aversive motives	Goal significance	Importance
	Certainty	Certainty	Concern relevance Outcome probability	Certainty
Agency	Intent/Self-other	Agency	Cause: agent Cause: motive	Human agency
Norms/values	Value relevance		Compatibility with standards External Internal	Legitimacy

claim office. The investigators then interviewed the travelers about their appraisals of the situation and about their subjective feelings. As expected by appraisal theory, individuals varied in their emotional reactions to the same experience of losing luggage. Moreover, and consistently with most appraisal theories, the more that the event was perceived as obstructing one's current goals, the more the individual experienced anger and, to some degree, worry.

In a laboratory study that tested the same hypothesis of differing emotional reactions as a function of divergent appraisals, an experimenter gave ambiguous, negative feedback to participants as they engaged in a difficult task (Siemer, Mauss, & Gross, 2007). The feedback caused different emotions across participants. Some felt shame, some guilt, some anger, and some reported experiencing sadness. Appraisals of the feedback situation, especially in terms of how important it was for the self, who caused it, and whether or not it was expected, predicted which of those negative emotions the participants reported feeling.

Causes of Emotion: Specific Appraisal Patterns

In appraisal theories, specific emotions result from distinct patterns of appraisals. To be able to predict a given person's emotional reaction, therefore, appraisal researchers first map out the relationships between a particular appraisal pattern (the cause) and the resulting specific emotion, such as fear, anger, joy, or sadness (e.g., Roseman, 2013; Siemer, Mauss, & Gross, 2007). In studies designed to extract the precise pattern of appraisals that determine specific emotions, participants are asked to recall an emotional event from their past and then to rate it on the appraisal dimensions nominated by the researcher, such as those in Table 1.2 (e.g., Frijda, Kuipers, & Ter Schure, 1989; Kuppens et al., 2007; Fischer & Roseman, 2007). Other evidence comes from studies in which participants read descriptions of events that have been designed to elicit specific patterns of appraisal and then rate their expected emotional reactions (e.g., Ellsworth & Smith, 1988; Reisenzein & Hofmann, 1990). Perhaps most compelling are the studies in which emotions are manipulated or measured in real-life circumstances while specific appraisals are manipulated or measured at the same time (Kreibig, Gendolla, & Scherer, 2010; Moors & De Houwer, 2001; Smith & Kirby, 2009).

A summary of the various findings has allowed appraisal theorists to assert, for instance, that fear occurs when circumstances are appraised as novel, negative, uncontrollable, and inconsistent with expectations. A visual summary of some regular patterns of appraisals found to be associated with different basic emotions is presented in Figure 1.5 (based on Smith & Ellsworth, 1985).

More recently, some appraisal theorists have backed away from the claim that appraisals are antecedent causes of emotions (Clore & Ortony, 2008; Moors, 2013; Scherer, 2009). In this view, the appraisals serve to describe one's experience of the emotion rather than trigger it per se. Such theories may harken back to the Two-Factor Theory and, as we shall see, to the ideas of William James (1890), in that some kind of bodily reaction is present before the appraisal cognitions.

Biological Givens: Valence and Novelty Appraisals

Magda Arnold (1960) described appraisals in terms that sounded innate. She proposed that organisms are constantly evaluating whether the environment is beneficial or harmful for them. Later theorists distinguished between primary appraisals that are adaptive in being very fast and clear-cut and secondary appraisals that involve high-order mental processes and are probably learned (Scherer, 2001). For instance, whereas a primary appraisal might judge a snake as dangerous, a secondary, more deliberate appraisal might involve the nuanced judgment that this particular snake is actually dead or a harmless variety and thus can be easily coped with.

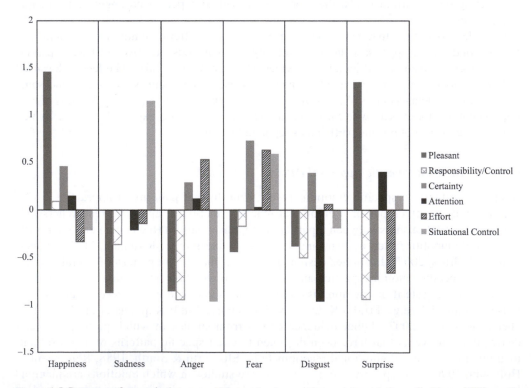

Figure 1.5 Patterns of appraisal across different basic emotions. Adapted from Smith and Ellsworth (1985).

The primary appraisals that could be considered innate are the appraisals of novelty and of valence (Scherer, 2001). The appraisal of novelty is the detection of new or changed elements of the environment. An ability to detect novelty is present in newborns and is shared with other animals. The parts of the brain that are responsible for this appraisal are also evolutionarily old. For example, the amygdala, a structure deep in the brain's limbic system (see Chapter 3), seems to control orienting responses (Holland & Gallagher, 1999) and is activated when an organism is exposed to novel objects (Schwartz et al., 2003; Wright et al., 2006). Lesions to the amygdala also disrupt primates' typical responses to novelty (Prather et al., 2001).

Whereas novelty tells an organism if there is something significant to pay attention to, the assessment of valence tells the organism whether it should be approached or avoided. Appraisals of valence also seem to be present in newborns and animals. In human adults, the amygdala also responds to positive and negative faces (e.g., Zald, 2003), scenes (e.g., Anders et al., 2008), words (e.g., Posner et al., 2009), and odors (e.g., Anderson et al., 2003). Moreover, the detection of valence triggers the same cardiovascular systems as the detection of novelty (Mendes et al., 2007). However, even if they share old neural systems, novelty appraisals and pleasantness appraisals are separate detectors (Weierich et al., 2009). In other words, if something is novel, we can't know if it is also positive. We need both appraisals.

The Integration of Experience: Independent Components

Some appraisal theorists believe that all of the components of emotion are elicited as a package upon the occurrence of an appraisal. This idea is reflected in Frijda's (1988, pp. 349) assertion; "[i]nput some event with its particular meaning; out comes an emotion of a particular kind." Although initially appraisal theories were developed to predict experiences that are usually labeled with discrete category labels such as "joy" and "fear," contemporary appraisal theorists think that the components of emotion are not triggered in an all-or-none fashion.

Such appraisal theories are called "componential theories" (e.g., Scherer, 2009). In this view, the different components of emotion can be caused independently by different appraisals. Fear, for instance, might be characterized by several component parts: a facial expression, ANS arousal, a tendency toward flight. The componential theorist is interested more in those components than in linking them to an overall state. So instead of trying to predict the occurrence of joy or fear, these theories may try to predict tendencies to reject, freeze, or approach (Moors, 2013). Or they may try to predict how the activation of different facial muscles are caused by different appraisals rather than linking them to the expression of a single emotional state (Scherer & Ellgring, 2007a, 2007b). Thus, the components of emotion could be caused by different objects or events and proceed independently, or else combine in innumerable ways to produce highly nuanced emotional experiences (Clore & Ortony, 2000; Ellsworth & Scherer, 2003).

Indeed, componential theorists focus on evidence suggesting that components of emotion actually do not typically cohere. (Bradley & Lang, 2000; Cacioppo et al., 2000; Reisenzein, 2000). Although some research found relationships between facial expression and reported emotion, Reisenzein, Studtmann, and Horstmann (2013) reviewed evidence of the relationship between reported feelings and appearance of specific facial expressions (based on Ekman, 1972, 1993) of amusement, disgust, surprise, sadness, anger, and fear. Except for amusement, the emotions and the facial expressions did not reliably co-occur.

The reality is that the question of whether emotions are tightly bound packages or sets of loosely connected pieces is one that is very hard to answer. It could be that in real-life, naturally occurring, and high-intensity emotions, the components are usually coherent. After all, the apparent decoupling of the component parts is based on observations from laboratory demonstrations in which experimental participants were induced to experience emotions but did not need to *act* on those emotions. If individuals do not have to act, or cannot act due to features of the laboratory environment, then certain parts of the emotion may not occur. Perhaps the component processes usually cohere and all point to the same emotional experience only, but very quickly until other processes come into play to decouple them. For example, it could be that after all components of anger come together, other processes intervene to control or change that emotion if it is unacceptable in the current social situation. For example, social norms within a culture can dictate the regulation of emotion and thus exert an especially strong influence the on its outward expression of an emotion. For example, social norms within a culture can influence the outward expression of an emotion. Thus, an individual in an industrialized Western country might feel like laughing at a funeral because she suddenly remembers a funny joke about a priest and a rabbi. However, especially after a particular age, she would probably control her laughter, suppress a smile or tendency to giggle, and display sadness at least on her face, if not also in bodily gestures (Cole, Zahn-Waxler, & Smith, 1994; Diener & Mangelsdorf, 1999; Eisenberg & Morris, 2002). Still, the fact that emotion components can be decoupled over time does not necessarily mean that they do not initially occur in a coherent way, particularly if the opportunity to act on emotion is present.

In sum, an emotion from the perspective of appraisal theories is illustrated in Figure 1.6. Circumstances are detected as important and appraised along a set of dimensions, including novelty, valence, and controllability. Distinct patterns of appraisal reliably elicit the components of emotion, including expressive, physiological, and cognitive responses, as well as action tendencies, although they do not have to occur in one package. Components of emotion may be augmented or prevented due to social or cultural rules. The resulting responses constitute the total emotion.

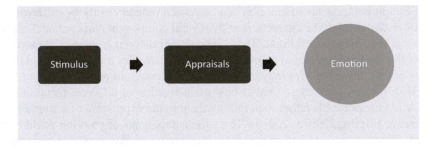

Figure 1.6 A schematic diagram of appraisal theories.

Psychological Constructionism

Whereas evolutionary psychologists study the function of emotion and appraisal theorists study why different people have different emotions in the same circumstances, psychological constructionism tries to explain the huge variation—both within and across individuals—in how emotions look and feel (Barrett, 2006; Cunningham & Brosch, 2012; Kirkland & Cunningham, 2012; Lindquist & Gendron, 2013; Russell, 2003, 2009; Widen, 2013). These theorists ask questions like is there really such a thing as anger, or are there actually many different experiences that we call "anger," just for convenience's sake? Psychological constructionists treat variability in emotion language, knowledge, and responding as indications that the things we call "sadness" and "disgust," for example, are created in the mind of the person experiencing the emotion at that time; emotions are first and foremost psychological realities.

An interest in the construction of specific emotions can be traced in part to the Two-Factor Theory of emotion, which we encountered earlier in the chapter, but even more strongly to the writings of William James (1890). James famously noted that most people of his time (scientists and laypeople alike) seemed to believe that having an emotion involved perceiving an emotionally arousing stimulus (he usually referred to a bear in the woods), feeling an emotion, and then taking action (running away from the bear). That is not right, James claimed. Instead, he argued that people perceive the emotionally arousing stimulus, get all jazzed up and take action, and later introspect on their actions and body to fashion an emotion. Constructing the emotional experience involved thinking about their state in their own way and through their own understanding of the situation. In other words, James thought people took a bunch of elemental biological and psychological states and constructed a personal emotional experience for themselves (Lindquist, 2013).

Both William James's ideas and the Two-Factor Theory of emotion were simple ideas that foreshadowed modern constructionist theories. In constructionist theories, primitive feeling states that have a biological basis are shaped into a psychological reality—into the experiences called "joy" or "disgust"—by the mental processes of perception and interpretation. Modern constructionist theories, in contrast to Schachter and Singer (1962), try to specify how people's knowledge of emotion categories shapes core affect into specific emotional experiences.

Causes of Emotion: Categorizing Affect Responses

From a constructionist perspective, emotions are not elicited by signal stimuli, but through principles of associative learning (Barrett & Bliss-Moreau, 2009). For instance, if a child sees a parent express pain at being bitten by a dog, the dog will come to produce generally negative feelings in the child. The novel contribution of psychological constructionists is the causes of specific emotions: specific emotions are caused by applying learned categories to experience. Whether or not experience is categorized as an emotion depends upon many things, including the individual's own knowledge and sophistication about emotion (Kashdan, Barrett, & McKnight, 2015), as well as the cultural and linguistic context in which the individual lives (Tsai, Simeonova, & Watanabe, 2004). Once categorization gets going, moreover things get interesting.

Categorization is the mental process that takes experience and gives it structure and meaning (Barrett, 2006; Lindquist, 2013). Categories contain information about the probable causes of general feelings, the relationships among the bodily changes, and predictions about what behavior should be taken (Fehr & Russell, 1984; Russell & Fehr, 1994). Most constructionists believe that when you learn to recognize a particular emotion (e.g., what sadness looks like, feels like, and motivates people to do) and to label that emotion (e.g., "sadness"), you start to shape general affective responses into discrete emotional experiences. Sometimes theorists call this a "conceptual act" (Lindquist & Barrett, 2008). Once you engage in the conceptual act of categorizing your emotions, you are more able to fully experience them as distinct and informative states.

Constructionist theories can easily account for similarity and variation in experiences of emotions across cultures. Some emotion categories exist across most societies, perhaps because they relate to universal concerns that arise from living in large, complex groups. Other emotion categories are culture specific and perhaps exist to solve problems associated with the ecological challenges or social values of that particular group. This can be appreciated by noting that languages describe emotions in very distinct ways. For instance, in Anuak, a language in the Sudan, emotions are described by reference to the liver. Sadness is having a "heavy liver." In

Marshallese, a language in Micronesia, emotions are described by reference to the throat. Pride is having a "high throat." Associating emotions with different body parts will give them slightly different meanings.

The existence of a specific set of emotion categories within a given culture and language group is presumed to come from social consensus about the most useful way to differentiate feeling states. In this view, feeling states are labeled for reasons that correspond to real social motivations and social problems, but not because biological entities exist called "disgust," "fear," and "sadness" (Barrett, 2009). Just what is biologically given in this view?

Biological Givens: Core Affect

In psychological constructionist theories, the innate component of emotion is core affect. Core affect is generally thought to be composed of two fundamental dimensions of conscious experience. The two dimensions correspond to the degree to which a state is pleasant versus unpleasant (**valence**) and the degree to which a state is activated versus deactivated (**activation**) (e.g., Barrett & Russell, 1999; Feldman, 1995a, 1995b; Lang, Bradley, & Cuthbert, 1990; Larsen & Diener, 1992; Mayer & Gaschke, 1988; Reisenzein, 1994; Russell, 1980, 1989; Watson & Tellegen, 1985). To express the same quality as pleasant versus unpleasant, some researchers have used the labels good–bad, pleasure–pain, approach–avoidance, rewarding–punishing, or positive–negative. But all such terms more or less refer to the subjective state that stands for "how well one is doing" (Russell & Barrett, 1999). In addition, labels other than activation have been used, such as arousal, tension, and activity, but such labels all refer to the level of experienced energy or mobilization of the state.

The dimensions of valence and activation have been demonstrated using the statistical techniques of **factor analysis** and **multidimensional scaling**. These tools show that the two dimensions best describe how people arrive at judging the similarity between the meaning of two emotion words (Reisenzein, 1994; Russell, 1979) or between two facial expressions of emotion (Russell & Bullock, 1985), how they describe their mood using typical emotion words (Barrett, 1996; Mayer & Gaschke, 1988), and even the way that the body responds to emotional stimulation (Cacioppo, Gardner, & Berntson, 1999; Lang, 1995). There is also evidence that the basic sensations of pleasantness and arousal are the product of two independent neurophysiological systems (Posner, Russell, & Peterson, 2005). Pleasantness–unpleasantness is associated with asymmetric activation of the frontal lobes and projections to and from parts of the limbic system of the brain, such as the amygdala (Davidson, 1992; Heller, 1990; Tomarken et al., 1992). Activation–deactivation is associated with right parietotemporal activation in the brain and projections to the reticular activation system in the brainstem (Heller, 1990, 1993).

The evidence for two dimensions comes from statistical modeling of self-reported feelings. It is interpreted as meaning that states we call happy and sad and angry can be reduced to the biological dimensions of pleasantness and activation and that any given emotion can be described as a blend of pleasantness and activation. For example, many states that we call *anger* could be characterized as highly unpleasant and moderately activated. And many states of fear could be described as moderately unpleasant and highly activated (e.g., Russell & Barrett, 1999).

In another view, the structure of emotion is best described as a circumplex (e.g., Barrett, 2004; Barrett & Russell, 2009; Larsen & Diener, 1992; Russell, 1989; Watson & Tellegen, 1985). Very simply, a circumplex is a circle and a set of axes. The circle illustrates people's perceptions of similarity between the objects. The axes represent the psychological properties that explain what is similar and different about people's perceptions of those objects. An affect circumplex represents how people perceive similarities and differences in their experience of emotion.

Figure 1.7 shows the circumplex and some of the emotion states that define its perimeter. The circumplex is useful because it provides a good description of how people generally experience their emotional state, while also suggesting hypotheses about individual differences in affective experience (Barrett & Niedenthal, 2004).

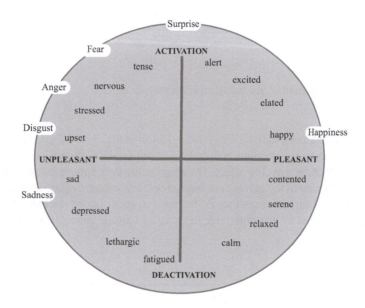

Figure 1.7 Circumplex of emotion. From Russell & Barrett, 1999.

The Integration of Experience

Most psychological constructionists believe that the components of emotion do not necessarily happen inevitably, all at the same time. Whether facial expression, autonomic activity, or specific mental processes occur depends upon the category that is used to construct an emotion in the situation in which it is occurring (Lindquist, 2013). For instance, if you are having a pleasant experience with a partner, you might be very likely to smile because your specific experience of happiness in the situation involves communicating the happiness with the other person. Some of your experiences of happiness when alone might not include smiling.

Variability in how emotion components fit together may be caused by stable individual differences. Some people may react to all emotional events primarily with facial expressions, whereas others may mostly show strong autonomic responses (Marwitz & Stemmler, 1998). There are individual differences in the complexity of cardiac responses across different experiences of stress that are provoked in the laboratory (Friedman, 2003). Psychological constructionists also suggest that the components of emotion are controlled by distinct neural and bodily systems that respond to particular features of the event in which an emotion was experienced (Russell, 2003; Stemmler, 2003). In their view, then, an emotion emerges from conceptualizations that trigger multiple response systems rather than one affect program.

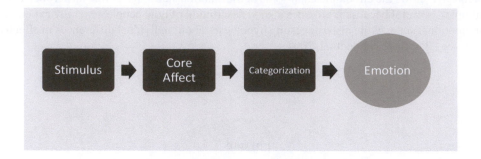

Figure 1.8 A schematic diagram of psychological constructionism.

An emotion from the perspective of psychological constructionist theories is illustrated in Figure 1.8. When events are encountered that have acquired emotional significance through learning, they cause a change in core affect. The changes are conceptualized in terms of emotion categories that are relevant to the current circumstances. The categorization may trigger some of the components of emotion, although they do not have to occur in one package. Components of emotion can be augmented or prevented due to social or cultural rules. The resulting responses constitute the total emotion.

Summary

- Theories of emotion are testable statements about 1) the causes of an emotion, 2) what people are born with (biological givens), and 3) how different components of emotion come together in the emotional expressions.
- Evolutionary theories of emotion hold that emotions are biologically evolved, functional responses to certain opportunities and challenges posed by the environment. One of the key predictions of the evolutionary theory of emotion, which we will revisit several times in this book, is that a set of universally recognized facial expressions of emotion exists.
- The major contribution of cognitive appraisal theories of emotion is the idea that emotions are elicited and differentiated by evaluations (appraisals) of the environment with respect to the current goals and interests of the individual experiencing the emotion.
- The psychological constructionist theory of emotion states that emotions are phenomena that are given shape by the process of categorization. Emotions are not stable biological entities, but rather elaborated within linguistic and cultural contexts.
- Appraisal and constructionist theories agree that the different components of emotion can be quite separate and have separate time courses and that an inevitable set of components does not accompany all emotional episodes.

Learning Links

1. Experience this documentary essay on the basic emotions. https://www.youtube.com/watch?v=V_b_jctSKZM
2. Read an interview with Dr. Lisa Barrett on psychological constructionism and emotion. http://emotionresearcher.com/lisa-feldman-barrett-why-emotions-are-situated-conceptualizations/
3. Learn about computational modeling of emotion based on appraisal theories of emotion. https://vimeo.com/112594888

References

Anders, S., Eippert, F., Weiskopf, N., & Veit, R. (2008). The human amygdala is sensitive to the valence of pictures and sounds irrespective of arousal: An fMRI study. *Social Cognitive and Affective Neuroscience*, *3*(3), 233–243. doi:10.1093/scan/nsn017.

Anderson, A. K., Christoff, K., Stappen, I., Panitz, D., Ghahremani, D. G., Glover, G., . . . Sobel, N. (2003). Dissociated neural representations of intensity and valence in human olfaction. *Nature Neuroscience*, *6*(2), 196–202. doi:10.1038/nn1001.

Arnold, M. B. (1960). *Emotion and personality*. New York: Columbia University Press.

Barrett, L. F. (1996). Hedonic tone, perceived arousal, and item desirability: Three components of self-reported mood. *Cognition & Emotion*, *10*(1), 47–68. doi:10.1080/026999396380385.

Barrett, L. F. (2004). Feelings or words? Understanding the content in self-report ratings of experienced emotion. *Journal of Personality and Social Psychology*, *87*(2), 266. doi:10.1037/0022–3514.87.2.266.

Barrett, L. F. (2006). Are emotions natural kinds? *Perspectives on Psychological Science*, *1*(1), 28–58. doi:10.1111/j.1745–6916.2006.00003.x.

Barrett, L. F. (2009). Variety is the spice of life: A psychological construction approach to understanding variability in emotion. *Cognition and Emotion*, *23*(7), 1284–1306. doi:10.1080/02699930902985894.

Barrett, L. F., & Bliss-Moreau, E. (2009). Affect as a psychological primitive. *Advances in Experimental Social Psychology*, *41*, 167–218. doi:10.1016/s0065–2601(08)00404–8.

Barrett, L. F., & Niedenthal, P. M. (2004). Valence focus and the perception of facial affect. *Emotion*, *4*(3), 266–274. doi:10.1037/1528–3542.4.3.266.

Barrett, L. F., Ochsner, K. N., & Gross, J. J. (2007). On the automaticity of emotion. *Social Psychology and the Unconscious: The Automaticity of Higher Mental Processes*, *173*, 217.

Barrett, L. F., & Russell, J. A. (1999). The structure of current affect controversies and emerging consensus. *Current Directions in Psychological Science, 8*(1), 10–14. doi:10.1111/1467–8721.00003.

Barrett, L. F., & Russell, J. A. (2009). The circumplex model of affect. In D. Sanders & K. Scherer (Eds.), *Oxford companion to emotion and the affective sciences.* New York: Oxford University Press, pp. 85–88.

Barrett, L. F., & Salovey, P. (Eds.). (2002). *The wisdom in feeling: Psychological processes in emotional intelligence.* New York: Guilford Press.

Bonanno, G., & Keltner, D. (2004). Brief report the coherence of emotion systems: Comparing "on-line" measures of appraisal and facial expressions, and self-report. *Cognition and Emotion, 18*(3), 431–444. doi:10.1080/02699930341000149.

Bradley, M. M., & Lang, P. J. (2000). Affective reactions to acoustic stimuli. *Psychophysiology, 37*(2), 204–215. doi:10.1111/1469–8986.3720204.

Buck, R. (1983). Emotional development and emotional education. In R. Plutchik & H. Kellerman (Eds.), *Emotion in early development* (pp. 259–293). New York: Academic Press.

Buck, R. (1999). The biological affects: A typology. *Psychological Review, 106*(2), 301. doi:10.1037/0033–295x.106.2.301.

Buck, R., Losow, J., Murphy, M., & Costanzo, P. (1992). Social facilitation and inhibition of emotional expression and communication. *Journal of Personality and Social Psychology, 63*(6), 962–968.

Cacioppo, J. T., Berntson, G. G., Larsen, J. T., Poehlmann, K. M., & Ito, T. A. (2000). The psychophysiology of emotion. *Handbook of Emotions, 2*, 173–191.

Cacioppo, J. T., Gardner, W. L., & Berntson, G. G. (1999). The affect system has parallel and integrative processing components: Form follows function. *Journal of Personality and Social Psychology, 76*(5), 839. doi:10.1037/0022–3514.76.5.839.

Clore, G. L., & Ortony, A. (2000). Cognition in emotion: Always, sometimes, or never. In R. D. Lane & L. Nadel (Eds.), *Cognitive Neuroscience of Emotion* (pp. 24–61). New York: Oxford University Press.

Cole, P. M., Martin, S. E., & Dennis, T. A. (2004). Emotion regulation as a scientific construct: Methodological challenges and directions for child development research. *Child Development, 75*(2), 317–333. doi:10.1111/j.1467–8624.2004.00673.x.

Cole, P. M., Zahn-Waxler, C., & Smith, K. D. (1994). Expressive control during a disappointment: Variations related to preschoolers' behavior problems. *Developmental Psychology, 30*(6), 835. http://dx.doi.org/10.1037/0012–1649.30.6.835.

Cosmides, L., & Tooby, J. (2000). Evolutionary psychology and the emotions. In M. Lewis & J. M. Haviland-Jones (Eds.), *Handbook of emotions* (2nd ed., pp. 91–115). New York: Guilford Press.

Cunningham, W. A., & Brosch, T. (2012). Motivational salience amygdala tuning from traits, needs, values, and goals. *Current Directions in Psychological Science, 21*(1), 54–59. doi:10.1177/0963721411430832.

Damasio, A. (1999). *The feeling of what happens: Body and emotion in the making of consciousness.* New York: Harcourt, Inc.

Darwin, C. (1872/1998). *The expression of emotions in man and animals.* New York: Philosophical Library. doi:10.1037/10001–000.

Davidson, R. J. (1992). Anterior cerebral asymmetry and the nature of emotion. *Brain and Cognition, 20*(1), 125–151. doi:10.1016/0278–2626(92)90065-t.

Diener, M. L., & Mangelsdorf, S. C. (1999). Behavioral strategies for emotion regulation in toddlers: Associations with maternal involvement and emotional expressions. *Infant Behavior and Development, 22*(4), 569–583. doi:10.1016/s0163–6383(00)00012–6.

Eisenberg, N., & Morris, A. S. (2002). Children's emotion-related regulation. In R. Kail (Ed.), *Advances in child development and behavior* (Vol. 30, pp. 190–229). Amsterdam: Academic Press.

Ekman, P. (1972). Universals and cultural differences in facial expression of emotion. In J. R. Cole (Ed.), *Nebraska symposium on motivation* (pp. 207–283). Lincoln, NE: University of Nebraska Press.

Ekman, P. (1992). An argument for basic emotions. *Cognition & Emotion, 6*(3–4), 169–200. doi:10.1080/02699939208411068.

Ekman, P. (1993). Facial expression and emotion. *American Psychologist, 48*(4), 384. doi:10.1037/0003–066x.48.4.384.

Ekman, P. (1994). All emotions are basic. In P. Ekman & R. Davidson (Eds.), *The nature of emotion: Fundamental questions* (pp. 15–19). New York: Oxford University Press.

Ekman, P. (1999). Facial expressions. *Handbook of Cognition and Emotion, 53,* 226–232.

Ekman, P., & Cordaro, D. (2011). What is meant by calling emotions basic. *Emotion Review, 3*(4), 364–370. doi:10.1177/1754073911410740.

Ekman, P., & Friesen, W. V. (1971). Constants across cultures in the face and emotion. *Journal of Personality and Social Psychology, 17*(2), 124. doi:10.1037/h0030377.

Ekman, P., & Friesen, W. V. (1975). *Unmasking the human face: A guide to recognizing emotions from facial expressions.* Palo Alto, CA: Consulting Psychologists' Press.

Ekman, P., & Rosenberg, E. (2005). *What the face reveals* (2nd ed.). New York: Oxford Press.

Ekman, P., Sorenson, E. R., & Friesen, W. V. (1969). Pan-cultural elements in facial displays of emotion. *Science, 164*(3875), 86–88. doi:10.1126/science.164.3875.86.

Ellsworth, P. C., & Scherer, K. R. (2003). Appraisal processes in emotion. In R. J. Davidson, K. R. Scherer & H. H. Goldsmith (Eds.), *Handbook of affective sciences* (pp. 572–595). New York: Oxford University Press.

Ellsworth, P. C., & Smith, C. A. (1988). From appraisal to emotion: Differences among unpleasant feelings. *Motivation and Emotion, 12,* 271–302.

Fehr, B., & Russell, J. A. (1984). Concept of emotion viewed from a prototype perspective. *Journal of Experimental Psychology: General, 113*(3), 464. doi:10.1037/0096–3445.113.3.464.

Feldman, L. A. (1995a). Valence focus and arousal focus: Individual differences in the structure of affective experience. *Journal of Personality and Social Psychology, 69*(1), 153. doi:10.1037/0022–3514.69.1.153.

Feldman, L. A. (1995b). Variations in the circumplex structure of mood. *Personality and Social Psychology Bulletin, 21*(8), 806–817. doi:10.1177/0146167295218003.

Fischer, A. H., & Roseman, I. J. (2007). Beat them or ban them: The characteristics and social functions of anger and contempt. *Journal of Personality and Social Psychology, 93*(1), 103. doi:10.1037/0022–3514.93.1.103.

Fredrickson, B. L. (2001). The role of positive emotions in positive psychology: The broaden-and-build theory of positive emotions. *American Psychologist, 56*(3), 218. doi:10.1037/0003–066x.56.3.218.

Fridlund, A. J., Ekman, P., & Oster, H. (1987). Facial expressions of emotion. In A. W. Siegman & S. Feldstein (Eds.), *Nonverbal behavior and communication* (2nd ed., pp. 143–223). Hillsdale, NJ: Erlbaum.

Friedman, B. H. (2010). Feelings and the body: The Jamesian perspective on autonomic specificity of emotion. *Biological Psychology, 84*(3), 383–393. doi:10.1016/j.biopsycho.2009.10.006.

Frijda, N. H. (1986). *The emotions.* Cambridge: Cambridge University Press.

Frijda, N. H. (1988). The laws of emotion. *American Psychologist, 43*(5), 349. doi:10.1037/0003–066x.43.5.349.

Frijda, N. H., Kuipers, P., & Ter Schure, E. (1989). Relations among emotion, appraisal, and emotional action readiness. *Journal of Personality and Social Psychology, 57*(2), 212. doi:10.1037/0022–3514.57.2.212.

Heller, W. (1990). The neuropsychology of emotion: Developmental patterns and implications for psychopathology. In N. L. Stein, B. Leventhal, T. Trabasso, N. L. Stein, B. Leventhal & T. Trabasso (Eds.), *Psychological and biological approaches to emotion* (pp. 167–211). Hillsdale, NJ: Lawrence Erlbaum Associates.

Heller, W. (1993). Neuropsychological mechanisms of individual differences in emotion, personality, and arousal. *Neuropsychology, 7*(4), 476. doi:10.1037/0894–4105.7.4.476.

Holland, P. C., & Gallagher, M. (1999). Amygdala circuitry in attentional and representational processes. *Trends in Cognitive Sciences, 3*(2), 65–73. doi:10.1016/s1364–6613(98)01271–6.

Horstmann, G. (2003). What do facial expressions convey: Feeling states, behavioral intentions, or actions requests? *Emotion, 3*(2), 150. doi:10.1037/1528–3542.3.2.150.

Izard, C. E. (1977). *Human emotions.* New York: Plenum Press.

Izard, C. E. (2007). Basic emotions, natural kinds, emotion schemas, and a new paradigm. *Perspectives on Psychological Science, 2*(3), 260–280. doi:10.1111/j.1745–6916.2007.00044.x.

James, W. (1890). *The principles of psychology* (Vol. 1). New York: Holt.

Johnson-Laird, P. N., & Oatley, K. (1992). Basic emotions, rationality, and folk theory. *Cognition & Emotion, 6*(3–4), 201–223. doi:10.1080/02699939208411069.

Kashdan, T. B., Barrett, L. F., & McKnight, P. E. (2015). Unpacking emotion differentiation transforming unpleasant experience by perceiving distinctions in negativity. *Current Directions in Psychological Science, 24*(1), 10–16. doi:10.1177/0963721414550708.

Keltner, D., & Ekman, P. (2000). Facial expression of emotion. *Handbook of Emotions*, 2(236–249), 2–17.

Keltner, D., Ekman, P., Gonzaga, G. C., & Beer, J. (2003). In R. Davidson, K. Scherer & H. Goldsmith (Eds.), *Handbook of affective sciences: Series in affective science* (pp. 411–559). New York: Oxford University Press.

Keltner, D., & Gross, J. J. (1999). Functional accounts of emotions. *Cognition & Emotion*, 13(5), 467–480. doi:10.1080/026999399379140.

Keltner, D., & Haidt, J. (2001). Social functions of emotions. In T. J. Mayne & G. A. Bonanno (Eds.), *Emotions: Current issues and future directions* (pp. 192–213). New York: Guilford Press.

Keltner, D., & Kring, A. M. (1998). Emotion, social function, and psychopathology. *Review of General Psychology*, 2(3), 320. doi:10.1037/1089–2680.2.3.320.

Kirkland, T., & Cunningham, W. A. (2012). Mapping emotions through time: How affective trajectories inform the language of emotion. *Emotion*, 12(2), 268. doi:10.1037/a0024218.

Kreibig, S. D. (2010). Autonomic nervous system activity in emotion: A review. *Biological Psychology*, 84(3), 394–421. doi:10.1016/j.biopsycho.2010.03.010.

Kreibig, S. D., Gendolla, G. H., & Scherer, K. R. (2010). Psychophysiological effects of emotional responding to goal attainment. *Biological Psychology*, 84(3), 474–487. doi:10.1016/j.biopsycho. 2009.11.004.

Kuppens, P., Van Mechelen, I., Smits, D. J., De Boeck, P., & Ceulemans, E. (2007). Individual differences in patterns of appraisal and anger experience. *Cognition and Emotion*, 21(4), 689–713. doi:10.1080/02699930600859219.

Lang, P. J. (1995). The emotion probe: Studies of motivation and attention. *American Psychologist*, 50(5), 372. doi:10.1037/0003–066x.50.5.372.

Lang, P. J., Bradley, M. M., & Cuthbert, B. N. (1990). Emotion, attention, and the startle reflex. *Psychological Review*, 97(3), 377. doi:10.1037/0033–295x.97.3.377.

Larsen, J. T., Berntson, G. G., Poehlmann, K. M., Ito, T. A., & Cacioppo, J. T. (2008). The psychophysiology of emotion. In M. Lewis, J. M. Haviland-Jones & L. F. Barrett (Eds.), *Handbook of emotions* (3rd ed., pp. 180–195). New York: Guilford Press.

Larsen, R. J., & Diener, E. (1992). Promises and problems with the circumplex model of emotion. In M. S. Clark (Ed.), *Emotion* (pp. 25–59). Thousand Oaks, CA: Sage.

Lazarus, R. S. (1966). *Psychological stress and the coping process*. New York: McGraw-Hill.

Lazarus, R. S. (1991). *Emotion and adaptation*. New York: Oxford University Press.

Lazarus, R. S., Averill, I. R., & Opton, E. M. (1970). Towards a cognitive theory of emotion. In M. B. Arnold (Ed.), *Feelings and emotions: The Loyola symposium* (pp. 207–232). New York: Academic Press.

Levenson, R. W., Ekman, P., & Friesen, W. V. (1990). Voluntary facial action generates emotion-specific autonomic nervous system activity. *Psychophysiology*, 27(4), 363–384. doi:10.1111/j.1469–8986.1990. tb02330.x.

Levenson, R. W., Ekman, P., Heider, K., & Friesen, W. V. (1992). Emotion and autonomic nervous system activity in the Minangkabau of West Sumatra. *Journal of Personality and Social Psychology*, 62(6), 972. doi:10.1037/0022–3514.62.6.972.

Lewis, M. (2007). Self-conscious emotional development. In J. L. Tracy, R. W. Robins & J. P. Tangney (Eds.), *The self-conscious emotions: Theory and research* (pp. 134–149). New York: Guilford Press.

Lindquist, K. A. (2013). Emotions emerge from more basic psychological ingredients: A modern psychological constructionist model. *Emotion Review*, 5(4), 356–368. doi:10.1177/1754073913489750.

Lindquist, K. A., & Barrett, L. F. (2008). Constructing emotion the experience of fear as a conceptual act. *Psychological Science*, 19(9), 898–903. doi:10.1111/j.1467–9280.2008.02174.x.

Lindquist, K. A., & Gendron, M. (2013). What's in a word? Language constructs emotion perception. *Emotion Review*, 5(1), 66–71. http://dx.doi.org/10.1177/1754073912451351.

MacLean, P. D. (1993). Cerebral evolution of emotion. In M. Lewis & J. M. Haviland (Eds.), *Handbook of emotions* (pp. 67–87). New York: Guilford Press.

Marsh, A. A., & Ambady, N. (2007). The influence of the fear facial expression on prosocial responding. *Cognition and Emotion*, 21(2), 225–247. doi:10.1080/02699930600652234.

Marwitz, M., & Stemmler, G. (1998). On the status of individual response specificity. *Psychophysiology*, 35(1), 1–15.

Mauss, I. B., Levenson, R. W., McCarter, L., Wilhelm, F. H., & Gross, J. J. (2005). The tie that binds? Coherence among emotion experience, behavior, and physiology. *Emotion*, *5*(2), 175. doi:10.1037/1528–3542.5.2.175.

Mayer, J. D., & Gaschke, Y. N. (1988). The experience and meta-experience of mood. *Journal of Personality and Social Psychology*, *55*(1), 102. doi:10.1037/0022–3514.55.1.102.

Mehu, M., & Dunbar, R. I. (2008). Naturalistic observations of smiling and laughter in human group interactions. *Behaviour*, *145*(12), 1747–1780. doi:10.1163/156853908786279619.

Mendes, W. B., Blascovich, J., Hunter, S., Lickel, B., & Jost, J. (2007). Threatened by the unexpected: Physiological responses during social interactions with expectancy-violating partners. *Journal of Personality and Social Psychology, 92*, 698–716.

Moors, A. (2013). On the causal role of appraisal in emotion. *Emotion Review*, *5*(2), 132–140. doi:10.1177/1754073912463601.

Moors, A., & De Houwer, J. (2001). Automatic appraisal of motivational valence: Motivational affective priming and Simon effects. *Cognition & Emotion*, *15*(6), 749–766. doi:10.1080/02699930143000293.

Niedenthal, P. M., & Brauer, M. (2012). Social functionality of human emotion. *Annual Review of Psychology*, *63*(1), 259–285. doi:10.1146/annurev.psych.121208.131605.

Öhman, A. (1986). Face the beast and fear the face: Animal and social fears as prototypes for evolutionary analyses of emotion. *Psychophysiology*, *23*(2), 123–145. doi:10.1111/j.1469–8986.1986.tb00608.x.

Öhman, A., & Mineka, S. (2001). Fears, phobias, and preparedness: Toward an evolved module of fear and fear learning. *Psychological Review*, *108*(3), 483. doi:10.1037/0033–295x.108.3.483.

Ortony, A., & Turner, T. J. (1990). What's basic about basic emotions? *Psychological Review*, *97*(3), 315–331. doi:10.1037/0033–295X.97.3.315.

Panksepp, J. (1998). *Affective neuroscience: The foundations of human and animal emotions*. Oxford: Oxford University Press.

Panksepp, J. (2007). Criteria for basic emotions: Is DISGUST a primary 'emotion'? *Cognition and Emotion*, *21*(8), 1819–1828. doi:10.1080/02699930701334302.

Parkinson, B., & Manstead, A. S. R. (1992). Appraisal as a cause of emotion. In M. Clarke (Ed.), *Emotion* (pp. 112–149). Thousand Oaks, CA: Sage.

Parr, L. A., Waller, B. M., Vick, S. J., & Bard, K. A. (2007). Classifying chimpanzee facial expressions using muscle action. *Emotion*, *7*(1), 172. doi:10.1037/1528–3542.7.1.172.

Plutchik, R. (1980). A general psychoevolutionary theory of emotion. In R. Plutchik & H. Kellerman (Eds.), *Theories of emotion* (pp. 3–33). New York: Academic Press.

Plutchik, R. (1984). Emotions: A general psychoevolutionary theory. In K. R. Scherer & P. Ekman (Eds.), *Approaches to emotion* (pp. 197–219). Hillsdale, NJ: Lawrence Erlbaum Associates.

Pollak, S. D. (2012). The role of parenting in the emergence of human emotion: New approaches to the old nature-nurture debate. *Parenting*, *12*(2–3), 232–242. doi:10.1080/15295192.2012.683363.

Pollak, S. D. (2013). Emotion and Learning: New approaches to the old nature-nurture debate. In S. Gelman & M. Banaji (Eds.), *Navigating the social world: What infants, children, and other species can teach us* (pp. 54–57). New York: Oxford University Press.

Posner, J., Russell, J. A., Gerber, A., Gorman, D., Colibazzi, T., Yu, S., . . . Peterson, B. S. (2009). The neurophysiological bases of emotion: An fMRI study of the affective circumplex using emotion-denoting words. *Human Brain Mapping*, *30*(3), 883–895. doi:10.1002/hbm.20553.

Posner, J., Russell, J. A., & Peterson, B. S. (2005). The circumplex model of affect: An integrative approach to affective neuroscience, cognitive development, and psychopathology. *Development and Psychopathology*, *17*(3), 715–734. doi:10.1017/s0954579405050340.

Prather, M. D., Lavenex, P., Mauldin-Jourdain, M. L., Mason, W. A., Capitanio, J. P., Mendoza, S. P., & Amaral, D. G. (2001). Increased social fear and decreased fear of objects in monkeys with neonatal amygdala lesions. *Neuroscience*, *106*(4), 653–658. doi:10.1016/s0306–4522(01)00445–6.

Rainville, P., Bechara, A., Naqvi, N., & Damasio, A. R. (2006). Basic emotions are associated with distinct patterns of cardiorespiratory activity. *International Journal of Psychophysiology*, *61*(1), 5–18. doi:10.1016/j.ijpsycho.2005.10.024.

Reisenzein, R. (1994). Pleasure-arousal theory and the intensity of emotions. *Journal of Personality and Social Psychology*, *67*(3), 525. doi:10.1037/0022–3514.67.3.525.

Reisenzein, R. (2000). Exploring the strength of association between the components of emotion syndromes: The case of surprise. *Cognition & Emotion, 14*(1), 1–38. doi:10.1080/026999300378978.

Reisenzein, R. (2001). Appraisal processes conceptualized from a schema-theoretic perspective. In K. R. Scherer, A. Schorr & T. Johnstone (Eds.), *Appraisal processes in emotion* (pp. 187–201). Oxford, UK: Oxford University Press.

Reisenzein, R., & Hofmann, T. (1990). An investigation of dimensions of cognitive appraisal in emotion using the repertory grid technique. *Motivation and Emotion, 14*(1), 1–26. doi:10.1007/bf00995546.

Reisenzein, R., Studtmann, M., & Horstmann, G. (2013). Coherence between emotion and facial expression: Evidence from laboratory experiments. *Emotion Review, 5*(1), 16–23. doi:10.1177/1754073912457228.

Roseman, I. (1984). Cognitive determinants of emotions: A structural theory. In P. Shaver (Ed.), *Review of personality and social psychology: Vol. 5. Emotions, relationships, and health* (pp. 11–36). Beverly Hills, CA: Sage.

Roseman, I. J. (1991). Appraisal determinants of discrete emotions. *Cognition & Emotion, 5*(3), 161–200.

Roseman, I. J. (2013). Appraisal in the emotion system: Coherence in strategies for coping. *Emotion Review, 5*(2), 141–149. doi:10.1177/1754073912469591.

Roseman, I. J., & Smith, C. A. (2001). Appraisal theory: Overview, assumptions, varieties, controversies. In K. R. Scherer, A. Schorr & T. Johnstone (Eds.), *Appraisal processes in emotion: Theory, methods, research* (pp. 3–19). London: London University Press.

Russell, J. A. (1979). Affective space is bipolar. *Journal of Personality and Social Psychology, 37*(3), 345. doi:10.1037/0022–3514.37.3.345.

Russell, J. A. (1980). A circumplex model of affect. *Journal of Personality and Social Psychology, 39*(6), 1161. doi:10.1037/h0077714.

Russell, J. A. (1989). Measures of emotion. In R. Plutchik & H. Kellerman (Eds.), *Emotion: Theory, research, and experience* (Vol. 4, pp. 83–111). Toronto. Ontario, Canada: Academic Press.

Russell, J. A. (2003). Core affect and the psychological construction of emotion. *Psychological Review, 110*(1), 145. doi:10.1037/0033–295x.110.1.145.

Russell, J. A. (2009). Emotion, core affect, and psychological construction. *Cognition and Emotion, 23*(7), 1259–1283. doi:10.1080/02699930902809375.

Russell, J. A., & Barrett, L. F. (1999). Core affect, prototypical emotional episodes, and other things called emotion: Dissecting the elephant. *Journal of Personality and Social Psychology, 76*(5), 805–819. doi:10.1037/0022–3514.76.5.805.

Russell, J. A., & Bullock, M. (1985). Multidimensional scaling of emotional facial expressions: Similarity from preschoolers to adults. *Journal of Personality and Social Psychology, 48*(5), 1290. doi:10.1037/0022–3514.48.5.1290.

Russell, J. A., & Fehr, B. (1994). Fuzzy concepts in a fuzzy hierarchy: Varieties of anger. *Journal of Personality and Social Psychology, 67*(2), 186. doi:10.1037/0022–3514.67.2.186.

Saarni, C. (2008). The interface of emotional development with social context. In M. Lewis, J. M. Haviland-Jones, L. F. Barrett, M. Lewis, J. M. Haviland-Jones & L. F. Barrett (Eds.), *Handbook of emotions* (3rd ed., pp. 332–347). New York: Guilford Press.

Saarni, C., Campos, J. J., Camras, L. A., & Witherington, D. (2008). Principles of emotion and emotional competence. In W. Damon, R. M. Lerner, D. Kuhn, R. Siegler & N. Eisenberg (Eds.), *Child and adolescent development: An advanced course* (pp. 361–405). Hoboken, NJ: John Wiley & Sons.

Schachter, S., & Singer, J. (1962). Cognitive, social, and physiological determinants of emotional state. *Psychological Review, 69*(5), 379. doi:10.1037/h0046234.

Scherer, K. R. (1984). Emotion as a multicomponent process: A model and some cross-cultural data. *Review of Personality & Social Psychology* (Vol. 5, pp. 37–63). Beverly Hills, CA: Sage.

Scherer, K. R. (2001). Appraisal considered as a process of multilevel sequential checking. *Appraisal Processes in Emotion: Theory, Methods, Research, 92*, 120.

Scherer, K. R. (2009). The dynamic architecture of emotion: Evidence for the component process model. *Cognition and Emotion, 23*(7), 1307–1351. doi:10.1080/02699930902928969.

Scherer, K. R., & Ceschi, G. (1997). Lost luggage: A field study of emotion–antecedent appraisal. *Motivation and Emotion, 21*(3), 211–235. doi:10.1023/a:1024498629430.

Scherer, K. R., & Ellgring, H. (2007a). Multimodal expression of emotion: Affect programs or componential appraisal patterns? *Emotion, 7*(1), 158. doi:10.1037/1528–3542.7.1.158.

Scherer, K. R., & Ellgring, H. (2007b). Are facial expressions of emotion produced by categorical affect programs or dynamically driven by appraisal? *Emotion, 7*(1), 113. doi:10.1037/1528–3542.7.1.113.

Schwartz, C. E., Wright, C. I., Shin, L. M., Kagan, J., & Rauch, S. L. (2003). Inhibited and uninhibited infants "grown up": Adult amygdalar response to novelty. *Science, 300*(5627), 1952–1953. doi:10.1126/science.1083703.

Scott, J. P. (1958). *Animal behavior.* Chicago, IL: University of Chicago Press.

Siemer, M., Mauss, I., & Gross, J. J. (2007). Same situation—different emotions: How appraisals shape our emotions. *Emotion, 7*(3), 592. doi:10.1037/1528–3542.7.3.592.

Smith, C. A. (1989). Dimensions of appraisal and physiological response in emotion. *Journal of Personality and Social Psychology, 56*(3), 339. doi:10.1037/0022–3514.56.3.339.

Smith, C. A., & Ellsworth, P. C. (1985). Patterns of cognitive appraisal in emotion. *Journal of Personality and Social Psychology, 48*(4), 813–838. doi:10.1037/0022–3514.48.4.813.

Smith, C. A., & Kirby, L. D. (2009). Putting appraisal in context: Toward a relational model of appraisal and emotion. *Cognition and Emotion, 23*(7), 1352–1372. doi:10.1080/02699930902860386.

Smith, C. A., & Lazarus, R. S. (1990). Emotion and adaptation. In L. Pervin (Ed.), *Handbook of personality: Theory and research* (pp. 609–637). New York, NY: Guilford Press.

Stemmler, G. (2003). Methodological considerations in the psychophysiological study of emotion. In R. J. Davidson, K. R. Scherer & H. Goldsmith (Eds.), *Handbook of affective sciences* (pp. 225–255). New York: Oxford University Press.

Stemmler, G., & Wacker, J. (2010). Personality, emotion, and individual differences in physiological responses. *Biological Psychology, 84*(3), 541–551. doi:10.1016/j.biopsycho.2009.09.012.

Stemmler, G., Heldmann, M., Pauls, C. A., & Scherer, T. (2001). Constraints for emotion specificity in fear and anger: The context counts. *Psychophysiology, 38*(2), 275–291. doi:10.1111/1469–8986.3820275.

Susskind, J. M., Lee, D. H., Cusi, A., Feiman, R., Grabski, W., & Anderson, A. K. (2008). Expressing fear enhances sensory acquisition. *Nature Neuroscience, 11*(7), 843–850. doi:10.1038/nn.2138.

Tomarken, A. J., Davidson, R. J., Wheeler, R. E., & Doss, R. C. (1992). Individual differences in anterior brain asymmetry and fundamental dimensions of emotion. *Journal of Personality and Social Psychology, 62*(4), 676. doi:10.1037/0022–3514.62.4.676.

Tomkins, S. S. (1962). *Affect, imagery, consciousness: Vol. I: The positive affects.* New York: Springer-Verlag.

Tomkins, S. S. (1963). *Affect, imagery, consciousness: Vol. 2: The negative affects.* New York: Springer-Verlag.

Tomkins, S. S., & McCarter, R. (1964). What and where are the primary affects? Some evidence for a theory. *Perceptual and Motor Skills,* 18, 119–158. doi:10.2466/pms.1964.18.1.119.

Tooby, J., & Cosmides, L. (1990). The past explains the present: Emotional adaptations and the structure of ancestral environments. *Ethology and Sociobiology, 11*(4), 375–424. doi:10.1016/0162–3095(90)90017-z.

Tracy, J. L., & Robins, R. W. (2004). Show your pride: Evidence for a discrete emotion expression. *Psychological Science, 15*(3), 194–197. doi:10.1111/j.0956–7976.2004.01503008.x.

Tsai, J. L., Simeonova, D. I., & Watanabe, J. T. (2004). Somatic and social: Chinese Americans talk about emotion. *Personality and Social Psychology Bulletin, 30*(9), 1226–1238. doi:10.1177/0146167204264014.

Waller, B. M., & Dunbar, R. I. (2005). Differential behavioural effects of silent bared teeth display and relaxed open mouth display in chimpanzees (Pan troglodytes). *Ethology, 111*(2), 129–142. doi:10.1111/j.1439–0310.2004.01045.x.

Watson, D., & Tellegen, A. (1985). Toward a consensual structure of mood. *Psychological Bulletin, 98*(2), 219. doi:10.1037/0033–2909.98.2.219.

Weierich, M. R., Wright, C. I., Negreira, A., Dickerson, B. C., & Barrett, L. F. (2010). Novelty as a dimension in the affective brain. *Neuroimage, 49*(3), 2871–2878. doi:10.1016/j.neuroimage.2009.09.047.

Widen, S. C. (2013). Children's interpretation of facial expressions: The long path from valence-based to specific discrete categories. *Emotion Review, 5*(1), 72–77. http://dx.doi.org/10.1177/1754073912451492.

Zald, D. H. (2003). The human amygdala and the emotional evaluation of sensory stimuli. *Brain Research Reviews, 41*(1), 88–123. doi:10.1016/s0165–0173(02)00248–5.

2   Methods for the Science of Emotion

Contents at a Glance

When you were younger, you might have tried to scare your siblings by telling them ghost stories. Or maybe you hid in the basement with a moose head that had been preserved by a taxidermist. Then when your six-year-old cousin came down the stairs, you made the head peek around the corner and appear to talk. (This happened to one of the authors.) Did that moose head method work? Could you do it again and again to get a similar reaction from people of other ages or other cultural backgrounds? In order to conduct research on human emotions, affective scientists attempt to create replicable experiments in the laboratory to induce emotional states.

They also try to measure emotions—both inside and outside of the laboratory. How do they elicit and measure emotions reliably? The answer is the content of this chapter. For the remainder of this book, we will refer back to these methods quite often.

Manipulating Emotions

One reason a researcher would induce an emotion in the laboratory is, of course, to test predictions of a specific theory of emotion. For example, an affective scientist might want to know which facial expressions or physiological changes co-occur with a particular self-reported emotion. The researcher would first find a method of inducing the emotion or emotions of interest. Then she would elicit those states in a large number of experimental participants and measure the self-reported, expressive, and physiological components of the resulting states. She may then confirm her predictions about how people facially express, say, disgust or fear.

Another reason a researcher might induce an emotion in experimental participants is in order to test whether that state reliably causes a particular behavior, such as increases in eating (Evers, Stok, & de Ridder, 2010) or helping (Schaller & Cialdini, 1990) behaviors. After eliciting an emotion in the laboratory, the researcher could give participants the opportunity to eat and measure the amount they consume. Finally, they might want to study how emotions influence cognitive behaviors such as reasoning or decision making (Blanchette & Richards, 2010). Here again the researcher could induce an emotion and then invite participants to solve moral dilemmas or evaluate risks of solutions to hypothetical problems.

Before we consider a number of ways to induce emotions in the laboratory, we need to appreciate that certain guidelines regulate the ethics of manipulation of emotions in the first place.

Ethical Guidelines

Exposing a six-year-old to a talking moose head is fine in the privacy of one's own house, but affective scientists cannot do anything they please to elicit emotions in experimental settings. They are required to conform to a set of **ethical guidelines**. In North America, such guidelines are specified by the American Psychological Association (APA). For example, scientists should not create a situation in which the intensity of participants' emotions surpasses those that they typically experience in daily life. In addition, experimentally induced emotions should be prompted by experiences that are, or are likely to be, encountered in everyday life rather than by very unusual interventions. And finally, the emotions should be extinguishable—particularly if they are negative or painful—and alleviated before the participant leaves the laboratory. The importance of debriefing to alleviate the effects of emotion inductions has been well documented (e.g., Brock & Becker, 1966).

Ethical guidelines were not in place in the 1950s, and so an example of a well-known experiment conducted in 1953 demonstrates the type of experimental manipulation of emotion that could not be conducted today. The researcher, Ax, wanted to find out whether anger and fear were characterized by specific patterns of autonomic nervous system activity. He measured 14 different indicators of autonomic nervous system activity such as heart rate, respiration, blood pressure, and muscle tension. Under the cover story of testing the validity of polygraphs, or lie detectors, Ax (1953) hooked participants up to a number of devices, such as an electric shock generator. Then, as their autonomic nervous system indicators were being recorded, for some of the participants Ax staged a malfunction of the shock generator; the generator spewed sparks, and the experimenter became overtly distressed. Predictably, the participants experienced high levels of fear. Participants who had been assigned to an anger condition were scolded for five minutes by a rude polygraph operator. This treatment indeed elicited high levels of anger. In fact, Ax (1953) found relative specificity in the patterns of participants' autonomic nervous system activity. However, it is no longer possible to conduct a study with such extreme dishonesty and unusual level of provocation. Furthermore, as we shall see in discussing research throughout this book, such extreme provocation is not necessary. We turn next to the methods that can be and are most often used to influence emotional responses in the laboratory.

Affective Images—The International Affective Picture System

Some research requires that many brief emotional reactions are elicited in a single participant throughout an experimental session. For instance, a researcher might be interested in how attention is allocated to information that causes feelings of joy versus feelings of fear.

The International Affective Picture System (IAPS, pronounced eye-aps) is a set of emotion-inducing images. Over half of the IAPS images contain scenes involving human beings in interactions. The remaining images contain animals, objects, or scenes that do not contain humans. Some examples appear in Figure 2.1. In extensive development and validation research, the full set of images has been presented to participants in different countries so that norms exist that summarize the positivity and arousal level of the typical self-reported affective reaction to each image (Lang, Bradley, & Cuthbert, 2005). Other research has

Figure 2.1 From top to bottom: high arousal positive, high arousal negative, and neutral images from Open Access Affective Standardized Image S (OASIS), a set of online, open access emotion-inducing images (Kurdi, Lozano, & Banaji, 2016).

investigated emotional responses to the IAPS images with measures of skin conductance (Bradley et al., 2001), cardiovascular response (Bradley et al., 2001), and neural electrophysiology (Cuthbert et al., 2000).

The IAPS images were developed in order to allow researchers all over the world to reliably elicit affective responses. By using the exact same images, researchers can then compare and even replicate each other's work.

Recall of Emotional Memories

Whereas some research questions require the scientist to produce a brief emotional reaction, as can be accomplished with the IAPS slides, other research questions require that a more prolonged emotional reaction be induced in experimental participants. One way experimenters in the laboratory induce emotional states that last longer than a few seconds is to ask participants to get active in the process of experiencing emotion. In the recall method for inducing emotions, participants are instructed to retrieve memories of events that they experienced personally and to relive the emotion they felt.

Strack, Schwarz, and Geschneidinger (1985) and Schwarz and Clore (1983) systematically investigated the retrieval of emotional memories to induce emotional states in the laboratory. They showed that the way in which the memory is retrieved determines whether an emotion is felt. Specifically, they demonstrated that the retrieval of emotional memories in a pallid way—a way that does not focus on the emotional parts of the experience but still accurately describes the situation—does not reactivate the original emotion. On the other hand, a retrieval that involves attention to the vivid emotional aspects of the situation tends to reactivate the original emotion. This is an important demonstration because it shows that we are not obliged to re-experience an entire emotional event each time that we think back about it. The way that we think about it influences the impact that memory has on our present emotional state.

Films

A third method for eliciting emotions in the laboratory is to show participants short films or film segments—even from well-known movies—that have been demonstrated in pilot testing to produce a particular emotion or reaction in *most* individuals (Gross & Levenson, 1995). You might wonder how we know which films produce which emotions. Researchers must always study the emotional effects of the method before using it in an experiment.

Philippot (1993) conducted a study of the emotional impact of a number of film segments. The segments lasted between three and six minutes and were selected to generate five different emotions (anger, disgust, sadness, happiness, and fear) and a neutral state in the viewer. Participants watched each clip and reported how it made them feel on a self-report questionnaire. Results showed that the movies provoked very specific emotions in most individuals. For example, the segments preselected to induce joy did induce joy quite specifically and more so than any other emotion. Subsequently, Gross and Levenson (1995) also developed a set of 16 movie segments that successfully induced specific emotions of amusement, anger, contentment, disgust, sadness, surprise, a neutral state, and fear, although their manipulation of fear was somewhat weak. Using neutral film clips as comparison, Hewig et al. (2005) more recently replicated tests of the effectiveness of Gross and Levenon's films with German university students and found strong support for the selective impact of the clips on emotional states a decade after the initial study and also in a different country. Table 2.1 lists some of the films used to induce the emotions.

Table 2.1 A sample of films used to induce emotion. From Hewig et al. (2005).

Film Source	Target Emotion	Clip Description
When Harry Met Sally (1989)	Amusement	Harry and Sally discuss about whether Harry would notice it if a woman could fake an orgasm./A man and a woman are talking to each other in a restaurant.
Hannah and her Sisters (1986)	Neutral	Hannah and Holly go shopping. They are talking about last night./ Two women stroll through a shopping center.
Cry Freedom (1987)	Anger	A group of Blacks is protesting against the racial discrimination laws in South Africa. In peaceful demonstrations they are walking through their villages./A group of black people is attacked by soldiers.
Pink Flamingos (1972)	Disgust	John makes unusual films. One day he films a transvestite with a poodle./A transvestite eats a dog's feces.
Silence of the Lambs (1991)	Fear	Clarice, a young FBI agent, is searching for a serial killer. In her investigation she also questions the tailor James./A woman follows a dangerous killer into a basement.
An Officer and a Gentleman (1982)	Sadness	Zack and Paula are looking for their friend Sid. They knock on the door of his motel room. As no one answers they enter the room./A couple finds a dead friend.

Many researchers have used the film segments developed by Philippot and Gross to conduct research both on the components of emotions and on the effects of emotion on other psychological processes. Sometimes researchers find their own films to use. Researchers who preferred to use segments that they themselves select are, of course, required to demonstrate empirically that their movies have the desired emotional effect (Boiten, 1998; Niedenthal & Dalle, 2001; Tomarken, Davidson, & Henriques, 1990). It should be noted that most of the films used to induce emotion in laboratory research are complex and realistic. However, they are also more benign than many currently popular television shows!

Music

Music also causes people to feel emotions and can be used to elicit certain emotions in the laboratory (Scherer, 2004; Västfjäll, 2002; Westermann et al., 1996). At first pass, you might think that the reason a specific song causes a very individual emotional state in a particular person is because, for him or her, that music is associated with a very personal emotional event or period of their life. Maybe you fell in love for the first time when a particular song was popular on the radio. You now associate the song with that time of being in love, and so the song always produces a particular feeling (either joy or perhaps sadness) in you. If the effects of music were this specific to each person, then it would be labor intensive to manipulate emotion with music. The researcher would have to find out which music makes each experimental participant feel which emotion and then go out and find those pieces of music and compile them before bringing those participants into the laboratory—a possible strategy, and one that works well, but that is also time consuming (e.g., Ellard, Farchione, & Barlow, 2012).

More often, researchers rely on general—rather than idiosyncratic—effects of music on people's experience of emotion (Sloboda, 1992). And these effects of music on emotion seem to be quite basic, at least in Western cultures (Costa, Fine, & Ricci Bitti, 2004). For example, Costa, Bitti, and Bonfiglioli (2000) found that dissonant (compared to consonant) bichords are perceived as unstable, furious, and tense. As a consequence, a piece of music with many dissonant chords will likely make the listener feel somewhat anxious. In addition, people tend to perceive minor chords as sadder and gloomier than major chords, and high-pitched tones are associated with positive emotions, whereas low-pitched tones tend to express negative emotions. Tempo is another powerful way of expressing emotional states in music. Slow tempos tend to express low-arousal emotions, whereas fast tempos are associated with high-arousal emotional states (Gagnon & Peretz, 2003). These different qualities of music can also be combined to produce an endless palette of emotional expressions in music: in a given piece of classical music, the adagio typically sounds much sadder than the allegro, which sounds more joyful.

Music has been shown to influence emotion as indexed by self-report (Sloboda & O'Neill, 2001), physiological reactions (Bartlett, 1996), activity in the brain (Koelsch, Fritz, Müller, & Friederici, 2006), and facial expression of emotion (Becker, 2004). However, the emotions elicited by music may not correspond to the basic emotions. Some researchers have demonstrated that music induces subtle states that are described by language that refers to nuanced feelings such as sensual, spiritual, radiant, and meditative (Scherer & Zentner, 2001).

Scripted Social Interaction

Similar to the Ax (1953) experiment, but under the supervision of ethics boards, modern social psychological studies of emotion sometimes involve a cover story (deception) about the experimental hypothesis and the use of a scripted social interaction involving the experimenter or fake participant (a **confederate**) who is working with the experimenter. Scripted social interactions to induce emotions in the laboratory are particularly useful when the emotion under study is difficult to elicit with images, films, and music and when a very realistic state is desired (Harmon-Jones, Amodio, & Zinner, 2007). Examples of these emotions include anger, fear, guilt, and embarrassment.

Stemmler and colleagues (2001), for example, induced anger to examine the coherence of the components of emotion (discussed in Chapter 1). Under a cover story that the experiment was designed to investigate "stress and strain," the participant performed a difficult mental task in which they had to count backwards in steps of 1, 2, 3, and so forth from a large initial number. As the participant counted, the experimenter interrupted them rudely through an intercom several times and made scripted comments about their poor performance. At the end of the task, the participant was asked for the result and the experimenter stated that the resulting number was incorrect. On self-report questions, participants who have undergone this manipulation, or one similar to it, indicate that the interaction indeed made them angry (e.g., Evers et al., 2014; Mauss et al., 2006).

Guilt, another emotion that is difficult to induce with films, music, or images, has also been induced with scripted interaction. For example, Konecni (1972) developed a procedure used in the field (i.e., outside the laboratory in the real world) in which participants feel as if they are responsible for making a confederate drop some new books on the ground. In another method, Brock and Becker (1966) famously designed an apparatus rigged so that when participants pressed buttons on it as instructed, it appeared that they had inadvertently caused a low or a high amount of damage to the device. In the high damage condition, specifically designed to induce guilt, the apparatus suddenly made a loud noise and produced clouds of thick white smoke. To add to the guilt, the experimenter said, "What happened? I'll never get my master's now. What did you do to the machine? Well, I guess that ends the experiment. The machine is broken" (Brock & Becker, 1966, p. 317). Subsequently, researchers have designed other apparatuses rigged to fall apart or fail in such a way to suggest that the participant is at fault. Manipulation checks have shown that these scripted interactions are effective elicitors of guilt in the laboratory and the field.

Finally, in an early study, Apsler (1975) found that requesting participants to perform any one of the following four behaviors in front of the experimenter or other audience served as a powerful induction of embarrassment: 1) dance to rock music for a minute, 2) laugh for 30 seconds as if having just heard a funny joke, 3) sing "The Star Spangled Banner" (with the lyrics provided), and 4) imitate a five-year-old throwing a temper tantrum to avoid going to bed for 30 seconds. Subsequent research has relied heavily on these treatments. For example, requesting participants to sing "The Star Spangled Banner" in front of a video camera and the experimenter is a frequently used (and highly effective!) induction method (Harris, 2001; Miller, 1987).

You can see that scripted interaction inductions of emotions are useful for eliciting strong and complex emotions. However, they are often very time consuming for research personnel and usually require a high level of social coordination and training (Aronson & Carlsmith, 1985).

Developmental Detail

Getting Little Ones Emotional (Ethically)

Speaking of ethics, as we did at the beginning of the chapter, how might researchers ethically induce emotions, or at least the expression of emotion, in infants and children?

Not surprisingly, the mother is often enlisted to help generate emotional responding. For instance, in order to look at the effects of facial expressions on the emotional expression of infants, Haviland and Lelwica (1987) had mothers make happy, sad, and anger facial expressions at their 10-week-olds while saying sentences that conveyed the same emotion. One difficulty with the procedure is that not all caretakers are good actors. Nevertheless, this study and others found evidence that the babies were likely to match their facial expressions to their mothers' (Termine & Izard, 1988).

At a slightly later age, scripted interactions can also be used to elicit emotions. For example, Stenberg, Campos, and Emde (1983) elicited anger responses in seven-month-old babies by having the mother or the experimenter give their baby a Gerber teething biscuit and then take it away (and out of reach!). Because babies at this age are usually not independently mobile, manipulations such as this, which involve control over the baby's outcomes, successfully induce frustration and anger. Interest and joy responses as well as fear responses can also be elicited by the introduction of low-intensity and high-intensity toys, respectively (Putnam & Stifter, 2002). You know how you jump when you play with a jack-in-the-box? Babies jump too!

Finally, films have been developed to induce emotional states in even older children. Eisenberg and colleagues (Eisenbery et al., 1988) showed films to five-year-olds that portrayed another child experiencing anxiety/distress (during a thunderstorm) and sadness (due to the death of a pet bird). The five-year-olds' emotional reactions matched those depicted in the films.

Naturally Occurring Emotions

A second important way to conduct research on emotions is to examine the behaviors of individuals who are experiencing different states naturally due to events in their lives. There are at least two ways to use naturally occurring emotions to study emotion processes. One is to find groups of people who have a strong probability of all being in a similar and predictable emotional state (because of the consensual meaning of the situation in that culture) and compare them to people in another situation who are feeling little emotion or something different. The second is to measure ongoing emotion in the laboratory or in daily life using online assessments and relate their reported emotions to the behavior of interest.

Quasi-Experimental Designs

Quasi-experimental studies are studies in which there are experimental and control conditions, but participants are not randomly assigned to them. The emotion-eliciting event might be naturally occurring or arranged by the experimenter. In emotion research, a scientist might examine the behavior of people who, because of something about their current situation, are thought a priori to be likely to be in a particular emotion state and compare the behavior to people who are thought to be in a more neutral state, or a different state altogether. For example, you might predict, based on our discussion of the emotional impact of some films, that individuals leaving a cinema after having seen a film known to be very depressing will be, on average, in a very sad state. And you could expect that people reading in a library at the same time might be in a rather neutral state. The behavior of these two groups of individuals could be compared in order to draw conclusions about how sadness influences behavior such as helping, socializing, consuming food or drink, or any of a number of behaviors.

In an example of a quasi-experimental field study, Niedenthal and Dalle (2001) wanted to see how a happy state affected categorization. They predicted that during any strong emotional state, individuals would temporarily form mental categories of objects and events that elicit the same emotion. An example would be a category of all things that "make a person feel disgust." This would suggest, the researchers thought, that people spontaneously create "emotional response categories" when feeling emotions. To test the idea that individuals naturally experiencing happiness (versus neutral mood) also tend to categorize on the basis of emotional equivalencies, Niedenthal and Dalle recruited participants at two actual wedding celebrations. The expectation was that the invitees at those weddings, if recruited for the study before drinking but after the ceremony, would be in a very happy (and still sober) state. At the same time, another experimenter recruited individuals walking down the street at more or less the same time. The expectation was that those people would be, on average, in a more neutral state.

Individuals at the weddings and on the street were approached and asked to participate in a brief psychological experiment, which involved completing two short questionnaires. The first questionnaire measured categorization, and the second measured emotional state. Results of the first questionnaire showed that individuals at the weddings tended to form categories based on emotional equivalences between objects significantly more than did individuals who were recruited while walking down the street (see Niedenthal & Dalle, 2001, for details about the measure of categorization). Results of the emotion measure showed that, as expected, invitees at the weddings were much happier than individuals walking down the street, who were in a generally neutral state.

Notice therefore that Niedenthal and Dalle (2001) could study groups of participants who were in naturally occurring emotional states and draw conclusions about how the emotions are related to other cognitive processes without needing to bring individuals into the laboratory to receive a treatment that evokes an emotion. This type of study thus enhances the *ecological validity* of the hypothesis—in this case, the idea of emotional response categorization—as it shows that the phenomenon occurs in daily life and not just in the laboratory.

Correlational Designs

You probably recall that in correlational research two behaviors or events are measured in order to quantify the direction (positive or negative) and strength (from 0 to 1.0) of the relationship between them. Some researchers want to measure naturally occurring emotions and other behaviors as they occur in everyday life.

Emotions can be studied as they occur "online," or almost so, in real life. In **experience sampling**, participants access the Internet or use apps on their smartphones to complete questionnaires about their emotions throughout the day (e.g., Feldman, 1995). The questionnaires can ask the respondent to indicate which emotions they are experiencing, rate the intensity of those emotions, and indicate what happened to cause the emotion, for example.

There are three basic schedules for the collection of experience-sampling data. First, researchers may request that participants fill out the computer-based questionnaires at regular times throughout the day, such as morning, noon, and in the evening. This is called **interval-contingent responding**. Second, the researcher may ask participants to fill out the questionnaires in response to specific types of events—for instance, whenever they have an emotion that lasts a certain amount of time. This is called **event-contingent responding**. And finally, the researcher may ask the participant to complete the questionnaires whenever the palmtop computer signals them to do so. This is called **signal-contingent responding**. Much more detail about the use of experience-sampling techniques can be found in Christensen et al. (2003) and Feldman Barrett and Barrett (2001).

In an excellent example of experience-sampling research, Carstensen and colleagues (2011) investigated developmental changes in emotional experience. Participants reported on their emotions at five randomly selected times each day for one week. The emotions of the same participants were then investigated in the same way 5 and then again 10 years later. The findings showed that emotional well-being improved with age (see also Chapters 8 and 9 for more detail). Furthermore, emotions were linked to mortality: participants who experienced more positive than negative emotions in everyday life were less likely to have died over the period of the study.

Induction Methods Are Not All the Same

One question you might have is how you would ever decide which emotion induction method to use. There are ways in which the methods can be compared that help you decide which is the best for the particular research question (Rottenberg, Ray, & Gross, 2007). Perhaps the most important dimensions are:

- Experimental demand
- Standardization
- Complexity
- Ecological validity

Experimental demand refers to how easy it is for experimental participants to guess what a study is designed to test. Experimental demand is high if the participant can very easily guess, and this is undesirable in cases in which the participant is motivated and able to change their behavior in order to either help or hurt the experimenter. Exposure to clearly happy or sad films, images, or music can seem to participants like obvious attempts to manipulate mood or emotional response. This might be particularly true when the participant is exposed to multiple emotion conditions or emotional stimuli because the very comparison will make it that much more apparent that the experimenter is manipulating emotion. Further, a link between the induction of emotion and the dependent variable may also be obvious: if the participant is exposed to a happy movie and is then asked to complete a measure of psychological well-being, the participant might easily conclude that the experiment concerns the effects of happiness on self-reports of well-being. If participants guess the expectations of the experimenter, they may alter their behavior, thereby compromising the validity of the study. To avoid such influences, researchers use a **cover story** to mask the true purpose of the study. For example, sometimes they simply assert that the two parts of the study (the task that includes the emotion induction and the task that measures the dependent variable) are not related or constitute two separate studies.

Standardization is the extent to which the method to induce emotions has been pilot-tested for effectiveness and reliability across people and contexts. The IAPS images were specifically developed for use with participants of many ages and from many countries. The films that are presented in Table 2.1 have also been extensively pilot-tested and used in subsequent research, making them somewhat better standardized than other induction methods such as music and scripted interaction.

Complexity and **ecological validity** are related ideas. Whereas complexity refers to invoking many components of the emotion in the laboratory experience, ecological validity is the extent to which the experience is similar to what might be experienced in daily life. The emotional experience in the laboratory is influenced and sometimes constrained by the methods being used by the experimenter (see next section). For instance, when participants are lying in a magnetic resonance imaging (MRI) scanner observing IAPS slides, the complexity and ecological validity of the emotional response must be viewed as limited. Not only do the slides not produce a complex state, but the fact that the participant may not move limits the extent to which the body can be involved in the experience of the emotional response. On the other hand, there are occasions (such as while driving a car) when we are bombarded with emotional stimuli to which our responses are constrained. We allocate attention to them, but perhaps do not engage in bodily response. Presenting IAPS images in an MRI scanner, therefore, can be said to be a model of some real-life emotional experiences, but not all.

There are also other considerations in the selection of emotion induction such as expense (we have seen that scripted social interaction is costly) and the specificity of response or state that is elicited (some procedures elicit positive or negative affective responses, whereas others seem to elicit quite discrete emotions, such as happiness, anger, fear, or guilt). Even with all of these issues in mind, however, the most important thing is that the researcher starts with a theory of emotion and then selects an induction method that elicits emotional states or reactions that the theory was intended to explain.

Measuring Emotions

In Chapter 1 we learned that emotions have many components. Measuring emotion also requires that the experimenter endorse a particular theory of emotion and try to assess the component or components of emotion specified by the theory. Here we describe five types of measures that assess different components of emotion. Each measure does not assess emotions to the same degree of specificity. Some measure the dimensions of "core affect" (valence and activation), and others measure more discrete emotional states.

Questionnaires

Think of the times you have been asked to rate some aspect of your experience on a scale from 1 (not at all) to 10 (very much) with intermediate numbers standing for intermediate amounts. It happens often, right? Such a rating system is called a Likert (pronounced lick-ert) response scale, and because the numerical assessments in Likert and Likert-type responses can be converted into words (not at all, a little, moderate, etc.), we call such questionnaires a **verbal measure**. Questionnaires with nonverbal formats, in which not words but pictures represent feeling states, have also been developed to measure conscious subjective feeling states.

One of the most often-used instruments for measuring global (or "core") affect is the Positive and Negative Affect Schedule (PANAS) developed by Watson, Clark, and Tellegen (1988). The PANAS is a brief, reliable, and valid questionnaire that consists of 20 feeling words. Respondents rate each word on a continuous numerical scale from 1 (very slightly or not at all) to 5 (extremely), according to how much they are feeling that state (Figure 2.2). Instructions to the respondent refer to a particular time frame, such as "right now," "in the past week," "in the past month," or "in general." The questionnaire can be used to calculate a negative affect (NA) score (by averaging responses to certain negative feeling words), as well as a positive affect (PA) score (by averaging responses to certain positive feeling words). The Multiple Affect Adjective Checklist—Revised (MAAC-R; Zuckerman & Lubin, 1985), the Current Mood Questionnaire (Feldman Barrett & Russell, 1998), and the Brief Mood Introspection Scale (BMIS; Mayer & Gaschke, 1988) are other instruments that can also be used to measure general positive and negative affect and high and low aroused states.

In contrast, the Differential Emotions Scale (Izard et al., 1974) was developed to measure discrete emotional states. The scale lists words that belong to 10 emotion categories: interest, joy, sadness, anger, fear, anxiety, disgust, scorn, surprise, and happiness. Respondents rate each word according to how much they feel that way at any given time (from "not at all" to "very strongly"). The experimenter can average the ratings of the three words for each category in order to know how much joy, anger, interest, and so forth the respondent felt.

The Self-Assessment Manikin (SAM; see Figure 2.3) is an instrument designed to measure the valence and arousal components of affect using nonverbal scales (Bradley & Lang, 1994). It is composed of a series of drawings of a figure whose face changes incrementally from

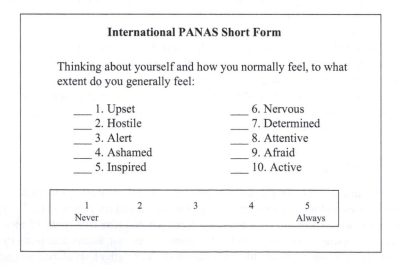

Figure 2.2 The International PANAS Short Form (I-PANAS-SF), a validated, shortened version of the full 20-item instrument. Adapted from Thompson (2007).

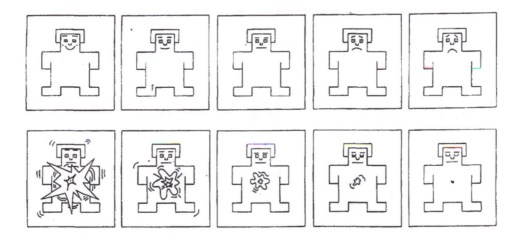

Figure 2.3 The Self-Assessment Manikin as developed by Bradley and Lang (1994).

smiling (happy) to frowning (unhappy) to represent valence, and a second series of drawings of the same figure that changes from appearing excited and wide-eyed to relaxed and sleepy to represent arousal. Respondents check the circle underneath the figure according to how well it corresponds to their feeling state at that moment. These ratings can then be converted into scores, with valence ratings on a scale of 1 (pleasant) to 9 (unpleasant) and arousal ratings on a scale of 1 (calm) to 9 (excited).

An advantage of the SAM, and indeed any nonverbal measure of emotion, is that it can be used to measure affect in both children and adults. In addition, because SAM is a language-free measurement, it can be used across countries and cultures (Morris, 1995).

Facial Expression

The study of facial expression can be traced to the French physiologist Guillaume-Benjamin Duchenne de Boulogne (1862/1990), who investigated how different combinations of facial muscles contribute to producing different expressions of emotion. Duchenne de Boulogne induced the contraction of facial muscles with the use of electric currents and took photographs of the resulting expressions. In so doing he foreshadowed one way to measure facial expression: the so-called **component method**. These days, affective scientists who use component methods rely on objective coding systems that were inspired in part by Duchenne de Boulogne's observations.

Ekman and Friesen (1978) developed the widely used, anatomically based coding system, the Facial Action Coding Scheme (FACS). FACS measures the appearance of changes in the face caused by muscular movements. Facial expressions are described by a combination of action units (AU). There are 44 AUs, which singly or in combination, account for all visible and distinguishable facial muscle movements. FACS scoring requires the careful observation of the contraction of facial muscles as well as the intensity of the contraction (Figure 2.4). Coders usually rely on photographs, but preferably on video recordings, to annotate minute changes in face morphology. A substantial level of training is required, over 100 hours, and in general the coding effort is very time consuming (Cohn & Ekman, 2005). For example, one minute of video takes approximately an hour to score. Some evidence for the validity of the FACS comes from

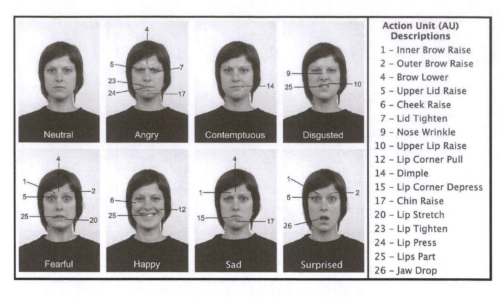

Figure 2.4 Posed expressions of eight different emotions, with labels for the key muscle movements involved, based on FACS action units. From the validated Radboud Faces Database; Langner et al., 2010.

studies that used self-reports of expressers' feelings or that relied on observers' judgment of emotion to identify the AUs implicated in the spontaneous facial expressions of basic emotions (Ekman & Friesen, 1982).

Because FACS coding is so time consuming, computer-assisted FACS coding software has also been developed (Cohn, Ambadar, & Ekman, 2007). The Computer Expression Recognition Toolbox (CERT) is one such measure of visible facial mimicry (Littlewort et al., 2011). CERT automatically codes the intensity of 19 different facial actions taken from the Facial Action Unit Coding System (Ekman & Rosenberg, 2005), as well as the degree to which six prototypical emotion expressions are present (Figure 2.4). It is more cost effective and less invasive than electromyography (EMG) (see above), which often limits researchers to just a few action units. CERT as described by Littlewort and colleagues is now commercially available from the company Emotient. FAST-FACS (Simon et al., 2011), which was specifically developed for emotion researchers, is another software tool available for computer-assisted FACS coding.

The techniques for measuring facial expressions that we have overviewed so far involve visual inspection of the face. Sometimes small but very important expressions occur that signal the presence of an emotional reaction without necessarily being readily detectable by visual inspection. Facial EMG measures the electrical discharge of contracted facial muscles with small surface electrodes that are placed on the face (Cacioppo & Petty, 1981; Cacioppo, Tassinary, & Fridlund, 1990). EMG recording thus can provide an accurate assessment of both visible and nonvisible, voluntary and spontaneous facial behavior. Existing descriptions of the muscles that comprise particular facial expressions can be used to guide electrode placement.

A second approach to measuring facial expressions, the **judgment method**, is not concerned with facial muscle movements themselves, but with the information that an observer can infer from a facial expression. The method was introduced by Darwin (1872/1998) and is commonly used for studying facial expressions when testing the hypothesis of the universality and innateness of facial expression. Judgment studies are based on the assumption that an observer can accurately recognize emotions from the face alone, in the absence of any information about the emotion-eliciting situation. In the standard judgment study, observers are presented with still photographs of facial expressions and are asked to identify the emotion expressed by the person by selecting a single emotional word from a short list (i.e., the forced-choice response format). Accuracy is inferred when the observer agrees either with a consensus view about the emotion being expressed (established in a pilot study) or when the label she chooses corresponds with the self-report of the individual whose facial expression has been photographed.

Central Nervous System

The nervous system is traditionally divided into two parts. These are the central and peripheral nervous systems. The **central nervous system** (CNS), which includes the brain and the spinal cord, plays an important role in our emotional responding. Scientists who study the neural bases of emotion look for neural biomarkers for emotional experience and expression. This means that they look for the systems of the brain that occur at the same time as an emotional event, such as a reaction to the sight of two puppies playing. Another way to say this is that they are looking for correlations between events in the brain and emotional responding. Electroencephalography and neuroimaging methods—in particular, functional magnetic resonance imaging—are two measures that have been developed to assess emotion processes in the CNS.

Electroencephalography (EEG)

Neurons in the brain communicate using electricity and neurochemicals. When neurons become active, they depolarize, meaning that their electrical potential, which is normally negative compared to the extracellular space, quickly changes in polarity, and if a threshold is reached, an electric impulse (a so-called action potential) travels down the axon. The axon divides in many branches, which each almost touch many other neurons. These points of near-contact between two neurons are called synapses. Because the synapse is actually a gap and the two neurons do not touch, the arriving action potential leads to the release of neurotransmitters, which jump the gap to make contact with receptors on the other neurons. If enough neurotransmitters reach the other neuron, its electric potential will also change, and if a threshold is reached, an action potential will be fired and sent to even more neurons. The changes in the electrical potential of groups of neurons can be measured over time with an electrode "headcap" placed on the scalp (see Figure 2.5). This is what EEG does. However, due to the fact that the electrical signals must pass between tissue and the skull before reaching electrodes and that only the upper part of the head is sampled, EEG is mostly confined to recording from the outer layers of the brain (the cortex) and is not very precise in localizing where in the brain the signal comes from. Instead, EEG can assess activation in larger regions of the brain such as the anterior (i.e., front) versus posterior (i.e., back) and/or the left hemisphere versus right hemisphere. Researchers have used EEG to test some hypotheses about the role of the different hemispheres of the brain in generating positive and negative emotions, which are discussed in the next chapter.

Scientists also use EEG measures to assess the timing of responses to a perceived emotional object, usually called an "event" (Bradley et al., 2007; Olofsson & Polich, 2007). Researchers can calculate event-related potential (ERP) waveforms by averaging the EEG over many trials to give an idea of the timing of responses to emotional information under different task conditions. ERPs consist of a series of positive and negative voltage changes, which are called P for positive and N for negative. The P and N responses are further identified in terms of the time in milliseconds at which they occur after the onset of a perceived event. For instance, the P100 (also P1) component is a positive voltage deflection that occurs about 100 milliseconds after an event occurs. Moreover, ERP components are associated with a specific topography, that is,

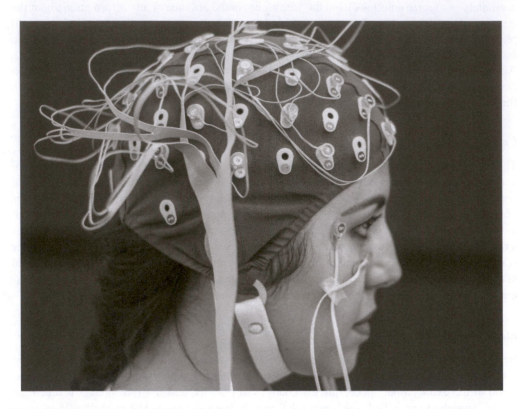

Figure 2.5 An example of an EEG headcap.

a distribution of positive and negative voltage over the scalp. The P100, for example, occurs over the back of the scalp and is thought to originate in visual cortices. Studies have shown that events (e.g., pictures) with unpleasant valence produce larger P1 amplitudes than pleasant and neutral images (Delplanque et al., 2004).

Functional Magnetic Resonance Imaging

Magnetic resonance imaging is a measure that is taken inside a cylindrical tube called a scanner and that uses a strong magnetic field (typically of 3 Tesla) and pulses of radio wave energy to make images of structures inside the body (Figure 2.6). The resulting image is called a scan. The scan is digital in nature so it can be stored on a computer and subjected to different kinds of analysis. Functional MRI, or fMRI, uses MRI scanning in a slightly different way, because it takes an image of the brain while the brain is working (performing a function). When a part of the brain is in use, blood oxygenation and flow to that region increase. The fMRI of the brain detects blood oxygenation and blood flow changes. Based on the scans, activation maps are computed, showing which parts of the brain are involved (statistically activated) in solving a particular task or making a particular judgment. Thus, rather than showing the state of a structure in the body (the goal of the MRI scan), the fMRI helps a researcher draw conclusions about what different parts of the brain are used to perform specific tasks.

With regard to emotions, fMRI research has addressed questions about whether there are neural biomarkers for basic emotions such as happiness, disgust, and fear (Barrett & Wager, 2006; Phan et al., 2002;

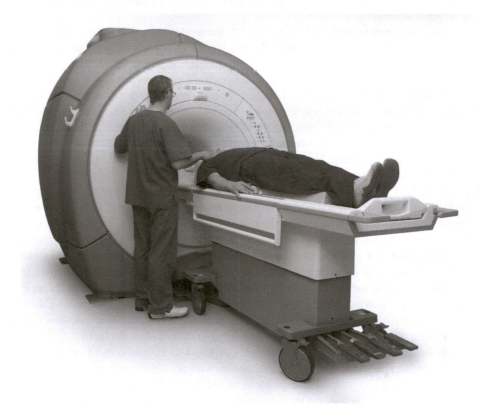

Figure 2.6 An MRI scanner.

Posner et al., 2009; Sprengelmeyer et al., 1998). Because fMRI is relatively imprecise in mapping subcortical, and especially brainstem, regions (which are small and lie deep in the brain), this technique is most effectively used to better understand the roles of cortical regions in emotions. Because cortical regions are important for executive functions, fMRI has been most informative in studies of the regulation of emotion rather than the discovery of biomarkers for emotion. The regulation and inhibition of emotion are thought to be driven by the prefrontal cortex, which is easier to visualize in fMRI (Kalisch, 2009; Ochsner et al., 2002; Wager et al., 2008).

There has been an acceleration in research using fMRI to answer questions in the affective sciences. This is probably due to a number of factors. One is that fMRI techniques, especially the way that the signals are processed and analyzed, are now more sophisticated in ways that make resulting data more precise and reliable. In addition, the technique has been refined so that more insight into the timing of mental events can be gained. In the past, questions of timing have been left to other measures such as EEG, which cannot speak to the location or neural circuitry involved in a mental process.

Peripheral Nervous System

The **peripheral nervous system** (PNS) lies outside of the brain and spinal cord and includes the cranial nerves, the spinal nerves, and the autonomic nerves. These nerves connect the CNS to sensory organs, such as the eyes and ears. It also connects the CNS to other organs of the body, as well as to muscles, blood vessels, and glands. The PNS can be further broken down into the somatic and autonomic nervous systems.

The **somatic nervous system** (SNS) functions to innervate skeletal muscles, including those of the face, that are under voluntary control. We rely on our SNS when we execute plans to make the movements that are necessary to walk, run, get dressed, and pick up a coffee cup or a cell phone. The **autonomic nervous system** (ANS), in contrast, supports automatic functions of the body. For example, the ANS regulates the internal balance of your body when you are faced with changing circumstances and adjusting innervation of smooth muscles—such as the heart—and glands. The ANS is further divided into the sympathetic nervous system and the parasympathetic nervous system. Whereas the **sympathetic nervous system** functions to prepare the body for action, the **parasympathetic nervous system** has restorative functions. These functions are sometimes called the "fight or flight" and the "rest and digest" systems, respectively.

Most researchers who study the physiology of emotion try to measure ANS responses because they are interested in automatic emotional responses. A number of ways to measure the ANS are summarized in Table 2.2. As the table illustrates, most aspects of physiology, such as heart rate, are recorded by placing sensors on the surface of the skin. Because of the use of sensors and the fact that an experimenter must place them on the participant, physiological recording is considered an intrusive procedure. By intrusive we mean that the participant knows that something is being measured and that the measurement technique might be experienced as stressful or uncomfortable. There are two exceptions to the use of sensors, and those are measures of pupillary response and eye blinks. These two responses can be assessed with eye tracking devices, although sometimes eye blinks are also measured with electrodes.

After electrodes are attached, the participant is exposed to the stimulus of interest. Stimuli can range from interpersonal, such as an interaction with a rude experimenter, to perceptual, such as visual or auditory stimuli like pictures of facial expressions or loud noises. During exposure to the stimulus, the electrodes capture the electrical potential (i.e., voltage) generated near the electrode sites in response to the stimulus. The digitized record of the electrical potential is then compared to recordings from a neutral baseline. Comparisons between recordings from a neutral baseline and those recorded during exposure to the stimulus of interest allow the researcher to see whether exposure to the stimulus had a biological impact on the participant and in which physiological system (i.e., heart rate, electrodermal response, etc.). The researcher can then link the physiological response to related emotions.

Because the ANS controls automatic reactions—things outside of a person's control—it is considered an accurate measure of "raw" emotion. However, so far no physiological biomarkers for the basic emotions (perhaps other than fear and anger) have been identified. Rather, researchers study physiological indicators to learn about other aspects of emotion such as novelty, intensity, and valence (Mauss & Robinson, 2009).

Table 2.2 A list of physiological measures that are taken in order to make some inferences about emotion processes such as fear and stress

Measurement	Instrument	Indicator
Electrodermal activity	Electrodes	Novelty, Intensity of Affect
Heart rate/period	Electrocardiograph	Fear, Anger, Focused Attention
Blood pressure	Sphygmomanometer	Engagement in Task, Anger, Stress
Blood volume	Plethysmograph	Startle, Fear, Anxiety
Pupillary response	Eye tracker	Fatigue, Novelty, Emotionality of Stimulus
Eye blink	Electro-oculogram, Eye tracker	Negative Affect, Nervousness, Stress

Assessment Methods Are Not All the Same

Just as available methods for inducing emotions do not all accomplish exactly the same thing, neither do methods for measuring emotions. Measurement methods vary in ways that make them more or less useful or accurate, depending upon the purpose of the empirical question or goals (Scherer, 2005). The important considerations for choosing a way to measure emotions in research are whether the method is:

• Language-based
• Subjective versus objective
• Measuring discrete or more global states of emotion
• Invasive
• Expensive

Language-based measurements include self-report scales. Some researchers believe that self-report is the "gold standard" for measuring emotions. The thinking is "if you want to know how someone is feeling, just ask them!" (Barrett, 2004). However, there are also problems with self-report using words for emotion. One is that these measures are open to experimental demand, which we discussed earlier in the chapter: If you ask me how I am feeling, I may arrange my answers to suit you the experimenter (e.g., tell you what you want to hear) or to suit me (e.g., perhaps I don't want to admit how I am feeling). In addition, language-based measures might not be useful or possible with younger children because they might not understand the words. Translations to other languages are always possible for cross-cultural research. But translating emotion words is very difficult and open to many types of errors that might make the research findings misleading (e.g., Hurtado de Mendoza et al., 2010).

Self-reports of emotion are also subjective. They are thus vulnerable to a number of reporting biases. For instance, it takes attention to decide if one is having an emotion, and maybe you don't have the inclination or the capacity to pay attention to your emotions at the time you are asked. Some researchers would rather have an objective measure of emotions. But because there is no perfect objective measure, an "objective" measure of emotion might not actually indicate the occurrence of a specific emotion.

Indeed, many methods for measuring emotion are not useful for quantifying specific emotions such as anger, guilt, and disgust. Some self-report questionnaires that we introduced you to can be used to derive scores for specific emotions (including the basic emotions). However, physiological and neural biomarkers for the basic emotions have not been conclusively found. When trying to measure emotions objectively, therefore, the best strategy is to measure many components of emotion, including facial expression, physiology, and even behavior.

Another problem is that many of the objective measures are both invasive and expensive. How would you like to be hooked up to electrodes on your chest, head, or other part of the body? Such invasiveness can affect how much emotion is produced by an emotion induction method and even which emotion is likely to be elicited. In addition, for some people who find such methods stressful, the invasive measures can actually cause emotions, including fear. Although MRI scanners allow for some progress toward identifying complex neural circuitry for specific emotions, they are constraining and uncomfortable. And the collection and analysis of MRI scans are very expensive.

In sum, there are many ways to measure the components of emotion. As with selecting a method to induce an emotion, the researcher must start with a theory of emotion and select measurement methods that assess the parts of emotion that the theory was intended to explain.

Summary

In this chapter we introduced the methods that affective scientists use to study emotions in and out of the laboratory:

- We described many ways to (ethically) induce emotional states in the laboratory, including the use of film, music, scripted interaction, and the presentation of emotional images.
- We noted that emotions can also be studied by harnessing naturally occurring emotions. Outside of the laboratory experience, sampling techniques can be used to collect reports about emotions as they occur in real-life situations.
- There are also many techniques for measuring individuals' emotional states, including the use of questionnaires, the assessment of facial expression, and the recording of physiology and brain states.
- By using many methods and assessing many parts of the whole elephant that we call an emotion, we can start to get closer to some truths about the components of emotion and their harmony or disharmony; about the involvement of all of "human nature"—the processes of the mind and the body—that make up an emotional experience; and about the role that emotions play in social life, the topic of the remainder of the book.

Learning Links

1. Watch a talk on affective computing and the use of computers to measure facial expression by Dr. Rana el Kaliouby. http://www.npr.org/2015/09/11/439190272/will-our-screens-soon-be-able-to-read-our-emotions

2. Discover this exploration of the use of emotion measures to assess and predict consumer behavior. https://vimeo.com/146308492

3. Learn about measurement and meaning of emotional intelligence. http://www.unh.edu/ emotional_intelligence/index.html

4. Read a Smithsonian.com article on the use of sad films to induce emotions. http://www.smithsonianmag.com/arts-culture/the-saddest-movie-in-the-world-33826787/?no-ist

References

Apsler, R. (1975). Effects of embarrassment on behavior toward others. *Journal of Personality and Social Psychology, 32*(1), 145. doi:10.1037/h0076699.

Aronson, E. B., & Carlsmith, M. J. M. (1985). Experimentation in social psychology. In G. Lindzey & E. Aroson (Eds.), *The handbook of social psychology* (2nd ed., Vol. 2, pp. 1–79). Reading, MA: Addison-Wesley.

Ax, A. F. (1953). The physiological differentiation between fear and anger in humans. *Psychosomatic Medicine, 15*(5), 433–442. doi:10.1097/00006842–195309000–00007.

Barrett, L. F. (2004). Feelings or words? Understanding the content in self-report ratings of experienced emotion. *Journal of Personality and Social Psychology, 87*(2), 266–281. doi:10.1037/0022–3514.87.2.266.

Barrett, L. F., & Barrett, D. J. (2001). An introduction to computerized experience sampling in psychology. *Social Science Computer Review, 19*(2), 175–185. doi:10.1177/089443930101900204.

Barrett, L. F., & Wager, T. D. (2006). The structure of emotion evidence from neuroimaging studies. *Current Directions in Psychological Science, 15*(2), 79–83. doi:10.1111/j.0963–7214.2006.00411.x.

Bartlett, D. L. (1996). Physiological responses to music and sound stimuli. In D. A. Hodges (Ed.), *Handbook of music psychology* (pp. 343–385). San Antonio, TX: Institute for Music Research Press.

Becker, J. O. (2004). *Deep listeners: Music, emotion, and trancing*. Bloomington, IN: Indiana University Press.

Blanchette, I., & Richards, A. (2010). The influence of affect on higher level cognition: A review of research on interpretation, judgement, decision making and reasoning. *Cognition & Emotion, 24*(4), 561–595. doi:10.1080/02699930903132496.

Boiten, F. A. (1998). The effects of emotional behavior on components of the respiratory cycle. *Biological Psychology, 49*(1), 29–51. doi:10.1016/s0301–0511(98)00025–8.

Bradley, M. M., Codispoti, M., Cuthbert, B. N., & Lang, P. J. (2001). Emotion and motivation I: Defensive and appetitive reactions in picture processing. *Emotion, 1*(3), 276. doi:10.1037//1528–3542.1.3.276.

Bradley, M. M., Hamby, S., Löw, A., & Lang, P. J. (2007). Brain potentials in perception: Picture complexity and emotional arousal. *Psychophysiology, 44*(3), 364–373. doi:10.1111/j.1469–8986.2007.00520.x.

Bradley, M. M., & Lang, P. J. (1994). Measuring emotion: The self-assessment manikin and the semantic differential. *Journal of Behavior Therapy and Experimental Psychiatry, 25*(1), 49–59. doi:10.1016/0005–7916(94)90063–9.

Brock, T. C., & Becker, L. A. (1966). "Debriefing" and susceptibility to subsequent experimental manipulations. *Journal of Experimental Social Psychology, 2*(3), 314–323. doi:10.1016/0022–1031(66)90087–4.

Cacioppo, J. T., & Petty, R. E. (1981). Social psychological procedures for cognitive response assessment: The thought-listing technique. In T. Merluzzi, C. Glass & M. Genest (Eds.), *Cognitive assessment* (pp. 309–342). New York: Guilford Press.

Cacioppo, J. T., Tassinary, L. G., & Fridlund, A. J. (1990). The skeletomotor system. In J. T. Cacioppo & L. G. Tassinary (Eds.), *Principles of psychophysiology: Physical, social, and inferential elements* (pp. 325–384). New York: Cambridge University Press.

Carstensen, L. L., Turan, B., Scheibe, S., Ram, N., Ersner-Hershfield, H., Samanez-Larkin, G. R., . . . Nesselroade, J. R. (2011). Emotional experience improves with age: Evidence based on over 10 years of experience sampling. *Psychology and Aging, 26*(1), 21. doi:10.1037/a0021285.

Christensen, T. C., Barrett, L. F., Bliss-Moreau, E., Lebo, K., & Kaschub, C. (2003). A practical guide to experience-sampling procedures. *Journal of Happiness Studies, 4*(1), 53–78. doi:10.1023/a:102360 9306024.

Cohn, J. F., Ambadar, Z., & Ekman, P. (2007). Observer-based measurement of facial expression with the facial action coding system. In J. A. Coan & J. J. B. Allen (Eds.), *The handbook of emotion elicitation and assessment. Oxford University Press Series in Affective Science* (pp. 203–221). New York: Oxford University.

Cohn, J. F., & Ekman, P. (2005). Measuring facial action by manual coding, facial EMG, and automatic facial image analysis. In J. A. Harrigan, R. Rosenthal & K. Scherer (Eds.), *Handbook of nonverbal behavior research methods in the affective sciences* (pp. 9–64). New York: Oxford.

Costa, M., Bitti, P. E. R., & Bonfiglioli, L. (2000). Psychological connotations of harmonic musical intervals. *Psychology of Music, 28*(1), 4–22. doi:10.1177/0305735600281002.

Costa, M., Fine, P., & Ricci Bitti, P. E. (2004). Interval distributions, mode, and tonal strength of melodies as predictors of perceived emotion. *Music Perception, 22*(1), 1–14. doi:10.1525/mp.2004.22.1.1.

Cuthbert, B. N., Schupp, H. T., Bradley, M. M., Birbaumer, N., & Lang, P. J. (2000). Brain potentials in affective picture processing: Covariation with autonomic arousal and affective report. *Biological Psychology, 52*(2), 95–111. doi:10.1016/s0301–0511(99)00044–7.

Darwin, C. (1998/1872). *The expression of the emotions in man and animals.* New York/Oxford: Oxford University Press.

Delplanque, S., Lavoie, M. E., Hot, P., Silvert, L., & Sequeira, H. (2004). Modulation of cognitive processing by emotional valence studied through event-related potentials in humans. *Neuroscience Letters, 356*(1), 1–4. doi:10.1016/j.neulet.2003.10.014.

Duchenne de Boulogne, G. B. (1862/1990). *The mechanism of human facial expression.* New York: Cambridge University Press.

Eisenberg, N., Fabes, R. A., Bustamante, D., Mathy, R. M., Miller, P. A., & Lindholm, E. (1988). Differentiation of vicariously induced emotional reactions in children. *Developmental Psychology, 24*(2), 237–246. doi:10.1037/0012–1649.24.2.237.

Ekman, P., & Friesen, W. (1978). *The facial action coding system (FACS): A technique for the measurement of facial movement.* Palo Alto, CA: Consulting Psychologists Press.

Ekman, P., & Rosenberg, E. (Eds.). (2005). *What the face reveals* (2nd ed.). New York: Oxford University Press.

Ellard, K. K., Farchione, T. J., & Barlow, D. H. (2012). Relative effectiveness of emotion induction procedures and the role of personal relevance in a clinical sample: A comparison of film, images, and music. *Journal of Psychopathology and Behavioral Assessment, 34*(2), 232–243. doi:10.1007/s10862–011–9271–4.

Evers, C., Hopp, H., Gross, J. J., Fischer, A. H., Manstead, A. S., & Mauss, I. B. (2014). Emotion response coherence: A dual-process perspective. *Biological Psychology, 98*, 43–49. doi:10.1016/j.biopsycho.2013.11.003.

Evers, C., Stok, F. M., & de Ridder, D. T. (2010). Feeding your feelings: Emotion regulation strategies and emotional eating. *Personality and Social Psychology Bulletin.* doi:10.1037/e524372011–025.

Feldman, L. A. (1995). Valence focus and arousal focus: Individual differences in the structure of affective experience. *Journal of Personality and Social Psychology, 69*(1), 153. doi:10.1037/0022–3514.69.1.153.

Feldman Barrett, L., & Russell, J. A. (1998). Independence and bipolarity in the structure of fcurrent affect. *Journal of Personality and Social Psychology, 74*(4), 967. doi:10.1037//0022–3514.74.4.967.

Gagnon, L., & Peretz, I. (2003). Mode and tempo relative contributions to "happy-sad" judgements in equitone melodies. *Cognition & Emotion, 17*(1), 25–40. doi:10.1080/02699930302279.

Gross, J. J., & Levenson, R. W. (1995). Emotion elicitation using films. *Cognition & Emotion, 9*(1), 87–108. doi:10.1080/02699939508408966.

Harmon-Jones, E., Amodio, D. M., & Zinner, L. R. (2007). Social psychological methods in emotion elicitation. In J. A. Coan & J. J. B. Allen (Eds.), *Handbook of emotion elicitation and assessment* (pp. 91–105). NewYork: Oxford University Press.

Harris, C. R. (2001). Cardiovascular responses of embarrassment and effects of emotional suppression in a social setting. *Journal of Personality and Social Psychology, 81*(5), 886. doi:10.1037/e323152004–003.

Haviland, J. M., & Lelwica, M. (1987). The induced affect response: 10-week-old infants' responses to three emotion expressions. *Developmental Psychology, 23*(1), 97–104. doi:10.1037/0012–1649.23.1.97.

Hewig, J., Hagemann, D., Seifert, J., Gollwitzer, M., Naumann, E., & Bartussek, D. (2005). Brief report. *Cognition & Emotion, 19*(7), 1095–1109. doi:10.1080/02699930541000084.

Hurtado de Mendoza, A., Fernández-Dols, J. M., Parrott, W. G., & Carrera, P. (2010). Emotion terms, category structure, and the problem of translation: The case of shame and vergüenza. *Cognition & Emotion, 24*(4), 661–680. doi:10.1080/02699930902958255.

Izard, C. E., Dougherty, F. E., Bloxom, B. M., & Kotsch, N. E. (1974). *The differential emotion scale: A method of measuring the meaning of subjective experience of discrete emotions*. Nashville, TN: Vanderbilt University, Department of Psychology.

Kalisch, R. (2009). The functional neuroanatomy of reappraisal: Time matters. *Neuroscience & Biobehavioral Reviews*, *33*(8), 1215–1226. doi:10.1016/j.neubiorev.2009.06.003.

Koelsch, S., Fritz, T., Müller, K., & Friederici, A. D. (2006). Investigating emotion with music: An fMRI study. *Human Brain Mapping*, *27*(3), 239–250. doi:10.1002/hbm.20180.

Konecni, V. J. (1972). Some effects of guilt on compliance: A field replication. *Journal of Personality and Social Psychology*, *23*, 30–32. doi:10.1037/h0032875.

Kurdi, B., Lozano, S., & Banaji, M. R. (2016). Introducing the open affective standardized image set (OASIS). *Behavior Research Methods*, 1–14. doi:10.3758/s13428–016–0715–3.

Lang, P. J., Bradley, M. M., & Cuthbert, B. N. (2005). *International affective picture system (IAPS): Digitized photographs, instruction manual, and affective ratings* (Tech. Rep. No. A-6). Gainesville: University of Florida, Center for Research in Psychophysiology.

Langner, O., Dotsch, R., Bijlstra, G., Wigboldus, D. J., Hawk, S. T., & van Knippenberg, A. (2010). Presentation and validation of the radboud faces database. *Cognition and Emotion*, *24*(8), 1377–1388. doi:10.1080/02699930903485076.

Littlewort, G., Whitehill, J., Wu, T., Fasel, I., Frank, M., Movellan, J., & Bartlett, M. (2011). The computer expression recognition toolbox (CERT). *Face and Gesture, 2011*, 298–305. doi:10.1109/fg.2011.5771414.

Mauss, I. B., Evers, C., Wilhelm, F. H., & Gross, J. J. (2006). How to bite your tongue without blowing your top: Implicit evaluation of emotion regulation predicts affective responding to anger provocation. *Personality and Social Psychology Bulletin*, *32*(5), 589–602. doi:10.1177/0146167205283841.

Mauss, I. B., & Robinson, M. D. (2009). Measures of emotion: A review. *Cognition and Emotion*, 23(2), 209–237. doi:10.1080/02699930802204677.

Mayer, J. D., & Gaschke, Y. N. (1988). The experience and meta-experience of mood. *Journal of Personality and Social Psychology*, *55*(1), 102. doi:10.1037/0022–3514.55.1.102.

Miller, S. M. (1987). Monitoring and blunting: Validation of a questionnaire to assess styles of information seeking under threat. *Journal of Personality and Social Psychology*, *52*(2), 345. doi:10.1037//0022–3514.52.2.345.

Morris, J. D. (1995). Observations: SAM: The self-assessment manikin; an efficient cross-cultural measurement of emotional response. *Journal of Advertising Research*, *35*(6), 63–68.

Niedenthal, P. M., & Dalle, N. (2001). Le mariage de mon meilleur ami: Emotional response categorization and naturally induced emotions. *European Journal of Social Psychology*, *31*(6), 737–742. doi:10.1002/ejsp.66.

Ochsner, K. N., Bunge, S. A., Gross, J. J., & Gabrieli, J. D. (2002). Rethinking feelings: An FMRI study of the cognitive regulation of emotion. *Journal of Cognitive Neuroscience*, *14*(8), 1215–1229. doi:10.1162/089892902760807212.

Olofsson, J. K., & Polich, J. (2007). Affective visual event-related potentials: Arousal, repetition, and time-on-task. *Biological Psychology*, *75*(1), 101–108. doi:10.1016/j.biopsycho.2006.12.006.

Phan, K. L., Wager, T., Taylor, S. F., & Liberzon, I. (2002). Functional neuroanatomy of emotion: A meta-analysis of emotion activation studies in PET and fMRI. *Neuroimage*, *16*(2), 331–348. doi:10.1006/nimg.2002.1087.

Philippot, P. (1993). Inducing and assessing differentiated emotion-feeling states in the laboratory. *Cognition & Emotion*, *7*(2), 171–193. doi:10.1080/02699939308409183.

Posner, J., Russell, J. A., Gerber, A., Gorman, D., Colibazzi, T., Yu, S., . . . Peterson, B. S. (2009). The neurophysiological bases of emotion: An fMRI study of the affective circumplex using emotion-denoting words. *Human Brain Mapping*, *30*(3), 883–895. doi:10.1002/hbm.20553.

Putnam, S. P., & Stifter, C. A. (2002). Development of approach and inhibition in the first year: Parallel findings from motor behavior, temperament ratings and directional cardiac response. *Developmental Science*, *5*(4), 441–451. doi:10.1111/1467–7687.00239.

Rottenberg, J., Ray, R. D., & Gross, J. J. (2007). Emotion elicitation using films. In J. A. Coan & J. B. Allen (Eds.), *Handbook of emotion elicitation and assessment* (pp. 9–28). New York: Oxford University Press.

Schaller, M., & Cialdini, R. B. (1990). Happiness, sadness, and helping: A motivational integration. In E. T. Higgins & R. M. Sorrentino (Eds.), *Handbook of motivation and cognition: Foundations of social behavior* (Vol. 2, pp. 265–296). New York: Guilford.

Scherer, K. R. (2004). Which emotions can be induced by music? What are the underlying mechanisms? And how can we measure them? *Journal of New Music Research, 33*(3), 239 251. doi:10.1080/09298 21042000317822.

Scherer, K. R. (2005). What are emotions? And how can they be measured? *Social Science Information, 44*(4), 695–729. doi:10.1177/0539018405058216.

Scherer, K. R., & Zentner, M. R. (2001). Emotional effects of music: Production rules. In P. N. Juslin & J. A. Sloboda (Eds.), *Music and emotion: Theory and research* (pp. 361–392). Oxford, UK: Oxford University Press.

Schwarz, N., & Clore, G. L. (1983). Mood, misattribution, and judgments of well-being: Informative and directive functions of affective states. *Journal of Personality and Social Psychology, 45*(3), 513. doi:10.1037/0022–3514.45.3.513.

Simon, T. K., De la Torre, F., Ambadar, Z., & E, J. F. (2011). Fast-FACS: A computer vision assisted system to increase the speed and reliability of manual FACS coding. *Proceedings of the HUMAINE Association Conference on Affective Computing and Intelligent Interaction.* Memphis, Tennessee.

Sloboda, J. A. (1992). Empirical studies of emotional response to music. In M. Reiss-Jones & S. Holleran (Eds.), *Cognitive bases of musical communication* (pp. 33–46). Washington, DC: American Psychological Association. doi:10.1037/10104–003.

Sloboda, J. A., & O'Neill, S. A. (2001). Emotions in everyday listening to music. In P. N. Juslin & J. A. Sloboda (Eds.), *Music and emotion: Theory and research* (pp. 71–104). New York: Oxford University Press.

Sprengelmeyer, R., Rausch, M., Eysel, U. T., & Przuntek, H. (1998). Neural structures associated with recognition of facial expressions of basic emotions. *Proceedings of the Royal Society of London B: Biological Sciences, 265*(1409), 1927–1931. doi:10.1098/rspb.1998.0522.

Stemmler, G., Heldmann, M., Pauls, C. A., & Scherer, T. (2001). Constraints for emotion specificity in fear and anger: The context counts. *Psychophysiology, 38*(2), 275–291. doi:10.1111/1469–8986.3820275.

Stenberg, C. R., Campos, J. J., & Emde, R. N. (1983). The facial expression of anger in seven-month-old infants. *Child Development, 54*(1), 178–184. doi:10.2307/1129875.

Strack, F., Schwarz, N., & Geschneidinger, E. (1985). Happiness and reminiscing: The role of time perspective, affect, and mode of thinking. *Journal of Personality and Social Psychology, 49*(6), 1460. doi:10.1037/0022–3514.49.6.1460.

Termine, N. T., & Izard, C. E. (1988). Infants' responses to their mothers' expressions of joy and sadness. *Developmental Psychology, 24*(2), 223–229. doi:10.1037/0012–1649.24.2.223.

Thompson, E. R. (2007). Development and validation of an internationally reliable short-form of the positive and negative affect schedule (PANAS). *Journal of Cross-Cultural Psychology, 38*(2), 227–242. doi:10.1177/0022022106297301.

Tomarken, A. J., Davidson, R. J., & Henriques, J. B. (1990). Resting frontal brain asymmetry predicts affective responses to films. *Journal of Personality and Social Psychology, 59*(4), 791. doi:10.1037/0022–3514.59.4.791.

Västfjäll, D. (2002). Emotion induction through music: A review of the musical mood induction procedure. *Musicae Scientiae, 5*(1 suppl), 173–211. doi:10.1177/10298649020050s107.

Wager, T. D., Davidson, M. L., Hughes, B. L., Lindquist, M. A., & Ochsner, K. N. (2008). Prefrontal-subcortical pathways mediating successful emotion regulation. *Neuron, 59*(6), 1037–1050. doi:10.1016/j.neuron.2008.09.006.

Watson, D., Clark, L. A., & Tellegen, A. (1988). Development and validation of brief measures of positive and negative affect: The PANAS scales. *Journal of Personality and Social Psychology, 54*(6), 1063. doi:10.1037/0022–3514.54.6.1063.

Westermann, R., Spies, K., Stahl, G., & Hesse, F. W. (1996). Relative effectiveness and validity of mood induction procedures: A meta-analysis. *European Journal of Social Psychology, 26*(4), 557–580. doi:10.1002/(sici)1099–0992(199607)26:4<557::aid-ejsp769>3.0.co;2–4.

Zuckerman, M., & Lubin, B. (1985). The multiple affect adjective check list revised. *San Diego: Educational and Industrial Testing Service.* doi:10.1037/t06153–000.

3 The Emotional Brain

In everyday metaphors, emotions are associated with the heart. We say that people get their hearts broken. People's hearts also sink, they may have heavy hearts, and they can even have their hearts set on something. As we learned in Chapter 1, the heart does play a role in emotions. However, scientists now know that the brain controls the cardiovascular system. So as far as emotions go, it is more accurate to say that the head and the heart work together.

Now that affective scientists have tools for observing the brain's function, we know a lot more about the role of the brain in the generation of emotion in the self and in the perception of emotion in others. There are so many reasons to want to know where emotions take place in the brain. One of the most important is to better understand variability in all components of emotional experience and especially disorders of emotion processing such as depression and anxiety. Affective scientists can also answer some foundational questions about emotion: Are specific emotions the product of specific brain areas, or rather of a distributed network encompassing many interconnected brain areas? Is the right hemisphere more emotional than the left? Which brain areas allow us to recognize emotions expressed by somebody else? In this chapter we provide answers to some of these exciting questions.

First, however, we will introduce the basics of brain anatomy and neuroscientific investigation. In order to best understand the relevant research, you should recall from the previous chapter that electroencephalography (EEG), the measure of changes in electrical potential of groups of neurons, can be measured over time with electrodes placed on the scalp. Functional magnetic resonance imaging (fMRI) is taken inside a cylindrical tube called a scanner and uses a combination of a powerful static magnetic field and radiofrequency waves coming from many angles to create images of blood oxygenation and blood flow changes in the brain. Both methods are ways to measure brain activity and to assess the roles of areas of the brain in the components of emotion.

Throughout the chapter we will refer to different areas of the brain. Therefore, in the first section we will review fundamental elements of the central and peripheral nervous systems and introduce you to brain anatomy.

The Peripheral Nervous System

The nervous system is composed of a peripheral and a central branch. The **central nervous system** (CNS) includes the brain and spinal cord (see next section). The nerves and ganglia that lie outside of the CNS are called the **peripheral nervous system** (PNS). This distinction is somewhat arbitrary, however, because many of the PNS neurons extend their axons into the periphery, but have their cell bodies lying in the brain or spinal cord. The PNS can be divided into the somatic and the autonomic nervous systems. The **somatic sensory system** includes both motor and sensory neurons, which allow for muscular movement and somatosensation (feeling of touch, pain, and proprioception, i.e., the position of our limbs in space). The **autonomic nervous system** (ANS), which itself can be divided into a sympathetic and a parasympathetic branch, regulates the functions of internal organs, such as the heart and the intestines, and it can modulate, for example, heart rate, digestion, and respiration rate. Activation of the **sympathetic nervous system** prepares the organism to react to an important event, as during the "fight or flight" response to threatening stimuli. The **parasympathetic system**, in contrast, is associated with rest, digestion, and restoration of the body. We all experience the effects of increased sympathetic or parasympathetic nervous system activity. For example, you might feel agitated before an exam (sympathetic) and drowsy after a meal (parasympathetic).

The Central Nervous System

As we have already seen, the human CNS can be divided into the brain and the spinal cord. The brain includes:

- The cortex (the outer layer), which is the most complex in terms of neural organization and function, and is crucial for memory, attention, language, consciousness, etc.
- The midbrain (diencephalon), which includes a collection of smaller nuclei like the thalamus and hypothalamus, many of which are involved in early stages of sensory processing
- The brainstem, which sits at the top of the spinal cord, houses most motor and sensory fibers innervating the face and neck, and plays a major role in vital functions such as cardiac and respiratory regulation
- The cerebellum, at the lower back of the brain, which is mostly involved in fine motor control

The human brain can also be divided into two hemispheres, which are connected by a densely packed fiber tract called the corpus callosum. Each hemisphere comprises four lobes: the frontal, parietal, occipital, and temporal (see Figure 3.1). Locations in the brain are also referred to based on three axes, dividing the brain into anterior-posterior (or rostral-caudal), superior-inferior (or dorsal-ventral), and lateral-medial regions. Subdivisions of the lobes can be referred to based on these axes (e.g., the prefrontal cortex, or PFC, is the anterior part of the frontal lobe), based on the vicinity to other lobes (e.g., the temporo-parietal junction, or TPJ, is at the intersection of the temporal and parietal lobes), based on other anatomical landmarks (e.g., the orbitofrontal cortex, or OFC, is the part of the frontal lobe that lies just above the eyes; see Figure 3.3), or based on the "ridges" (gyri) and "furrows" (sulci) of the folded cortex (e.g., the superior temporal gyrus, or STG, and the superior temporal sulcus, or STS).

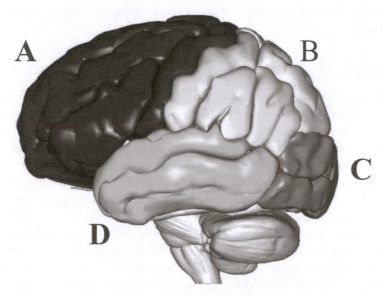

Figure 3.1 The frontal (A), parietal (B), occipital (C), and temporal (D) lobes of the brain. Image created with BodyParts3D. From Mitsuhashi et al. (2009).

A very common distinction in neuroscience, especially when it comes to the neural bases of emotion and its regulation, is between the cerebral (or neo) cortex, which lies on the outside, and the subcortical areas underneath and in the center of the brain.

Neurotransmitters

Neurons, the central building blocks of the nervous system, communicate both electrically and chemically (Kandel et al., 2013). When neurons depolarize past a certain threshold, they fire an action potential, which travels down the axon to the many synapses, which are the contact points with other neurons. At the level of the synapse, communication is (most of the time) chemical in nature. The presynaptic neuron releases chemical substances, called neurotransmitters, which, like keys in a lock, "fit into" corresponding receptors on the postsynaptic neurons. Many substances have been identified that act as neurotransmitters and can be divided into two major classes: small molecule transmitters and neuroactive peptides (Schwartz & Javitch, 2013). The most common excitatory neurotransmitter is glutamate, and the most common inhibiting neurotransmitter is gamma-aminobutyric acid (GABA).

Models of the Emotional Brain

Much of the research about the neural basis of emotion was inspired by evolutionary theory. For example, there is widespread belief that whenever something emerges during evolution that works, in the sense of solving problems of survival, it is preserved and incorporated in future generations and in more sophisticated organisms. Phylogenetically older structures (those that appeared earlier in evolution) are preserved and located in lower and medial areas of the brain, whereas newer parts get added on around and on top. Moreover, it is often believed that in humans, emotions are mostly generated by these older subcortical structures and are regulated by parts of the younger cortex. The origin of these ideas dates back to the beginning of the twentieth century. To better understand them, we briefly summarize earlier models about emotions in the brain.

Historical Models

One of the first models of emotions in the brain goes back to the late 1920s and early 1930s, when experiments by two scientists named Cannon and Bard showed that decorticated cats (in which the outer layer of the brain had been surgically removed) were still able to display emotions, such as sudden and ill-directed anger attacks called "sham rage" (Cannon, 1927.) This led to the conclusion that the hypothalamus, a subcortical area located deep in the brain, is at the source of the emotional response and is commonly inhibited by evolutionarily more recent cortical areas. Once the cortex is removed, the hypothalamus is no longer inhibited, and emotions become uncontrolled.

Another landmark model of emotions in the brain was also based on work on aggression in animals and was proposed by Papez in 1937 (Papez, 1995). The "Papez circuit" included many more areas than the hypothalamus and is therefore larger than the model by Cannon and Bard. It includes mostly medial and subcortical areas, such as the hypothalamus, thalamus, hippocampus, and cingulate cortex, as well as their connecting fibers.

Paul MacLean included the amygdala in the Papez circuit, which he relabeled the limbic system, reintroducing the term originally used by the famous nineteenth-century French physician Paul Broca (Lambert, 2003; MacLean, 1949). Consistent with his belief in evolutionary theory, MacLean proposed a "triune brain" model (Figure 3.2). The model proposed that three different brain systems, each with distinctive characteristics, have emerged throughout evolution and now coexist in humans. These systems (actually called complexes) are, in order of increasing complexity and decreasing phylogenetic age, the reptilian complex, the paleomammalian complex (the limbic system), and the neomammalian complex (the neocortex). MacLean placed drives and emotions in the reptilian and paleomammalian systems and higher cognitive functions, including top-down regulation of emotions, in the neomammalian complex.

Although popular in folk psychology, MacLean's triune brain theory is generally known to be incorrect by today's emotion scientists, and the hippocampus is no longer seen as an important structure in producing emotional responses (LeDoux, 1996). However, the concept of a limbic system remains well established (even though its precise anatomical boundaries remain debated), and so does the idea of emotions being generated subcortically and kept in check by the cortex (but see the constructionist view here later).

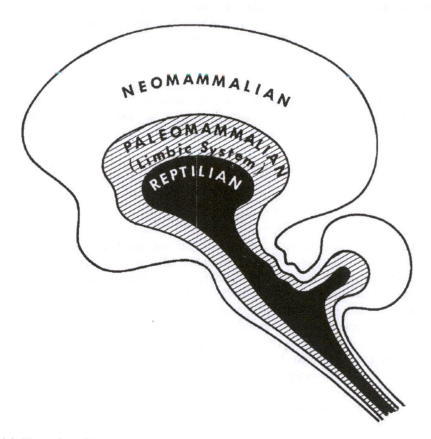

Figure 3.2 Illustration of the triune brain. From MacLean (1967).

Contemporary Models

Today, there are several different models and theories about how and where in the human brain emotions arise. Partly, this abundance of theory reflects neuroscience's struggle to pinpoint the neural correlates of emotions, a difficult task due to the complexity of human emotions, which cannot be reduced to behavioral or physiological responses, as is the case in animal behavior. Currently, there are two main opposing conceptualizations about the neural correlates of human emotions. Here, we will refer to them as *locationist* and *constructionist* approaches, consistent with a recent review (Lindquist et al., 2012). Additional models of the neural basis of emotions, such as hemispheric specialization hypotheses, will also be discussed.

Throughout our discussion, brain areas underlying the expression of emotions and those underlying the perception of other people's emotions are often discussed jointly. One reason for this is that these two phenomena are difficult to disentangle. For example, if a group of like-minded people receives the same saddening news (e.g., the death of a loved one), they most likely will all experience and express the same emotion of sadness. This will lead to simultaneous production and perception of emotions. Many researchers therefore consider visually perceived facial expressions to act as conditioned stimuli. Over the course of a person's lifetime, facial expressions become associated with biologically relevant events and with the emotional reactions to them. Therefore, when pictures of facial expressions are presented in an experiment, they tend to evoke at least part of the associated emotional response.

Another reason is more practical and concerns the difficulties (including ethical constraints) of eliciting strong emotions in the laboratory. Especially when imaging the brain—for instance, in the MRI scanner—the participant must undergo many repetitions of the same type of event (such as the feeling of anger) in order to have sufficient statistical power to confidently distinguish neural activity specific to the task or stimulus of interest. Brain imaging also requires the participant to lie as still as possible, which is difficult, if not impossible, if they were to experience full-blown emotions, because strong emotional feelings are usually accompanied by movements of the face and head. However, there is also a more interesting reason for why we decided to discuss jointly the brain activity pertaining to the experience and expression of emotions. Indeed, as we discuss later on in the chapter, many scholars believe that there is a biological reason for why overlapping brain circuits underlie the perception and production of emotion.

Locationism

Locationist approaches assume that specific areas of the brain are responsible for specific emotions. Although their precise views can differ, scientists who endorse the notion of locationism usually think of emotions as an evolutionarily shaped set of distinctive physiological, behavioral, and expressive reactions to specific stimuli. An important and practical aspect of locationism is that many features of emotions, including their brain anatomy, are thought to be the same in humans, other primates, and even smaller mammals like rodents. This makes it possible to study emotions, or at least aspects of them, invasively in animals (Panksepp, 1998). This is not to say, however, that human and animal emotions are equivalent in every aspect. Humans' highly developed cortex makes their emotional reactions less stereotypical and more complex and allows for regulation of and awareness about emotional reactions. Most locationists assume that emotions are generated subcortically, or in ventral and medial areas of the prefrontal cortex that are seen as part of the limbic system. Here, we will highlight a few of the areas linked to specific emotions (see Figure 3.3).

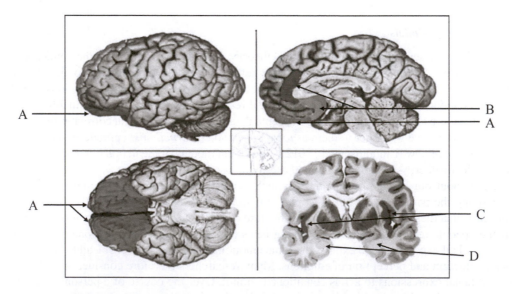

Figure 3.3 Some of the brain structures that locationist approaches assume to be associated with specific emotions. Fear is in the amygdala (D), disgust in the insula (C), anger in the orbitofrontal cortex (A), and sadness in the anterior cingulate cortex (B). From Lindquist et al. (2012).

Developmental Detail

Emotion and Developing Brains

The brains we are describing in the chapter are typically developing brains. But some brains are not so typical. Children who are maltreated, the victims of early abuse, or neglected, often develop social-behavioral problems. For instance, they show detriments in responding to emotional expressions of, and in forming emotional attachments to, their caregivers (Pollak, 2008). These detriments may be due to the fact that the stress of abuse and neglect negatively affects brain maturation. Consistent with this idea, a neuroimaging study found that the prefrontal cortex—an area important for emotion regulation—was smaller in children who had been maltreated than in matched control children who had not been so treated (Tupler & DeBellis, 2006).

Early childhood adversity also changes the neurochemistry of the developing brain. This was demonstrated in a study comparing the brains of children who had been in orphanages as infants and then later adopted into families with family-reared children who had not suffered maltreatment (Fries et al., 2005). The researchers were particularly interested in the neuropeptides oxytocin (OT) and arginine vasopressin (AVP), both of which increase during social interactions involving rewarding sensory experiences such as pleasant touch and odors—sensations typical of maternal or otherwise homey interactions. The two samples of children were tested at their homes in interaction with their mothers. After the interaction, the family-reared children, but not the children who had experienced early adversity, showed rises in OT levels. In addition, the two groups differed in their stable levels of AVP. The reduced AVP and suppressed OT reactivity could have long-term detrimental effects on both affiliative behaviors and stress regulation of maltreated children as they mature. Indeed, other studies show that early maltreatment is related to dysregulation of cortisol during social interactions, suggesting an inability to manage stress. Results such as these are of urgent concern because they show that neglect and abuse have long-term effects that go deep into the brain.

The *amygdala* is undoubtedly one of the brain structures best known for being associated with a specific emotion. This almond-shaped structure, composed of several subareas (or nuclei), is located in the medial temporal lobes (see Figures 3.3 and 3.4). It is common belief among scientists and the general public that the amygdala plays a pivotal role in the experience and expression of fear, anxiety, and related states (LeDoux, 2007; Öhman, 2009). Indeed, empirical findings support this assumption.

First, there is convincing evidence in animal studies that used electrical recording, electrical stimulation, or lesioning of brain areas that the amygdala plays a pivotal role in fear and fear conditioning (Fendt & Fanselow, 1999). Second, much of research in humans points in the same direction, although results are less clear-cut. Because it is not possible to lesion the amygdala in humans for obvious ethical reasons, indirect evidence must be obtained from naturally occurring

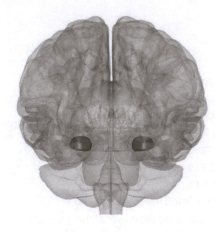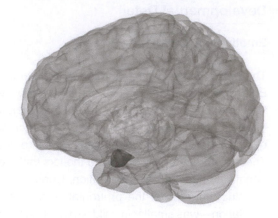

Figure 3.4 Position of the amygdala in the brain. Image created with BodyParts3D. From Mitsuhashi et al. (2009).

amygdala damage. For example, a rare condition called Urbach-Wiethe disease results in focal bilateral amygdala damage. One famous patient with this disease, called SM, does not express or experience fear, even when exposed to live snakes and spiders or when taken on a tour of a haunted house (Feinstein et al., 2011). Moreover, SM can recognize all emotions in faces except fear (Adolphs et al., 1994). In addition to the study of SM and similar patients, evidence linking the amygdala to fear comes from neuroimaging. A large number of neuroimaging studies reported greater amygdala activation during the experience or perception of fear or anxiety-related states compared to other emotions (Taylor & Whalen, 2015). However, as we will see later, the link between fear and the amygdala in humans may not be as firmly established as in animal models.

Another brain structure associated with a specific emotion is the *insula*, which is a part of the cortex deep in the lateral sulcus, hidden by parts of the frontal and temporal lobes. Several lines of evidence suggest that the insula is linked to experience and perception of disgust. Electrical stimulation of the insula in macaque monkeys elicits behavior, facial expressions, and physiological responses of disgust (Caruana et al., 2011). In humans, the insula is more activated during the perception of facial expressions of disgust than other emotions, both in neuroimaging studies and during intracranial electrical recording (Krolak-Salmon et al., 2003; Phillips et al., 1997). Electrical stimulation of the human insula reduces accuracy of disgust recognition (Papagno et al., 2016). Moreover, overlapping areas of the insula become activated both when inhaling disgusting odorants and when observing other people's expressions of disgust (Wicker et al., 2003). Finally, a patient with lesions in the left insula and putamen was selectively impaired in the recognition of disgust faces and sounds, and also reported experiencing disgust less often than other emotions and than control participants (Calder et al., 2000; but see Boucher et al., 2015).

In addition to the examples of the amygdala and insula, other brain structures have been linked to specific emotions (see Lindquist et al., 2012). The anterior cingulate cortex (ACC), located medially and frontally in the cortex, may be at the origin of sadness (Killgore & Yurgelun-Todd, 2004; but see Caruana et al., 2015). Anger, instead, may originate from the orbitofrontal cortex (OFC), whereas the supplementary motor area (a medial part of the cortex involved in motor control) has been associated with happiness (Fried et al., 1998; Krolak-Salmon et al., 2006; Rochas et al., 2013).

In addition, animal neurophysiologists have emphasized the role of small parts of the midbrain and brainstem. There, separated but highly intertwined circuits have been found in rodents that, when electrically stimulated, generate distinct emotions, including behavioral and physiological responses (Panksepp, 1998). This line of work is very relevant for the cross-species understanding of emotions, but the noninvasive techniques used in humans such as neuroimaging currently do not allow for that level of precision.

Constructionism

Although locationism remains strong in contemporary emotion research, competing views have emerged and recently regained acceptance. Criticisms of locationism are mostly based on the difficulty of finding brain areas that are consistently and specifically associated with discrete emotions (Lindquist et al., 2012).

For example, the link between the amygdala and fear may not be as strict as suggested by the research that we just summarized. Indeed, not all patients with bilateral amygdala damage are impaired in recognizing fearful faces, leading to the hypothesis that the amygdala might instead be specialized for responding to threatening or dangerous stimuli (Adolphs et al., 1999) or in general to stimuli that are relevant for the organism (Sander, Grafman, & Zalla, 2003). Results from recent brain imaging studies are also inconclusive. In such studies, amygdala activation has been found during the perception and experience of several other emotions besides fear (Adolphs, 2013; Lindquist et al., 2012).

Similarly, the association between disgust and the insula has not always been confirmed. In fact, increased insula activation is found in brain imaging studies using all sorts of stimuli and tasks. The insula has been associated with an astonishingly large number of functions other than emotion, including interoceptive awareness, pain, empathy, fairness, and speech production (Corradi-Dell'Acqua et al., 2016; Craig, 2009; Nieuwenhuys, 2012). Although we can't dismiss locationism entirely, the difficulties in consistently linking specific brain areas and emotions have led to the development of alternative models of the neural basis of emotions. One of these is called constructionism.

Psychological constructionism was presented as a general theory of emotion and was discussed in detail in Chapter 1 (Gendron & Barrett, 2009). Scientists who endorse this theory believe that discrete emotions such as fear, anger, disgust, and joy result from basic psychological and neural operations that are not specific to each particular emotion category, or even to emotions in general. That is, any particular emotion we experience arises from the interplay between our biological responses to an event or object and our psychological understanding of those responses. The theory's main basic principles, some of which we learned about in Chapter 1, are:

- Core affect, the conscious experience of bodily changes
- Conceptualization, the linking of bodily changes with the sensory perception of an object or event
- Executive attention, which helps to select the most important elements of bodily and environmental change
- Language, which is a means of categorizing and communicating about emotions

Because the psychological constructionist approach assumes these fundamental building blocks, which underlie most of human perception and thinking, they explicitly argue against specific correlates for discrete emotions.

In a series of brain imaging (fMRI) reviews, Barrett and colleagues provided evidence for a distributed emotional network (Kober et al., 2008; Lindquist et al., 2012). Using data-driven statistical methods such as **cluster analysis**, they defined six different functional groups of brain regions that are generally activated together, even across different studies. The neural networks, and the psychological operations they perform, are not specific to discrete emotional categories or to emotion per se (see Figure 3.5). Nevertheless, in the complex and intertwined neural networks that basically span the entire brain, including cortical, subcortical, and brainstem structures, some specificity for emotion categories can also be found (Wager et al., 2015).

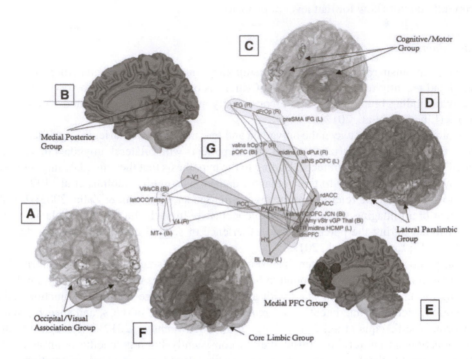

Figure 3.5 Six functional groups revealed by a meta-analysis of imaging studies. Core affect originates in
the core limbic (F) and the lateral paralimbic group (D); conceptualization in the medial PFC
(E) and posterior group (B); language and executive attention in the cognitive/motor group
(C). The central image (G) represents a flattened view of some of the areas in these functional
groups and the way they interact. From Kober et al. (2008).

Hemispheric Specialization

Most likely, you have heard this idea in the popular media or have seen an image depicting
it: the two hemispheres of the brain are very different in the functions they perform (see Figure 3.6). Indeed, it is common belief in folk psychology that the right hemisphere is specialized
for emotion, creativity, imagination, and spatial abilities, whereas the left hemisphere is specialized for abstract and logical thinking, computation, and language comprehension. There is
some scientific evidence backing this dichotomy, mostly based on studies of patients who have
suffered brain damage.

Modern laterality research is based on locationist theory and was also influenced by early
nineteenth-century "phrenology." Phrenologists believed that the mind has a set of mental faculties, with each particular faculty represented in a different area of the brain. An example
of a mental faculty was "love of offspring." In theory, the size of an area corresponded to an
individual's propensity, something like a personality trait. So, locations on an individual's skull
had to change size to accommodate the more developed mental functions housed by enlarged
brain areas (Harrington, 1995). This belief led to the practice of reading the bumps on people's
skulls in order to assess their personality traits. Although phrenology was later dismissed as a
scientific theory, locationism and its idea that many psychological functions are served by specialized and separated areas or circuits of the brain is very much alive in modern neuroscience.

To a large extent, however, scientific findings have been overinterpreted in popular culture
and media, often leading to the idea that two fully independent and antagonistic souls (one in

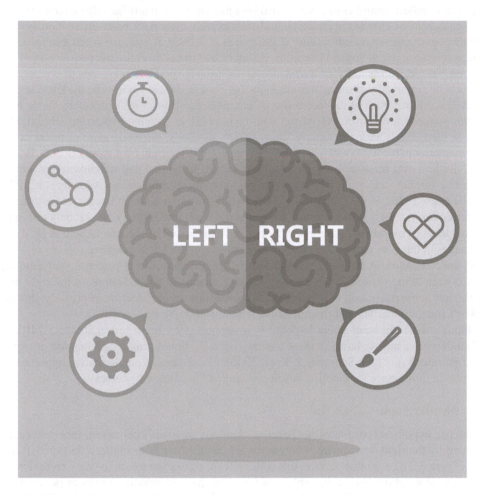

Figure 3.6 How we have historically thought about the two hemispheres of the brain.

each hemisphere) reside in our head (Figure 3.6). In reality, hemispheric differences are often more subtle. You also need to keep in mind that in the healthy brain, the two hemispheres work together, continuously exchanging information via the corpus callosum connecting them. In the next section, we will review some of the relevant scientific evidence and three theories about the hemispheric specialization of emotions. The reader interested in the hemispheric lateralization of other mental functions should consult some of the monographs on the topic (Davidson & Hugdahl, 1995; Hugdahl & Westerhausen, 2010).

RIGHT HEMISPHERE HYPOTHESIS

The right hemisphere hypothesis of emotion posits that the expression, perception, and experience of positive and negative emotions are predominantly carried out by the right hemisphere. The father of this hypothesis may be Jules Bernard Luys, a nineteenth-century neuroanatomist (Harrington, 1995). Luys reported that patients who suffered left-side body paralysis after brain damage (e.g., stroke) became emotionally volatile, manic, and delusional. This was not the case in patients paralyzed on the right side. Because each half of the body is mostly under the control of the contralateral (opposite) hemisphere, Luys inferred that the right hemisphere might contain an emotion control center, which had become damaged in left-lateralized patients. Similar observations of changes in character and emotionality after right hemisphere damage were made throughout the twentieth century (Demaree et al., 2005). It was also noted that hysterical hemianesthesia, a psychological condition without clear organic origin that causes loss of sensation on one side of the body, occurred almost exclusively on the left.

It has been empirically observed that emotions are expressed more strongly on the left side of the face. Because innervation of the face is mostly contralateral (Rinn, 1984), especially in the lower half, this suggests a dominant role of the right hemisphere in emotion expression (Borod, Haywood, & Koff, 1997; Sackeim, Gur, & Saucy, 1978). Similarly, the recognition of facial expressions is superior in the left visual field, which is connected to the right hemisphere (Ley & Bryden, 1979). Studies with brain-lesioned patients have shown that visual and somatosensory areas of the right hemisphere are implicated in the recognition of facial expressions (Adolphs et al., 2000; Adolphs et al., 1996). Finally, anesthesia of the right hemisphere through injection of a drug into the internal carotid artery (this procedure, known as the Wada test, is reversible and only lasts a few minutes) leads to perceiving lower intensity in facial expressions of emotion (Ahern et al., 1991). No changes in intensity ratings are found after anesthesia of the left hemisphere.

The specialization of the right hemisphere for the expression and perception of emotions has also been demonstrated in the auditory sensory modality. There, lesions of the right more than the left hemisphere lead to impairments in perception and production of prosody, that is, a speaker's tone, intonation, and rhythm (Ross, Thompson, & Yenkosky, 1997).

Although the right hemisphere hypothesis is supported by brain lesion studies, fMRI and EEG studies have mostly failed to show a strong lateralization during the perception or expression of emotions (e.g., see Schirmer & Kotz, 2006). Consequently, an alternative hypothesis of hemispheric dominance for emotion developed, called the valence hypothesis.

THE VALENCE HYPOTHESIS

The valence hypothesis postulates that negative emotions are mainly perceived, experienced, and expressed by the right hemisphere, whereas the left hemisphere is specialized for positive emotions (Figure 3.7). In another variant, this right–left specialization exists for the expression and experience of emotion, but the perception of both positive and negative emotions occurs in the right hemisphere. Some support for the valence hypothesis comes from studies looking at brain damage or inhibition of one hemisphere. For example, sedation of the left hemisphere (again via the Wada test) results in depressed mood, whereas sedation of the right hemisphere results in smiling, laughing, and positive mood (Demaree et al., 2005). Moreover, right hemisphere damage may impair the recognition of negative emotions, but not of happiness (Adolphs et al., 1996). However, patient data regarding hemispheric specialization of emotion recognition are often mixed. Stronger support has come from studies relying on EEG studies, which repeatedly find, even in 10-month-old infants, greater activity (measured as decreased power in the 10-Hz range) over frontal electrodes of the right hemisphere during perception or expression of negative emotional states and of the left hemisphere during positive emotional states (Davidson & Fox, 1982; Davidson & Irwin, 1999). However, more recent neuroimaging research has mostly failed to confirm this hemispheric difference (Hamann, 2012; Lindquist et al., 2012; Phan et al., 2002).

THE APPROACH–WITHDRAWAL HYPOTHESIS

One way to categorize emotions is as approach or withdrawal emotions, which refers to whether they motivate us to move toward or away from interacting with another. The approach–withdrawal hypothesis of hemispheric lateralization posits that approach action tendencies are mediated by prefrontal areas of the left hemisphere, whereas withdrawal tendencies stem from

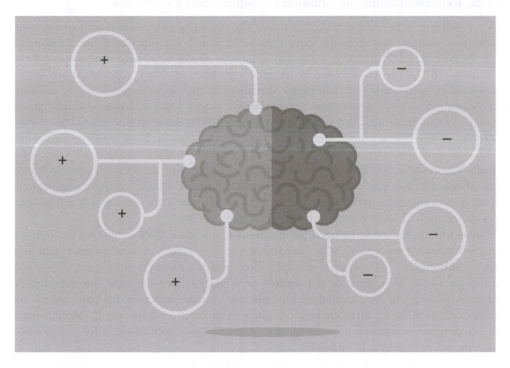

Figure 3.7 The valence hypothesis holds that negative feelings are processed in the right hemisphere and positive feelings are processed in the left hemisphere.

the right hemisphere (Harmon-Jones, Gable, & Peterson, 2010). When it comes to specific emotions, the approach–withdrawal hypothesis is, for the most part, identical to the valence hypothesis. Positive emotions are still the specialty of the left hemisphere and most negative emotions of the right hemisphere. However, the crucial difference between the two hypotheses is the lateralization of anger, an emotion with negative valence, which is now attributed to the left hemisphere. Like it was for the previously presented valence hypothesis, most of the support for the approach–withdrawal hypothesis comes from EEG studies. These studies have found, for example, that voluntarily producing facial expressions of anger and joy (approach emotions) results in greater left frontal activation, whereas production of expressions of fear and sadness (withdrawal emotions) results in relatively greater right frontal activation (Coan, Allen, & Harmon-Jones, 2001).

Summary of Hemispheric Specialization

In this section we have reviewed three distinct theories that propose an emotional specialization for the cerebral hemispheres. According to the right hemisphere hypothesis, emotions are experienced, perceived, and expressed by the right hemisphere. The valence hypothesis suggests that both hemispheres play a role in emotion, with negative affect being anchored in the right hemisphere and positive affect in the left hemisphere. Finally, the approach–withdrawal hypothesis is very similar but postulates that the negative (and approach-related) emotion of anger is also produced by the left hemisphere. As new techniques continue to be developed to investigate the brain in action, such as fMRI, research will help decide which hypothesis best fits the data.

Shared Representations for Emotion Perception and Production

In line with theories of embodied cognition (see Chapter 8), neuroscience largely assumes that overlapping brain circuits become active both when somebody experiences an emotion and when she perceives the emotion expressed by somebody else (Decety & Sommerville, 2003; de Vignemont, 2013; Niedenthal et al., 2010). This hypothesis of shared representations for self and other also extends to actions and bodily sensations, including pain and touch. The activation of emotional (or motor or somatosensory) areas during perception contributes to the recognition of others' emotions, actions, and sensations (Iacoboni, 2009; Keysers, Kaas, & Gazzola, 2010; Niedenthal, 2007; Wood et al., 2016). In line with this assumption, brain imaging studies have found considerable overlap in the brain activity accompanying the production and observation of facial expressions. This neural overlap includes motor and somatosensory cortices (Van der Gaag, Mindera, & Keysers, 2007). Moreover, damage to somatosensory cortices, which process and integrate somatosensory feedback from one's own face and body, leads to reduced accuracy in the recognition of facial expressions (Adolphs et al., 2000).

Similar results, including reduced facial mimicry, are found after temporary inhibition of motor and somatosensory areas, which can be induced with a method called **transcranial magnetic stimulation**, or TMS (Korb et al., 2015; Pitcher et al., 2008; Pourtois et al., 2004). TMS involves the use of a magnetic field generator, or "coil," which is held just above the head of the person undergoing the procedure. Using electromagnetic induction, the coil causes small electric currents in the region of the brain, resulting in the creation of so-called "virtual lesions." The virtual lesions serve to inhibit a brain area (typically only cortical ones) for a brief period via strong but short magnetic impulses.

Because motor and somatosensory areas are activated during emotion expression, their activation during passive watching of facial expressions and the fact that their inhibition or damage leads to impaired recognition of facial expressions all strongly suggest that these brain areas also play a role in emotion recognition.

Mirror Neurons and Emotions

The hypothesis of shared representations for self and other originated with the discovery of *mirror neurons*. Mirror neurons constitute a special class of motor neurons and were discovered by an Italian group of physiologists in the frontal and parietal cortex of macaque monkeys (di Pellegrino et al., 1992). They got their intriguing name when it became clear that they activate both during the production (e.g., monkey grasps a peanut) and the perception (monkey observes experimenter grasping the peanut) of an action. This was interpreted as the brain's elegant way of using a single system to do two separate things: act upon the environment and understand the goals of others' actions (Gallese et al., 1996).

For years, the existence of mirror neurons in humans was disputed, primarily because ethical reasons prevented researchers from doing single-neuron recordings in humans, forcing them instead to use more indirect measures of neuronal activity (EEG, fMRI, TMS). Today, the presence of a human mirror neuron system is generally accepted (Molenberghs, Cunnington, & Mattingley, 2012; Mukamel et al., 2010), although its precise anatomical boundaries, functional roles, and phylogenetic origins remain matters of intense debate (Cook et al., 2014; Heyes, 2010a, 2010b).

Importantly, the human mirror neuron system (MNS) is more extended and includes many more brain areas than those originally found in macaque monkeys. In addition to the ventral premotor cortex and the inferior parietal lobule, where mirror neurons were originally found, the human MNS includes the supplementary motor area, the hippocampus and parahippocampal gyrus, the entorhinal cortex, and likely also the primary motor and somatosensory cortices (Figure 3.8; Keysers, Kaas, & Gazzola, 2010; Keysers & Gazzola, 2010; Mukamel et al., 2010).

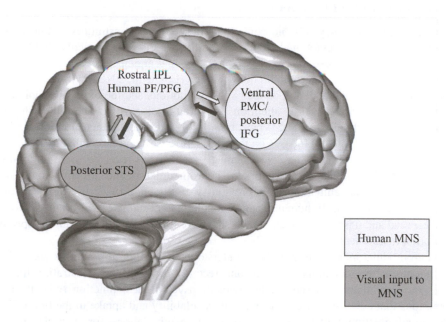

Figure 3.8 Classical areas of the human MNS (in white) and an associated area in the posterior superior temporal sulcus (STS). IPL = inferior parietal lobule; PMC = premotor cortex; IFG = inferior frontal gyrus. From Iacoboni & Dapretto (2006). Image re-created using BodyParts3D. From Mitsuhashi et al. (2009).

A number of brain imaging studies have found overlapping brain activation during either emotion experience and emotion perception or emotion expression and perception, allowing for a role of the MNS in emotion recognition. For example, similar and highly overlapping brain activity was found in the anterior insula when participants inhaled disgusting odors or watched facial expressions of disgust (Wicker et al., 2003). Another study found overlapping brain activity in an extended network, including the insula, the amygdala, and the somatosensory cortex, during passive watching and active imitation of facial expressions of happiness, disgust, and fear (van der Gaag, Mindera, & Keysers, 2007).

Other studies have shown that inhibition or damage to parts of the MNS can lead to impaired or delayed emotion recognition. For example, inhibition of the right somatosensory cortex with TMS leads to impaired emotion recognition (Pitcher et al., 2008; Pourtois et al., 2004) and even reduced facial mimicry in women (Korb et al., 2015). Damage to the same and neighboring areas similarly impairs the recognition of facial expressions of emotion (Adolphs et al., 2000).

In summary, due to their theoretical appeal, mirror neurons have been claimed to under-lie a large variety of psychological functions, including understanding of others' goals and states, imitation, speech perception, embodied simulation (see Chapter 8), empathy, and emotion recognition. As mirror neuron research is starting to become scrutinized more critically, at least some of the many speculations about their roles will likely be reconsidered (Lamm & Majdandžić, 2015). Nevertheless, compelling evidence links the human MNS to emotion understanding. Future research will help us decide about the precise role of mirror neurons in emotion understanding, as well as in many of the other functions they may facilitate.

The Neurochemistry of Emotions

We now discuss the role played by neuromodulators (i.e. neurotransmitters and hormones) in generating and sustaining emotional responses. Unfortunately, this particular field of neuroscience has not been explored very well. So far, very few attempts have been made to map specific emotions to distinct neuromodulators systems (Lövheim, 2012; Panksepp, 1998). And in most review articles and textbook chapters about emotions and the brain, the topic is either completely lacking or receives little attention compared to discussions about the role of brain areas and circuits (Dalgleish, 2004). When the role of neuromodulators in emotions is mentioned, the discussion typically focuses on the topics of reward and mood disorders rather than on specific emotions (although the neurochemistry of fear has received more attention, e.g., see Adolphs, 2013). The majority of work on neuromodulators and affective states is being carried out in nonhuman animals that, as previously discussed, provide useful but incomplete models of human emotion. In humans, neuromodulators act on extended brain networks and have widespread and unspecific effects—facts that have further kept them from the spotlight of most emotion researchers.

The neuromodulators that are now best understood in relation to emotions are called serotonin, noradrenaline, dopamine, opioids, and recently oxytocin. Demonstrating the role of a single neuromodulator in a specific behavior or psychological function typically requires manipulations that either increase or decrease its availability and uptake in the brain. This can include the administration of drugs, but also genetic manipulations, for example, in mice, to remove or reduce the concentration of certain neuromodulators in the brain.

Dopamine was originally believed to be the main source of pleasure in the brain (Wise, 1980). Anatomically speaking, neurons of the ventral tegmental area (VTA) of the midbrain release dopamine into subcortical areas like the nucleus accumbens (NAc), the ventral striatum, and the amygdala, as well as to the prefrontal cortex.

However, dopamine seems to play a larger role in the wanting (seeking, craving) than the liking (pleasure) aspects of reward (Berridge & Kringelbach, 2015). Although wanting and liking are often positively related to each other, they can be shown to be dissociated behaviors and mental states. For example, genetically modified mice who have dopamine levels elevated by 70% show more wanting of a sweet reward (they work harder to receive it), but do not show greater liking reactions, as measured through their orofacial expressions (Peciña et al., 2003). Similarly, Parkinson's patients who received high doses of dopamine agonists (leading to a net increase in the available dopamine and an improvement of the patients' motor behavior) shop and gamble compulsively, but do not report experiencing greater pleasure from these activities (Berridge & Kringelbach, 2015).

Liking and wanting also seem to be associated with the opioid system, as suggested by an interesting study carried out in human participants (Chelnokova et al., 2014). Administration of morphine (an opioid agonist) makes male participants press a button longer (wanting) to see attractive female faces, which they also rate as more attractive (liking). The same participants, however, exert less effort and rate female faces as less attractive after receiving naltrexone, an opioid receptor antagonist.

As exciting as these and other findings can be, more research is needed to clearly understand the role and interplay of the dopamine and opioid systems in animal and human reward. Similarly, the role of other neuromodulators in emotions is just starting to be understood, and many important discoveries in this field occurred by chance. For example, the role of serotonin in the regulation of mood was discovered serendipitously about 50 years ago, when the administration of a new drug for the treatment of tuberculosis resulted in elevated mood and generally increased energy (Castrén, 2005; Mukherjee, 2012). This and further drugs with antidepressant activity were later shown to increase concentrations of serotonin and noradrenaline, both of which are monoamines, in the brain. The resulting monoamine hypothesis proposed that depression is caused by a deficiency of these two neuromodulators which remain today the main target of antidepressant medication. However, the efficacy of monoamine-increasing drugs, and of the underlying theory that serotonin and noradrenaline depletion are the main cause of depression, are now being called into serious question (Castrén, 2005; Mukherjee, 2012).

Another neuromodulator that has received enormous attention in the last decade, both in the scientific community and among the general public, is oxytocin. Oxytocin is both a hormone and a neuropeptide and has been implicated in a vast array of behaviors and has played a key role in the evolution of social behaviors, in particular, in attachment, exploration, and sexuality (Carter et al., 2008; Donaldson & Young, 2008; Meyer-Lindenberg et al., 2011). In humans, oxytocin is often administered through nasal spray, although the precise mechanism of how it passes the blood–brain barrier and enters the brain is not well understood (Churchland & Winkielman, 2012). Still, the importance of oxytocin in human bonding and cooperative behavior is of such great interest that its molecular structure is becoming easily recognized and even used in the creation of jewelry and greeting cards (Figure 3.9)!

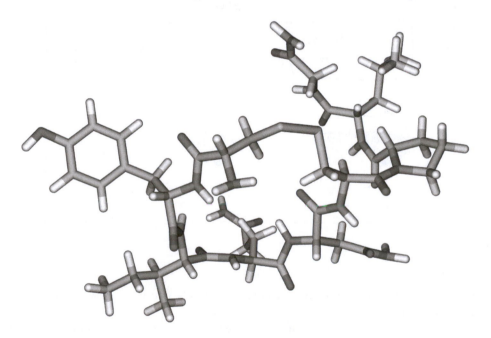

Figure 3.9 The molecular structure of oxytocin.

There is currently great interest in the positive effects of oxytocin on the perception of social stimuli, such as facial expressions, and there is hope that its administration could help alleviate some of the social symptoms of autism spectrum disorders (Anagnostou et al., 2012; Bartz et al., 2011; Domes et al., 2007; Macdonald & Macdonald, 2010; Meyer-Lindenberg et al., 2011). In a study carried out in healthy male participants, intranasal oxytocin was shown to increase facial mimicry, especially for distressed infants (Korb et al., 2016). This finding suggests that oxytocin could improve the accurate identification of facial expression by increasing facial mimicry (see Chapter 5 for a discussion about the role of facial mimicry in emotion recognition).

In summary, the emotional neurochemistry of the brain remains largely unknown. Without a doubt, exciting discoveries in this field are likely to be made in the near future—be they the result of planned experimentation or of serendipitous neuropharmacological findings.

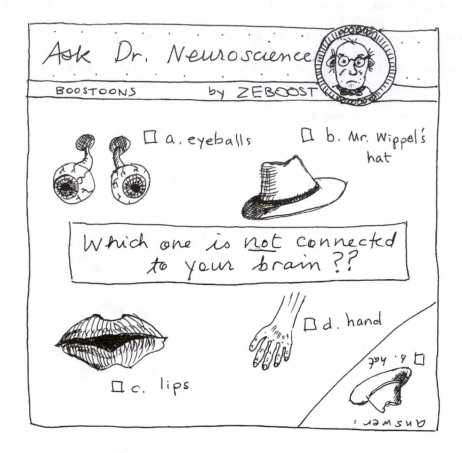

Summary

- Neuroscientific theories of emotion can be roughly put into two categories: locationism and constructivism.
- Locationism refers to the belief that specific areas of the brain are responsible for the experience of particular emotions. According to locationism, each emotion category (e.g., fear, anger, happiness) arises from largely subcortical, separate brain areas or networks, which are homologous with other animals.
- There are also several theories that specify roles of the two cerebral hemispheres in emotional experience.
- Constructionism holds that emotions are the result of fundamental cognitive functions, which are not specific to emotion and which result from widespread and flexible cortical–subcortical networks.
- Theories of embodied cognition are influential in neuroscientific research about emotions because overlapping brain areas have been shown to activate during both the experience/expression of emotions and the perception of other people's emotional expressions.

- Although little is known about the neurochemistry of specific emotions in humans, dopamine, serotonin, and oxytocin are implicated in certain aspects of emotion life.
- More research, utilizing a variety of scientific methods, is needed to truly discover the neural bases of emotions and to bridge the gap between research in humans and other animals.

Learning Links

1. Read a summary of challenges for the neuroscience of emotions. http://www.brain facts.org/sensing-thinking-behaving/mood/articles/2016/feeling-our-way-the-challenge-of-studying-emotion-and-the-brain-011216/
2. Hear a talk by Dr. David Anderson about the study of brains of mice and fruit flies and how this sheds light on the neural bases of emotion in humans. http://www.npr.org/2015/11/06/453995372/what-can-fruit-flies-tell-us-about-human-emotions
3. Listen to Dr. Richard Davidson speak about how social and emotional learning changes the brain. https://www.youtube.com/watch?v=o9fVvsR-CqM
4. Watch an animated video representing one view of the role of the right hemisphere in emotion. https://www.youtube.com/watch?v=JuyB7NO0EYY

References

Adolphs, R. (2013). The biology of fear. *Current Biology: CB*, *23*(2), R79–93. doi:10.1016/j.cub.2012.11.055.

Adolphs, R., Damasio, H., Tranel, D., Cooper, G., & Damasio, A. R. (2000). A role for somatosensory cortices in the visual recognition of emotion as revealed by three-dimensional lesion mapping. *Journal of Neuroscience*, *20*(7), 2683–2690.

Adolphs, R., Damasio, H., Tranel, D., & Damasio, A. R. (1996). Cortical systems for the recognition of emotion in facial expressions. *The Journal of Neuroscience: The Official Journal of the Society for Neuroscience*, *16*(23), 7678–7687.

Adolphs, R., Tranel, D., Damasio, H., & Damasio, A. (1994). Impaired recognition of emotion in facial expressions following bilateral damage to the human amygdala. *Nature*, *372*(6507), 669–672.

Adolphs, R., Tranel, D., Hamann, S., Young, A. W., Calder, A. J., Phelps, E. A., . . . Damasio, A. R. (1999). Recognition of facial emotion in nine individuals with bilateral amygdala damage. *Neuropsychologia*, *37*(10), 1111–1117.

Ahern, G. L., Schomer, D. L., Kleefield, J., Blume, H., Cosgrove, G. R., Weintraub, S., & Mesulam, M. M. (1991). Right hemisphere advantage for evaluating emotional facial expressions. *Cortex; a Journal Devoted to the Study of the Nervous System and Behavior*, *27*(2), 193–202.

Anagnostou, E., Soorya, L., Chaplin, W., Bartz, J., Halpern, D., Wasserman, S., . . . Hollander, E. (2012). Intranasal oxytocin versus placebo in the treatment of adults with autism spectrum disorders: A randomized controlled trial. *Molecular Autism*, *3*(1), 16. doi:10.1186/2040-2392-3–16.

Bartz, J. A., Zaki, J., Bolger, N., & Ochsner, K. N. (2011). Social effects of oxytocin in humans: Context and person matter. *Trends in Cognitive Sciences*, *15*(7), 301–309. doi:16/j.tics.2011.05.002.

Berridge, K. C., & Kringelbach, M. L. (2015). Pleasure systems in the brain. *Neuron*, *86*(3), 646–664. doi:10.1016/j.neuron.2015.02.018.

Borod, J. C., Haywood, C. S., & Koff, E. (1997). Neuropsychological aspects of facial asymmetry during emotional expression: A review of the normal adult literature. *Neuropsychology Review*, *7*(1), 41–60. doi:10.1007/BF02876972.

Boucher, O., Rouleau, I., Lassonde, M., Lepore, F., Bouthillier, A., & Nguyen, D. K. (2015). Social information processing following resection of the insular cortex. *Neuropsychologia*, *71*, 1–10. doi:10.1016/j.neuropsychologia.2015.03.008.

Calder, A. J., Keane, J., Manes, F., Antoun, N., & Young, A. W. (2000). Impaired recognition and experience of disgust following brain injury. *Nature Neuroscience*, *3*(11), 1077–1078.

Cannon, W. B. (1927). The James-Lange theory of emotions: A critical examination and an alternative theory. *The American Journal of Psychology*, (39), 106–124. doi:10.2307/1422695.

Carter, C. S., Grippo, A. J., Pournajafi-Nazarloo, H., Ruscio, M. G., & Porges, S. W. (2008). Oxytocin, vasopressin and sociality. *Progress in Brain Research, 170*, 331–336. doi:10.1016/S0079-6123 (08)00427-5.

Caruana, F., Avanzini, P., Gozzo, F., Francione, S., Cardinale, F., & Rizzolatti, G. (2015). Mirth and laughter elicited by electrical stimulation of the human anterior cingulate cortex. *Cortex*. doi:10.1016/j. cortex.2015.07.024.

Caruana, F., Jezzini, A., Sbriscia-Fioretti, B., Rizzolatti, G., & Gallese, V. (2011). Emotional and social behaviors elicited by electrical stimulation of the insula in the macaque monkey. *Current Biology: CB, 21*(3), 195–199. doi:10.1016/j.cub.2010.12.042.

Castrén, E. (2005). Is mood chemistry? *Nature Reviews Neuroscience, 6*(3), 241–246. doi:10.1038/ nrn1629.

Chelnokova, O., Laeng, B., Eikemo, M., Riegels, J., Løseth, G., Maurud, H., . . . Leknes, S. (2014). Rewards of beauty: The opioid system mediates social motivation in humans. *Molecular Psychiatry, 19*(7), 746–747. doi:10.1038/mp.2014.1.

Churchland, P. S., & Winkielman, P. (2012). Modulating social behavior with oxytocin: How does it work? What does it mean? *Hormones and Behavior, 61*(3), 392–399. doi:10.1016/j. yhbeh.2011.12.003.

Coan, J. A., Allen, J. J. B., & Harmon-Jones, E. (2001). Voluntary facial expression and hemispheric asymmetry over the frontal cortex. *Psychophysiology, 38*(6), 912–925.

Cook, R., Bird, G., Catmur, C., Press, C., & Heyes, C. (2014). Mirror neurons: From origin to function. *The Behavioral and Brain Sciences, 37*(2), 177–192. doi:10.1017/S0140525X13000903.

Corradi-Dell'Acqua, C., Tusche, A., Vuilleumier, P., & Singer, T. (2016). Cross-modal representations of first-hand and vicarious pain, disgust and fairness in insular and cingulate cortex. *Nature Communications, 7*, 10904. doi:10.1038/ncomms10904.

Craig, A. D. (2009). How do you feel—now? The anterior insula and human awareness. *Nature Reviews Neuroscience, 10*(1), 59–70. doi:10.1038/nrn2555.

Dalgleish, T. (2004). The emotional brain. *Nature Reviews Neuroscience, 5*(7), 582–589.

Davidson, R. J., & Fox, N. A. (1982). Asymmetrical brain activity discriminates between positive and negative affective stimuli in human infants. *Science, 218*(4578), 1235–1237.

Davidson, R. J., & Hugdahl, K. (Eds.). (1995). *Brain asymmetry*. Cambridge, MA: MIT Press. Retrieved from https://mitpress.mit.edu/books/brain-asymmetry.

Davidson, R. J., & Irwin, W. (1999). The functional neuroanatomy of emotion and affective style. *Trends in Cognitive Science, 3*(1), 11–21.

de Vignemont, F. (2013). Shared body representations and the "Whose" system. *Neuropsychologia. 55*, 128–136, doi:10.1016/j.neuropsychologia.2013.08.013

Decety, J., & Sommerville, J. A. (2003). Shared representations between self and other: A social cognitive neuroscience view. *Trends in Cognitive Sciences, 7*(12), 527–533.

Demaree, H. A., Everhart, D. E., Youngstrom, E. A., & Harrison, D. W. (2005). Brain lateralization of emotional processing: Historical roots and a future incorporating "dominance." *Behavioral and Cognitive Neuroscience Reviews, 4*(1), 3–20. doi:10.1177/1534582305276837.

di Pellegrino, G., Fadiga, L., Fogassi, L., Gallese, V., & Rizzolatti, G. (1992). Understanding motor events: A neurophysiological study. *Experimental Brain Research, 91*(1), 176–180.

Domes, G., Heinrichs, M., Michel, A., Berger, C., & Herpertz, S. C. (2007). Oxytocin improves "mind-reading" in humans. *Biological Psychiatry, 61*(6), 731–733. doi:10.1016/j.biopsych.2006.07.015.

Donaldson, Z. R., & Young, L. J. (2008). Oxytocin, vasopressin, and the neurogenetics of sociality. *Science, 322*(5903), 900–904. doi:10.1126/science.1158668.

Feinstein, J. S., Adolphs, R., Damasio, A., & Tranel, D. (2011). The human amygdala and the induction and experience of fear. *Current Biology: CB, 21*(1), 34–38. doi:10.1016/j.cub.2010.11.042.

Fendt, M., & Fanselow, M. S. (1999). The neuroanatomical and neurochemical basis of conditioned fear. *Neuroscience and Biobehavioral Reviews, 23*(5), 743–760.

Fried, I., Wilson, C. L., MacDonald, K. A., & Behnke, E. J. (1998). Electric current stimulates laughter. *Nature, 391*(6668), 650.

Fries, A. B. W., Ziegler, T. E., Kurian, J. R., Jacoris, S., & Pollak, S. D. (2005). Early experience in humans is associated with changes in neuropeptides critical for regulating social behavior. *Proceedings of the*

National Academy of Sciences of the United States of America, *102*(47), 17237–17240. doi:10.1073/pnas.0504767102.

Gallese, V., Fadiga, L., Fogassi, L., & Rizzolatti, G. (1996). Action recognition in the premotor cortex. *Brain*, *119*, 593–609.

Gendron, M., & Barrett, L. F. (2009). Reconstructing the past: A century of ideas about emotion in psychology. *Emotion Review*, *1*(4), 316–339. doi:10.1177/1754073909338877.

Hamann, S. (2012). Mapping discrete and dimensional emotions onto the brain: Controversies and consensus. *Trends in Cognitive Sciences*, *16*(9), 458–466. doi:10.1016/j.tics.2012.07.006.

Harmon-Jones, E., Gable, P. A., & Peterson, C. K. (2010). The role of asymmetric frontal cortical activity in emotion-related phenomena: A review and update. *Biological Psychology*, *84*(3), 451–462. doi:10.1016/j.biopsycho.2009.08.010.

Harrington, H. (1995). Unfinished business: Models of laterality in the nineteenth century. In R. J. Davidson & K. Hugdahl (Eds.), *Brain asymmetry* (pp. 3–28). Cambridge, MA: MIT Press. Retrieved from https://mitpress.mit.edu/books/brain-asymmetry.

Heyes, C. (2010a). Mesmerising mirror neurons. *NeuroImage*, *51*(2), 789–791. doi:10.1016/j.neuroimage.2010.02.034.

Heyes, C. (2010b). Where do mirror neurons come from? *Neuroscience and Biobehavioral Reviews*, *34*(4), 575–583. doi:10.1016/j.neubiorev.2009.11.007.

Hugdahl, K., & Westerhausen, R. (2010). *The two halves of the brain: Information processing in the cerebral hemispheres*. Cambridge, MA: MIT Press.

Iacoboni, M. (2009). Imitation, empathy, and mirror neurons. *Annual Review of Psychology*, *60*, 653–670. doi:10.1146/annurev.psych.60.110707.163604.

Iacoboni, M., & Dapretto, M. (2006). The mirror neuron system and the consequences of its dysfunction. *Nature Review Neuroscience*, *7*(12), 942–951. doi:nrn2024 [pii] 10.1038/nrn2024.

Kandel, E. R., Schwartz, G. H., Thomas, M. J., Siegelbaum, S. A., & Hudspeth, A. J. (Eds.). (2013). *Principles of neural science* (5th ed.). New York: McGraw-Hill.

Keysers, C., & Gazzola, V. (2010). Social neuroscience: Mirror neurons recorded in humans. *Current Biology*, *20*(8), R353–R354. doi:10.1016/j.cub.2010.03.013.

Keysers, C., Kaas, J. H., & Gazzola, V. (2010). Somatosensation in social perception. *Nature Reviews Neuroscience*, *11*(6), 417–428. doi:10.1038/nrn2833.

Killgore, W. D. S., & Yurgelun-Todd, D. A. (2004). Activation of the amygdala and anterior cingulate during nonconscious processing of sad versus happy faces. *NeuroImage*, *21*(4), 1215–1223. doi:10.1016/j.neuroimage.2003.12.033.

Korb, S., Malsert, J., Rochas, V., Rihs, T. A., Rieger, S. W., Schwab, S., ... Grandjean, D. (2015). Gender differences in the neural network of facial mimicry of smiles—An rTMS study. *Cortex*, *70*, 101–114. doi:10.1016/j.cortex.2015.06.025.

Korb, S., Malsert, J., Strathearn, L., Vuilleumier, P., & Niedenthal, P. (2016). Sniff and mimic—Intranasal oxytocin increases facial mimicry in a sample of men. *Hormones and Behavior*, *84*, 64–74.

Kober, H., Barrett, L. F., Joseph, J., Bliss-Moreau, E., Lindquist, K., & Wager, T. D. (2008). Functional grouping and cortical–subcortical interactions in emotion: A meta-analysis of neuroimaging studies. *NeuroImage*, *42*(2), 998–1031. doi:10.1016/j.neuroimage.2008.03.059.

Krolak-Salmon, P., Hénaff, M.-A., Isnard, J., Tallon-Baudry, C., Guénot, M., Vighetto, A., ... Mauguière, F. (2003). An attention modulated response to disgust in human ventral anterior insula. *Annals of Neurology*, *53*(4), 446–453. doi:10.1002/ana.10502.

Krolak-Salmon, P., Henaff, M. A., Vighetto, A., Bauchet, F., Bertrand, O., Mauguiere, F., & Isnard, J. (2006). Experiencing and detecting happiness in humans: The role of the supplementary motor area. *Ann Neurol*, *59*(1), 196–199.

Lambert, K. G. (2003). The life and career of Paul MacLean: A journey toward neurobiological and social harmony. *Physiology & Behavior*, *79*(3), 343–349. doi:10.1016/S0031–9384(03)00147–1.

Lamm, C., & Majdandžić, J. (2015). The role of shared neural activations, mirror neurons, and morality in empathy—A critical comment. *Neuroscience Research*, *90C*, 15–24. doi:10.1016/j.neures.2014.10.008.

LeDoux, J. E. (1996). *The emotional brain*. New York: Simon & Schuster.

LeDoux, J. E. (2007). The amygdala. *Current Biology: CB*, *17*(20), R868–R874. doi:10.1016/j.cub.2007.08.005.

Ley, R. G., & Bryden, M. P. (1979). Hemispheric differences in processing emotions and faces. *Brain and Language, 7*(1), 127–138.

Lindquist, K. A., Wager, T. D., Kober, H., Bliss-Moreau, E., & Barrett, L. F. (2012). The brain basis of emotion: A meta-analytic review. *The Behavioral and Brain Sciences, 35*(3), 121–143. doi:10.1017/S0140525X11000446.

Lövheim, H. (2012). A new three-dimensional model for emotions and monoamine neurotransmitters. *Medical Hypotheses, 78*(2), 341–348. doi:10.1016/j.mehy.2011.11.016.

Macdonald, K., & Macdonald, T. M. (2010). The peptide that binds: A systematic review of oxytocin and its prosocial effects in humans. *Harvard Review of Psychiatry, 18*(1), 1–21. doi:10.3109/10673220903523615.

MacLean, P. D. (1949). Psychosomatic disease and the visceral brain; recent developments bearing on the Papez theory of emotion. *Psychosomatic Medicine, 11*(6), 338–353.

MacLean, P. D. (1967). The brain in relation to empathy and medical education. *Journal of Nervous and Mental Disease, 144*(5), 374–382. doi:10.1097/00005053-196705000-00005.

Meyer-Lindenberg, A., Domes, G., Kirsch, P., & Heinrichs, M. (2011). Oxytocin and vasopressin in the human brain: Social neuropeptides for translational medicine. *Nature Reviews Neuroscience, 12*(9), 524–538. doi:10.1038/nrn3044.

Mitsuhashi, N., Fujieda, K., Tamura, T., Kawamoto, S., Takagi, T., & Okubo, K. (2009). BodyParts3D: 3D structure database for anatomical concepts. *Nucleic Acids Research, 37*(suppl 1), D782-D785. doi:10.1093/nar/gkn613.

Molenberghs, P., Cunnington, R., & Mattingley, J. B. (2012). Brain regions with mirror properties: A meta-analysis of 125 human fMRI studies. *Neuroscience and Biobehavioral Reviews, 36*(1), 341–349. doi:10.1016/j.neubiorev.2011.07.004.

Mukamel, R., Ekstrom, A. D., Kaplan, J., Iacoboni, M., & Fried, I. (2010). Single-neuron responses in humans during execution and observation of actions. *Current Biology, 20*(8), 750–756. doi:10.1016/j.cub.2010.02.045.

Mukherjee, S. (2012, April 19). The Science and History of Treating Depression. *The New York Times Magazine.* Retrieved from http://www.nytimes.com/2012/04/22/magazine/the-science-and-history-of-treating-depression.html.

Niedenthal, P. M. (2007). Embodying emotion. *Science, 316,* 1002–1005. doi:10.1126/science.1136930.

Niedenthal, P. M., Mermillod, M., Maringer, M., & Hess, U. (2010). The simulation of smiles (SIMS) model: Embodied simulation and the meaning of facial expression. *The Behavioral and Brain Sciences, 33*(6), 417–433.

Nieuwenhuys, R. (2012). The insular cortex: A review. *Progress in Brain Research, 195,* 123–163. doi:10.1016/B978-0-444-53860-4.00007-6.

Öhman, A. (2009). Of snakes and faces: An evolutionary perspective on the psychology of fear. *Scandinavian Journal of Psychology, 50*(6), 543–552. doi:10.1111/j.1467-9450.2009.00784.x.

Panksepp, J. (1998). *Affective neuroscience.* New York: Oxford University Press.

Papagno, C., Pisoni, A., Mattavelli, G., Casarotti, A., Comi, A., Fumagalli, F., . . . Bello, L. (2016). Specific disgust processing in the left insula: New evidence from direct electrical stimulation. *Neuropsychologia, 84,* 29–35. doi:10.1016/j.neuropsychologia.2016.01.036.

Papez, J. W. (1995). A proposed mechanism of emotion. 1937. *Journal of Neuropsychiatry and Clinical Neurosciences, 7*(1), 103–112.

Peciña, S., Cagniard, B., Berridge, K. C., Aldridge, J. W., & Zhuang, X. (2003). Hyperdopaminergic mutant mice have higher "wanting" but not "liking" for sweet rewards. *The Journal of Neuroscience: The Official Journal of the Society for Neuroscience, 23*(28), 9395–9402.

Phan, K. L., Wager, T., Taylor, S. F., & Liberzon, I. (2002). Functional neuroanatomy of emotion: A meta-analysis of emotion activation studies in PET and fMRI. *Neuroimage, 16*(2), 331–348.

Phillips, M. L., Young, A. W., Senior, C., Brammer, M., Andrew, C., Calder, A. J., . . . David, A. S. (1997). A specific neural substrate for perceiving facial expressions of disgust. *Nature, 389*(6650), 495–498.

Pitcher, D., Garrido, L., Walsh, V., & Duchaine, B. C. (2008). Transcranial magnetic stimulation disrupts the perception and embodiment of facial expressions. *Journal of Neuroscience, 28*(36), 8929–8933.

Pollak, S. D. (2008). Mechanisms linking early experience and the emergence of emotions: Illustrations from the study of maltreated children. *Current Directions in Psychological Science, 17*(6), 370–375. doi:10.1111/j.1467-8721.2008.00608.x.

Pourtois, G., Sander, D., Andres, M., Grandjean, D., Reveret, L., Olivier, E., & Vuilleumier, P. (2004). Dissociable roles of the human somatosensory and superior temporal cortices for processing social face signals. *European Journal of Neuroscience*, 20(12), 3507–3515.

Rinn, W. E. (1984). The neuropsychology of facial expression: A review of the neurological and psychological mechanisms for producing facial expressions. *Psychological Bulletin*, 95(1), 52–77.

Rochas, V., Gelmini, L., Krolak-Salmon, P., Poulet, E., Saoud, M., Brunelin, J., & Bediou, B. (2013). Disrupting pre-SMA activity impairs facial happiness recognition: An event-related TMS study. *Cerebral Cortex (New York: 1991)*, 23(7), 1517–1525. doi:10.1093/cercor/bhs133.

Ross, E. D., Thompson, R. D., & Yenkosky, J. (1997). Lateralization of affective prosody in brain and the callosal integration of hemispheric language functions. *Brain and Language*, 56(1), 27–54. doi:10.1006/brln.1997.1731.

Sackeim, H. A., Gur, R. C., & Saucy, M. C. (1978). Emotions are expressed more intensely on the left side of the face. *Science*, 202, 434–436.

Sander, D., Grafman, J., & Zalla, T. (2003). The human amygdala: An evolved system for relevance detection. *Rev Neurosci*, 14(4), 303–316.

Schirmer, A., & Kotz, S. A. (2006). Beyond the right hemisphere: Brain mechanisms mediating vocal emotional processing. *Trends in Cognitive Sciences*, 10(1), 24–30. doi:10.1016/j.tics.2005.11.009.

Schwartz, J. H., & Javitch, J. A. (2013). Neurotransmitters. In E. R. Kandel, G. H. Schwartz, M. J. Thomas, S. A. Siegelbaum & A. J. Hudspeth (Eds.), *Principles of neural science* (5th ed., pp. 289–306). New York: McGraw-Hill.

Taylor, J. M., & Whalen, P. J. (2015). Neuroimaging and anxiety: The neural substrates of pathological and non-pathological anxiety. *Current Psychiatry Reports*, 17(6), 49. doi:10.1007/s11920-015-0586-9.

Tupler, L. A., & De Bellis, M. D. (2006). Segmented hippocampal volume in children and adolescents with posttraumatic stress disorder. *Biological psychiatry*, 59(6), 523–529. doi:10.1016/j.biopsych.2005.08.007.

van der Gaag, C., Minderaa, R. B., & Keysers, C. (2007). Facial expressions: What the mirror neuron system can and cannot tell us. *Social Neuroscience*, 2(3–4), 179–222.

Wager, T. D., Kang, J., Johnson, T. D., Nichols, T. E., Satpute, A. B., & Barrett, L. F. (2015). A Bayesian model of category-specific emotional brain responses. *PLoS Computational Biology*, 11(4), e1004066. doi:10.1371/journal.pcbi.1004066.

Wicker, B., Keysers, C., Plailly, J., Royet, J. P., Gallese, V., & Rizzolatti, G. (2003). Both of us disgusted in my insula: The common neural basis of seeing and feeling disgust. *Neuron*, 40(3), 655–664.

Wise, R. A. (1980). The dopamine synapse and the notion of "pleasure centers" in the brain. *Trends in Neurosciences*, 3(4), 91–95. doi:10.1016/0166-2236(80)90035-1.

Wood, A., Rychlowska, M., Korb, S., & Niedenthal, P. M. (2016). Fashioning the face: Sensorimotor simulation contributes to facial expression recognition. *Trends in Cognitive Sciences*, 20(3), 227–240. doi:10.1016/j.tics.2015.12.010.

4   Functions of Emotion

Contents at a Glance

Have you ever asked yourself what emotions are good for? Perhaps you haven't because emotions are so common. You have them, your mother has them, your friends have them. Why even ask the question? If emotions were not good for anything, we as a society might try to get rid of them or reduce their frequency in our social interactions. Would it be better if most people were like Mr. Spock in *Star Trek*? What would happen if we started to spend our days with virtual friends? Would life change if we left our babies with robot caretakers all day? Would it be a good idea if computer scientists tried to design robots that had emotions just like humans? In order to answer these questions, we need an understanding of what emotions are good for, if anything.

In Chapter 1 we learned that over the past few decades, most affective scientists have come to believe that emotions are functional (e.g., Barrett, 2006; Barrett & Campos, 1987; Cosmides & Tooby, 2000; Frijda, 1986; Johnson-Laird & Oatley, 1992; Keltner, Haidt, & Shiota, 2006; Niedenthal & Brauer, 2012; Plutchik, 1980). Although we initially associated the idea that emotions are functional with Darwin and evolutionary theories of emotion, it is not necessary to accept that emotions are encoded in our genes to think that emotions are functional. Most appraisal theorists and psychological constructionists also see emotions as useful, problem-solving phenomena. Even if emotions are not innate, they can be learned and culturally transmitted in order to solve problems of social living.

In this chapter, we explore the functions of various emotions for social units of varying sizes. Keltner and Haidt (1999, 2001) posit three types of social units: the individual, the dyad, and the group. For each unit, emotion functions in one of three distinct ways: a basic survival function (individual), a communication function (dyad), and a social coordination function (group). It's worth noting, again, that in talking about emotions as functional, we are not referring to pathological states of emotion, such as clinical depression or anxiety. The question is not whether it is useful to be depressed or anxious. We remain faithful to our initial definition of emotion as "episodic, relatively short-term, biologically-based patterns of perception, experience, physiology, action, and communication that occur in response to specific physical and social challenges and opportunities" (Keltner & Gross, 1999).

How to Know That Emotions Are Functional

As you have learned, Darwin aside, psychologists and philosophers have not always believed that emotions are functional. Even within the past century some theorists advanced the view that emotions are animalistic and disruptive. It is possible that you also think emotions are animalistic and disruptive. If you've ever labeled someone "too emotional," you typically mean the person's emotions were unhelpful or dysfunctional, at least in a particular situation. Why would scientists argue that emotions are, on average, useful to us (Parrott, 2001)?

Consequences of Emotion Deficits

One way to discover if emotions are functional is to study what happens when people's emotions or emotional development are atypical. Psychologists have studied what happens when individuals do not express their emotions to others in circumstances that are emotionally arousing (Butler et al., 2003; Impett et al., 2014; Srivastava et al., 2009) and when people fail to discuss their emotions with others in conversation after experiencing emotional events (Rimé, 2007). They have also studied what happens when a person has deficits in understanding emotions expressed by other individuals. These deficits may be caused by brain lesions (e.g., Heberlein et al., 2008; Kennedy et al., 2009), by the development of diseases such as Parkinson's (Wieser et al., 2006), by autism (e.g., Clark, Winkielman, & McIntosh, 2008; McIntosh et al., 2006), or by childhood maltreatment (Pollak, 2008).

What happens in these cases is, as a rule, not so functional. Impairments in identifying facial expressions are associated with antisocial behavior (Fairchild et al., 2009; Marsh & Blair, 2008). For example, people who are unable to identify facial expressions that signal distress (such as fear or sadness) in another individual are more likely to engage in aggressive or otherwise harmful behavior, probably due to a lack of empathy for the distress (Blair, 2005). Impairment in other emotion processes can also lead to ineffective behavioral regulation (Tranel, Bechara, & Damasio, 2000). For example, when people do not remember and use their prior emotional reactions to objects and events in decision making, their decisions can be poor (Hinson, Jameson, & Whitney, 2002). In general, that is, problems with emotion processes—deficits in the abilities to understand, express, experience, and regulate emotion—lead to bad choices, limited social engagement, and even failure of economic viability.

Benefits of Emotional Intelligence

In contrast, people who are particularly good at emotions are more likely to have positive outcomes in life (e.g., Mayer, Salovey, & Caruso, 2004; Salovey et al., 2003). Salovey and Mayer (1990) introduced the concept of **emotional intelligence**, a capacity to pay attention to and understand one's own emotions and those of others, and subsequently to use those emotions to guide behavior and decisions. People "high" in emotional intelligence, compared to low, attend more to emotions, interpret their own and other's emotions more accurately, and use the emotions, when pertinent, to make choices with positive outcomes.

Research shows that people with high emotional intelligence are more successful in a number of domains of life (Mayer, Salovey, & Caruso, 2008). For instance, they are less likely to engage in bullying and violent behavior (Rubin, 1999) and less likely to abuse drugs and alcohol (Brackett, Mayer, & Warner, 2004). They also tend to have more successful relationships, be judged as more interpersonally sensitive (Brackett et al., 2006; Lopes, Salovey, & Straus, 2003), and be better managers in organizational settings than individuals with low emotional intelligence (Rosete, 2007).

Disruptions in emotion-processing capacity cause bad outcomes and well-developed emotion skills yield good outcomes. These facts suggest that emotions are, on average, functional. But just how and for whom?

Survival Function of Emotion for the Individual

One of the questions we can ask, when considering the function of emotions for the individual, is whether our emotions aid our ability to survive and thrive in the face of challenges and opportunities. As a general principle, although a feeling may be subjectively unpleasant, or although the endocrine or autonomic part of the emotion may be costly to the body, on average, there is a beneficial survival function that emotions serve for most people, most of the time. Next we discuss three ways in which emotions are functional for the individual. In particular, we show how 1) the physiology of emotion supports adaptive action, 2) the feelings of emotion regulate the pursuit of goals, and 3) action tendencies of emotion promote the selective responses to the world that results in a broadening of the individual's repertoire of cognitive and behavioral responses. The functionality of facial expression for the individual is discussed in detail in Chapter 5.

Physiology

The emotions we experience vary in their degree of physiological arousal (Levenson, 2003). The main system of the body that regulates arousal and other relatively automatic biological processes (e.g., breathing, sweating, digesting) is the **autonomic nervous system** (ANS), which we also discussed in Chapter 3. The ANS is composed of two subsystems that typically work in opposition. The **sympathetic nervous system** (SNS) is excitatory, augmenting activity in ANS-regulated systems (e.g., increase in heart rate). Activity of the SNS becomes dominant during physical or psychological stress, producing arousal to aid in mobilizing the energy needed to respond to the challenge. Due to its excitatory function, the SNS is commonly referred to as the "fight or flight" portion of the ANS. On the other hand, the **parasympathetic nervous system** (PNS) is inhibitory, decreasing activity in ANS-regulated systems (e.g., decrease in heart rate) while also controlling core biological maintenance functions (e.g., digestion). In periods of relative calm and safety, activity of the PNS is dominant, maintaining a lower degree of physiological arousal. Due to its inhibitory and biological maintenance functions, the PNS is commonly referred to as the "rest and digest" portion of the ANS.

The following example often helps students understand the SNS/PNS distinction and further solidifies a functional intuition regarding the ANS subsystems. Suppose you and your friends are camping in the forest. You all recently finished a delicious, campfire-cooked dinner after a long day of hiking and canoeing. Everyone is settling in around the fire for scary stories and s'mores when you hear a rustling noise and a deep growl behind you in the trees. Immediately, your body responds to help you deal with the situation. Your heart starts to race, you start to sweat, and you quickly grab a nearby marshmallow-roasting stick in preparation to defend yourself. This is your excitatory, sympathetic nervous system coming online, preparing you to meet the demands of your current situation. Before you have time to run away, your friend Marie steps out of the trees, growling and slashing at everyone with her "bear claws." Relieved, everyone laughs while Marie sits down and helps the group roast marshmallows. You can feel your heart rate slow while you calm down. This is your inhibitory, parasympathetic nervous system calming your body down and preparing you for biologically necessary rest and relaxation. Later, when you snuggle into your sleeping bag, dreaming of your friend Marie riding grizzly bears through the forest, your PNS is controlling your digestion, helping your body recover and preparing it for your next adventure.

Research shows that ANS changes occurring during emotion-eliciting events provide bodily support for taking appropriate action. Specific emotions mobilize specific functional actions, such as flight in fear and attack in anger (e.g., Levenson, 1992; Stemmler et al., 2001). For example, Stemmler, Aue, and Wacker (2007) measured the ANS activity of club soccer players imagining themselves in anger- or fear-inducing, scripted soccer scenarios. Both emotions were associated with patterns of SNS activity that support the kinds of swift and vigorous behavior needed in these situations. Anger was accompanied by relatively stronger **noradrenergic** responses (i.e., responses mediated by cells sensitive to noradrenaline). Fear was accompanied by relatively stronger **adrenergic** responses (i.e., responses mediated by cells sensitive to adrenaline) and/or relatively larger withdrawal from the vagus nerve, the major parasympathetic pathway from the central nervous system. These findings support the idea that fear and anger involve biological responses in ANS systems that prepare the body for action that is appropriate and useful in light of the current environmental challenges.

In terms of arousal, sadness is the counterpart to anger and fear, which involve high states of arousal. Sadness is usually associated with behavioral withdrawal and energy conservation (i.e., a state of low arousal), often due to irrevocable loss of something or someone important. Such behaviors are adaptations that assure self-preservation (Kelsey et al., 2002). In terms of underlying physiology, conservation–withdrawal types of behavior have been shown to be associated with greater PNS activity, including heart rate deceleration (e.g., Bosch et al., 2001; Ritz et al., 2000). Thus, the physiological states involved in anger, fear, and sadness each serve distinct functions in accordance with the challenge(s) that elicited the emotion in the first place (Kreibig et al., 2007).

Polyvagal Theory

Porges (1995, 2001, 2007) proposed an evolution-based theory that attempts to explain how the ANS links the physiological states of emotion with functional, adaptive behavior. He argued that distinct portions of the **vagus nerve** (the tenth cranial nerve, the major PNS pathway connecting the brain with the rest of the body) have evolved in mammals to mediate functionally distinct behavioral and biological outcomes, thus earning his theory the name Polyvagal.

According to **Polyvagal Theory**, the ANS evolved in mammals through three global stages, with each stage suiting environmental demands at that point in evolutionary time. The mammalian ANS has retained structural vestiges of these three evolutionary phases, which were specifically implicated in immobilization (e.g., freezing), mobilization (e.g., fight–flight), and social communication (e.g., facial expression), respectively. First in mammalian phylogenetic history, the immobilization system involves the **unmyelinated vagus**, a primitive branch of the vagus nerve shared with most vertebrates. Because myelin (a fat-and-protein–based sheath that surrounds many nerve cells) electrically insulates the cell, unmyelinated nerves are slower to conduct electricity than their myelinated counterparts. An ANS where the central feature is an unmyelinated vagus is relatively slow and inefficient, limiting the range of possible biological responses to environmental demands available to the organism. The Polyvagal Theory states that, in part due to increasingly complex environments, the mammalian ANS underwent a second phase of development. Retaining the unmyelinated vagus and building upon it, the second phase of the evolutionary development of the mammalian ANS resulted in the mobilization system, the chief component being the sympathetic nervous system. The mobilization system adds to the immobilization system by allowing for more (and faster) biological responses to environmental demands; when highly activated, the mobilization system allows for the production of very fast and vigorous behavior. The last in the phylogenetic development of the mammalian ANS in this view is the **myelinated vagus**. A branch of the vagus nerve, the myelinated vagus counteracts sympathetic stimulation of the heart and quiets the hypothalamic-pituitary-adrenal axis (HPA; the neural pathway leading to the secretion of the stress hormone cortisol from the adrenal glands). Further, Polyvagal Theory posits that the myelinated vagus is responsible for a "social communication" system. Recent experimental work provides preliminary evidence that individuals with a vagus nerve that is highly responsive to the environment may be more socially sensitive (Muhtadie et al., 2015).

Taken together, the three systems (i.e., immobilization, mobilization, and social engagement) posited in Polyvagal Theory can be thought of as producing appropriate biological responses to the constantly changing safe, dangerous, and life-threatening circumstances in the environment. Notice that in this view, the ANS has subsystems that produce general classes of physiological and behavioral states that facilitate and constrain adaptive emotional responses. However, so far, scientists have not discovered brain circuits that link each basic emotion to specific autonomic states (Quigley & Barrett, 2014). And some scientists warn that the measurement of activity of the vagus nerve is very complicated and not yet well understood (Berntson, Cacioppo, & Grossman, 2007; Grossman & Taylor, 2007).

Emotions and Goal Adjustment

An integrative account of the function of emotion for individual survival was proposed by Oatley and Johnson-Laird (1987) in their **Cognitive Theory of Emotion**. Oatley and Johnson-Laird (1987), like evolutionary theorists, believe that emotions are adaptations to environmental challenges and opportunities posed repeatedly over the course of evolution and that the emotions serve the primary function of coordinating adaptive behavior. However, these theorists see emotions as serving a regulatory capacity in terms of managing our goals. In their view, emotions come about when individuals, consciously or unconsciously, note that their behavior requires some adjustment. That is, specific emotions occur when progress on specific types of goals—which happen to be universal and highly repetitive—is interrupted. In Oatley and Johnson-Laird's view, the emotion then reorganizes and redirects the individual's activity in the service of a new goal, or at least in such a way as to deal with what has just occurred.

Table 4.1 presents what Oatley and Johnson-Laird propose, based on both empirical and theoretical considerations, to be the five basic emotions. Each emotion is triggered by a *juncture*, an interruption of the current goal/activity, and each emotion causes a *transition* to a subsequent state. You can see that, from this view, if an individual experiences a failure of an important plan or a loss of an active goal, this will activate the experience of sadness. Sadness is then associated with the tendency to stay still or withdraw (which has the important benefit of soliciting caretaking) or else search for a new plan (which has the benefit of alleviating the sadness). Oatley and his colleagues (e.g., Oatley & Duncan, 1992, 1994) have found some support for these ideas using diary study methodology. These authors argue that emotions are functional in that they provide an internal evaluation of ongoing goal-directed activity and then guide behavior in a way so as to respond to the meaning of that emotional response.

Table 4.1 A cognitive theory of emotion. From Oatley & Johnson-Laird (1987).

Emotion	Juncture of Current Plan	State at which Transition Occurs
Happiness	Subgoals being achieved	Continues with plan, modifying as necessary
Sadness	Failure of major plan or loss of active goal	Do nothing/search for new plan
Anxiety	Self-preservation goal threatened	Stop, attend vigilantly to environment and/or escape
Anger	Active plan frustrated	Try harder, and/or aggress
Disgust	Gustatory goal violated	Reject substance and/or withdraw

From Oatley, K., & Johnson-Laird, P. N. (1987). Towards a cognitive theory of emotions. *Cognition and Emotion, 1,* 29–50.

The Broaden-and-Build Theory of Positive Emotions

Notice that so far we have talked mostly about the function of negative emotions such as fear, anger, and disgust. Fredrickson (1998, 2013) proposed the **broaden-and-build theory**, which describes the ways in which the positive emotions such as joy, interest, and contentment help an individual respond to opportunities to thrive.

The model suggests, first, that positive emotional states temporarily *broaden* the individual's repertoire of thoughts and actions. Fredrickson notes, for example, that positive emotions are associated with an expansion, or widening, of the focus of visual attention (Derryberry & Tucker, 1994). Instead of focusing exclusively on details, individuals in positive emotional states take into account a wider number of cues and meanings from the environment (e.g., Bless et al., 1996; Isen et al., 1985). Relatedly, people in happy states explore visual scenes more extensively, pay more attention to the periphery of the scene (Wadlinger & Isaacowitz, 2006), and generally show greater flexibility of visual and semantic attention (Johnson, Waugh, & Fredrickson, 2010; Rowe, Hirsh, & Anderson, 2007). That is, they can more easily change their focus of attention and more easily access new or unusual word meanings. People's bodily movements are even broader, or more expansive, when they are in positive states (Gross, Crane, & Fredrickson, 2012).

Here is an example of broadening of attention: Fredrickson and Branigan (2005) used films to produce a high arousal, positive emotion (amusement), a low arousal one (contentment), or neutral feelings (control) in their participants. Then, to measure the breadth of attention, they showed all participants "global–local items" such as those in Figure 4.1. When participants viewed each global–local item, they had to say which of the two bottom groupings of shapes was most similar to the target grouping at the top. Broad attentional focus is associated with the tendency to respond "left" for every global–local item. Note that in each item, the leftmost

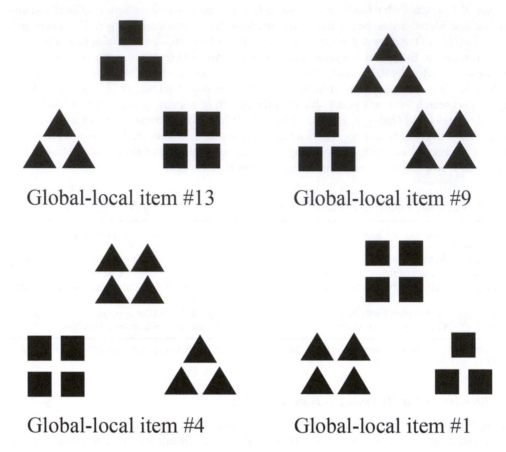

Global-local item #13   Global-local item #9

Global-local item #4   Global-local item #1

Figure 4.1 Examples of global–local items. From Fredrickson & Branigan (2005).

grouping is similar on a "global" level. That is, the overall shape of the grouping matches the overall shape of the target grouping. Narrow attention, on the other hand, focuses "locally," homing in on the pieces rather than the overall shape of the target grouping. Those with narrow focus thus had a tendency to respond "right." Fredrickson and Branigan found that participants who were feeling both amusement and contentment made the broad attention response significantly more often than those in the control condition. Important limits on these discoveries continue to be made, and the context for the effects of positive emotion on attention have to be considered. These will be discussed in Chapter 8 (Harmon-Jones, Gable, & Price, 2013).

An important consequence, perhaps *the* important consequence, of broadening the full set of attentional and behavioral responses available to the individual in the moment, according to Fredrickson (1998), is that positive emotions then lead to a building of lasting physical and psychological resources that can be relied on in the future. The desire to play that is shown by juveniles of many species when they are happy results in the development of new physical skills, for example. Rough-and-tumble play, as it is called in the animal world, serves both to promote muscular and vascular fitness and to rehearse a number of skills that will be important later in life, including the negotiation of danger and social confrontations. More generally, correlational studies show that people who regularly experience and express positive emotions are more resilient, meaning that they are able to recover from negative experiences and respond well to changing life demands (Fredrickson et al., 2003). Frequent positive emotions also lead to people having stronger social connections with other people (Gable, Gonzaga, & Strachman, 2006; Waugh & Fredrickson, 2006). An important consequence of the building of psychological and social resources is that positive emotions are associated with a number of positive health outcomes (e.g., Kok & Fredrickson, 2010). The full broaden-and-build model is illustrated in Figure 4.2.

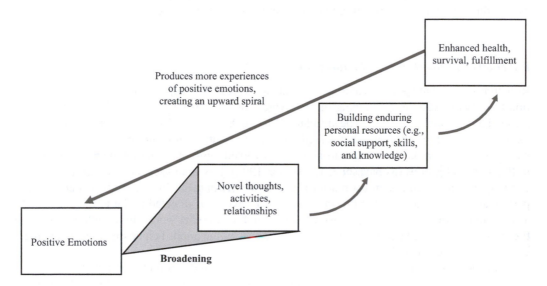

Figure 4.2 The broaden-and-build theory of emotions. Adapted from Fredrickson and Cohn (2008).

One reason that positive emotions may be good for health is that they undo the harmful physiological effects of negative emotions. During states of fear and anger, for example, a person's autonomic nervous system is typically highly active. We learned earlier in this chapter that autonomic nervous system changes during those emotions support functional action. However, it is not healthy for the ANS to remain in very aroused states over long periods because lasting aroused states wear down the body. Positive emotions help to re-establish equilibrium following negative emotional arousal of this kind. In a study of this hypothesis, Fredrickson and Levenson (1998) had experimental participants watch a film that uniformly induced fear and heightened cardiovascular activity. The participants were then randomly assigned to watch one of four additional films. The four films elicited contentment, mild amusement, sadness, or neutral emotion. Participants who watched the films that produced one of the two positive emotions returned to their baseline levels of cardiovascular activation more quickly than those who watched the film that elicited neutral emotion and much more quickly than those who watched the sad film. In this sense, the positive emotions repaired the physical symptoms of fear induced by the initial film, symptoms that are metabolically costly for the body. By returning the body to quiescence after an experience of a costly negative emotion such as fear and anger, positive emotions can, over time, protect the physical health of the body itself.

In sum, the physiology of emotions and the motivating component of emotions themselves appear to help individuals respond adaptively to environmental threats and opportunities. But these benefits all serve the individual, not the group. Once we start to examine the smallest of groups, the dyad, we can see how the purpose of emotions extends beyond survival.

Communication Function of Emotion for the Dyad

Dyads are two people who are interacting in some way. In dyadic interaction, we need to know what the other individual is feeling. If we know their emotions, we can understand what they are doing and why, as well as what we should be doing in the same situation (Buck, 1983, 1988). Through bodily movement, voice, and facial expression, emotions efficiently communicate information about the goals of two people, who they are to each other, and how the present situation will or should unfold over time (Buck, 1983; Keltner & Kring, 1998; Shiota et al., 2004). This is the communication function that Darwin proposed, but subsequent theory and research have taken the idea much further since Darwin's time.

Function of Features of Facial Expressions

Research shows that specific features of our facial expressions help us communicate information to someone else. Eye widening in fear expressions, for example, is an easily seen social signal that tells another person to be afraid too (Marsh, Adams, & Kleck, 2005). This communicative feature of the fear expression is facilitated by the contrast of white sclera in human eyes, which is unique among primates and may have evolved along with human beings' tendency to live in social groups (Kobayashi & Kohshima, 1997). Research shows that observers of the eye part of a fear expression learn a lot about their environment. In one study, experimental participants had to say whether the gaze of a pair of eyes was directed to the left or the right. They could do this faster if the eyes were wide, as in fear. In other words, they could tell where the eyes were looking because the increased white around the pupils helped them see where the eyes were directed (Lee, Susskind, & Anderson, 2013).

Eye widening not only helped observers cue in on the pupil direction faster, but also allowed them to subsequently follow the gaze to locate targets (potential threats) faster. In another study (Lee et al., 2013), over many trials, participants saw a set of schematic eyes that were either wide (as in fear) or not wide and that were gazing straight ahead. The gaze then turned to the left or right. Finally, an asterisk appeared, and participants had to indicate as quickly as possible whether it was on the right or the left of the computer screen. Fear eyes did a better job of cuing the participant to find the asterisk. Thus, if the fear eyes gazed to the left and the asterisk also appeared on the left, the participants found the asterisk faster than if neutral eyes gazed left. If the fear eyes gazed to the right and the asterisk appeared on the left, participants were slower because they were taking their cue from those wide eyes (see Figure 4.3).

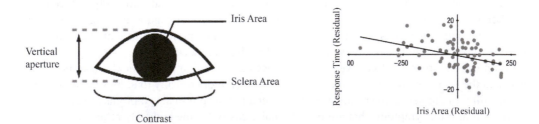

Figure 4.3 Amount of iris area predicts response time to correctly cued peripheral targets. The illustration (a) shows the four features extracted from each unique pair of schematic eyes. The graph (b) shows the relationship between the visible iris area revealed by eye widening and response times for correctly cued targets ($r = -0.378$). Axes represent iris area after controlling for baseline vertical-gaze perception using data collected in a separate experiment. Adapted from Lee, Susskind, & Anderson (2013).

The eyes are clearly an important social cue. And indeed, the same effect of fear faces for cuing spatial location is also seen in children, suggesting that they are used as such possibly as soon as the visual system is fully developed (Dawel et al., 2015). From a young age, children need the information communicated by the features of facial expression.

Facial Expressions as Behavior Regulators

Facial expressions of emotion also communicate more general types of information and are particularly useful because they are **nonverbal** and even **preverbal**. Studies using different research methods indicate that by one year of age, infants can discriminate between facial expressions (Schwartz et al., 1985; Young-Browne, Rosenfeld, & Horowitz, 1977). For example, by three months infants can discriminate between happy and surprised faces (Young-Browne, Rosenfeld, & Horowitz, 1977) and happy and angry faces (Barrera & Maurer, 1981). In addition, infants at the same age can also discriminate among different exemplars of the same expression (happy) that vary in intensity (Kuckuck, Vibbert, & Bornstein, 1986). By seven months, infants can reliably discriminate between varying intensities of happy and angry facial expressions (Striano, Brennan, & Vanman, 2002) and between anger and fear (Kobiella et al., 2008).

Facial expressions of emotion help guide the behavior of developing infants in several ways. The first is by communicating punishment and reward. Although there may be hardwired emotional responses to particular challenges and opportunities in the environment (Mineka & Cook, 1993), caretakers must teach infants to have specific emotional reactions to (initially) ambiguous objects and events in order to generate in them appropriate and effective behavior. Objects that conduct electricity are an example of an ambiguous stimulus in the sense that they are such a recent technological development that there is no reason to believe that humans would be hardwired to be fearful of them in their current appearance (i.e., as distinct from lightning, for instance). By expressing fear when a toddler approaches an electrical outlet or an exposed wire, a caretaker can elicit fear in the toddler. This is a good lesson, and in typically developing children the perception of fear in a caretaker results in the appropriate avoidance behavior of outlets in the future (Askew & Field, 2007; Hertenstein & Campos, 2004). It is in this sense that Campos and colleagues (2003) aptly call facial expressions of emotion "behavior regulators": facial expressions function as rewards (Matthews & Wells, 1999) and punishments (Blair, 1995) that serve to increase and decrease behaviors, as in operant conditioning (for review, see Blair, 2003; Gerull & Rappe, 2002; Mumme et al., 1996).

In a classic study, Klinnert (1984) showed that caretakers' facial expressions can effectively guide infants' behavior. In the study, 12- and 18-month-old infants were confronted with an unfamiliar toy. When the toy was presented, the infant's mother expressed either joy or fear, or else she maintained a neutral expression. Compared to the neutral condition, when the mother expressed fear about the toy, her infant moved toward her (for comfort), and when she expressed joy, the infant felt confident enough to move away (to explore or otherwise go on with life). Klinnert et al. (1986) showed the same effect when the expression of joy or fear was displayed by a familiar experimenter.

In the first year of life, infants also develop the capacity to discriminate between vocal expressions of emotion (Walker-Andrews & Lennon, 1991). Adults talk to infants and, perhaps precisely because infants cannot yet understand the words, adults largely use emotion in their voice to communicate (Trainor, Austin, & Desjardins, 2000). Furthermore, like facial expression, vocal expressions of emotion are behavioral regulators (Mumme, Fernald, & Herrera, 1996). For example, Vaish and Striano (2004) employed a **visual cliff paradigm**, in which infants are placed on a piece of Plexiglas that gives the impression that if the infant advances, it will fall off the cliff. In the study, the mother stood on the other side of the visual cliff and (in one condition) provided vocal expressions of positive emotion. Findings showed that infants used the positive emotion expressed by the mother as a sign that it was safe to cross the visual cliff and join her on the other side. This same finding had been demonstrated with facial expressions in the absence of voice. Vocal expressions of emotion work just like facial expressions of emotion to regulate infants' behavior (Grossmann, 2010).

Functions of Smiles in Dyadic Interaction

Some theories have proposed that a particular facial expression, the smile, serves specific functions of communication (Niedenthal et al., 2010). In theory, there are smiles of **reward**, **affiliation**, and **dominance**. The functions that smiles accomplish, respectively, are 1) rewarding the self and other for pleasurable or adaptive behavior, 2) forging and maintaining social bonds, and 3) negotiating social hierarchies.

Developmental Detail

A Baby's Cries Go Right to the Mother's Brain

Have you ever been stuck on an airplane flight with a crying infant? It was probably no fun. However, infant crying is functional. In particular, crying reliably elicits caretaking responses from parents and thereby seems to serve the evolutionary function of ensuring the survival of the infant (Bell, 1974). Indeed, the distress cries of all mammal infants are markedly similar, and scientists found that mother deer will respond to the recorded distress cries of human, seal, cat, bat, and dog infants that were adjusted for variation in pitch. Although you might have heard the idea that babies make acoustically different cries to signal specific needs (such as hunger versus pain), there is no empirical evidence that caretakers perceive distinct meanings in cries and respond to them with specific actions. Rather, cries seem to vary along an acoustic continuum that reflects the degree to which the infant is distressed (Porter, Porges, & Marshall, 1988). Highly distressed cries elicit a prototypical pattern of caretaker behavior that involves approach, soothing, and attempts to identify and address specific causes such as illness, fear, or other discomfort (Gustafson & Harris, 1990).

Infant cries have effects on the maternal brain that are consistent with the behavioral effects. Lorberbaum and his colleagues exposed mothers to babies' cries and white noise (a control stimulus) while imaging the mother's brains in an MRI scanner (Lorberbaum et al., 2002). They found increased activity in areas of the brain that prior research showed to be involved in the maternal behavior of rodents. In addition, babies' cries activated neural circuitry for human empathy (i.e., anterior and posterior cingulate, thalamus, hypothalamus, dorsal and ventral striatum, medial prefrontal cortex, and right orbitofrontal and insular regions). It seems pretty clear, then, that although they can't ask for help using language, babies come into the world with an emotional signaling system that helps them get their needs met.

Niedenthal and colleagues suggest that reward smiles are closely related to the so-called true or enjoyment smiles and reflect the fact that the smiler is feeling a positive social or sensory experience. The main function of the reward smile is to increase the probability that the social or sensory experience that caused the smile will be repeated in the future. For instance, if you liked to be kissed by someone and flashed a reward smile, the individual who kissed you should be more likely to kiss you again. The smile makes this happen because it feels good both to the person who is smiling and the person who receives the smile (see Chapter 5). The category of affiliative smiles, on the other hand, may include different subclasses of smiles, including smiles that have been called polite, embarrassed, and greeting smiles. When people make these smiles, they are signaling that they are approachable and that they mean no harm (Cashdan, 1998). Part of what communicates affiliation might be the way the lips over the teeth in this smile (see Figure 4.4) suggest that the smiler does not want to be aggressive. Finally, dominance smiles are produced to show and maintain (perceived, not necessarily sanctioned) social or moral status, and thus help to define one's position in a given hierarchy. This category of smiles may involve displays of contempt (Ekman, 1992), derision, and pride (Tracy & Robins, 2007). Unlike reward and affiliative smiles, dominance smiles are predicted to convey and elicit negative feelings.

Initial evidence for the existence of these three smiles was provided by a cross-cultural study of smiles in North America, Europe, Asia, and the Pacific Rim (Rychlowska et al., 2015). The researchers assessed the endorsement of motives and feelings that cause smiling in these countries. Statistical analysis (called factor analysis) suggested that the motives and feelings really divided themselves into three broad groups. Consistent with the theory, participants' responses grouped into clusters corresponding to reward, bonding, and hierarchy-managing functions of smiles.

Other research showed that the three smiles looked different because they were composed by the contraction of separate groups of muscles (Figure 4.4). The representations of French and American participants were significantly correlated. Reward smiles involved symmetrical action of the smile muscle and eyebrow flashes. The affiliation smile contained more stretching and pressing of the lips over the mouth. And the dominance smile was rather asymmetric and contained evidence of disgust (Niedenthal et al., 2016).

Social Functional Theories

Emotions are coordinated sets of responses that go beyond the face and voice, which are only manifestations of emotions. **Social functional theories** of emotion, inspired by evolutionary psychology, were specifically developed to understand the function of each emotion in its

Figure 4.4 Reward, affiliation, and dominance smiles.

entirety for social communication (Dunbar, 1993; Gonzaga et al., 2001; Shiota et al., 2004; Spoor & Kelly, 2004).

In addition to assuming the importance of evolutionary forces, social functional theories take for granted that emotions are also influenced by cultural factors. Because each emotion is assumed to serve a distinct social function, we can consider each separately (Keltner, Haidt, & Shiota, 2006), investigating how it communicates to other people our potential relationship with them, our needs, and our demands (van Kleef, 2009).

Sadness is a good example. A 2015 Pixar movie, *Inside Out*, tells the story of a little girl, Riley, who moves to another city with her family and misses her life back home in Minnesota where she loves to play pond hockey. It is not until the end of the movie that Riley finally expresses her sadness to her parents, not only in words but with her body and voice, and in this moment the viewer understands the function of sadness: its display is a signal that calls out for support and care (Figure 4.5). When you are sad, you often slow down and become drooping or even fold up into yourself, communicating a need for care from others (Leary, Koch, & Hechenbleikner, 2001).

Figure 4.5 When Riley expresses sadness in the movie *Inside Out*, she gets the care from her parents that she needs.

Anger signals a different kind of need. In one model, anger evolved as a bargaining tool to help the angry individual resolve conflicts in her favor (Tooby et al., 2008). The idea is that we get angry when we believe that another person is not concerned enough with our own welfare. By showing anger, we communicate to the other person a need to increase this concern. Whether or not people respond as we wish to our anger depends upon our ability to inflict costs or to withhold benefits from them. Otherwise, they might not care. If we are able to inflict more cost or are able to withhold benefits, we can use our anger successfully to make the person we are angry at "recalibrate" (i.e., increase) her attention to our needs.

Many characteristics of an individual are linked to the potential to inflict cost or confer benefits, but two with evolutionary significance are strength and attractiveness. A man's upper body strength, for example, is related to his ability to inflict costs through physical harm. Likewise,

Table 4.2 Social function of emotion. From Keltner, Haidt, & Shiota (2006).

Problem	Emotions	Specific Function
Finding a mate	Desire	Increase likelihood of sexual contact
	Love	Commit to long-term bond
Keeping mate	Jealousy	Protect mate from rivals
Protecting offspring	Love	Increase bond between parent, offspring

Adapted from Keltner, D., Haidt, J., & Shiota, M. N. (2006). Social functionalism and the evolution of emotions. In M. Schaller, J. Simpson & D. Kenrick (Eds.), *Evolution and Social Psychology* (pp. 115–142). New York, NY: Psychology Press.

attractiveness is a characteristic that signals health and, in women, fertility, which increases an attractive individual's value as a sexual partner. So, attractive individuals, especially women, have the ability to withhold benefits (i.e., become unavailable as a mate), and therefore a better bargaining position. This reasoning suggests that strong and attractive individuals 1) feel more entitled to better treatment (because they have greater leverage over the potential target of their anger), 2) get angry when they do not receive this better treatment (are more prone to anger), and 3) should prevail more in conflicts than others. The theory also predicts that attractiveness is more important for women and strength more important for men in conflicts. Sell, Tooby, and Cosmides (2009) tested these hypotheses in a series of experiments. They found that stronger men felt more entitled to better treatment in comparison to weaker men. They also found that strength was positively correlated with how easily or often men were angered and with how often they use and endorse the efficacy of aggression in conflicts. Strength was even positively correlated with the extent to which men endorsed the efficacy of the use of military force in international affairs and against internal transgressors. In addition, the researchers found that a woman's self-rated attractiveness was positively correlated with her proneness to anger, feelings of entitlement, success in conflict, and attitudes on the efficacy of anger in interpersonal and political conflict. In essence, attractive women used anger just like strong men.

In addition to managing loss, threats, and injustice, people have to find mates and friends, bond with their offspring, maintain stable relationships, and form social hierarchies to get things done in groups (Buss, 1989, 1994; Hrdy, 1999). By considering social opportunities in addition to social challenges, social functionalist theories add to other evolutionary approaches a focus on positive emotions. Emotions such as desire, love, and compassion play an important role in assuring that the creation and maintenance of social bonds—necessary for reproductive success—are successfully accomplished (Keltner, Haidt, & Shiota, 2006). For example, love is a reliable communication of long-term commitment, which is necessary for the maintenance of a relationship such as marriage. Some of these emotions and their functions are presented in Table 4.2.

In sum, emotions communicate appropriate behavioral responses from adults and infants, they signal information about the relationship between standards and behavior, and they communicate much about the nature of intentions and motivations within a dyad (Buck, 1988).

Social Coordination Function for the Group

Some researchers have examined the functions emotions have, not within individuals or between dyads, but among bigger groups of people and in societies at large (Frijda & Mesquita, 1994; Haidt, 2003; Keltner & Haidt, 1999, 2001). Emotions play a functional role in the creation of groups, the maintenance of group boundaries, and for long-term commitment to actions that achieve the goals of the group (Chekroun & Brauer, 2002, 2004; Frijda & Mesquita, 1994; Haidt, 2003; Keltner & Haidt, 1999).

Group Formation

First, emotions cause groups to form in the first place (Spoor & Kelly, 2004). Group identi-fication and cohesion are created particularly by positive emotions, including joy, awe, and ecstasy. Sharing such emotions makes members of groups feel more similar to each other, and this fosters even greater feelings of "groupiness" (Walter & Bruch, 2008). When the fans of a winning team all experience joy at the end of a sporting event, for example, they come to feel even more cohesive. Furthermore, they may at least temporarily show explicit signs of their group membership by wearing clothing or other insignias for a period of time after the event (Cialdini et al., 1976; Figure 4.6).

Figure 4.6 When members of a group all experience the same emotion, the group becomes more cohesive.

However, negative emotions may also bring people together because individuals who feel sadness or grief often prefer to be with others who have shared the common, difficult fate and are experiencing similar emotions (Gump & Kulik, 1997). For example, during highly emo-tional national elections, members of a losing candidate's party may feel very closely related and highly identified with each other, and they may draw a sharp boundary, perhaps sharper than usual, between themselves and members of the opposing party or parties.

Similar group dynamics are also observed when members of groups experience anxiety (Wohl, Branscombe, & Reysen, 2010). In a demonstration of this exclusive group identification, Wilder and Shapiro (1989) induced high (or low) levels of anxiety in four-person groups by having them compete (or cooperate) with another group. After working together on a task, the members of the group watched another four-person group give them feedback on their own performance through a TV monitor. Although the "real" group of participants did not know it, the second group was composed of confederates of the experimenter. Three of the four members of the ostensible other group gave negative feedback, whereas one gave positive feedback and was in this sense an atypical group member. Later, the real participants judged the members of the ostensible evaluating group. Group anxiety caused the judgments of the atypical member to be assimilated toward those of the other three group members, such that the high-anxiety participants rated that person significantly more negatively than did low-anxiety participants. Such findings have been replicated with other manipulations of anxiety as well, and together they suggest that group emotions in intergroup settings make the demarcations between in-group and out-group more sharply defined and sometimes more visible (van Zomeren, Fischer, & Spears, 2007).

Bringing Group Members Back into Line

Emotions are also used to make sure that members of groups continue to engage in behaviors that the group condones or desires. For instance, public shaming rituals have been used to get people to conform to group norms and to remind both the shamed person and all other group members of those norms (Scheff, 1988). A well-known criminal museum in Rothenburg, Germany, that documents instruments of torture and punishment from medieval times displays various "masks of shame." Some medieval societies made the violator of a law or norm wear such a mask in order to elicit ridicule from other group members as a punishment. One particularly interesting mask is the "flute of shame" (*die Schandflöte*), which was used to punish those who violated norms for the quality of music played in the king's court (see Figure 4.7)! Some countries even in this day and age have considered the possibility of requiring former prisoners to wear tee shirts that announce the crime for which they were incarcerated. As Frijda and Mesquita (1994) have noted: "Shame stimulates behavior that leads to acceptance by the group, in addition to stimulating behavior that flees group rejection; agreeing with the group norm is one of these behaviors. Therefore, it may be seen as stimulating group cohesion" (p. 78).

Group Governance

Another important function of emotions for groups is their role in solving the problem of group governance (Keltner, Haidt, & Shiota, 2006; Shioto et al., 2004). In order to provide group governance, social groups typically produce, either by explicit or implicit means, a hierarchy of individuals or subgroups. As with emotion communicated within dyads, certain emotions such as anger, contempt, and pride communicate superiority and power to lower-status group members. Such emotions communicated to the group can elicit feelings of awe in lower-status group members, which serve to preserve the higher-status individual's authority (Fiske, 1991). In careful experimental work, Keltner and colleagues have also shown that embarrassment displayed by lower-status group members also communicates submissiveness to higher-status group members and serves an appeasement function (e.g., Keltner et al., 1998).

In an ingenious laboratory study, for example, Keltner and colleagues arranged for two high- and two low-status members of American university fraternities to tease each other. Analyses of the teasing behavior showed that when teased by higher-status individuals, the lower-status individuals expressed more embarrassment and smiling, apparently to appease the teasers. When teased by lower-status individuals, the higher-status individuals expressed more facial hostility, presumably in order to reassert their position in the social hierarchy.

When leaders want to signal to a group that they are on top, they use the expression of pride (Gilbert, 2001). When individuals display pride, they are perceived to be more dominant by the other members of the group and they receive a number of positive benefits from the group. For instance, they are more likely to get promoted or win awards (Shiota, Campos, & Keltner, 2003).

Figure 4.7 The flute of shame (*die Schandflöte*). Used in the Middle Ages to induce shame and public humiliation of individuals. Photograph provided by the Kriminalmuseum, Rothenburg,
Germany.

Collective Action

Finally, emotions, especially group emotions, which are discussed in Chapter 10, play an important role in causing and sustaining collective action, meaning the processes by which all or most
members of a group try to exert a societal change. When groups of people feel guilt, for example,
they are more likely to call for apologies and reparations on the part of governments and institutions (Berndsen & McGarty, 2010; Branscombe, Doosje, & McGarty, 2002; Doosje et al., 1998;
McGarty et al., 2005; Wohl & Branscombe, 2005). And when members of groups feel moral

outrage and anger, the group shows a greater commitment to collective action aimed at righting social inequalities, including discrimination and prejudice (Crisp et al., 2007; Leach, Iyer, & Pedersen, 2006; Thomas & McGarty, 2009; van Zomeren et al., 2004; Wakslak et al., 2007).

Group emotions can also accumulate and function to cause societal-level change. **Emotional climate** is the accumulation of repeated group emotional responses to societal events or sociopolitical conditions, which can produce a general and lasting emotional tone of the nation or society, as well as the likely emotional responses to events (Bar-Tal et al., 2007). For instance, de Rivera and Páez (2007) have characterized the emotional climate of countries in terms of the degree to which individuals feel social trust as well as social anger and fear. Such climates are, by the way, independent of the degree to which the country endorses a culture of peace. Research conducted during or after specific political events has documented acute emotional climates. These events include terrorist attacks in Spain (e.g., Conejero & Etxebarria, 2007) and genocide in Rwanda (Kanyangara et al., 2007). Emotional climate thus seems to play an important role in signaling the need for and motivating collective action as well as gauging its success.

In sum, for the group, emotions serve to define group boundaries and maintain social structure and norms within the group. Living in groups is, of course, a challenge because of the possibility of conflicting interests, opinions, and natures (Trivers, 1971). Without fundamental ways to make people feel that they want to facilitate the functioning of the group, adhere to group rules and norms, and recognize group leaders, societies would probably fail. Emotions seem to be at least part of the solution to living successfully in groups.

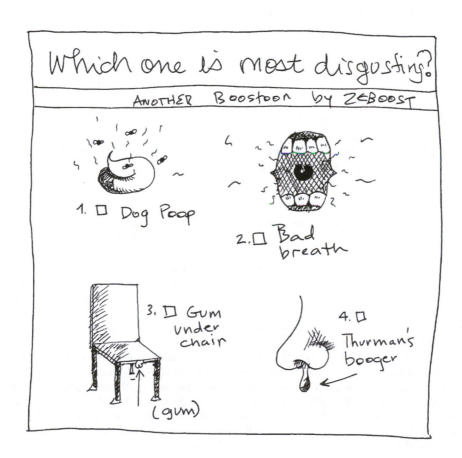

Summary

It is widely accepted that emotions are functional, but there are many ways of thinking about just *how* they are functional. Furthermore, the functions can vary depending on the size of the social unit. In this chapter, we described the function of emotion for three social units: the individual, the dyad, and the group.

- The function for the individual is a basic survival function. The body's physiology, distinct facial expressions, and the broaden-and-build forces of positive emotions all serve to help the individual deal with challenges and opportunities relevant to survival that are posed by the environment.
- For two people interacting, dyads, emotions—both features of emotions such as parts of facial expressions and tone of voice, in addition to the entire experience of emotion—serve the function of communication of critical information. Our emotions serve to tell others where to look and whether we and they are in danger. They also convey a need to be cared for or that one's welfare needs more consideration. Social functional theories of emotion hold that this communication serves to solve many tasks of social living, including positive ones of finding partners and bonding with our babies.
- At the larger group level, emotions serve functions involving social coordination. Emotions help us strengthen group coherence and define the boundaries of acceptable behavior. They are also used to signal the nature of the social hierarchy in the group. Finally, emotions are important to groups because they help the members mobilize their energy to produce a single desired effect, called collective action.

Learning Links

1. Explore this report on how the function of emotion is represented in the Pixar movie *Inside Out*. http://www.npr.org/sections/health-shots/2015/06/13/413980258/science-of-sadness-and-joy-inside-out-gets-childhood-emotions-right
2. See how robots are developed to engage in social referencing. https://www.youtube.com/watch?v=7ddlVsSoQJg
3. Read an interesting article on the function of emotions elicited by music. http://www.ncbi.nlm.nih.gov/pmc/articles/PMC3872313/

References

Askew, C., & Field, A. P. (2007). Vicarious learning and the development of fears in childhood. *Behaviour Research and Therapy, 45*(11), 2616–2627. doi:10.1016/j.brat.2007.06.008.

Barrera, M. E., & Maurer, D. (1981). Recognition of mother's photographed face by the three-month-old infant. *Child Development, 52*(2), 714–716. doi:10.1111/j.1467–8624.1981.tb03102.x.

Barrett, K. C., & Campos, J. J. (1987). Perspectives on emotional development: II. A functionalist approach to emotions. In J. D. Osofsky (Ed.), *Handbook of infant development* (2nd ed., pp. 555–578). New York: Wiley.

Barrett, L. F. (2006). Are emotions natural kinds? *Perspectives on Psychological Science, 1*(1), 28–58. doi:10.1111/j.1745–6916.2006.00003.x.

Bar-Tal, D., Halperin, E., & De Rivera, J. (2007). Collective emotions in conflict situations: Societal implications. *Journal of Social Issues, 63*(2), 441–460. doi:10.1111/j.1540–4560.2007.00518.x.

Bell, R. Q. (1974). Contributions of human infants to caregiving and social interaction. In M. Lewis & L. Rosenblum (Eds.), *The effect of the infant on its caregiver* (p. 264). Oxford, England: Wiley-Interscience.

Berndsen, M., & McGarty, C. (2010). The impact of magnitude of harm and perceived difficulty of making reparations on group-based guilt and reparation towards victims of historical harm. *European Journal of Social Psychology, 40*(3), 500–513. doi:10.1002/ejsp.642.

Berntson, G. G., Cacioppo, J. T., & Grossman, P. (2007). Whither vagal tone. *Biological Psychology*, *74*(2), 295–300. doi:10.1016/j.biopsycho.2006.08.006.

Blair, R. J. R. (1995). A cognitive developmental approach to morality: Investigating the psychopath. *Cognition*, *57*(1), 1–29. doi:10.1016/0010–0277(95)00676-p.

Blair, R. J. R. (2003). Facial expressions, their communicatory functions and neuro-cognitive substrates. *Philosophical Transactions of the Royal Society B: Biological Sciences*, *358*(1431), 561–572. doi:10.1098/rstb.2002.1220.

Blair, R. J. R. (2005). Responding to the emotions of others: Dissociating forms of empathy through the study of typical and psychiatric populations. *Consciousness and Cognition*, *14*(4), 698–718. doi:10.1016/j.concog.2005.06.004.

Bless, H., Clore, G. L., Schwarz, N., Golisano, V., Rabe, C., & Wölk, M. (1996). Mood and the use of scripts: Does a happy mood really lead to mindlessness? *Journal of Personality and Social Psychology*, *71*(4), 665. doi:10.1037/0022–3514.71.4.665.

Bosch, J. A., de Geus, E. J., Kelder, A., Veerman, E. C., Hoogstraten, J., & Amerongen, A. V. (2001). Differential effects of active versus passive coping on secretory immunity. *Psychophysiology, 38*, 836–846. doi:10.1111/1469–8986.3850836.

Brackett, M. A., Mayer, J. D., & Warner, R. M. (2004). Emotional intelligence and its relation to everyday behaviour. *Personality and Individual Differences*, *36*(6), 1387–1402. doi:10.1016/s0191–8869(03)00236–8.

Brackett, M. A., Rivers, S. E., Shiffman, S., Lerner, N., & Salovey, P. (2006). Relating emotional abilities to social functioning: A comparison of self-report and performance measures of emotional intelligence. *Journal of Personality and Social Psychology*, *91*(4), 780. doi:10.1037/0022–3514.91.4.780.

Branscombe, N. R., Doosje, B., & McGarty, C. (2002). Antecedents and consequences of collective guilt. In D. M. Mackie & E. R. Smith (Eds.), *From Prejudice to Intergroup Emotions: Differentiated Reactions to Social Groups* (pp.49–66). Philadelphia, PA: Psychology Press. doi:10.1177/1368430206064637.

Buck, R. (1983). Emotional development and emotional education. In R. Plutchik & H. Kellerman (Eds.), *Emotions in early development* (pp. 209–242). Beverly Hills, CA: Sage. doi:10.1016/b978–0–12–558702–0.50015–7.

Buck, R. (1988). The perception of facial expression: Individual regulation and social coordination. In T. R. Alley & L. S. Mark (Eds.), *Social and applied aspects of perceiving faces* (pp. 141–165). Hillsdale, NJ: Lawrence Erlbaum.

Buss, D. M. (1989). Sex differences in human mate preferences: Evolutionary hypotheses tested in 37 cultures. *Behavioral and Brain Sciences*, *12*(1), 1–14. doi:10.1017/s0140525x00023992.

Buss, D. M. (1994). Individual differences in mating strategies. *Behavioral and Brain Sciences*, *17*(3), 581–582. doi:10.1017/s0140525x00036062.

Butler, E. A., Egloff, B., Wlhelm, F. H., Smith, N. C., Erickson, E. A., & Gross, J. J. (2003). The social consequences of expressive suppression. *Emotion*, *3*(1), 48. doi:10.1037/1528–3542.3.1.48.

Campos, J. J., Thein, S., & Owen, D. (2003). A Darwinian legacy to understanding human infancy. *Annals of the New York Academy of Sciences*, *1000*(1), 110–134. doi:0.1196/annals.1280.040.

Cashdan, E. (1998). Smiles, speech, and body posture: How women and men display sociometric status and power. *Journal of Nonverbal Behavior*, *22*(4), 209–228. doi:10.1023/A:1022967721884.

Chekroun, P., & Brauer, M. (2002). The bystander effect and social control behavior: The effect of the presence of others on people's reactions to norm violations. *European Journal of Social Psychology*, *32*(6), 853–867. doi:10.1002/ejsp.126.

Chekroun, P., & Brauer, M. (2004). Controˆle social et effet spectateur: L'impact de l'implication personnelle [Social control and the bystander effect: The impact of personal implication]. *L'Anneˊe Psychologique*, *104*, 83102. doi:10.3406/psy.2004.3928.

Cialdini, R. B., Borden, R. J., Thorne, A., Walker, M. R., Freeman, S., & Sloan, L. R. (1976). Basking in reflected glory: Three (football) field studies. *Journal of Personality and Social Psychology*, *34*(3), 366. doi:10.1037/0022–3514.34.3.366.

Clark, T. F., Winkielman, P., & McIntosh, D. N. (2008). Autism and the extraction of emotion from briefly presented facial expressions: Stumbling at the first step of empathy. *Emotion*, *8*(6), 803. doi:10.1037/a0014124.

Conejero, S., & Etxebarria, I. (2007). The impact of the Madrid bombing on personal emotions, emotional atmosphere and emotional climate. *Journal of Social Issues*, *63*(2), 273–287. doi:10.1111/j.1540–4560.2007.00508.x.

Cosmides, L., & Tooby, J. (2000). Evolutionary psychology and the emotions. *Handbook of Emotions*, *2*, 91–115.

Crisp, R. J., Heuston, S., Farr, M. J., & Turner, R. N. (2007). Seeing red or feeling blue: Differentiated intergroup emotions and ingroup identification in soccer fans. *Group Processes & Intergroup Relations*, *10*(1), 9–26. doi:10.1177/1368430207071337.

Dawel, A., Palermo, R., O'Kearney, R., Irons, J. & McKone, E. (2015), Fearful faces drive gaze-cueing and threat bias effects in children on the lookout for danger. *Developmental Science*, 18: 219–231. doi:10.1111/desc.12203.

de Rivera, J., & Páez, D. (2007). Emotional climate, human security, and cultures of peace. *Journal of Social Issues*, *63*(2), 233–253. doi:10.1111/j.1540–4560.2007.00506.x.

Derryberry, D., & Tucker, D. M. (1994). Motivating the focus of attention. In P. M. Niedenthal & S. Kitayama (Eds.), *The heart's eye: Emotional influences in perception and attention* (pp. 167–196). San Diege, CA: Academic Press. doi:10.1016/b978–0–12–410560–7.50014–4.

Doosje, B., Branscombe, N. R., Spears, R., & Manstead, A. S. (1998). Guilty by association: When one's group has a negative history. *Journal of Personality and Social Psychology*, *75*(4), 872. doi:10.1037//0022–3514.75.4.872.

Dunbar, R. I. (1993). Coevolution of neocortical size, group size and language in humans. *Behavioral and Brain Sciences*, *16*(4), 681–694. doi:10.1017/s0140525x00032325.

Ekman, P. (1992). An argument for basic emotions. *Cognition & Emotion*, *6*(3–4), 169–200. doi:10.1080/02699939208411068.

Fairchild, G., Van Goozen, S. H., Calder, A. J., Stollery, S. J., & Goodyer, I. M. (2009). Deficits in facial expression recognition in male adolescents with early-onset or adolescence-onset conduct disorder. *Journal of Child Psychology and Psychiatry*, *50*, 627–636. doi:10.1111/j.1469–7610.2008.02020.x.

Fiske, A. P. (1991). *Structures of social life: The four elementary forms of human relations: Communal sharing, authority ranking, equality matching, market pricing.* New York, NY: Free Press. doi:10.1086/229892.

Fredrickson, B. L. (1998). What good are positive emotions? *Review of General Psychology*, *2*(3), 300. doi:10.1037/1089–2680.2.3.300.

Fredrickson, B. L. (2013). Positive emotions broaden and build. *Advances in Experimental Social Psychology*, *47*, 1–53. doi:10.1016/b978–0–12–407236–7.00001–2.

Fredrickson, B. L., & Branigan, C. (2005). Positive emotions broaden the scope of attention and thought-action repertoires. *Cognition & Emotion*, *19*(3), 313–332. doi:10.1080/02699930441000238.

Fredrickson, B. L., & Cohn, M. A. (2008). Positive emotions. In M. Lewis, J. Haviland-Jones & L. F. Barrett (Eds.), *Handbook of emotions* (3rd ed., pp. 777–796). New York: Guilford Press.

Fredrickson, B. L., & Levenson, R. W. (1998). Positive emotions speed recovery from the cardiovascular sequelae of negative emotions. *Cognition & Emotion*, *12*(2), 191–220. doi:10.1080/026999398379718.

Fredrickson, B. L., Tugade, M. M., Waugh, C. E., & Larkin, G. R. (2003). What good are positive emotions in crisis? A prospective study of resilience and emotions following the terrorist attacks on the United States on September 11th, 2001. *Journal of Personality and Social Psychology*, *84*(2), 365. doi:10.1037/0022–3514.84.2.365.

Friijda, N. H. (1986). *The emotions.* Cambridge, UK: Cambridge University Press.

Frijda, N. H., & Mesquita, B. (1994). The social roles and functions of emotions. In S. Kitayama & H. Marcus (Eds.), *Emotion and culture: Empirical studies of mutual influence* (pp. 51–87). Washington, DC: American Psychological Association. doi:10.1037/10152–002.

Gable, S. L., Gonzaga, G. C., & Strachman, A. (2006). Will you be there for me when things go right? Supportive responses to positive event disclosures. *Journal of Personality and Social Psychology*, *91*(5), 904. doi:10.1037/0022–3514.91.5.904.

Gerull, F. C., & Rapee, R. M. (2002). Mother knows best: Effects of maternal modeling on the acquisition of fear and avoidance behaviour in toddlers. *Behaviour Research and Therapy*, *40*(3), 279–287. doi:10.1016/s0005–7967(01)00013–4.

Gilbert, P. (2001). Evolution and social anxiety: The role of attraction, social competition, and social hierarchies. *Psychiatric Clinics of North America*, *24*(4), 723–751. doi:10.1016/s0193–953x(05)70260–4.

Gonzaga, G. C., Keltner, D., Londahl, E. A., & Smith, M. D. (2001). Love and the commitment problem in romantic relations and friendship. *Journal of Personality and Social Psychology*, *81*(2), 247. doi:10.1037/0022–3514.81.2.247.

Gross, M. M., Crane, E. A., & Fredrickson, B. L. (2012). Effort-shape and kinematic assessment of bodily expression of emotion during gait. *Human Movement Science*, *31*(1), 202–221. doi:10.1016/j. humov.2011.05.001.

Grossman, P., & Taylor, E. W. (2007). Toward understanding respiratory sinus arrhythmia: Relations to cardiac vagal tone, evolution and biobehavioral functions. *Biological Psychology*, *74*(2), 263–285. doi:10.1016/j.biopsycho.2005.11.014.

Grossmann, T. (2010). The development of emotion perception in face and voice during infancy. *Restorative Neurology and Neuroscience*, *28*(2), 219. doi:10.3233/RNN-2010–0499.

Gump, B. B., & Kulik, J. A. (1997). Stress, affiliation, and emotional contagion. *Journal of Personality and Social Psychology*, *72*(2), 305. doi:10.1037/0022–3514.72.2.305.

Gustafson, G. E., & Harris, K. L. (1990). Women's responses to young infants' cries. *Developmental Psychology*, *26*(1), 144–152. doi:10.1037/0012–1649.26.1.144.

Haidt, J. (2003). The moral emotions. In R. J. Davidson, K. R. Scherer & H. H. Goldsmith (Eds.), *Handbook of affective sciences* (pp. 853–870). Oxford: Oxford University Press.

Harmon-Jones, E., Gable, P. A., & Price, T. F. (2013). Does negative affect always narrow and positive affect always broaden the mind? Considering the influence of motivational intensity on cognitive scope. *Current Directions in Psychological Science*, *22*(4), 301–307. doi:10.1177/0963721413481353.

Heberlein, A. S., Padon, A. A., Gillihan, S. J., Farah, M. J., & Fellows, L. K. (2008). Ventromedial frontal lobe plays a critical role in facial emotion recognition. *Journal of Cognitive Neuroscience*, *20*(4), 721–733. doi:10.1162/jocn.2008.20049.

Hertenstein, M. J., & Campos, J. J. (2004). The retention effects of an adult's emotional displays on infant behavior. *Child Development*, *75*(2), 595–613. doi:10.1111/j.1467–8624.2004.00695.x.

Hinson, J. M., Jameson, T. L., & Whitney, P. (2002). Somatic markers, working memory, and decision making. *Cognitive, Affective, & Behavioral Neuroscience*, *2*(4), 341–353. doi:10.3758/cabn.2.4.341.

Hrdy, S. B. (1999). *Mother nature: A history of mothers, infants, and natural selection*. New York: Pantheon.

Impett, E. A., Le, B. M., Kogan, A., Oveis, C., & Keltner, D. (2014). When you think your partner is holding back the costs of perceived partner suppression during relationship sacrifice. *Social Psychological and Personality Science*, *5*(5), 542–549. doi:10.1177/1948550613514455.

Isen, A. M., Johnson, M. M., Mertz, E., & Robinson, G. F. (1985). The influence of positive affect on the unusualness of word associations. *Journal of Personality and Social Psychology*, *48*(6), 1413. doi:10.1037/0022–3514.48.6.1413.

Johnson, K. J., Waugh, C. E., & Fredrickson, B. L. (2010). Smile to see the forest: Facially expressed positive emotions broaden cognition. *Cognition and Emotion*, *24*(2), 299–321. doi:10.1080/02699930903384667.

Johnson-Laird, P. N., & Oatley, K. (1992). Basic emotions, rationality, and folk theory. *Cognition & Emotion*, *6*(3–4), 201–223. doi:10.1080/02699939208411069.

Kanyangara, P., Rimé, B., Philippot, P., & Yzerbyt, V. (2007). Collective rituals, emotional climate and intergroup perception: Participation in "Gacaca" tribunals and assimilation of the Rwandan genocide. *Journal of Social Issues*, *63*(2), 387–403. doi:10.1111/j.1540–4560.2007.00515.x.

Kelsey, R. M., Ornduff, S. R., Reiff, S., & Arthur, C. M. (2002). Psychophysiological correlates of narcissistic traits in women during active coping. *Psychophysiology*, *39*, 322–332 doi:10.1111/1469–8986.3930322.

Keltner, D., & Gross, J. J. (1999). Functional accounts of emotions. *Cognition & Emotion*, *13*(5), 467–480. doi:10.1080/026999399379140.

Keltner, D., & Haidt, J. (1999). Social functions of emotions at four levels of analysis. *Cognition & Emotion*, *13*(5), 505–521. doi:10.1080/026999399379168.

Keltner, D., & Haidt, J. (2001). Social functions of emotions. In T. J. Mayne & G. A. Bonanno (Eds.), *Emotions: Current issues and future directions* (pp. 192–213). New York: Guilford Press.

Keltner, D., Haidt, J., & Shiota, M. N. (2006). Social functionalism and the evolution of emotions. In M. Schaller, J. A. Simpson & D. T. Kenrick (Eds.), *Evolution and social psychology* (pp. 115–142). New York: Psychology Press.

Keltner, D., & Kring, A. M. (1998). Emotion, social function, and psychopathology. *Review of General Psychology*, *2*(3), 320. doi:10.1037/1089–2680.2.3.320.

Keltner, D., Young, R. C., Heerey, E. A., Oemig, C., & Monarch, N. D. (1998). Teasing in hierarchical and intimate relations. *Journal of Personality and Social Psychology, 75*(5), 1231. doi:10.1037/0022–3514.75.5.1231.

Kennedy, D. P., Gläscher, J., Tyszka, J. M., & Adolphs, R. (2009). Personal space regulation by the human amygdala. *Nature Neuroscience, 12*(10), 1226–1227. doi:10.1038/nn.2381.

Klinnert, M. D. (1984). The regulation of infant behavior by maternal facial expression. *Infant Behavior and Development, 7*(4), 447–465. doi:10.1016/s0163–6383(84)80005–3.

Klinnert, M. D., Emde, R. N., Butterfield, P., & Campos, J. J. (1986). Social referencing: The infant's use of emotional signals from a friendly adult with mother present. *Developmental Psychology, 22*(4), 427. doi:10.1037/0012–1649.22.4.427.

Kobayashi, H., & Kohshima, S. (1997). Unique morphology of the human eye. *Nature, 387*, 767–768. doi:10.1006/jhev.2001.0468.

Kobiella, A., Grossmann, T., Reid, V., & Striano, T. (2008). The discrimination of angry and fearful facial expressions in 7-month-old infants: An event-related potential study. *PCEM, 22*(1), 134–146. doi:10.1080/02699930701394256.

Kok, B. E., & Fredrickson, B. L. (2010). Upward spirals of the heart: Autonomic flexibility, as indexed by vagal tone, reciprocally and prospectively predicts positive emotions and social connectedness. *Biological Psychology, 85*(3), 432–436. doi:10.1016/j.biopsycho.2010.09.005.

Kreibig, S. D., Wilhelm, F. H., Roth, W. T., & Gross, J. J. (2007). Cardiovascular, electrodermal, and respiratory response patterns to fear- and sadness-inducing films. *Psychophysiology, 44*(5), 787–806. doi:10.1111/j.1469–8986.2007.00550.x.

Kuckuck, A., Vibbert, M., & Bornstein, M. H. (1986). The perception of smiling and its experiential correlates in 3-month-olds. *Child Development, 57*, 1054–1061. doi:10.1111/j.1467–8624.1986.tb00266.x.

Leach, C. W., Iyer, A., & Pedersen, A. (2006). Anger and guilt about ingroup advantage explain the willingness for political action. *Personality and Social Psychology Bulletin, 32*(9), 1232–1245. doi:10.1177/0146167206289729.

Leary, M. R., Koch, E. J., & Hechenbleikner, N. R. (2001). Emotional responses to interpersonal rejection. In M. R. Leary (Ed.), *Interpersonal rejection* (p. 145–166). New York: Oxford University Press.

Lee, D. H., Susskind, J. M., & Anderson, A. K. (2013). Social transmission of the sensory benefits of eye widening in fear expressions. *Psychological Science, 24*(6), 957–965. doi:10.1177/0956797612464500.

Levenson, R. W. (1992). Autonomic nervous system differences among emotions. *Psychological Science, 3*, 23–27. doi:10.1111/j.1467–9280.1992.tb00251.x.

Levenson, R. W. (2003). Blood, sweat, and fears. *Annals of the New York Academy of Sciences, 1000*(1), 348–366. doi:10.1196/annals.1280.016.

Lopes, P. N., Salovey, P., & Straus, R. (2003). Emotional intelligence, personality, and the perceived quality of social relationships. *Personality and Individual Differences, 35*(3), 641–658. doi:10.1016/s0191–8869(02)00242–8.

Lorberbaum, J. P., Newman, J. D., Horwitz, A. R., Dubno, J. R., Lydiard, R. B., Hamner, M. B., . . . George, M. S. (2002). A potential role for thalamocingulate circuitry in human maternal behavior. *Biological Psychiatry, 51*(6), 431–445. doi:10.1016/S0006–3223(01)01284–7.

Marsh, A. A., Adams, R. B., & Kleck, R. E. (2005). Why do fear and anger look the way they do? Form and social function in facial expressions. *Personality and Social Psychology Bulletin, 31*(1), 73–86. doi:10.1177/0146167204271306.

Marsh, A. A., & Blair, R. J. R. (2008). Deficits in facial affect recognition among antisocial populations: A meta-analysis. *Neuroscience & Biobehavioral Reviews, 32*(3), 454–465. doi:10.1016/j.neubiorev.2007.08.003.

Matthews, G., & Wells, A. (1999). The cognitive science of attention and emotion. In T. Dalgleish & M. Power (Eds.), *Handbook of cognition and emotion* (pp. 171–192). New York: Wiley. doi:10.1002/0470013494.ch9.

Mayer, J. D., Salovey, P., & Caruso, D. R. (2004). Emotional Intelligence: Theory, Findings, and Implications. *Psychological inquiry, 15*(3), 197–215. doi:10.1207/s15327965pli1503_02.

Mayer, J. D., Salovey, P., & Caruso, D. R. (2008). Emotional intelligence: New ability or eclectic traits? *American Psychologist, 63*(6), 503. doi:10.1037/0003–066x.63.6.503.

McGarty, C., Pedersen, A., Wayne Leach, C., Mansell, T., Waller, J., & Bliuc, A. M. (2005). Group-based guilt as a predictor of commitment to apology. *British Journal of Social Psychology*, *44*(4), 659–680. doi:10.1348/014466604x18974.

McIntosh, D. N., Reichmann-Decker, A., Winkielman, P., & Wilbarger, J. L. (2006). When the social mirror breaks: Deficits in automatic, but not voluntary, mimicry of emotional facial expressions in autism. *Developmental Science*, *9*(3), 295–302. doi:10.1111/j.1467–7687.2006.00492.x.

Mineka, S., & Cook, M. (1993). Mechanisms involved in the observational conditioning of fear. *Journal of Experimental Psychology: General*, *122*(1), 23. doi:10.1037/0096–3445.122.1.23.

Muhtadie, L., Koslov, K., Akinola, M., & Mendes, W. B. (2015). Vagal flexibility: A physiological predictor of social sensitivity. *Journal of Personality and Social Psychology*, *109*(1), 106–120. doi:10.1037/pspp0000016.

Mumme, D. L., Fernald, A., & Herrera, C. (1996). Infants' responses to facial and vocal emotional signals in a social referencing paradigm. *Child Development*, *67*(6), 3219–3237. doi:10.2307/1131775.

Niedenthal, P. M., & Brauer, M. (2012). Social functionality of human emotion. *Annual Review of Psychology*, *63*(1), 259–285. doi:10.1146/annurev.psych.121208.131605.

Niedenthal, P. M., Korb, S., Wood, A., & Rychlowska, M. (2016). Smiles of love, sympathy and war and how we know one when we see it. In U. Hess (Ed.), *Emotional mimicry in social context*. Cambridge: Cambridge University Press.

Niedenthal, P. M., Mermillod, M., Maringer, M., & Hess, U. (2010). The simulation of smiles (SIMS) model: Embodied simulation and the meaning of facial expression. *Behavioral and Brain Sciences*, *33*(6), 417–433. doi:10.1017/S0140525X10000865.

Oatley, K., & Duncan, E. (1992). Episode of emotion in daily life. In K. T. Strongman (Ed.), *International review of studies on emotion* (Vol. 2, pp. 249–293). Chichester: John Wiley & Sons.

Oatley, K., & Duncan, E. (1994). The experience of emotions in everyday life. *Cognition & Emotion*, *8*(4), 369–381. doi:10.1080/02699939408408947.

Oatley, K., & Johnson-Laird, P. N. (1987). Towards a cognitive theory of emotions. *Cognition and Emotion*, *1*, 29–50. doi:10.1080/02699938708408362.

Parrott, W. G. (2001). Implications of dysfunctional emotions for understanding how emotions function. *Review of General Psychology*, *5*(3), 180–186. doi:10.1037/1089–2680.5.3.180.

Plutchik, R. (1980). *Emotion: A psycho-evolutionary synthesis*. New York: Harper & Row.

Pollak, S. D. (2008). Mechanisms linking early experience and the emergence of emotions illustrations from the study of maltreated children. *Current Directions in Psychological Science*, *17*(6), 370–375. doi:10.1111/j.1467–8721.2008.00608.x.

Porges, S. W. (1995). Orienting in a defensive world: Mammalian modifications of our evolutionary heritage. A polyvagal theory. *Psychophysiology*, *32*(4), 301–318. doi:10.1111/j.1469–8986.1995.tb01213.x.

Porges, S. W. (2001). The polyvagal theory: Phylogenetic substrates of a social nervous system. *International Journal of Psychophysiology*, *42*(2), 123–146. doi:10.1016/s0167–8760(01)00162–3.

Porges, S. W. (2007). The polyvagal perspective. *Biological Psychology*, *74*(2), 116–143. doi:0.1016/j.biopsycho.2006.06.009.

Porter, F. L., Porges, S. W., & Marshall, R. E. (1988). Newborn pain cries and vagal tone: Parallel changes in response to circumcision. *Child Development, 59*(2), 495–505. doi:10.2307/1130327.

Quigley, K. S., & Barrett, L. F. (2014). Is there consistency and specificity of autonomic changes during emotional episodes? Guidance from the conceptual act theory and psychophysiology. *Biological Psychology*, *98*, 82–94. doi:10.1016/j.biopsycho.2013.12.013.

Rimé, B. (2007). Interpersonal emotion regulation. In J. J. Gross (Ed.), *Handbook of emotion regulation* (pp. 466–485). New York: Guilford Press.

Ritz, T., Steptoe, A., De Wilde, S., & Costa, M. (2000). Emotions and stress increase respiratory resistance in asthma. *Psychosomatic Medicine, 62*, 401–412. doi:10.1097/00006842–200005000–00014.

Rosete, D. (2007). Does emotional intelligence play an important role in leadership effectiveness? (Unpublished doctoral dissertation). University of Wollongong, Wollongong, New South Wales, Australia.

Rowe, G., Hirsh, J. B., & Anderson, A. K. (2007). Positive affect increases the breadth of attentional selection. *Proceedings of the National Academy of Sciences*, *104*(1), 383–388. doi:10.1073/pnas.0605198104.

Rubin, M. M. (1999). Emotional intelligence and its role in mitigating aggression: A correlational study of the relationship between emotional intelligence and aggression in urban adolescents. (Unpublished dissertation). Immaculata College, Immaculata, Pennsylvania.

Rychlowska, M., Miyamoto, Y., Matsumoto, D., Hess, U., Gilboa-Schechtman, E., Kamble, S., . . . Niedenthal, P. M. (2015). Heterogeneity of long-history migration explains cultural differences in reports of emotional expressivity and the functions of smiles. *PNAS Proceedings of the National Academy of Sciences of the United States of America*, *112*(19), E2429–E2436. doi:10.1073/pnas.1413661112.

Salovey, P., & Mayer, J. D. (1990). Emotional intelligence. *Imagination, Cognition and Personality*, *9*(3), 185–211. doi:10.2190/dugg-p24e-52wk-6cdg.

Salovey, P., Mayer, J. D., Caruso, D., & Lopes, P. N. (2003). Measuring emotional intelligence as a set of abilities with the Mayer-Salovey-Caruso emotional intelligence test. In C.R. Snyder (Ed.), *Positive psychological assessment: A handbook of models and measures*, (pp. 251–265). Washington, DC: American Psychological Association. doi:10.1037/10612–016.

Scheff, T. J. (1988). Shame and conformity: The deference-emotion system. *American Sociological Review*, 53(3), 395–406. doi:10.2307/2095647.

Schwartz, G. M., Izard, C. E., & Ansul, S. E. (1985). The 5-month-old's ability to discriminate facial expressions of emotion. *Infant Behavior and Development*, *8*(1), 65–77. doi:10.1016/S0163–6383(85)80017–5.

Sell, A., Tooby, J., & Cosmides, L. (2009). Formidability and the logic of human anger. *Proceedings of the National Academy of Sciences*, *106*(35), 15073–15078. doi:10.1073/pnas.0904312106.

Shiota, M. N., Campos, B., & Keltner, D. (2003). The faces of positive emotion. *Annals of the New York Academy of Sciences*, *1000*(1), 296–299. doi:10.1196/annals.1280.029.

Shiota, M. N., Campos, B., Keltner, D., & Hertenstein, M. J. (2004). Positive emotion and the regulation of interpersonal relationships. In P. Philippot and R. Feldman (Eds.), *The Regulation of Emotion* (pp. 127–155). New York, NY: Psychology Press.

Shiota, M. N., Campos, B., Keltner, D., & Hertenstien, M. J. (2004). Positive emotion and the regulation of interpersonal relationships. In P. Philippot & R. S. Feldman (Eds.), *The regulation of emotion* (pp. 127–155). Mahwah, NJ: Erlbaum.

Spoor, J. R., & Kelly, J. R. (2004). The evolutionary significance of affect in groups: Communication and group bonding. *Group Processes & Intergroup Relations*, *7*(4), 398–412. doi:10.1177/1368430204046145.

Srivastava, S., Tamir, M., McGonigal, K. M., John, O. P., & Gross, J. J. (2009). The social costs of emotional suppression: A prospective study of the transition to college. *Journal of Personality and Social Psychology*, *96*(4), 883. doi:10.1037/a0014755.

Stemmler, G., Aue, T., & Wacker, J. (2007). Anger and fear: Separable effects of emotion and motivational direction on somatovisceral responses. *International Journal of Psychophysiology*, *66*(2), 141–153. doi:10.1016/j.ijpsycho.2007.03.019.

Stemmler, G., Heldmann, M., Pauls, C. A., & Scherer, T. (2001), Constraints for emotion specificity in fear and anger: The context counts. *Psychophysiology*, *38*, 275–291. doi:10.1111/1469–8986.3820275.

Striano, T., Brennan, P. A., & Vanman, E. J. (2002). Maternal depressive symptoms and 6-month-old infants' sensitivity to facial expressions. *Infancy*, *3*(1), 115–126. doi:10.1207/S15327078IN0301_6.

Thomas, E. F., & McGarty, C. A. (2009). The role of efficacy and moral outrage norms in creating the potential for international development activism through group-based interaction. *British Journal of Social Psychology*, *48*(1), 115–134. doi:10.1348/014466608x313774.

Tooby, J., Cosmides, L., Sell, A., Lieberman, D., & Sznycer, D. (2008). Internal regulatory variables and the design of human motivation: A computational and evolutionary approach. In Andrew J. Elliot (Ed.), *Handbook of approach and avoidance motivation* (pp. 251–271). Mahwah, NJ: Lawrence Erlbaum Associates. doi:10.4324/9780203888148.ch15.

Tracy, J. L., & Robins, R. W. (2007). Emerging insights into the nature and function of pride. *Current Directions in Psychological Science*, *16*(3), 147–150. doi:10.1111/j.1467–8721.2007.00493.x.

Trainor, L. J., Austin, C. M., & Desjardins, R. N. (2000). Is infant-directed speech prosody a result of the vocal expression of emotion? *Psychological Science*, *11*(3), 188–195. doi:10.1111/1467–9280.00240.

Tranel, D., Bechara, A., & Damasio, A. R. (2000). Decision making and the somatic marker hypothesis. In M. S. Gazzaniga (Ed.), *The New cognitive neurosciences* (pp. 1047–1061). Cambridge, MA: MIT Press/Bradford Books.

Trivers, R. L. (1971). The evolution of reciprocal altruism. *Quarterly Review of Biology*, *46*, 35–57. doi:10.1086/406755.

Vaish, A., & Striano, T. (2004). Is visual reference necessary? Contributions of facial versus vocal cues in 12-month-olds' social referencing behavior. *Developmental Science*, *7*(3), 261–269. doi:10.1111/j.1467–7687.2004.00344.x.

van Kleef, G. A. (2009). How emotions regulate social life the emotions as social information (EASI) model. *Current Directions in Psychological Science*, *18*(3), 184–188. doi:10.1111/j.1467–8721.2009.01633.x.

van Zomeren, M., Fischer, A. H., & Spears, R. (2007). Testing the limits of tolerance: How intergroup anxiety amplifies negative and offensive responses to out-group-initiated contact. *Personality and Social Psychology Bulletin*, *33*(12), 1686–1699. doi:10.1177/0146167207307485.

van Zomeren, M., Spears, R., Fischer, A. H., & Leach, C. W. (2004). Put your money where your mouth is! Explaining collective action tendencies through group-based anger and group efficacy. *Journal of Personality and Social Psychology*, *87*(5), 649. doi:10.1037/0022–3514.87.5.649.

Vermeulen, N., Godefroid, J., & Mermillod, M. (2009). Emotional modulation of attention: Fear increases but disgust reduces the attentional blink. *PLoS One*, *4*(11), e7924. doi:10.1371/journal.pone.0007924.

Wadlinger, H. A., & Isaacowitz, D. M. (2006). Positive mood broadens visual attention to positive stimuli. *Motivation and Emotion*, *30*(1), 87–99. doi:10.1007/s11031–006–9021–1.

Wakslak, C. J., Jost, J. T., Tyler, T. R., & Chen, E. S. (2007). Moral outrage mediates the dampening effect of system justification on support for redistributive social policies. *Psychological Science*, *18*(3), 267–274. doi:10.1111/j.1467–9280.2007.01887.x.

Walker-Andrews, A. S., & Lennon, E. (1991). Infants' discrimination of vocal expressions: Contributions of auditory and visual information. *Infant Behavior and Development*, *14*(2), 131–142. doi:10.1016/0163–6383(91)90001–9.

Walter, F., & Bruch, H. (2008). The positive group affect spiral: A dynamic model of the emergence of positive affective similarity in work groups. *Journal of Organizational Behavior*, *29*(2), 239–261. doi:10.1002/job.505.

Waugh, C. E., & Fredrickson, B. L. (2006). Nice to know you: Positive emotions, self–other overlap, and complex understanding in the formation of a new relationship. *The Journal of Positive Psychology*, *1*(2), 93–106. doi:10.1080/17439760500510569.

Wieser, M. J., Mühlberger, A., Alpers, G. W., Macht, M., Ellgring, H., & Pauli, P. (2006). Emotion processing in Parkinson's disease: Dissociation between early neuronal processing and explicit ratings. *Clinical Neurophysiology*, *117*(1), 94–102. doi:10.1016/j.clinph.2005.09.009.

Wilder, D. A., & Shapiro, P. N. (1989). Role of competition-induced anxiety in limiting the beneficial impact of positive behavior by an out-group member. *Journal of Personality and Social Psychology*, *56*(1), 60. doi:10.1037/0022–3514.56.1.60.

Wohl, M. J., & Branscombe, N. R. (2005). Forgiveness and collective guilt assignment to historical perpetrator groups depend on level of social category inclusiveness. *Journal of Personality and Social Psychology*, *88*(2), 288. doi:10.1037/0022–3514.88.2.288.

Wohl, M. J., Branscombe, N. R., & Reysen, S. (2010). Perceiving your group's future to be in jeopardy: Extinction threat induces collective angst and the desire to strengthen the ingroup. Personality and Social Psychology Bulletin, 37(7), 989-910. doi:10.1177/0146167210372505.

Young-Browne, G., Rosenfeld, H. M., & Horowitz, F. D. (1977). Infant discrimination of facial expressions. *Child Development*, *48*, 555–562. doi:10.2307/1128653.

5   Expression of Emotion

Faces are possibly the most important and attention-grabbing things humans see. They are the first thing babies see when they are born, and an infant's gaze is drawn to them (Kato & Konishi, 2013). There is a good reason for this. Until an infant develops language comprehension, it will be her caretakers' nonverbal behavior—particularly their facial expressions—that reward her for desirable behavior, alert her to potential dangers, and signal to her that a new food or toy is safe and good. But the importance of faces and facial expressions does not go away once we learn to communicate verbally. More than any other visual stimulus, faces demand our attention, and we are quick to detect them (sometimes too quick, given how often people claim to see faces in their toast or in the clouds). It is adaptive for us to pay attention to faces, because the facial expressions of those around us provide information about their emotions as well as their attitudes toward us and the objects in our environments (see Figure 5.1). This information then guides our own behavior and feelings. The communicative function of facial expressions becomes readily apparent when we can no longer see them, such as in written conversation. People's increasing use of emojis in text messages and emails highlights the importance of

Figure 5.1 From left to right, top to bottom: happy, neutral, sad, surprised, afraid, angry, and disgusted. Image
from http://blog.eiworld.org/facial-emotion-recognition-deficits-in-schizophrenia-patients/

facial expressions for revealing our internal states and adding nuance to our communication
with others. Although cartoonish and exaggerated, adding a smiling or frowning emoji can
clarify whether your text message to a friend saying, "I sure do love that guy," is sincere or
sarcastic.

For all the reasons just discussed, facial expressions have been a central area of focus for
emotion researchers, and you will learn about what they have found in this chapter. First we provide an overview of the mechanics and neurobiology of facial expressions, which are surprisingly complex. We next outline the function and origin of facial expressions and the question of
whether facial expressions are universal or culture specific. A third topic is related to the exact
nature of the information conveyed by the face. Here we show how facial expressions convey
information about the expresser's emotional state and their social motives and intentions. The
fourth section on facial expression explores how facial expressions may not just be a product
of an emotion state, but may even help create the feeling of an emotion. We will see how this
possibility allows for **facial mimicry** to help us understand the emotions of others. The final
section of the chapter reviews research into how the body and the voice convey emotion and
how all these signals, when combined, are perceived by others.

The Mechanics of Facial Expressions

Knowing how facial muscles are controlled is important if you want to generate hypotheses
about where facial expressions come from and why they occur. Facial expressions are produced
by the contraction of coordinated muscle groups, which create folds and wrinkles on the skin
of the face. Whereas other skeletal muscles in the body are anchored to bone so they can move
your skeleton through space, the 43 muscles involved in facial expression are anchored to your
skin (Cattaneo & Pavesi, 2014). This allows the muscles to both control the sensory organs on
the face (e.g., closing and opening the eyes and mouth, wrinkling the nose to expel a bad smell)
and, importantly, to change the shape and surface of the face to express emotion. Humans and
certain primate relatives have evolved to produce clear, recognizable facial expressions—in
fact, some primates (including us) may have less facial hair and more even-toned skin pigmen-
tation than other species so that our facial expressions are easily visible (Changizi, Zhang, &
Shimojo, 2006; Santana, Dobson, & Diogo, 2014).

Your facial muscles have a unique relationship with your brain. Most skeletal muscles in your body, like those in your arms, have **proprioceptors** that tell the brain how stretched or contracted the muscle is so you can know the position of your arm without looking at it. The facial muscles, however, lack these proprioceptors, so your brain relies on **mechanoreceptors** in your skin that provide information about changes in the position and warping of the skin of your face. Mechanoreceptors send stronger signals to your brain when your skin is moving than when it is still. Perhaps you have had the experience of making a facial expression and do not even realize it until a friend points it out.

Facial muscles receive signals from the cortex and subcortical areas in the brain via motor nerve cells originating in the brainstem (Rinn, 1984, 1991). The facial muscles of the forehead, the eyebrows, and the lips are innervated by the seventh cranial nerve, aptly called the **facial nerve**, and this nerve is the most important in causing the contraction of the muscles that make many facial expressions. The third cranial nerve, the **occulomotor nerve**, is also implicated in the lifting of the eyelids, as in surprise, and governs pupil dilation and the movements of the eyeball. The fifth cranial nerve, the **trigeminal nerve**, innervates the muscles used for chewing and for clenching the jaw. The trigeminal nerve is very complex, however, and also involved in sensations in the face. In particular, it is responsible for returning sensation from the face to the brain. The facial and trigeminal nerves are depicted in Figure 5.2.

Compared to the control of arm and leg movements, the brain systems responsible for generating facial movements are much more distributed and complex. Facial expressions are controlled by multiple cortical and subcortical brain systems, some of which are more important for generating spontaneous expressions of emotion (e.g., when you smile uncontrollably about a joke you hear), whereas others give us voluntary control over our facial muscles (e.g., when you smile for a photo). The facial motor nucleus, where the facial nerve originates in the brainstem, receives information from the motor cortex, similarly to how voluntary limb movement is

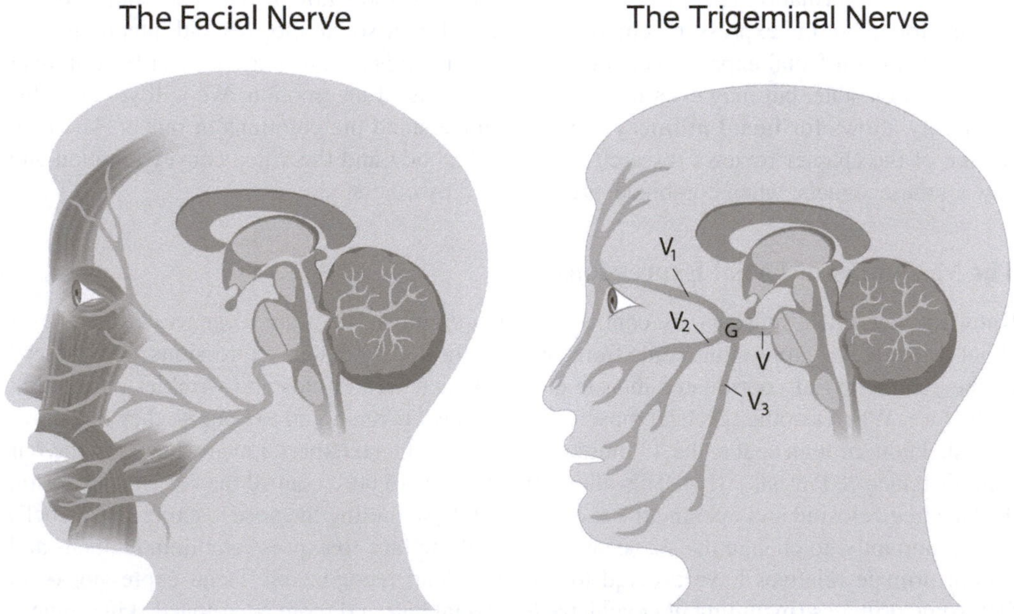

The Facial Nerve
The Trigeminal Nerve

Figure 5.2 Diagram of the facial (cranial nerve VII) and trigeminal (cranial nerve V) nerves. The facial nerve sends motor output signals to the muscles of facial expression, whereas the trigeminal nerve receives somatosensory feedback from the facial skin, among other functions.

generated, but it also receives indirect information from parts of the brain associated with emotion and more reflexive and homeostasis-related behaviors, like the amygdala, the brainstem, and the hypothalamus. That facial movements are caused by a wide range of brain systems, including subcortical brain areas associated with emotion, highlights facial expressions' tight relationship with emotion states.

In sum, the production of facial expressions differs from other types of muscle movement in several ways. The facial muscles are attached to the skin of your face and work in groups to move the skin, whereas other skeletal muscles of your body move joints. This allows facial muscle contractions to be visible to other people, rather than simply occurring below the skin. The way your brain receives feedback from your facial muscles about their current states is also unique because it relies on mechanoreceptors in the skin that are most sensitive to changes in position, unlike the proprioceptors in other muscles that provide constant information about muscle stretching and contraction and joint angle. More distributed brain systems are responsible for generating emotion expressions compared to voluntary limb movements. These differences between the facial and nonfacial motor systems underscore the unique functions of the face in several processes (sensation, consumption, verbal communication), but most importantly, in emotion expression.

Origin of Facial Expressions

A long-standing debate in emotion research is whether specific emotions are **universal**, meaning all humans (and perhaps our mammalian relatives) have the capacity to experience them, or are the product of cultural learning and socialization, and therefore vary across cultures in the way spoken language does. You may recognize this as yet another variation of the nature versus nurture debate (which we discussed in Chapter 1 on theories of emotion). From an evolutionary perspective, facial expressions of emotions are innate expressions of specific emotional states. Because they can be traced back to animal behavior, they should be universal, that is, shared by humans of any age, gender, race, and culture. On the other hand, facial expressions could be the nonverbal equivalent of language, in that all human cultures have them but they are the result of cultural, rather than genetic, evolution. In this case we would expect to find little or no similarity in facial expressions across cultures. The origins of facial expressions can therefore be explored by a) testing hypotheses about the adaptive functions of specific expressions and comparing human facial expressions to nonhuman animal facial gestures, and b) comparing human expressions across various cultures.

Evolution and Function of Facial Expressions

As we learned in Chapter 1, Darwin (1872/1998) claimed that facial expressions in humans have evolved from functional movements that were adaptive for our ancestors because they solved particular survival problems. For instance, your lip curls up in anger because, long ago in our evolutionary past, you would have been preparing to bite (thus this human expression is similar to the snarl of a dog). In addition to preparing the organism for adaptive action like biting, some expressions manipulate our faces to regulate the amount of stimulation taken in through our various sensory channels. The eyes take in visual information (sight), the nose takes in olfactory information (smell), and the mouth takes in gustatory information (taste). When we experience fear, as an example, we need to detect and escape from the present threat; Darwin thought that the facial expression of fear, and specifically the widening of the eyes, has evolved to increase an individual's ability to be vigilant in dangerous situations. The facial expression of disgust, Darwin proposed, helps an individual avoid ingesting contaminating stimuli (Rozin & Fallon, 1987).

In tests of Darwin's claims about the functions of the expressions of fear and disgust, Susskind and colleagues (2008) found that when experimental participants were led to make facial expressions of fear, they took in visual and olfactory information more efficiently than when they were led to make neutral expressions: their visual fields increased, they localized visual targets in space more quickly, and they inhaled more and faster through their nasal passages (also, West et al., 2011; the expression of surprise may have similar sensory benefits, Susskind & Anderson, 2008). Findings also showed that the disgust expression had the opposite effect. Compared to a neutral expression, the disgust expression served to shut the senses off to external input; the visual fields contracted and inhalation through the nasal passages was more restricted (see results for vision and olfaction on the upper and lower portions, respectively, of Figure 5.3). Because fear arises during threat and disgust arises during exposure to contamination, these relations seem highly functional (also, Krusemark & Li, 2011).

In most mammals, affect is communicated primarily through body and ear posture and vocalizations, rather than the face (Panksepp & Biven, 2012). It has therefore been proposed that in species that do look to the face for emotion information (like many primates), facial expressions

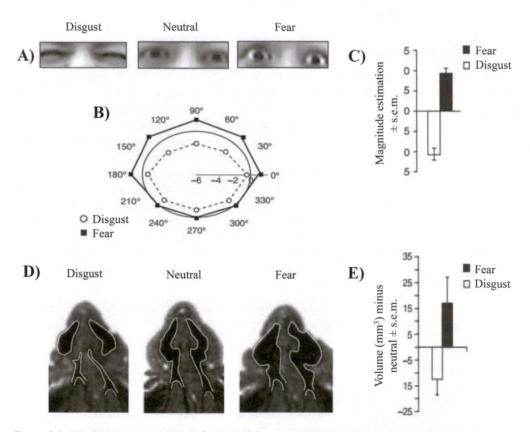

Figure 5.3 (A) Average eye opening from participants posing disgust, neutral, and fear expressions. (B) Changes in visual field estimation along horizontal, vertical, and oblique axes. Central ellipse is neutral baseline. Unit markings are in 9.5 degrees of visual angle. (C) Change in estimated visual field size (in standardized units) for fear and disgust expressions relative to neutral expressions, averaged across visual field location. (D) Passageways to the inferior turbinate of the respiratory mucosa. Relative to neutral expressions (middle panel), disgust (left) and fear (right) expressions resulted in closure and dilation, respectively. (E) Bar graphs represent average overall air cavity volume for fear and disgust expressions relative to neutral. Adapted from Susskind et al. (2008).

are just exaggerated, ritualized versions of the facial movements needed to produce the vocalizations associated with emotions (Andrew, 1963). For instance, smiling alters the shape of the mouth and vocal tract, which raises the pitch and increases the loudness of speech or vocalizations (Tartter, 1980). Higher-pitched vocalizations are considered submissive, friendly, and less threatening, whereas lower pitches across species often accompany aggression (probably because it creates the illusion that the vocalizing animal is larger and has the body to support low pitches). The facial movement required to produce high-pitched, nonthreatening sounds could then become a signal of positive emotion in itself, even in the absence of audible vocalizations (for evidence of this idea in chimpanzees, see Davila-Ross et al., 2015).

Once the expression becomes a communicative cue that tells others what the expresser is feeling, the communicative function may persist even if the original reason for the facial movement's existence disappears. In mammals with mobile ears, like horses and dogs, ear movements communicate a lot about the animal's intentions and social status. Even though most of us cannot move our ears, we still knit and raise our eyebrows when expressing emotion, possibly a vestigial leftover from when we could move our ears (van Hooff, 1976).

Besides identifying possible adaptive functions of the muscle movements involved in facial expressions, we can also compare expressions across species. Of course, it is difficult to know what an animal is feeling since it cannot tell us, but comparative psychologists and ethologists can identify which contexts and stimuli cause certain nonverbal displays and then consider whether the animals' displays are **homologous** (similar in evolutionary origin) to humans' expressions and behavior in similar types of contexts. As an example, during play, chimpanzees "smile" with relaxed, open mouths and produce a rhythmic panting that is possibly homologous to human laughter, just as humans laugh and smile when playing and having fun. Chimps produce a different "smile," called a silent bared-teeth display, to communicate affiliation and friendliness (see Figure 5.4; Parr & Waller, 2006; Waller & Dunbar, 2005). Interestingly, the smiles of enjoyment and social affiliation look different in humans, too (Niedenthal et al., 2010).

In sum, identifying plausible functions of emotion expressions and tracking their evolution through cross-species comparison is one way to answer the question of the origins of facial expressions.

Figure 5.4 Chimpanzees produce the play face (left) during play and when being tickled and produce the silent bared-teeth display (right) as a sign of affiliation and appeasement. These expressions are thought to be homologous to human smiles that signal enjoyment and friendly intentions, respectively. Photos courtesy of Dr. Lisa Parr.

The Question of Cultural Universality

Another approach that attempts to answer the question of whether specific facial expressions are evolutionarily endowed involves cross-cultural studies that look at whether people all over the world recognize the same expressions as signifying the same emotion (Ekman, 1972; Ekman, Sorenson, & Friesen, 1969; Izard, 1971). In such studies, observers in different cultures match photographs of posed facial expressions of six basic emotions—anger, happiness, sadness, fear, disgust, and surprise—with emotional labels selected from a short list of emotion words (the native language equivalents of each of those six words). People across the globe tended to label the expressions with the same emotion at rates greater than chance (for a meta-analysis, see Elfenbein & Ambady, 2002).

One problem with studies that claim to demonstrate universality of facial expressions is that for almost a century there has been extensive exposure across cultures to facial expressions, especially expressions made by people from Western cultures. That is, people in most countries of the world have seen films and television depicting facial expressions and the situations in which the expressions arose. So, maybe facial expressions and their meanings seem to be universal when, in fact, cross-cultural learning and influence have occurred. In order to address this possibility, Paul Ekman studied members of isolated, preliterate cultures, which likely had experienced no exposure to Western facial expressions. In several studies, members of the Fore tribe of Papua New Guinea were read simple stories about emotional situations, and they had to match the stories with photographs of posed facial expressions (Ekman, 1973; Ekman & Friesen, 1971). There was agreement across cultures in the facial expression that fit the situation. In addition to the six "basic" expressions, researchers have found high agreement for shame, embarrassment, amusement, compassion, contempt and three expressions associated with self-conscious emotions (tongue biting, gaping, and covering the face with the hand) (Haidt & Keltner, 1999).

The interpretation of the agreement in recognition of facial expressions across cultures as evidence for the universality thesis has been repeatedly criticized on technical and methodological grounds (for a critical review, see Nelson & Russell, 2013; Russell, 1994). People may, for instance, perform better than chance in multiple-choice designs by process of elimination (if they know the expression is not one of the emotions they are familiar with, they can pick the other label without knowing what that label means). It is therefore invaluable to look at studies in which researchers put subjects in a particular emotion state or observe them in naturally occurring emotional contexts and then code their expressions. Dozens of studies involving subjects from a range of cultures and a variety of emotion states demonstrate some cross-cultural consistency in facial expressions spontaneously generated during emotion episodes (for a review, see Matsumoto et al., 2008). For instance, the spontaneous facial expressions of Olympic athletes from 35 different countries were coded using Facial Action Coding Scheme (FACS) (described in Chapter 2). Gold medal winners tended to produce Duchenne smiles, in which the corners of the eyes crinkle, which is considered an expression of joy; silver medal winners (who had just lost a competition) were more likely to exhibit sadness or contempt (Matsumoto & Willingham, 2006).

The same psychologists then compared congenitally blind Paralympic medal winners' expressions to those of sighted athletes and found no difference in spontaneous facial expressions (Matsumoto & Willingham, 2009). Because congenitally blind people are unable to learn culturally constructed facial expressions by observing others' faces, this study provides compelling support that at least some emotion expressions are universal (see Figure 5.5; for a similar study of the expression of pride, see Tracy & Matsumoto, 2008). Furthermore, children with congenital blindness vary little from sighted children in their facial responses to typical emotion-eliciting situations such as smiling during social play, pouting during punishment, and

Figure 5.5 Blind (left) and sighted (right) athletes immediately upon losing a competition. From Matsumoto & Willingham (2009).

crying when in an unfamiliar environment (Darwin, 1872/1998; Eibl-Eibesfeldt, 1973; Thompson, 1941; for a more recent review, see Matsumoto & Willingham, 2009).

Even among researchers who think facial expressions are genetically inherited, there is substantial disagreement about what is innate (see Fridlund, 1994). An extreme position might be to say that humans are born with the ability to produce six highly stereotyped and reflexive facial expressions and that every time they feel an emotion, they produce that expression. If they do not produce that expression when feeling the emotion, it is because they have learned to suppress or mask it. A more moderate position might argue that the structure of the human face, combined with certain adaptive and evolved action tendencies (see Chapter 1), such as the urge to attack when angered, combine to produce patterns of facial expression that are similar across people (because we have shared facial morphology and action tendencies) and yet vulnerable to being shaped by learning, context, and culture.

Indeed, the strong position mentioned earlier is hard to reconcile with cross-cultural studies, as the magnitude of recognition accuracy varies across culture to some degree (Elfenbein & Ambady, 2002; Haidt & Keltner, 1999; Nelson & Russell, 2013). Researchers have repeatedly found that observers are more accurate when they judge expressions of members of their own culture, a bias called the **in-group advantage**. The in-group advantage can be partly explained by expression dialects: much as cultural differences evolve in speech dialects for a single language, different cultures might exhibit slight variants of innate expressions, sometimes due to norms about which emotions are appropriate to express in public. Interestingly, the in-group advantage decreases with increased exposure to members of other cultures (Elfenbein, 2013; Elfenbein & Ambady, 2002). These and other sources of cultural variations such as culture-specific situational elicitors and interpretations of facial expressions (e.g., Haidt & Keltner, 1999) and socially and culturally learned display rules (Ekman, 1972; Matsumato et al., 2005) will be discussed in detail in Chapter 12.

There is thus ample evidence for a strong innate component in facial expressions of emotion that is rooted in mammalian evolution. At the same time, cultural rules for interpretation and display influence the facial displays of emotion. Many scientists endorse an "interactionist perspective" in which both biological and social/cultural determinants of facial expressions are taken into account (Ekman, 1972, 1994; Elfenbein & Ambady, 2002).

What Facial Expressions Convey: Emotion Readout Versus Social Motivations

Whether innate or learned, facial expressions undeniably serve a communicative purpose in addition to any biological functions. A historical debate in the field is whether facial expressions communicate a person's true internal feelings or, instead, reflect the person's desire to influence other people.

Developmental Detail

Distressed and Smile Expressions Come First

In the first few months of life, infants display a range of facial reflexes, such as blinking, rooting and sucking to locate a nipple, and tongue thrusting to remove unwanted items from their mouths. These reflexes are a far cry from emotion expressions, not only because they are automatic responses to often innocuous sensory input (like being tapped on the cheek), but also because they do not have any clear communicative function. So, do infants make facial expressions of emotion? Some researchers say "no," arguing that facial expressions need to be learned through observing other people (Barrett, 2006), or that facial expressions emerge from these primitive facial reflexes later in development (Fridlund, 1994).

In distinguishing between reflexes and emotion expressions in babies, it is helpful to examine two facial expressions seen in infants that do have social communication functions: distress expressions and smiles. When newborns are distressed, their faces bunch up, their mouths open so everyone can hear their shrieks, and they turn red (see the left image in the figure). Distressed expressions trigger caretaking from parents, much like infant crying (Chapter 3; Donovan & Leavitt, 1985). More differentiated displays of negative emotion, such as adult-like fear and anger expressions, emerge later in development when the communicative situations for the underlying emotion have also developed. For instance, older, mobile infants express angry frustration when they are physically restrained (Stenberg & Campos, 1990).

At about six weeks of age, infants begin to smile in response to seeing or interacting with people. In fact, even blind infants smile in response to stimulation from parents (Trevarthen, 1979). Smiles are incredibly rewarding to parents and likely function to reinforce positive parent–infant bonding. Healthy parent–infant interactions involve constant mutual facial mimicry and engagement that rely heavily on smiles (Feldman, 2007). It seems then that within the first six weeks of life two expressions distinguish themselves from reflexes in that they have social-communicative functions for infant–parent interaction.

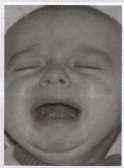

A baby's distress and smile expressions emerge early in life and are the major forms of communication with caretakers. From Gil et al. (2011).

Some research supports the idea that facial expressions reflect the expresser's internal emotional state (Ekman, 1972; Izard, 1971; Tomkins, 1962, 1963). In other words, when you feel an emotion like fear, your facial expression will honestly and accurately reveal that you are afraid. This **read-out** view states that there is a close relationship between emotion and expression and that this relationship is due to the functioning of an innate affect program (e.g., Buck, 1978; Camras, Holland, & Patterson, 1993; Johnson, Waugh, & Fredrickson, 2010; Manstead, Fischer, & Jakobs, 1999; Mauss et al., 2005). In the program for each of the basic emotions, it is the facial muscles that, so to speak, externalize the internal feelings. Through socialization you may learn to suppress or mask undesirable emotions, but your true feelings may "leak" out in the form of subtle facial muscle movements (Ekman & Friesen, 1969).

According to the **behavioral ecology** view, on the other hand, facial expressions evolved to communicate the expresser's social motives in a particular social situation (Fridlund, 1992, 1994, 1997). Facial expressions signal what the expresser intends to do and what the expresser wants others to do. For example, a smile signals the expresser's intention to affiliate, whereas a sad face signals request for assistance and comfort. Likewise, a jealous person may put up a sad face in front of the partner in order to avoid disapproval and anger and to elicit empathy and concern. The behavioral ecology view contends that facial expressions are usually displayed in interactive situations and that they are more or less intense depending on the real or imagined presence of others.

As an example, Kraut and Johnston (1979) found that bowlers smiled more when facing their co-players than when facing the bowling pins, independent of how well they scored (see also Ruiz-Belda et al., 2003). Another researcher filmed participants' facial expressions while they listened to stories about close calls—dramatic consequences that almost happened—in varyingly social contexts (Chovil, 1991). Participants heard the stories either on a tape recording, over the phone, from a confederate in the same room but visually separated by a partition, or in a face-to-face interaction. Displays of sympathetic distress, such as gasps, grimaces, and wincing, were more frequent the more social the context. Differences across social context can change how expressive people are, including the familiarity between the expresser and the audience, the valence of the emotional situation, and the intensity of the emotion elicitors (Buck et al., 1992; Hess, Banse, & Kappas, 1995; Jakobs, Manstead, & Fischer, 1999, 2001; Lee & Wagner, 2002). The behavioral ecology view also emphasizes that expressions of emotion are only a small percent of the complete repertoire of facial gestures people produce in daily life. For instance, people emphasize, reenact, and alter the meaning of what they are saying using facial muscle movements that are not typically classified as "emotion" expressions (Fridlund, 1994).

Facial expressions thus seem to communicate information about the expresser's feelings and about the expresser's social motives and behavioral intentions. This does not mean that facial expressions never reflect genuine states, but that they occur in agents who exert influence over their social environments.

Facial Expressions Influence the Experience and Perception of Emotions

Recall that the facial nerve contracts some of the muscles that make up facial expressions. The trigeminal nerve, meanwhile, sends sensory information from the face back to the brain. Facial expressions therefore might tell other people what we are feeling, but they may also cause us to feel certain things via sensory feedback. This idea is conveyed in expressions and songs that tell us that if we want to be happy, we should just put a smile on our face. The **facial feedback hypothesis** states that facial expressions contribute to our own emotional states through feedback from the face to the brain. Emotion theorists since Darwin, notably Izard (1971, 1990), Tomkins (1962, 1963), and Zajonc, Murphy, and Inglehart (1989), have developed the idea that facial behavior can activate or regulate emotion experience. They proposed that producing facial expressions and receiving sensory feedback from the face modulate the intensity of—or, in the strong formulation of the hypothesis, create—emotional experience (for reviews, see Adelmann & Zajonc, 1989; Buck, 1980; McIntosh, 1996).

According to the facial feedback hypothesis, the expression of congruent facial expressions enhances the corresponding feelings, whereas the inhibition of congruent facial expressions or the display of incongruent emotional expressions attenuates the feeling. For example, if you are already sad, the more you frown and pout, the sadder you feel. To test this idea, researchers explicitly instructed participants to exaggerate or to conceal their spontaneous emotional expression induced by electric shocks (Kopel & Arkowitz, 1974; Lanzetta, Cartwright-Smith, & Kleck, 1976), pleasant and unpleasant films (Zuckerman et al., 1981), pleasant and disgusting odors (Kraut, 1982), or an imagery task in which participants imagined several standardized happy ("winning in the lottery") and sad situations ("death of a family member"; McCanne & Anderson, 1987). Consistent with the hypothesis, inhibition of participants' facial expression attenuated their self-reported pleasantness ratings, whereas amplification increased their pleasantness ratings (see also Laird, 1974; Lewis, 2012; Hyniewska & Sato, 2015). You may have already noticed that this approach to studying facial feedback is vulnerable to **demand characteristics**, meaning the participants may have guessed what the researchers were studying and therefore told them what they wanted to hear.

To get around demand characteristics, researchers invented a more indirect way to enhance or inhibit participants' muscle contractions (Strack, Martin, & Stepper, 1988). Participants who believed that they were taking part in a study on psychomotor coordination rated the funniness of humorous cartoons while holding a pen either with their teeth only, which produced smiling, or with their lips only, which inhibited smiling, or with their nondominant hand (see Figure 5.6). The latter individuals served as a control group. Cartoons were rated as more amusing in the "teeth" condition and least amusing in the "lip" condition, with control group participants falling in between. In another study, participants induced to smile using a similar procedure were able to hold their hands in a bucket of ice water (a very painful procedure) for longer and had less of a stress response to the task compared to participants who were not made to smile (Kraft & Pressman, 2012). People instructed to imitate angry facial expressions had greater pupillary dilation and skin conductance (two indicators of autonomic arousal) than participants who were simply viewing the angry expressions (Lee et al., 2013).

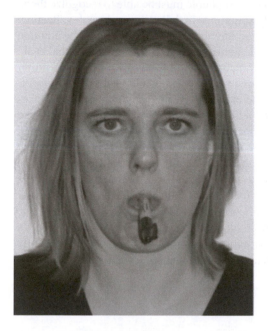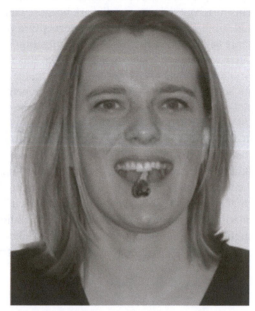

Figure 5.6 Researchers covertly manipulate participants' facial expressions to study the effects of facial feedback. Holding an object with your lips prevents smiling (left), whereas holding it with your teeth forces you to smile right. From Niedenthal (2007). Psychologists are now questioning whether such posed and prolonged smiling actually influences your emotion state, due to a highly-publicized failed replication of a study that used the pen technique (Wagenmakers et al., 2016).

The implications of the facial feedback hypothesis have also been explored in clinical populations. Patients suffering from major depression disorder showed reduced symptom severity when they received Botox injections (which paralyze facial muscles) to the muscles involved in eyebrow furrowing, a movement associated with negative emotions (Finzi & Rosenthal, 2014). In patients with facial paralysis, the more their zygomatic muscle (the smile muscle) was immobilized, the greater their depressive symptoms (VanSwearingen, Cohn, & Bajaj-Luthra, 1999). These findings suggest that long-term inability to produce certain facial expressions can reduce the intensity of associated emotions, which has consequences for mental health. Taken together, there exists strong empirical evidence that people's expressive behavior plays a role in their experience of emotion. However, these feedback effects are small to moderate (Matsumoto, 1987) and are in general smaller than the impact of emotion-eliciting events. In fact, a recent large-scale replication of the original Strack et al. study involving 17 psychology labs and hundreds of participants failed to find an effect of the pen manipulation on participants' funniness ratings, causing psychologists to question both the original study and the facial feedback hypothesis (Wagenmakers et al., 2016). While this "many-labs" replication casts strong doubt on the reliability of the 1988 findings, researchers should conduct preregistered replications of more recent demonstrations of the facial feedback hypothesis before dismissing the entire theory.

Embodied Simulation and Emotion Perception

Although facial feedback may prove to play only a modest role in the activation and modulation of emotion, it may be very important for the recognition of facial expression of emotion. If facial expressions serve a communicative function, other people must be able to recognize them. This turns out to be no simple task because facial expressions in daily life are complex, fleeting, and subtle. A theory of **emotion perception** (recognizing the meaning underlying the emotion expressions of others) that is gaining traction is called **embodied simulation** (Niedenthal et al., 2010; Wood et al., 2016). According to this theory, people can use their own brain and motor emotion systems to re-create, or simulate, the expressions of others, which gives them immediate access to the emotions underlying the perceived expressions. The simulation process takes place in the areas of the brain involved in the production of the perceived facial expression and sometimes involves the actual contraction of the perceiver's facial muscles, which is called **facial mimicry** (Figure 5.7). For instance, imagine that you glance at your friend to see what she is thinking and feeling. The corners of her mouth are pulled up, her jaw is slightly open, the skin around her eyes is bunched up, and she has raised eyebrows. Your brain rapidly simulates the motor and sensory experience of producing her facial expression embedded in the particular context (perhaps she is watching a funny YouTube video). Your facial muscles may even make minute contractions. This unconscious embodied simulation of her facial expression produces a slight version of the emotional state associated with the expression, allowing you to implicitly and seemingly effortlessly register that your friend is amused and somewhat shocked at what she is seeing.

Figure 5.7 Facial mimicry is an important basis of empathy and occurs most often in people who care about each other.

How do we know that this unconscious process is happening, and furthermore, that it is actually helping you recognize the emotions of others? A large body of research on emotional mimicry has shown that the exposure to photos or videos of facial expressions of emotion induces in observers an involuntary, unconscious, and rapid facial muscle activity (measured by electromyography [EMG]) that matches the observed facial display (Dimberg, Thunberg, & Grunedal, 2002; Künecke et al., 2014; for a review see Hess & Fischer, 2013). According to the embodied emotion approach (Niedenthal, 2007), facial mimicry reflects the embodied simulation of the observed facial expression and provides facial feedback, which, as we've learned, has been shown to influence individuals' emotional experience.

Some evidence that this mimicry is then used in the recognition of facial expressions of emotions comes from studies where participants' facial expressions were temporarily disrupted, for example, by having them hold a pen sideways in the mouth (Niedenthal et al., 2001), having them wear a mouth guard (Rychlowska et al., 2014), or by temporarily paralyzing the facial muscle activity via a Botox injection (Neal & Chartrand, 2011). Blocking facial mimicry generally impairs emotion recognition accuracy as well as speed of recognition (Stel & van Knippenberg, 2008).

Does this mean that emotion recognition is not possible without facial mimicry and/or embodied simulation? Of course not. Facial mimicry seems to be less important for the recognition of very prototypical facial expressions, which are easy to identify (Adolphs, 2002; Hess & Fischer, 2013) and much more important for extracting the nuanced meaning from dynamic, ambiguous expressions (Rychlowska et al., 2014; Sato & Yoshikawa, 2007). The social context also influences facial mimicry. Studies have found that people are more likely to mimic the facial expressions of liked, powerful, and/or socially close interaction partners (for a review, see Hess & Fischer, 2014). Facial and bodily mimicry, in turn, increases affiliation and liking (Lakin et al., 2003). This means that mimicry may help best in the recognition of certain people's facial expressions and not others'.

Beyond the Face: Other Components of Emotion Expression

So far we have focused on the expression of emotion in the face. But if emotion expressions are thought to be both biologically functional and communicative, we might expect emotions to produce corresponding changes in the body and voice. We will therefore review some of the emerging work on bodily and vocal expressions of emotion.

Bodily Expression of Emotion

Emotions prepare a person for appropriate action in response to a stimulus. For instance, people experiencing fear might freeze, cower, or prepare to run away; people experiencing anger might clench their fists and make themselves appear big and intimidating; and people experiencing joy might move energetically and with a playful bounce in their step. Notice that these behaviors all closely match a theoretical function of the emotions—to escape a threat, to aggress against a transgressor, and to playfully explore and socialize, respectively. If these movement patterns or action tendencies are components of emotions, we might expect aspects of the behaviors to be expressed during an emotion state even if their original purpose is no longer present. Maybe you have had the experience of being furious at someone who was not there and feeling the desire to hit a wall or a pillow, even though this aggression would not serve a purpose.

If there are specific patterns of body movement associated with emotions, then we would expect people to be able to identify what others are feeling based on their bodies alone. A common technique for testing this involves point-light display portrayals (e.g., Brownlow et al., 1997). In one study, researchers filmed actors in a darkened room portraying disgust, fear, anger, happiness, and sadness with body movements while wearing full-body suits with reflective material at a few important locations on the body (e.g., the wrists and head, see Figure 5.8; Atkinson et al., 2004). They then asked people to judge the emotion expressed in video clips

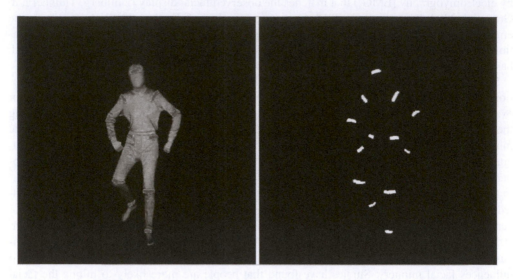

Figure 5.8 The same frame of an actor's dynamic portrayal of anger in both full-light (left) and point-
    light (right) displays. In the full-light version, the actor's face is covered so judges' ratings of
    the emotion expressed by the bodily movements will not be influenced by facial expressions.
    From Atkinson et al. (2004).

both when the actors' full bodies were visible and when only the reflective points on their suits
were visible. Participants had very high accuracy in categorizing the moves according to emotion, even for the point-light display versions, suggesting very little information is required to
detect an emotion in a body (De Meijer, 1989; Dittrich et al., 1996).

The actors tended to portray anger with erratic movements toward the camera, shaking fists,
and stamping feet. Fear involved cowering, contracting movements away from the camera,
often with hands raised in defense. Happiness involved expansive movements like skipping,
jumping up and down, and pumping the arms. Sadness frequently involved droopy posture
and self-soothing actions like putting the hands on the face or across the body. In displays
of disgust, actors often covered their mouths and noses, turned away from the camera, and
swiped their hands in front of their faces like they were waving away a bad smell (Atkinson
et al., 2004).

Other researchers have focused less on the specific gestures associated with particular emotions (such as cowering in fear), instead identifying features of movement (such as amplitude
and fluidity) that are associated with specific emotions (Castellano, Villalba, & Camurri,
2007). Scientists have gone even further than point-light displays in trying to distill emotion expressions in the body down to their key diagnostic features: one team used animated
bouncing balls instead of human forms to identify what aspects of movement convey particular emotions (for a fuller description of this work, see Chapter 12; Sievers, Polansky,
Casey, & Wheatley, 2013). For instance, erratic, rapid, and downward-focused movement
conveys anger.

To summarize, there are systematic and recognizable relationships between emotion states
and particular bodily gestures and/or qualities of movement. Feedback from the body may
modulate the intensity of an emotion state much as feedback from the face does (Flack, 2006),
and embodied simulation likely plays a role in recognizing emotion expressions in the bodily

movements of others. For example, when experienced dancers watch other people dance, they exhibit increased activity in motor areas of their brains (Cross, Hamilton, & Grafton, 2006). If embodied simulation supports dancers' perception and understanding of dance moves, it may also support people's understanding of others' bodily expression.

Emotion in the Voice

Our voices reveal our feelings through nonverbal vocalizations—such as a sigh or a laugh—and while we are speaking, via the nonlinguistic aspects of our voices called **prosody**. Vocal expressions signal our emotions to those around us and therefore exist partly to influence others, but they are also often automatic and uncontrollable. You know this if you have ever giggled uncontrollably in class, despite your best efforts to be quiet, or been unable to make your voice stop quavering with nervousness during an important presentation.

As with facial expressions, much research on vocal expressions has tried to identify distinct patterns of vocalizations that might correspond to specific emotion states. One way they test these ideas is by recording naturalistic or posed vocal expressions of emotion and analyzing the acoustic properties. These properties include pitch, loudness, rhythm, tempo, phonation features like breathiness and nasality, and glottal excitation, which describes characteristics of vocalizations that differ across vowels and consonants (see Figure 5.9 for a visualization of a laughter sound clip; Cummings & Clements, 1995).

The analysis of sounds produced by people feeling different emotions led some researchers to conclude that the voice conveys only a few aspects of affect, but not specific emotion states. Specifically, physiological arousal has a direct influence on the quality of your voice, and some have argued it is the only feature of emotion that you can detect in the voice (Bachorowski, 1999; Cowie, 2000). Other dimensions, such as valence, or even discrete emotion states, have been more elusive to describe in terms of acoustic properties. Anger and joy, as an example, are associated with similar increases in pitch and loudness, presumably because they are both high-arousal states (Johnstone & Scherer, 2000).

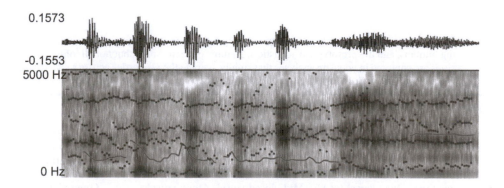

Figure 5.9 Visualization of a male laughter sound clip generated in Praat, a free program that analyzes the acoustic properties of vocalizations. The top *oscillogram* has time on the X axis, and the Y axis represents the intensity of the sound waves (each burst of activity is one "ha" in the laughter). The bottom spectrogram illustrates frequency, or pitch, on the Y axis. Darker shaded areas have a higher intensity at those frequencies. The thin line on the spectrogram is tracing pitch, and the dots represent the frequencies of formants, which are the layers of harmonic resonances in the voice. From Cummings & Clements (1995).

However, those who conclude there are no differences in emotion expressions might be looking at the wrong vocal properties (Juslin, 2013). Regarding the lack of differentiation between anger and joy mentioned earlier, it may be that combinations of other features of sound are more diagnostic, like attack (anger vocalizations are proposed to have a more abrupt onset than happy ones) and jitter (anger may sound more irregular with slight perturbations in pitch; Juslin & Scherer, 2005). Indeed, when researchers included a full range of acoustic properties, including irregularities in speech patterns and changes in phonation, they found that the combination of features could distinguish emotions in sentences spoken by actors (Johnstone & Scherer, 2000). The physiological features of laughter production—revealed in the degree to which the laugh sounds nasal, breathy, and open mouthed—are related to how spontaneous and "genuine" the laugh is (note that these features are not easily extracted from acoustic software like Praat [see Figure 5.8] and therefore require trained listeners; Lavan, Scott, & McGettigan, 2015).

Charles Snowdon argues that human music arose from fundamental features of emotion vocalizations in primates, and he therefore uses musical ideas of harmony to describe monkey calls (see Table 5.1 for the proposed cross-species acoustic features of affective communication). In particular, he suggests that monkeys and humans use *dissonant* pitch intervals (listen to Stravinsky's *Rite of Spring* to hear dissonant chords) to communicate threat and alarm, *minor* intervals (Beethoven's *Für Elise*) to communicate sympathy or sadness, and *major* intervals to communicate positive, lively affect (Mozart's *Eine Kleine Nachtmusik*; Snowdon & Teie, 2013). As this work suggests, researchers will need to consider the full range of quantitative and qualitative acoustic descriptors if they hope to identify specific categories of emotion vocalizations (e.g., Yang & Lugger, 2010).

Another way to determine whether the voice can convey discrete emotions is to have participants identify the emotions expressed by vocalizations and see how much consensus there is. Across 60 experiments and regardless of the raters' culture of origin and whether the vocalizations were spontaneous or posed, a meta-analysis suggested that raters' consensus was quite high for the expression of anger, fear, happiness, sadness, and tenderness (see also Sauter et al., 2010). One research team had actors produce many more emotion vocalizations than the few basic emotions typically studied; the team found judges could correctly identify

Table 5.1 Different affective–communicative signals thought to be important for social primates, including humans, and the prototypical acoustic signatures of each. Some, but not all, of these dimensions are captured in acoustic analyses that simply average the properties across a sound sample. From Snowdon & Teie (2013).

Soothing/affective:	Lively/affective:	Sympathetic/ expressive:	Threat	Alarm
Raised larynx	Raised larynx	Lowered larynx	Frontal vowels	Open vowels
Pure waveform	Vocal waveform	Vocal waveform	Complex waveform	Penetrating waveform
Closed vowel (oo)	Open vowel (ah)	Mid-closed vowel (oh)	Open vowels	Open vowels
Moderate tempo	Quick, short notes	Slow descending phrases	Accented notes	Sustained notes
High vocal range	Mid-high vocal range	Mid-low vocal range	Low vocal range	High vocal range
Open consonant intervals	Major diatonic intervals	Minor diatonic intervals	Dissonant intervals	Dissonant intervals
Quiet	Moderate	Quiet	Moderately loud	Loud

22 different emotions reliably, including compassion, interest, and embarrassment (Simon-Thomas et al., 2009).

The idea behind the facial feedback hypothesis discussed earlier can also apply to vocal expression. For instance, using a slow, quiet voice to discuss an anger-provoking topic reduces a speaker's self-reported anger and autonomic arousal compared to using a rapid, loud speaking style (Siegman, Anderson, & Berger, 1990). In a clever study, participants read text while wearing soundproof headphones through which they heard their own voices played back in real time (Aucouturier et al., 2016). The experimenters subtly manipulated the quality of some participants' voices so that they sounded happy, sad, or fearful, without the participants being made aware that their voices were altered. Participants in the sad condition reported feeling less positivity and those in the happy condition reported more positivity, but there was no effect for fear; all three feedback conditions had higher skin conductance (a measure of arousal) than control condition participants. It thus appears that sensory feedback about the emotional qualities of your voice, in addition to the movements of your facial muscles, can modify your experience of emotion.

Combining Emotion Expression Components in Context

So far we have considered how the face, the body, and the voice express emotion in isolation. But because faces tend to talk and have bodies attached, perceivers normally receive simultaneous information from all three channels. How are these cues integrated?

Perhaps unsurprisingly, videos of full-person emotion expressions are recognized with greater accuracy than videos of just the face or just the body, even when the video clips are extremely brief (250 milliseconds; Martinez et al., 2015). So more information allows for greater emotion recognition accuracy, but what happens when the different pieces of information are in conflict? Although a person's voice and face usually express the same emotion, researchers can use a variety of computerized techniques to construct incongruent pairs of facial expressions and vocalizations to better understand how the different cues are integrated to form a whole. These incongruent pairs are detected very early in perceptual processing, and congruent pairs facilitate processing, suggesting information from different modalities (auditory and visual) is rapidly integrated (de Gelder et al., 1999; Dolan, Morris, & de Gelder, 2001). Our brains want to combine all the emotion expressions a person is displaying to infer their feelings, and when that information is contradictory, it impairs our processing ability (Hassin, Aviezer, & Bentin, 2013; Meeren, Heijnsbergen, & de Gelder, 2005). For instance, when participants are instructed to categorize the emotion expressed by an actor's face or voice and ignore their body posture, they are slower when the body expresses an emotion that is incongruent with the face or voice (Van den Stock, Righart, & De Gelder, 2007).

In real life, the information from a single channel (e.g., face, voice, or body) is sometimes ambiguous or inconclusive, perhaps because the expresser's emotion is subtle or she has learned to suppress her expressions. It turns out that in extreme emotion states, facial expressions become less indicative of the underlying emotion because in extreme positive or negative states, people produce loud, scream-like vocalizations that take over their faces (Aviezer, Trope, & Todorov, 2012). In one study, researchers edited photos of tennis players during moments of peak positive (after winning a match) and negative (after losing a match) emotional intensity, combining losing faces with winning bodies (and vice versa; see Figure 5.10). Participants' ratings of the valence expressed by the athletes was entirely dependent on the body, such that an upset face looked happy if paired with a happy, winning body posture.

Researchers are now considering more seriously the importance of placing emotion expressions from one channel, like the face, in the context of the whole person and environment, and, as we have seen, some of the results so far are unexpectedly complicated.

Figure 5.10 Photos of athletes at moments of victory and loss were edited so that the same facial expression occurred with both a winning (1 and 2) and a losing (3 and 4) body. As you can see, the context of the body changes your interpretation of the extreme facial expression. From Aviezer, Trope, & Todorov (2012).

Summary

- Emotion expressions are probably the most important stimuli in social life. They attract attention, and they do so automatically (Lundqvist & Öhman, 2005). Facial expressions impart an enormous amount of information about the emotional state of the expresser, as well as his or her motives and needs.
- Certain facial expressions have functional origins, and similar facial movements are observed in other mammals. Many facial expressions occur in all humans, although culture and socialization do influence how and when emotions are expressed.
- Expressions reflect both underlying emotion states and the social intentions of the expresser.

- Research on the facial feedback hypothesis has shown that these facial expressions not only express, but also influence, the subjective state of the expresser. Indeed, because individuals imitate others' facial expressions, and because expressions can feed back on subjective states, they are useful pieces of information for better understanding and even empathizing with another individual (Zajonc et al., 1987).
- Although faces have received the most attention in emotion expression research, the body and voice are also important for the experience and expression of emotion. Future research on emotion expression will likely involve more whole-person (rather than just face or voice) analyses, as well as dynamic, moving people within environmental contexts as stimuli (e.g., Bänziger, Grandjean, & Scherer, 2009; these stimuli may even occur in immersive virtual reality paradigms, see Gutiérrez-Maldonado, Rus-Calafell, & González-Conde, 2014). In this way, laboratory experiments will come closer to replicating how we actually experience emotions and expressions in the real world.

Learning Links

1. Discover how Disney animates facial expressions. https://www.youtube.com/watch?v=wQYD9ioKLqQ
2. Explore a new technology for transferring the facial expressions of one person to another on computer. https://www.youtube.com/watch?v=9zvTgL2e044

3. Learn more about the muscles involved in producing facial expressions. https://www.you
    tube.com/watch?v=zGqfKY1rjkM
4. Look at how scientists try to produce bodily expression of emotion in robots. https://www.
    youtube.com/watch?v=euW9rKGxSEk

References

Adelmann, P. K., & Zajonc, R. B. (1989). Facial efference and the experience of emotion. *Annual Review of Psychology, 40*(1), 249–280. doi:10.1146/annurev.ps.40.020189.001341.

Adolphs, R. (2002). Neural systems for recognizing emotion. *Current Opinion in Neurobiology, 12*(2), 169–177. doi:10.1016/S0959–4388(02)00301-X.

Andrew, R. J. (1963). The origin and evolution of the calls and facial expressions of the primates. *Behaviour, 20*(1), 1–107.

Atkinson, A. P., Dittrich, W. H., Gemmell, A. J., & Young, A. W. (2004). Emotion perception from dynamic and static body expressions in point-light and full-light displays. *Perception, 33*(6), 717–746. doi:10.1068/p5096.

Aucouturier, J. J., Johansson, P., Hall, L., Segnini, R., Mercadié, L., & Watanabe, K. (2016). Covert digital manipulation of vocal emotion alter speakers' emotional states in a congruent direction. *Proceedings of the National Academy of Sciences, 114*(4), 948–953. doi:10.1073/pnas.1506552113.

Aviezer, H., Trope, Y., & Todorov, A. (2012). Body cues, not facial expressions, discriminate between intense positive and negative emotions. *Science, 338*(6111), 1225–1229. doi:10.1126/science.1224313.

Bachorowski, J. A. (1999). Vocal expression and perception of emotion. *Current Directions in Psychological Science, 8*(2), 53–57. doi:10.1111/1467–8721.00013.

Bänziger, T., Grandjean, D., & Scherer, K. R. (2009). Emotion recognition from expressions in face, voice, and body: The multimodal emotion recognition test (MERT). *Emotion, 9*(5), 691–704. doi:10.1037/a0017088.

Barrett, L. F. (2006). Are emotions natural kinds? *Perspectives on psychological science (Wiley-Blackwell), 1*(1), 28–58. doi:10.1111/j.1745–6916.2006.00003.x.

Brownlow, S., Dixon, A. R., Egbert, C. A., & Radcliffe, R. D. (1997). Perception of movement and dancer characteristics from point-light displays of dance. *The Psychological Record, 47*(3), 411–421.

Buck, R. (1978). The slide-viewing technique for measuring nonverbal sending accuracy: A guide for replication. *Catalog of Selected Documents in Psychology, 8*, 63.

Buck, R. (1980). Nonverbal behavior and the theory of emotion: The facial feedback hypothesis. *Journal of Personality and Social Psychology, 38*(5), 811–824. doi:10.1037/0022–3514.38.5.811.

Buck, R., Losow, J. I., Murphy, M. M., & Costanzo, P. (1992). Social facilitation and inhibition of emotional expression and communication. *Journal of Personality and Social Psychology, 63*(6), 962–968. doi:10.1037/0022–3514.63.6.962.

Camras, L. A., Holland, E. A., & Patterson, M. J. (1993). Facial expression. In M. Lewis & J. M. Haviland (Eds.), *Handbook of emotions* (pp. 199–208). New York: Guilford Press.

Castellano, G., Villalba, S. D., & Camurri, A. (2007). Recognising human emotions from body movement and gesture dynamics. In A. Paiva, R. Prada & R. Picard (Eds.), *Affective computing and intelligent interaction* (pp. 71–82). Berlin Heidelberg: Springer. doi:10.1007/978–3–540–74889–2_7.

Cattaneo, L., & Pavesi, G. (2014). The facial motor system. *Neuroscience and Biobehavioral Reviews*, 38, 135–159. doi:10.1016/j.neubiorev.2013.11.002.

Changizi, M. A., Zhang, Q., & Shimojo, S. (2006). Bare skin, blood and the evolution of primate colour vision. *Biology Letters, 2*(2), 217–221. doi:10.1098/rsbl.2006.0440.

Chovil, N. (1991). Social determinants of facial displays. *Journal of Nonverbal Behavior, 15*(3), 141–154. doi:10.1007/BF01672216.

Cross, E. S., Hamilton, A. F. D. C., & Grafton, S. T. (2006). Building a motor simulation de novo: Observation of dance by dancers. *Neuroimage, 31*(3), 1257–1267. doi:10.1016/j.neuroimage.2006.01.033.

Cummings, K. E., & Clements, M. A. (1995). Analysis of the glottal excitation of emotionally styled and stressed speech. *The Journal of the Acoustical Society of America, 98*(1), 88–98. doi:10.1121/1.413664.

Darwin, C. (1872/1998). *The expression of emotions in man and animals*. New York: Philosophical Library. doi:10.1037/10001–000.

Davila-Ross, M., Jesus, G., Osborne, J., & Bard, K. A. (2015). Chimpanzees (*Pan troglodytes*) produce the same types of 'laugh faces' when they emit laughter and when they are silent. *PLoS One*, *10*(6), e0127337. doi:10.1371/journal.pone.0127337.

de Gelder, B., Böcker, K. B., Tuomainen, J., Hensen, M., & Vroomen, J. (1999). The combined perception of emotion from voice and face: Early interaction revealed by human electric brain responses. *Neuroscience Letters*, *260*(2), 133–136. doi:10.1016/S0304-3940(98)00963-X.

De Meijer, M. (1989). The contribution of general features of body movement to the attribution of emotions. *Journal of Nonverbal Behavior*, *13*(4), 247–268. doi:10.1007/BF00990296.

Dimberg, U., Thunberg, M., & Grunedal, S. (2002). Facial reactions to emotional stimuli: Automatically controlled emotional responses. *Cognition & Emotion*, *16*(4), 449–471. doi:10.1080/02699930143000356.

Dittrich, W. H., Troscianko, T., Lea, S. E., & Morgan, D. (1996). Perception of emotion from dynamic point-light displays represented in dance. *Perception*, *25*(6), 727–738. doi:10.1068/p250727.

Dolan, R. J., Morris, J. S., & de Gelder, B. (2001). Crossmodal binding of fear in voice and face. *Proceedings of the National Academy of Sciences*, *98*(17), 10006–10010. doi:10.1073/pnas.171288598.

Donovan, W. L., & Leavitt, L. A. (1985). Physiology and behavior: Parents' responses to the infant cry. In B. M. Lester & C. F. Z. Boukydis (Eds.), *Infant crying: Theoretical and research perspectives* (pp. 241–261). New York: Plenum. doi:10.1007/978-1-4613-2381-5_11.

Eibl-Eibesfeldt, I. (1973). *Love and hate: On the natural history of basic behaviour patterns*. New York: Aldine de Gruyter.

Ekman, P. (1972). Universals and cultural different in facial expression of emotion. In J. R. Cole (Ed.), *Nebraska symposium on motivation* (pp. 207–283). Lincoln, NE: University of Nebraska Press.

Ekman, P. (1973). Cross-cultural studies of facial expression. In P. Ekman (Ed.), *Darwin and facial expression* (pp. 169–220). New York: Academic Press.

Ekman, P. (1994). All emotions are basic. In P. Ekman & R. Davidson (Eds.), *The nature of emotion: Fundamental questions* (pp. 15–19). New York: Oxford University Press.

Ekman, P., & Friesen, W. V. (1971). Constants across cultures in the face and emotion. *Journal of Personality and Social Psychology*, *17*(2), 124–129. doi:10.1037/h0030377.

Ekman, P., Sorenson, E. R., & Friesen, W. V. (1969). Pan-cultural elements in facial displays of emotion. *Science*, *164*(3875), 86–88. doi:10.1126/science.164.3875.86.

Elfenbein, H. A. (2013). Nonverbal dialects and accents in facial expressions of emotion. *Emotion Review*, *5*(1), 90–96. doi:10.1177/1754073912451332.

Elfenbein, H. A., & Ambady, N. (2002). On the universality and cultural specificity of emotion recognition: A meta-analysis. *Psychological Bulletin*, *128*(2), 203–235. doi:10.1037/0033-2909.128.2.203.

Feldman, R. (2007). Parent-infant synchrony and the construction of shared timing; physiological precursors, developmental outcomes, and risk conditions. *Journal of Child Psychology and Psychiatry*, *48*(3–4), 329–354. doi:10.1111/j.1469-7610.2006.01701.x.

Finzi, E., & Rosenthal, N. E. (2014). Treatment of depression with onabotulinumtoxina: A randomized, double-blind, placebo controlled trial. *Journal of Psychiatric Research*, *52*, 1–6. doi:10.1016/j.jpsychires.2013.11.006.

Flack, W. J. (2006). Peripheral feedback effects of facial expressions, bodily postures, and vocal expressions on emotional feelings. *Cognition and Emotion*, *20*(2), 177–195. doi:10.1080/02699930500359617.

Fridlund, A. J. (1992). The behavioral ecology and sociality of human faces. In M. S. Clark (Ed.), *Emotion* (pp. 90–121). Thousand Oaks, CA: Sage Publications.

Fridlund, A. J. (1994). *Human facial expression: An evolutionary view*. San Diego, CA: Academic Press.

Fridlund, A. J. (1997). The new ethology of human facial expressions. In J. A. Russell & J. M. Fernández-Dols (Eds.), *The psychology of facial expression* (pp. 103–129). Cambridge: Cambridge University Press. doi:10.1017/CBO9780511659911.007.

Gil, S., Teissèdre, F., Chambres, P., & Droit-Volet, S. (2011). The evaluation of emotional facial expressions in early postpartum depression mood: A difference between adult and baby faces? *Psychiatry Research*, *186*(2), 281–286. doi:10.1016/j.psychres.2010.06.015.

Gutiérrez-Maldonado, J., Rus-Calafell, M., & González-Conde, J. (2014). Creation of a new set of dynamic virtual reality faces for the assessment and training of facial emotion recognition ability. *Virtual Reality*, *18*(1), 61–71. doi:10.1007/s10055-013-0236-7.

Haidt, J., & Keltner, D. (1999). Culture and facial expression: Open-ended methods find more expressions and a gradient of recognition. *Cognition and Emotion*, *13*(3), 225–266. doi:10.1080/026999399379168.

Hassin, R. R., Aviezer, H., & Bentin, S. (2013). Inherently ambiguous: Facial expressions of emotions, in context. *Emotion Review*, *5*(1), 60–65. doi:10.1177/1754073912451331.

Hess, U., Banse, R., & Kappas, A. (1995). The intensity of facial expression is determined by underlying affective state and social situation. *Journal of Personality and Social Psychology*, *69*(2), 280–288. doi:10.1037/0022–3514.69.2.280.

Hess, U., & Fischer, A. (2013). Emotional mimicry as social regulation. *Personality and Social Psychology Review*, *17*(2), 142–157. doi:10.1177/1088868312472607.

Hess, U., & Fischer, A. (2014). Emotional mimicry: Why and when we mimic emotions. *Social and Personality Psychology Compass*, *8*(2), 45–57. doi:10.1111/spc3.12083.

Hyniewska, S., & Sato, W. (2015). Facial feedback affects valence judgments of dynamic and static emotional expressions. *Frontiers in Psychology*, *6*, 291. doi:10.3389/fpsyg.2015.00291.

Izard, C. E. (1971). *The face of emotion*. New York: Appleton-Century-Crofts.

Izard, C. E. (1990). Facial expressions and the regulation of emotions. *Journal of Personality and Social Psychology*, *58*(3), 487–498. doi:10.1037/0022–3514.58.3.487.

Jakobs, E., Manstead, A. S., & Fischer, A. H. (1999). Social motives and emotional feelings as determinants of facial displays: The case of smiling. *Personality and Social Psychology Bulletin*, *25*(4), 424–435. doi:10.1177/0146167299025004003.

Jakobs, E., Manstead, A. S., & Fischer, A. H. (2001). Social context effects on facial activity in a negative emotional setting. *Emotion*, *1*(1), 51–69. doi:10.1037/1528–3542.1.1.51.

Johnson, K. J., Waugh, C. E., & Fredrickson, B. L. (2010). Smile to see the forest: Facially expressed positive emotions broaden cognition. *Cognition and Emotion*, *24*(2), 299–321. doi:10.1080/02699930903384667.

Johnstone, T., & Scherer, K. R. (2000). Vocal communication of emotion. In M. Lewis & J. M. Haviland-Jones (Eds.), *Handbook of emotions* (2nd ed., pp. 226–235). New York: Guilford Press.

Juslin, P. N. (2013). From everyday emotions to aesthetic emotions: Towards a unified theory of musical emotions. *Physics of Life Reviews*, *10*(3), 235–266. doi:10.1016/j.plrev.2013.05.008.

Juslin, P. N., & Scherer, K. R. (2005). Vocal expression of affect. In J. A. Harrigan, R. Rosenthal & K. R. Scherer (Eds.), *The new handbook of methods in nonverbal behavior research* (pp. 65–135). New York: Oxford University Press.

Kato, M., & Konishi, Y. (2013). Where and how infants look: The development of scan paths and fixations in face perception. *Infant Behavior & Development*, *36*(1), 32–41. doi:10.1016/j.infbeh.2012.10.005.

Kopel, S. A., & Arkowitz, H. S. (1974). Role playing as a source of self-observation and behavior change. *Journal of Personality and Social Psychology*, *29*(5), 677–686. doi:10.1037/h0036675.

Kraft, T. L., & Pressman, S. D. (2012). Grin and bear it: The influence of manipulated facial expression on the stress response. *Psychological Science*, *23*(11), 1372–1378. doi:10.1177/0956797611244531.

Kraut, R. E. (1982). Social presence, facial feedback, and emotion. *Journal of Personality and Social Psychology*, *42*(5), 853–863. doi:10.1037/0022–3514.42.5.853.

Kraut, R. E., & Johnston, R. E. (1979). Social and emotional messages of smiling: An ethological approach. *Journal of Personality and Social Psychology*, *37*(9), 1539–1553. doi:10.1037/0022–3514.37.9.1539.

Krusemark, E. A., & Li, W. (2011). Do all threats work the same way? Divergent effects of fear and disgust on sensory perception and attention. *The Journal of Neuroscience*, *31*(9), 3429–3434. doi:10.1523/jneurosci.4394–10.2011.

Künecke, J., Hildebrandt, A., Recio, G., Sommer, W., & Wilhelm, O. (2014). Facial EMG responses to emotional expressions are related to emotion perception ability. *PLoS One*, *9*(1), e84053. doi:10.1371/journal.pone.0084053.

Laird, J. D. (1974). Self-attribution of emotion: The effects of expressive behavior on the quality of emotional experience. *Journal of Personality and Social Psychology*, *29*(4), 475–486. doi:10.1037/h0036125.

Lakin, J. L., Jefferis, V. E., Cheng, C. M., & Chartrand, T. L. (2003). The chameleon effect as social glue: Evidence for the evolutionary significance of nonconscious mimicry. *Journal of Nonverbal Behavior*, *27*(3), 145–162. doi:10.1023/A:1025389814290.

Lanzetta, J. T., Cartwright-Smith, J., & Eleck, R. E. (1976). Effects of nonverbal dissimulation on emotional experience and autonomic arousal. *Journal of Personality and Social Psychology*, *33*(3), 354–370. doi: 10.1037/0022-3514.33.3.354.

Lavan, N., Scott, S. K., & McGettigan, C. (2015). Laugh like you mean it: Authenticity modulates acoustic, physiological and perceptual properties of laughter. *Journal of Nonverbal Behavior*, *40*, 1–17. doi:10.1007/s10919–015–0222–8.

Lee, D. H., Susskind, J. M., & Anderson, A. K. (2013). Social transmission of the sensory benefits of eye widening in fear expressions. *Psychological Science*, *24*(6), 957–965. doi:10.1177/0956797612464500.

Lee, V., & Wagner, H. (2002). The effect of social presence on the facial and verbal expression of emotion and the interrelationships among emotion components. *Journal of Nonverbal Behavior*, *26*(1), 3–25. doi:10.1023/A:1014479919684.

Lewis, M. B. (2012). Exploring the positive and negative implications of facial feedback. *Emotion*, *12*(4), 852–859. doi:10.1037/a0029275.

Lundqvist, D., & Ohman, A. (2005). Emotion regulates attention: The relation between facial configurations, facial emotion, and visual attention. *Visual Cognition*, *12*(1), 51–84. doi: 10.1080/13506280444000085.

Manstead, A. R., Fischer, A. H., & Jakobs, E. B. (1999). The social and emotional functions of facial displays. In P. Philippot, R. S. Feldman & E. J. Coats (Eds.), *The social context of nonverbal behavior* (pp. 287–313). New York; Paris, France: Cambridge University Press.

Martinez, L., Falvello, V. B., Aviezer, H., & Todorov, A. (2015). Contributions of facial expressions and body language to the rapid perception of dynamic emotions. *Cognition and Emotion, 30*(5), 1–14. doi: 10.1080/02699931.2015.1035229.

Matsumoto, D. (1987). The role of facial response in the experience of emotion: More methodological problems and a meta-analysis. *Journal of Personality and Social Psychology*, *52*(4), 769–774. doi:10.1037/0022–3514.52.4.769.

Matsumoto, D., Keltner, D., Shiota, M. N., O'Sullivan, M., & Frank, M. (2008). Facial expressions of emotion. In M. Lewis, J. M. Haviland-Jones & L. F. Barrett (Eds.), *Handbook of emotions* (3rd ed., pp. 211–234). New York: Guilford Press.

Matsumoto, D., & Willingham, B. (2006). The thrill of victory and the agony of defeat: Spontaneous expressions of medal winners of the 2004 Athens Olympic games. *Journal of Personality and Social Psychology*, *91*(3), 568–581. doi:10.1037/0022–3514.91.3.568.

Matsumoto, D., & Willingham, B. (2009). Spontaneous facial expressions of emotion of congenitally and noncongenitally blind individuals. *Journal of Personality and Social Psychology*, *96*(1), 1–10. doi:10.1037/a0014037.

Matsumoto, D., Yoo, S. H., Hirayama, S., & Petrova, G. (2005). Development and validation of a measure of display rule knowledge: The display rule assessment inventory. *Emotion*, *5*(1), 23–40. doi:10.1037/1528–3542.5.1.23.

Mauss, I. B., Levenson, R. W., McCarter, L., Wilhelm, F. H., & Gross, J. J. (2005). The tie that binds? Coherence among emotion experience, behavior, and physiology. *Emotion*, *5*(2), 175–190. doi:10.1037/1528–3542.5.2.175.

McCanne, T. R., & Anderson, J. A. (1987). Emotional responding following experimental manipulation of facial electromyographic activity. *Journal of Personality and Social Psychology*, *52*(4), 759–768. doi:10.1037/0022–3514.52.4.759.

McIntosh, D. N. (1996). Facial feedback hypotheses: Evidence, implications, and directions. *Motivation and Emotion*, *20*(2), 121–147. doi:10.1007/BF02253868.

Meeren, H. K., van Heijnsbergen, C. C., & de Gelder, B. (2005). Rapid perceptual integration of facial expression and emotional body language. *Proceedings of the National Academy of Sciences of the United States of America*, *102*(45), 16518–16523. doi:10.1073/pnas.0507650102.

Neal, D. T., & Chartrand, T. L. (2011). Embodied emotion perception: Amplifying and dampening facial feedback modulates emotion perception accuracy. *Social Psychological and Personality Science*, *2*(6), 673–678. doi:10.1177/1948550611406138.

Nelson, N. L., & Russell, J. A. (2013). Universality revisited. *Emotion Review*, *5*(1), 8–15. doi:10.1177/1754073912457227.

Niedenthal, P. M. (2007). Embodying emotion. *Science*, *316*(5827), 1002–1005. doi:10.1126/science.1136930.

Niedenthal, P. M., Brauer, M., Halberstadt, J. B., & Innes-Ker, Å. H. (2001). When did her smile drop? Facial mimicry and the influences of emotional state on the detection of change in emotional expression. *Cognition & Emotion, 15*(6), 853–864. doi:10.1080/02699930143000194.

Niedenthal, P. M., Mermillod, M., Maringer, M., & Hess, U. (2010). The simulation of smiles (SIMS) model: Embodied simulation and the meaning of facial expression. *Behavioral and Brain Sciences, 33*(6), 417–433. doi:10.1017/S0140525X10000865.

Panksepp, J., & Biven, L. (2012). *The archaeology of mind: Neuroevolutionary origins of human emotion.* New York: W W Norton & Co.

Parr, L. A., & Waller, B. M. (2006). Understanding chimpanzee facial expression: Insights into the evolution of communication. *Social Cognitive and Affective Neuroscience, 1*(3), 221–228. doi:10.1093/scan/nsl031.

Rinn, W. E. (1984). The neuropsychology of facial expression: A review of the neurological and psychological mechanisms for producing facial expressions. *Psychological Bulletin, 95*(1), 52–77. doi:10.1037/0033–2909.95.1.52.

Rinn, W. E. (1991). Neuropsychology of facial expression. In R. S. Feldman & B. Rimé (Eds.), *Fundamentals of nonverbal behavior* (pp. 3–30). New York; Paris, France: Cambridge University Press.

Rozin, P., & Fallon, A. E. (1987). A perspective on disgust. *Psychological Review, 94*(1), 23–41. doi:10.1037/0033–295X.94.1.23.

Ruiz-Belda, M., Fernández-Dols, J., Carrera, P., & Barchard, K. (2003). Spontaneous facial expressions of happy bowlers and soccer fans. *Cognition and Emotion, 17*(2), 315–326. doi:10.1080/02699930302288.

Russell, J. A. (1994). Is there universal recognition of emotion from facial expressions? A review of the cross-cultural studies. *Psychological Bulletin, 115*(1), 102–141. doi:10.1037/0033–2909.115.1.102.

Rychlowska, M., Cañadas, E., Wood, A., Krumhuber, E. G., Fischer, A., & Niedenthal, P. M. (2014). Blocking mimicry makes true and false smiles look the same. *PloS One, 9*(3), e90876. doi:10.1371/journal.pone.0090876.

Santana, S. E., Dobson, S. D., & Diogo, R. (2014). Plain faces are more expressive: Comparative study of facial colour, mobility and musculature in primates. *Biology Letters, 10*(5), 20140275. doi:10.1098/rsbl.2014.0275.

Sato, W., & Yoshikawa, S. (2007). Spontaneous facial mimicry in response to dynamic facial expressions. *Cognition, 104*(1), 1–18. doi:10.1016/j.cognition.2006.05.001.

Sauter, D. A., Eisner, F., Ekman, P., & Scott, S. K. (2010). Cross-cultural recognition of basic emotions through nonverbal emotional vocalizations. *Proceedings of the National Academy of Sciences, 107*(6), 2408–2412. doi:10.1073/pnas.0908239106.

Siegman, A. W., Anderson, R. A., & Berger, T. (1990). The angry voice: Its effects on the experience of anger and cardiovascular reactivity. *Psychosomatic Medicine, 52*(6), 631–643.

Sievers, B., Polansky, L., Casey, M., & Wheatley, T. (2013). Music and movement share a dynamic structure that supports universal expressions of emotion. *Proceedings of the National Academy of Sciences, 110*(1), 70–75. doi:10.1073/pnas.1209023110.

Simon-Thomas, E. R., Keltner, D. J., Sauter, D., Sinicropi-Yao, L., & Abramson, A. (2009). The voice conveys specific emotions: Evidence from vocal burst displays. *Emotion, 9*(6), 838–846. doi:10.1037/a0017810.

Snowdon, C. T., & Teie, D. (2013). Emotional communication in monkeys: Music to their ears? In E. Altenmüller, S. Schmidt & E. Zimmermann (Eds.), *The evolution of emotional communication: From sounds in nonhuman mammals to speech and music in man* (pp. 133–151). Oxford: Oxford University Press.

Stel, M., & van Knippenberg, A. (2008). The role of facial mimicry in the recognition of affect. *Psychological Science, 19*(10), 984–985. doi:10.1111/j.1467–9280.2008.02188.x.

Stenberg, C. R., & Campos, J. J. (1990). The development of anger expressions in infancy. In N. L. Stein, B. Leventhal & T. Trabasso (Eds.), *Psychological and biological approaches to emotion* (pp. 447–282). Hillsdale, NJ, England: Lawrence Erlbaum Associates.

Strack, F., Martin, L. L., & Stepper, S. (1988). Inhibiting and facilitating conditions of the human smile: A nonobtrusive test of the facial feedback hypothesis. *Journal of Personality and Social Psychology, 54*(5), 768–777. doi:10.1037/0022–3514.54.5.768.

Susskind, J. M., & Anderson, A. K. (2008). Facial expression form and function. *Communicative & Integrative Biology, 1*(2), 148–149. doi:10.4161/cib.1.2.6999.

Susskind, J. M., Lee, D. H., Cusi, A., Feiman, R., Grabski, W., & Anderson, A. K. (2008). Expressing fear enhances sensory acquisition. *Nature Neuroscience, 11*(7), 843–850. doi:10.1038/nn.2138.

Tartter, V. C. (1980). Happy talk: Perceptual and acoustic effects of smiling on speech. *Perception & Psychophysics, 27*(1), 24–27.

Thompson, J. (1941). Development of facial expression of emotion in blind and seeing children. *Archives of Psychology (Columbia University), 264*, 47.

Tomkins, S. S. (1962). *Affect, imagery, consciousness: Vol. I: The positive affects.* New York: Springer-Verlag.

Tomkins, S. S. (1963). *Affect, imagery, consciousness: Vol. 2: The negative affects.* New York: Springer-Verlag.

Tracy, J. L., & Matsumoto, D. (2008). The spontaneous expression of pride and shame: Evidence for biologically innate nonverbal displays. *Proceedings of the National Academy of Sciences, 105*(33), 11655–11660.

Trevarthen, C. (1979). Communication and cooperation in early infancy: A description of primary intersubjectivity. In M. Bullowa (Ed.), *Before speech: The beginning of human communication* (pp. 321–347). New York: Cambridge University Press.

Van den Stock, J., Righart, R., & De Gelder, B. (2007). Body expressions influence recognition of emotions in the face and voice. *Emotion, 7*(3), 487–494. doi:10.1037/1528–3542.7.3.487.

van Hooff, J. (1976). The comparison of the facial expressions in man and higher primates. In M. con Craanach (Ed.), *Methods of inference from animal to human behavior* (3rd ed., pp. 165–196). Chicago, IL: Aldine.

VanSwearingen, J. M., Cohn, J. F., & Bajaj-Luthra, A. (1999). Specific impairment of smiling increases the severity of depressive symptoms in patients with facial neuromuscular disorders. *Aesthetic Plastic Surgery, 23*(6), 416–423. doi:10.1007/s002669900312.

Wagenmakers E.-J., Beek T., Dijkhoff L., Gronau Q. F., Acosta A., Adams R. B. Jr., . . . Zwaan R. A. (2016). Registered Replication Report: Strack, Martin, & Stepper(1988). Perspectives on Psychological Science, 11. doi:10.1177/1745691616674458.

Waller, B. M., & Dunbar, R. M. (2005). Differential behavioural effects of silent bared teeth display and relaxed open mouth display in chimpanzees (Pan troglodytes). *Ethology, 111*(2), 129–142. doi:10.1111/j.1439–0310.2004.01045.x.

West, G. L., Al-Aidroos, N., Susskind, J., & Pratt, J. (2011). Emotion and action: The effect of fear on saccadic performance. *Experimental Brain Research, 209*(1), 153–158. doi:10.1007/s00221–010–2508–8.

Wood, A., Rychlowska, M., Korb, S., & Niedenthal, P. (2016). Fashioning the face: Sensorimotor simulation contributes to facial expression recognition. *Trends in Cognitive Sciences, 20*(3), 227–240. doi:10.1016/j.tics.2015.12.010.

Yang, B., & Lugger, M. (2010). Emotion recognition from speech signals using new harmony features. *Signal Processing, 90*(5), 1415–1423. doi:10.1016/j.sigpro.2009.09.009.

Zajonc, R. B., Adelmann, P. K., Murphy, S. T., & Niedenthal, P. M. (1987). Convergence in the physical appearance of spouses. *Motivation and Emotion, 11*(4), 335–346. doi:10.1007/BF00992848.

Zajonc, R. B., Murphy, S. T., & Inglehart, M. (1989). Feeling and facial efference: Implications of the vascular theory of emotion. *Psychological Review, 96*(3), 395–416. doi:10.1037/0033–295X.96.3.395.

Zuckerman, M., Klorman, R., Larrance, D. T., & Spiegel, N. H. (1981). Facial, autonomic, and subjective components of emotion: The facial feedback hypothesis versus the externalizer–internalizer distinction. *Journal of Personality and Social Psychology, 41*(5), 929–944. doi:10.1037/0022–3514.41.5.929.

6   Self-Conscious Emotions

Contents at a Glance

Here is a question that students often ask when they take a class on the topic of human emotion: "Is it unhealthy to be jealous?" A boyfriend or girlfriend may have accused them of being too jealous. Or worse—their relationships fail because of their tendency to be jealous. Although in Chapter 1 we spent some time describing the so-called basic emotions, which we also examined in our functional analysis in Chapter 4, we look at yet more complex emotions that might be of even greater concern and interest to the average individual. These include jealousy, but also shame, guilt, envy, embarrassment, pride, and hubris—all of which have important inter-personal implications and social and moral functions (Fischer & Manstead, 2008; Haidt, 2003; Niedenthal & Brauer, 2012). In fact, the emotions discussed in this chapter—**self-conscious emotions**—occupy a central role in motivating and regulating almost all of people's thoughts, feelings, and behaviors (Fischer & Tangney, 1995). Most individuals spend a great deal of time avoiding social disapproval or rejection, which are the circumstances that can cause shame, guilt, or embarrassment to arise. People also organize their social lives in order to regulate the extent to which they must deal with feelings of jealousy or envy.

Defining Self-Conscious Emotions

In contrast to the basic emotions, self-conscious emotions 1) emerge later in development because they rely on mental abilities that are not fully in place until after about two years of age; 2) do not have distinct facial expressions, although some have universally recognizable gestures that involve the face and the body (Tracy, Robins, & Shrieber, 2009); and 3) most likely evolved for the management of social relationships rather than for individual survival (see Table 6.1 for summary). The management of social relationships, for both humans and many animals, typi-cally includes the tasks of creating and nurturing social bonds ("getting along") and acquiring social status ("getting ahead") (Fischer & Manstead, 2008; Tracy & Robins, 2004).

Cognitive Achievements Underlying Self-Conscious Emotions

Self-conscious emotions are **cognition-dependent** emotions (Izard, Ackerman, & Schultz, 1999). The name conveys the idea that these emotions do not occur fully until certain cognitive capacities have developed (Harter, 1999; Lewis et al., 1989; Tangney & Fischer, 1995).

The experience of self-conscious emotions requires that an individual is first capable of distinguishing the self as physically distinct from others (e.g., as separate from the mother; Figure 6.1). A **self-concept**, or a sense of self, develops in toddlerhood, beginning around the age of two. At this time, typically developing children begin to use pronouns such as "I," "me," and "mine." They also show evidence of self-awareness in an experimental task called the rouge test. In the rouge test, a small red dot is covertly applied to a child's nose. The child is then given the opportunity to look in a mirror. If the child touches the red dot on herself or tries to wipe it off, she is said to have developed a self-concept (Lewis & Brooks-Gunn, 1979). Without some recognition that the person in the mirror is herself, the child would make no effort to remove the anomaly from her own face. The role of a sense of self in self-conscious emotions is further emphasized by research demonstrating that primates, such as orangutans and chimpanzees, that engage in self-representational processes reliably display self-conscious emotions such as embarrassment and pride (Hart & Karmel, 1996; Russon & Galdikas, 1993).

Table 6.1 A comparison of basic and self-conscious emotions

Type of Emotion	Basic	Self-Conscious
Development	During first 9 months	After 18 months
Function	Individual survival	Group living
Cognitive achievement	Perception, categorization	Self-reflection, self-evaluation, social comparison
Universal display	Facial expression	Complex displays for some

Figure 6.1 After the age of two years, children start to have a sense of self that allows them to differentiate themselves from other people.

In contrast, animals that lack a sense of self appear not to experience such emotions (despite the fact that their owners might claim that they do).

Two other cognitive achievements arise from a child's self-concept: self-evaluation and self-comparison. In **self-evaluation**, which also develops after about two years of age, children begin to internalize standards and norms taught by caretakers and reinforced by society (Lewis, 2000). They then assess the extent to which they are conforming to such standards and norms and judge themselves and their behaviors as good or bad. In **social comparison**, which emerges much later than two years of age, children evaluate how attractive, shy, intelligent, or poor they are by contrast to the appearance, personality, intelligence, or wealth of other people. Social comparison is a process that almost all people use to figure out how they feel about themselves, their abilities, and their outcomes (Mussweiler, Rüter, & Epstude, 2004).

In the first section of this chapter, we review the **self-evaluative** emotions. These emotions, which include guilt, shame, embarrassment, pride, and hubris, are largely related to evaluations of the self, and are based on comparisons to personal standards, as well as moral values (what is right and wrong). In the second section of the chapter, we examine **social comparison** emotions. These emotions, envy and jealousy, largely involve comparisons of the self to qualities, possessions, and outcomes of other individuals.

Self-Evaluative Emotions

Self-evaluative emotions derive from the ability to make good/bad judgments about the self. The emotions of shame, guilt, and embarrassment arise when the self or something about the self is evaluated negatively; pride and hubris arise when the self or something about the self is evaluated positively (Taylor, 1985).

Guilt and Shame

Guilt and shame are punishing states, with distinct feelings and action tendencies (e.g., Lindsay-Hartz, 1984; Tangney, 1990, 1991; Tangney & Tracy, 2012). The feeling of guilt is one of heightened arousal and remorse. It arises when a person recognizes that she has engaged in an action that hurt someone else and falls short of her own or society's standards (Berndsen et al., 2004). People who feel guilt usually appraise themselves as being in control of and responsible for the situation, and also believe it is possible to set the situation right, at least by changing their behavior in the future (Wicker, Payne, & Morgan, 1983). The action tendencies associated with guilt are a desire to directly or indirectly make amends. Specifically, when feeling guilt, people experience a need to make things right, to reaffirm their beliefs about moral systems, and to seek forgiveness in some way for their hurtful actions (Frijda, Kuipers, & Ter Schure, 1989; Lindsay-Hartz, 1984).

Shame is thought to be the more painful and distressing of these two self-evaluative emotions. The feeling of **shame** is marked by hopelessness and the sense that one's entire self is worthless, powerless, and small (Lindsay-Hartz, 1984). Shame arises when a person recognizes that she has failed or violated a social norm and believes such failures stem from an aspect of herself that she cannot alter or control. Shame has been shown to be associated with specific action tendencies. These include the action tendency to run and hide or to become smaller and disappear from the situation (De Hooge, Zeelenberg, & Breugelmans, 2007). Shame (but not guilt) also appears to be associated with a distinct bodily expression. When feeling shame, people hang their head and shoulders, drop their arms to their sides, and gaze downward. This display is reliably recognized as related to shame in many cultures (Tracy & Robins, 2008). Furthermore, the display is shown by the congenitally blind (Tracy & Matsumoto, 2008), suggesting it is universal.

In studies of the events that give rise to guilt, individuals tend to describe specific moral transgressions that have harmed someone else (Ausubel, 1955; de Rivera, 1977; Lewis, 1971; Taylor, 1985). These include lying, cheating, stealing, and infidelity. Shame arises more often from situations that threaten one's social esteem, social status, or social acceptance (Kemeny, Gruenewald, & Dickerson, 2004), such as public failure or defeat, social rejection (including sexual rebuffs and contempt from others), and exposure or invasion of personal privacy. However, it should be noted that no situation is exclusively associated with one or the other of these two emotions. Moral transgressions also provoke shame, and failures also provoke guilt in some individuals (Tangney, 1992; Tracy & Robins, 2006).

Distinguishing Guilt and Shame

Because guilt and shame can arise in similar situations, one might wonder what makes one person react to a situation with guilt and another person react to the same situation with shame. Lewis (1971) proposed that it is a matter of the individual's assessment of the cause of the negative situation. Guilt arises when we focus on our unacceptable behavior as the cause, and shame arises when we focus on our entire self as the cause. Both are evaluations of the self, but the object of evaluation varies: "I feel guilty about my behavior" versus "I feel ashamed of myself." In order to make this distinction, imagine this scenario:

> Your good friend, who rarely dates, invites you to attend a party with him/her and his/her date, Chris. It is your friend's first date with Chris. You go along and discover that Chris is not only very attractive, but is also flirting with you. You flirt back. Although you are not seriously interested in him/her, at the end of the night you give Chris your phone number. The next day, your good friend raves to you about how much he/she liked Chris.
>
> (from Niedenthal, Tangney, & Gavanski, 1994)

Let's face it. If this happened to you, you would feel bad. But would you feel guilt or would you feel shame? According to Lewis (1971), if you evaluated your flirting and acquiring Chris's phone number as hurtful, you would feel guilt. But if you found yourself confessing, "I'm such a bad person," that would be shame.

Niedenthal, Tangney, and Gavanski (1994) found further confirmation of Lewis's distinction in their study of **counterfactual thinking**. Counterfactual thinking is the process of mentally "undoing" a situation that has already happened (Roese & Olson, 1995). Such thinking often takes this form: "If only something had been different, then this situation would not have occurred." For instance, if a man's car broke down on vacation, he might think, "If only I had had the car serviced before leaving town, it would not have broken down."

Importantly, the agent that people mentally change when reflecting on a past situation is the very thing that they think caused the situation (Wells & Gavanski, 1989). Thus, in the car situation, the person is implying that he identifies himself as the cause of the trouble because in his counterfactual thought, he mentally alters his own action, or, in this case, inaction: he did not have the car serviced. Alternatively, the man might think, "If only my wife had had the car serviced, it would not have broken down," reflecting the fact that he sees his partner as the cause, or he could think, "If only Fords were not such unreliable cars, my car would not have broken down," implicating a car company as the root of the problem.

Niedenthal and colleagues studied the content of counterfactual thinking following experiences that provoke guilt and shame. In one study, the researchers examined individuals' counterfactual thoughts about past autobiographical experiences of guilt and shame. In a second study, the researchers provided participants with scenarios designed to provoke feelings of guilt and others designed to provoke feelings of shame. For both studies, the participants were instructed to write down three counterfactual thoughts intended to undo the outcomes of the situations. The content of those thoughts constituted the data of interest.

Analyses of the counterfactuals revealed that, after recalling or imagining guilt-inducing situations, individuals mentally altered their behavior, thinking, "If only I had not [done a bad thing], then this would not have happened." In contrast, after recalling or imagining shame situations, individuals mentally altered themselves, thinking: "If only I weren't [a bad person], then this would not have happened." These findings and many others support Lewis's distinction between the attribution of causality: to behavior in guilt and to the self in shame (Tangney & Dearing, 2002; Tracy & Robins, 2006).

Functions of Guilt and Shame

Theorists tend to agree that shame and guilt play a role in regulating moral behavior (Tangney & Tracy, 2012). Both emotions often arise from the breaking of social norms and the receipt of formal and informal social sanctions (Dienstbier, 1984, 2000; Harris, 1989; Lewis, 1993). From childhood to adulthood, a standard socialization technique consists of inducing feelings of guilt or shame in an individual who has transgressed a norm or behaved inappropriately (Scheff, 1988, 1990; Scherer, 2001).

Phenomenological studies of guilt and shame indicate that these emotions do indeed heighten an individual's feelings of responsibility for his or her actions (e.g., Ferguson, Stegge, & Damhuis, 1991; Lindsay-Hartz, de Rivera, & Mascolo, 1995). So, a general function of these self-evaluative emotions is the development of self-control and the ability to refrain from committing immoral and self-incriminating acts (Tangney, 2002b). The two emotions also have specific functions linked to their action tendencies. Guilt seems to promote behaviors that set things right, and shame seems to promote behaviors that protect the self from further threat.

Many studies have documented the reparative function of guilt (Amodio, Devine, & Harmon-Jones, 2007). For example, Cryder, Springer, and Morewedge (2012) showed that guilt makes people more generous to those they have wronged. In that study, participants were exposed to some "background information" about the experiment they were about to take part in. However, none of the participants actually read the information because, by design of the experimenters, it was needlessly wordy and written in a tiny font. Participants then had the opportunity to taste either red apple–flavored or vomit-flavored jellybeans. Which would you choose? Almost everyone chose the red apple–flavored jellybeans. At this point, a method that had been shown in pilot-testing to be a very effective method of guilt was introduced: Half of the participants were told that the "background information" (which they had not read carefully) had specified that another participant, their partner for the remainder of the study, would have to taste whichever candy they had rejected, though, of course, the partner was a confederate working for the experimenter and did not have to taste any candy. (Control participants did not receive information about the partner having to taste the rejected candy.) Later, all participants played a "behavioral economics" game, in which they got to decide how much money to allocate to their partner. Those who believed they had relegated vomit-flavored jellybeans to their partner earlier in the session gave the partner significantly more money during the game. In other words, the participants who were feeling guilt tried to make up for their behavior and repair the relationship.

Other research also indicates that guilt is associated with heightened empathy (Joireman, 2004; Silfver et al., 2008). And, even when simply anticipating guilt, people tend to engage in more upstanding behavior, including self-constraint (Giner-Sorolla, 2001) and the avoidance of self-indulgent behavior (Zemack-Rugar, Bettman, & Fitzsimons, 2007).

In contrast to guilt, shame is linked to a tendency to exhibit less empathy and perspective taking than usual (Yang, Yang, & Chiou, 2010). A lack of empathy might be expected from a person who feels like hiding and is totally focused on the self. But these action tendencies are also functional for a person who feels the loss, or potential loss, of social esteem, social status, or social acceptance; by withdrawing and disengaging, the shamed individual is no longer putting herself "out there" to be further threatened. The bodily display of shame itself also works to reduce social threat. Such displays tend to elicit cooperation and reductions in aggressive or punitive behavior by interaction partners (Keltner, Young, & Buswell, 1997). Others seem to recognize that the expression of shame communicates that the shamed individual acknowledges his or her defeat, transgression, or failure. They may then be more forgiving of the shamed individual (Keltner, 1995). It seems, therefore, that guilt functions to keep people's behavior in line with social norms and prevents them from engaging in behaviors that hurt others, whereas shame functions to protect people from further loss of esteem and continued social threat (Tangney & Tracy, 2012).

In sum, although guilt and shame are both unpleasant emotions that involve negative evaluations of the self, eliciting guilt in someone appears to be a more productive way to shape their future behavior. The use of shame to change people's behavior may have some unfortunate side effects of limiting their empathic responding and their ability to make amends.

Embarrassment

Think of a time when you felt embarrassed. What happened? Maybe you belched or farted in a crowded elevator. Or maybe you walked into a large room when a university course was already in full swing, and the professor, who was in the middle of a sentence, stopped talking as you entered. You felt something unpleasant, marked by negative self-exposure. The feeling of embarrassment involves a sense of fluster, self-focus, and perhaps mortification, characterized by a sense of foolishness more than a sense of being worthless, as is experienced in shame (e.g., Buss, 1980; Plutchik, 1980).

Keltner (1995) documented a universal gesture of embarrassment. According to his analysis, embarrassment is expressed by a sequence of behaviors that involves, first, *gaze aversion*, then contraction of muscles around the face aimed at *inhibiting smiling*, followed by a *non-Duchenne smile* involving only the upturning of the lips and resembling a sheepish grin, then another attempt to *inhibit smiling*, then a downturn of the head, completed by a tendency to engage in *face touching* usually used to hide the mouth or eyes (Figure 6.2). Keltner and Buswell (1997), moreover, have demonstrated that this sequence does not accompany experiences of shame or amusement.

Embarrassment also has a unique physiological feature: the blush. Blushing, or the visible reddening of the cheeks and neck, accompanies embarrassment exclusively (Miller, 2004). The blush of embarrassment is distinguishable from the blush that is the result of exercise, sexual arousal, or intoxication (Leary et al., 1992). Individuals cannot control the extent to which they blush when embarrassed (Drummond, 2001). But they can control what they, in fact, do most often when they are embarrassed: apologize for their mistake and try to repair it. Unlike guilt, in which the repair involves undoing the harm done to others, in embarrassment, the repair involves redressing harm done to the **presented self**, or the self that others see.

Embarrassment arises in situations in which, compared to shame, much more trivial failures have occurred (Buss, 1980; Lewis, 1992). Parrott, Sabini, and Silver (1988) have proposed that embarrassment specifically results from disruptions in the performance of socially prescribed roles or **scripts**. The valedictorian of a high school graduating class is not following the script—which involves being particularly capable—when he or she trips on the way to the lectern, for instance. Embarrassment also seems to occur only in public, when there is a potential or real loss of esteem (Lewis, 1995). When a person discovers that others are watching while they inadvertently drag toilet paper from the heel of their shoe, they perceive a loss of esteem from

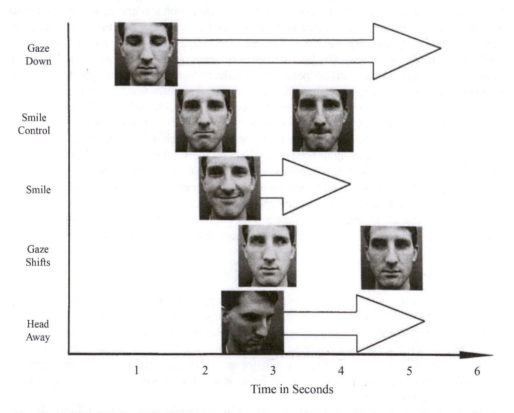

Figure 6.2 Representation of a prototypical embarrassment response. The mean duration of each action is equal to the interval beginning with the leftmost edge of the photograph and ending with the end of the arrow. From Keltner (1995).

others (Miller, 1996; Miller & Leary, 1992; Sabini et al., 2000). A final characteristic of the circumstances that give rise to embarrassment is surprise value. Embarrassment-provoking situations are usually more sudden and unexpected in their onset than are situations that elicit other self-conscious emotions (Gross & Stone, 1964).

Functions of Embarrassment

The function of the nonverbal communication of embarrassment is one of appeasement. This gesture expresses a desire for forgiveness and, thus, for reintegration into a group or relationship. Consistent with this idea, individuals show a need to overtly communicate their embarrassment and continue to feel quite flustered and mortified if this communication is in any way hindered (Leary, Landel, & Patton, 1996). Furthermore, the expression of embarrassment seems to have the prosocial effects that the embarrassed person desires. For example, questionnaire studies of responses to others' embarrassment reveal that we try to help those who express their embarrassment, most often by communicating our acceptance of the embarrassed person in spite of the gaffe or public exposure. When confronted by a display of embarrassment, we also like to share stories of similar embarrassing circumstances.

Developmental Detail

Embarrassment Emerges in Toddlerhood

Though we may think of young kids as being less self-conscious than adolescents, they are certainly not immune from embarrassment. Psychologist Michael Lewis charted the developmental emergence of embarrassment (Lewis, 1995; Lewis et al., 1989). He found two important things. First, there are two types of embarrassment, which he terms "exposure" embarrassment and "evaluation" embarrassment. Exposure embarrassment arises from being the center of attention, such as when you sneeze loudly and everyone turns to look at you. Evaluation embarrassment arises from doing something poorly, such as not completing a task well or in the time allotted. Second, Lewis demonstrated that exposure embarrassment emerges by the end of the second year of life. At that age, toddlers have just learned who they are and they know that everyone is looking at them! After learning more about distinguishing between what is good and bad and right and wrong, at least a year later, the child starts to show signs of evaluation embarrassment.

To further investigate the underlying feelings of exposure and evaluation embarrassment, Lewis and Ramsay (2002) arranged for four-year-old children to fail on a task in order to elicit evaluation embarrassment. Children were then put into situations of being the center of attention, such as dancing with the experimenter to "Old MacDonald," which tended to elicit exposure embarrassment. The child's cortisol (i.e., stress hormone) levels were also measured. Results showed that higher cortisol responses were related to evaluation embarrassment and lower cortisol responses were related to exposure embarrassment. This means that negative self-evaluative reactions are even more stressful than being the object of attention.

These prosocial reactions may be caused by the fact that people actually like individuals who express embarrassment after making a gaffe—even more than they like those who do not. In one laboratory demonstration, Semin and Manstead (1982) showed participants a video of a man who accidentally toppled over a tall pile of toilet paper rolls in a grocery store. In one version of the video, the man expressed embarrassment and in another he made no show of embarrassment. Participants liked the protagonist more if he expressed embarrassment than if he did not. Blushing has a similar effect of eliciting positive reactions. De Jong (1999) had participants read scenarios in which a shopper caused damage in a grocery store and then either blushed or did not blush. The shopper who blushed was evaluated more favorably than the one who did not blush. So bodily displays of embarrassment and blushing can serve to repair social relationships following an accidental violation of social expectations (Feinberg, Willer, & Keltner, 2012).

Pride and Hubris

Pride is an emotion that arises from a positive assessment of the self (Lewis, 2000b). It is a state that involves satisfaction with meeting one's own personal standards and goals, including internalized beliefs about right and wrong (Tangney, 2002a; Tracy & Robins, 2004b). Of course, if pride is nice sounding, one might ask, why do Judeo-Christian and other religious writings teach that "pride goeth before a fall?" Why does pride also have a negative connotation, as in a deadly sin, a feeling to be avoided and the expression of which should be inhibited?

Actually, there appear to be two types of pride, sometimes called **authentic pride** and **hubristic pride** (Tracy et al., 2014). We will call these "pride" and "hubris," respectively. Pride and hubris can be distinguished in a manner similar to the distinction between guilt and shame made earlier in the chapter: Pride involves pleasure in a job well done (a behavior), whereas hubris involves a smug satisfaction with the self in general (Tracy and Robins, 2014). When feeling pride, a person might say, "I worked hard in this particular course and as a result I received a high grade." In contrast, with hubris a person might believe, "I accomplished this because I am so great" (Tracy & Robins, 2007). This latter thought typifies the self-satisfied arrogance that we associate with sinful pride (Tracy et al., 2011).

Pride has different outcomes and behaviors than hubris does. For instance, pride has been related to positive outcomes in the area in which the individual is proud (Weiner, 1985) and to the development of a positive sense of self-esteem (Herrald & Tomaka, 2002). In a study directed at understanding the benefits of pride, Verbeke, Belschak, and Bagozzi (2004) examined the role of this emotion in the behavior of salespersons. Feelings of pride were associated with a heightened motivation to apply effective strategies and to work hard, as well as the experience of self-efficacy. Pride was also associated with more positive social or citizenship behaviors, such as helping others and promoting the company in general. It thus appears that pride can have the positive benefits of enhancing creativity, productivity, and altruism (Bagozzi, Gopinath, & Nyer, 1999; Fredrickson, 2001).

In contrast, hubris is associated with more negative outcomes, including a tendency toward aggression and hostility (Tangney, 1999). These reactions are likely to be due to the righteous indignation that results from narcissistic injuries, which are so frequently encountered when one thinks of himself or herself as especially worthy (Bushman & Baumeister, 1998; Morf & Rhodewalt, 2001). Consistent with this idea, hubris is not associated with high self-esteem, as one might expect, but with highly variable self-esteem that seems tied to momentary social feedback (e.g., Rhodewalt, Madrian, & Cheney, 1998). Furthermore, the arrogance and egoism communicated by hubris can be socially destructive; other individuals usually try to avoid, shun, or otherwise reject the hubristic person. Consequently, excessive feelings of hubris can cause conflict in and even terminate close relationships.

Figure 6.3 Pride expression: expansive posture, raised chin, and arms on hip or raised in victory. From Tracy, Robins, & Schriber (2009).

A gesture accompanies pride. It involves a smile, a backward tilt of the head and lifting of the chin, and arms resting on hips or raised above the head to show confidence or victory (see Figure 6.3). The gesture of pride is displayed spontaneously by children as young as three years old when they experience success or other situations that elicit reports of pride. It is also displayed by sighted, blind, and congenitally blind adults from many cultures in similar circumstances (Belsky, Domitrovich, & Crnic, 1997; Lewis, Alessandri, & Sullivan, 1992; Stipek, Recchia, & McClintic, 1992; Tracy & Matsumoto, 2008). Literate individuals in Italy and the United States can recognize the gesture of pride with greater-than-chance accuracy (Tracy & Robins, 2004b) and distinguish it from happiness or surprise. So can illiterate African tribe members who have had little to no exposure to Western culture (Tracy & Robins, 2004a), as well as Fijians (Tracy, Shariff, Zhao, & Henrich, 2013). The gesture of pride therefore seems to be universal. For what purpose has pride evolved?

Functions of Pride

Pride may have evolved as a mechanism of communicating success, thereby ensuring the person's status within a group, as well as his or her access to resources managed by the group. This idea is supported by research showing that chimpanzees who occupy positions of dominance perform displays that look like those of prideful humans, perhaps minus the smile (Tracy et al., 2014).

Manipulating feelings of pride in the laboratory also has the effect of increasing status behaviors. In one study, some participants were given positive feedback that elicited pride before working on a group task. Compared to those who were not feeling particularly proud, participants who were feeling proud were perceived by the group members and other observers as behaving in ways that indicated higher status. And they were also viewed as more likable (Williams & DeSteno, 2009). Overall, pride seems to be related to status attainment because it motivates the development of competence and self-confidence. Although hubris may also have evolved to facilitate the attainment of status, it may do so in a different, perhaps more socially costly, way. Hubris seems to facilitate the attainment of status through the use of dominance and aggression rather than through competence. In other words, pride promotes *prestige* and hubris promotes *dominance*, two very different ways of commanding a high-status position (Cheng, Tracy, & Henrich, 2010). At this point, much more is known about pride than hubris, however, and future research will continue to document more about this so-called deadly sin!

Social Comparison Emotions

Social comparison emotions emerge from the ability to be aware of and think about the self, as well as the ability to compare the self to others. The social comparison emotions we will consider in depth, envy and jealousy, both have these characteristics (Parrott, 1991; Salovey & Rothman, 1991; Silver & Sabini, 1978). That is, we assume that in most instances of the two emotions, a person's personality, appearance, abilities, or other qualities are compared to those of another person, and the resulting comparison, within specific social contexts, is an important precondition for the emotions.

Envy

Envy is an unpleasant emotion characterized by longing, dissatisfaction, and the impression of inferiority (Parrott & Smith, 1993; Smith & Kim, 2007). These feelings arise when an individual believes that another person has something that he or she wants but does not yet, or ever will, have. The self compares unfavorably to another.

Thus, the situation in which envy is experienced involves two people: the envious person and the envied person. But there are conditions on whom we envy. Usually we envy those who are similar to us in ways other than the possession of the coveted object or circumstance, as shown by Schaubroeck and Lam (2004) in a study conducted in a bank. These researchers asked employees of the bank to rate the similarity between themselves and their co-workers. Several months later, some employees had been promoted and others had not. The previous ratings of similarity predicted how much envy was felt. The more similar the employee perceived her promoted co-worker, the more envy she felt toward the promoted person. Another study showed that envy occurs when we are faced with comparisons that reveal our own shortcomings in areas of personal relevance (Salovey and Rodin, 1984). Participants in the study received feedback on a career aptitude test that suggested that their career prospects in their preferred field were either very bad or very good. They were then told about the performance of another participant who had done better or worse on the aptitude test for the same career or a different (less self-relevant) career. Envy arose only when participants learned that they had done poorly and another participant had done better on the test in the self-relevant career domain.

Like hubris, envy counts among the seven deadly sins. Also, like pride, there might be two different types. In some theories, **benign envy** is different from the envy of hatred and revenge, often called **malicious envy** (Neu, 1980; Rawls, 1971; Taylor, 1988). This distinction highlights the fact that envy can involve longing, disappointment with the self, and a desire to emulate the envied other person, on the one hand; or bitterness, ill will, and the desire to engage in destructive behaviors, on the other (Parrott, 1991). Malicious envy is, of course, the sin that religious writings speak of.

What is it about the envy situation that leads to feelings of hostility? When does envy become malicious? Apparently, feelings of hostility are due to the belief that the envied person had an unfair advantage in life (Smith et al., 1994). Smith and colleagues based their study, in part, on Fritz Heider's analysis of envy. Central to Heider's "balance theory" is the idea that similar people should have similar, or *balanced*, outcomes (Heider, 1958). If two similar people have very different outcomes, then the less well-off one might perceive the well-off one as unfairly advantaged. Notice the word *perceive*. It does not matter if the envied person objectively deserved her good fortune. If it is *perceived* as an unfair advantage, then the less well-off person will experience ill will and hatred (van de Ven, Zeelenberg, & Pieters, 2012).

Functions of Envy

In light of the distinction between benign and malicious envy, you might imagine that one is a more useful emotion than the other, and some research suggests that this is so. Van de Ven, Zeelenberg, and Pieters (2009) asked their Dutch participants about envy experiences and found that when thinking about a person whom they envied in a benign way, their participants liked and admired that individual more. Although they reported frustration, they also felt motivated to improve and become more like the envied person. Malicious envy was associated with frustration too, but also with a belief that an injustice had been done and with a desire to degrade or even hurt the envied person. These findings suggest that benign envy motivates self-improvement and the acquisition of new skills, but that malicious envy may not do so. Indeed, motivation and enhanced performance have been shown to result from benign envy caused by upward social comparison created in the laboratory (van de Ven, Zeelenberg, & Pieters, 2011). That is, other people's fortunes can sometimes be inspiring and used as cause for greater effort toward improvement (Smith & Kim, 2007).

Jealousy

Feelings of jealousy involve anger, fear of loss, and suspicion (Parrott & Smith, 1993; Salovey & Rothman, 1991). These feelings arise when *an individual believes that an important relationship is threatened by another individual*. So, jealousy requires three entities: the jealous person, the person with whom the jealous person has a relationship, and the rival who threatens that relationship. We often associate jealousy with romance, but siblings and co-workers may also feel jealous of another sibling or co-worker who threatens their relationship with a parent or superior, respectively (DeSteno, Valdesolo, & Bartlett, 2006; Harris, 2003). Although jealousy sounds very different from envy, these words are sometimes used interchangeably by laypeople. For this reason, we will first empirically distinguish the two emotions. We will then discuss two theories of jealousy: the evolutionary account of jealousy (Buss, 1995; Buss, Larsen, Westen, & Semmelroth, 1992), and the self-evaluation maintenance model of jealousy (DeSteno & Salovey, 1996b).

Distinguishing Envy from Jealousy

As we saw earlier, a situation that could give rise to envy is this: You have curly hair that makes you look like a clown when the humidity is high. Your friend has beautiful silky hair that seems to be perfect whether she is in a rain shower, hiking in the desert, or at a formal party. You want her hair, but you cannot have it. Do you say to yourself and others that you are "envious" of the friend? Or do you say you are "jealous" of her?

Now we can probably agree that you are envious of your friend because you want hair like hers and believe that will never be possible. Still, you might have said that you were "jealous." There are a number of ways to look at this apparent confusion in the uses of the words jealousy and envy. Smith, Kim, and Parrott (1988) asked experimental participants to describe examples of times in their lives when they were jealous and when they were envious. Judges then coded these descriptions in terms of whether the situations conformed, or not, to the scientific

Table 6.2 Research by Smith et al. (1988) showed that participants associated specific feeling states with jealousy and others with envy

Jealousy	Envy
Suspicion	Motivation to improve
Rejection	Wishful
Hostility	Longing
Anger at other(s)	Inferior
Fear of loss	Self-aware
Hurt	Self-critical
Cheated	Dissatisfied
Desire to get even	Frustration
Resentment	
Spite	
Malice	
Intensity	

definitions of the two terms. The findings showed that individuals used envy precisely and specifically as referring to situations in which they felt that someone had something (a personal quality, a possession, an achievement) that they did not have but wanted. When recalling situations of jealousy, they tended to describe both classic situations in which they believed that a significant relationship was threatened by a rival (jealousy) and situations in which another individual had something they wanted but did not have (envy).

Does this mean that jealousy is not distinct from envy? In other words, do such findings mean that the states are actually the same? Not according to other results of the same study. Analyses of the ratings of the feelings that characterize the two states suggested that jealousy and envy are quite distinct when many fine-grained feelings are considered (cf. Salovey & Rodin, 1986). Table 6.2 shows the feelings that Smith and colleagues' participants said characterize jealousy and envy. By and large, laypeople report a difference between the two states, with envy being characterized by senses of longing and inferiority and a motivation to improve, whereas jealousy involves more rejection, suspicion, and anger. Thus, although individuals seem to use jealousy more generally (and perhaps incorrectly) than the term envy, even laypeople report that the states feel distinct (as also confirmed by the results of another study by Parrott & Smith, 1993).

One reason the word jealousy is used in situations that actually involve envy is that people do not like the moral connotations of the word envy (Schoeck, 1969). Thus, there may be a strong aversion in many countries and cultures to using the word *envy* to denote a feeling because it has historically been considered a sin (Sabini & Silver, 1982).

Evolutionary Theory of Jealousy

As we learned in Chapter 1, an evolutionary approach to psychological functioning begins with the following question: What are the adaptive problems faced by members of this species? The next question is this: How has the species evolved to solve these problems? What is important for the study of jealousy is the fact that human males face some specific problems, due to their biology, which are different from those faced by females. As far as jealousy is concerned, an important difference is that because females experience internal fertilization and gestation, they do not ever face uncertainty in their maternity. They know who their offspring are with 100 percent certainty. Males do not. In the absence of DNA testing, males always experience some degree of uncertainty in their paternity. Thus, males always face the possibility of being **cuckolded**, or unknowingly raising children to whom they are not genetically related. A cuckolded human male risks investing time, energy, and other resources into offspring that do not assure the survival of his gene pool. This problem should lead to the evolution of anticuckoldry mechanisms. Such mechanisms have been identified in mammals, including lions (Bertram, 1975) and nonhuman primates (Hrdy, 1979), and they should be especially evolved in human males because humans make a greater investment in offspring after birth than any other mammal (Daly, Wilson, & Weghorst, 1982; Symons, 1979). Sexual jealousy would be an efficient anticuckoldry device.

As noted, females know who their offspring are most of the time (barring inadvertent switching of babies in the maternity ward). They do, however, face a different adaptive challenge regarding parental investment. The problem is that of maintaining the time, resources, and commitment of the male. The two situations in which females risk losing a male's investment in the offspring are 1) he has an affair and divides resources now between the two relationships; or 2) he leaves the female and her offspring altogether in order to invest in a new relationship. This second is most likely to happen when a deep emotional attachment has developed with another partner. The development of jealousy of emotional attachments would be an ideal mechanism for warding off loss of investment.

The evolutionary theory of jealousy is based on the preceding analysis. The theory holds that jealousy is a mechanism that has evolved to monitor and motivate behavior to maintain a relationship that entails parental investment. The theory makes at least two testable hypotheses about sex differences in jealousy that have been subject to intense empirical study: one that differentiates sexual and emotional infidelity, and one that focuses on the mate value of potential partners.

Sexual Versus Emotional Infidelity Hypothesis

One hypothesis generated by the evolutionary theory of jealousy is that threats to a relationship involving *sexual promiscuity* should be of particular concern to males, whereas threats to relationships involving *emotional attachment* should be of particular concern to women (Daly & Wilson, 1983). In a study of this hypothesis, Buss and his colleagues asked 202 undergraduates if they would be more upset if their romantic partner had sex or formed an emotional attachment with a rival to the relationship (Buss et al., 1992). More men reported that they would be most upset by sexual infidelity, and more women reported that they would be most upset if their partner formed an emotional bond.

In a second study, participants were instructed to form three different images: walking to class feeling neutral, their partner having sexual intercourse with a rival, and their partner falling in love and having a strong emotional attachment with a rival. Measures of electrodermal activity, pulse rate, and electromyographic activity in the brow (*corrugator supercilii*) were taken to assess how aroused they were while imagining each scene. As is shown by all measures illustrated in Figure 6.4, except for the pulse rate of women, which was not different for the two jealousy images, men showed more physiological reactivity to the sex image, whereas females showed more response to the emotional attachment image. This was taken as further evidence that males are more threatened by sexual rivals and that females are more threatened by rivals to their emotional attachment.

These sensational findings are not without critics. DeSteno and Salovey proposed a "double-shot" hypothesis to explain why the sex difference in jealousy-provoking situations is most often seen in studies using forced-choice questionnaires (i.e., what would bother you more, sexual *or* emotional infidelity?). DeSteno and Salovey (1996a) showed that most women believe that emotional infidelity by their partner implies sexual infidelity as well, but that sexual infidelity

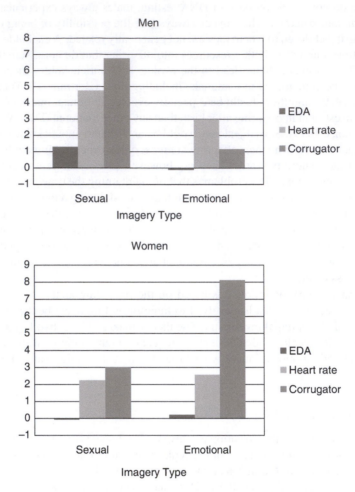

Figure 6.4 Means of physiological measures (electrodermal activity [EDA], heart rate, and contraction of corrugator muscle as indicated by EMG recording) during two imagery conditions. Adapted from Buss et al. (1992).

does not necessarily mean emotional involvement. Men do not hold such a belief about women (i.e., they believe women can have an emotional attachment without sex). They further demonstrated that these divergent beliefs, as opposed to something fundamental to biological sex, accounted for the sex difference in jealousy. Although women reported that both types of infidelity would cause them distress, they selected emotional infidelity as most distressing because it implied, in their minds, a double-shot of cheating (DeSteno & Salovey, 1996a). These findings and interpretations of them have led to a lively debate with some evidence for both sides (e.g., Buss et al., 1999; DeSteno et al., 2002; Harris & Christenfeld, 1996).

Research by Harris (2002, 2003) has also challenged demonstrations of sex differences in jealousy about sexual and emotion infidelity. Harris replicated the finding that a greater number of men than women indicate that they would be more jealous about sexual than emotional infidelity, but this finding was limited to forced-choice questions about hypothetical scenarios, and it disappeared when she asked about actual experiences of infidelity. This was the case for both heterosexual and homosexual individuals (Harris, 2002). Further, slightly modifying hypothetical scenarios used in past research yields results contrary to the evolutionary prediction (Harris, 2003). Specifically, when Harris modified the instructions to indicate that participants should imagine that the infidelity was a one-time occurrence, she found that both women and men indicated emotional infidelity as more upsetting, which she argues is consistent with the double-shot hypothesis.

Characteristics of Rivals to Relationships

Other evolutionary studies have tested the hypothesis that male jealousy targets very different rivals than female jealousy does. According to evolutionary theory, males have high **mate value** when they can provide resources and protection to a partner and their offspring. Females, by way of contrast, have high mate value when they are very fertile and can produce many healthy offspring. A focus on mate value suggests that males should be most jealous of rivals who possess physical strength and the ability to attain resources (as represented in status and financial prospects, for instance). In contrast, females should be most jealous of other females characterized by signs of fertility such as youth and beauty (Buss, 1989; Buss et al., 2000).

This hypothesis was supported in a study by Dijkstra and Buunk (2002). In the study, participants rated 56 characteristics that had been previously generated as possibly inducing jealousy; participants were asked how jealous they would be if their partner were to be seen flirting with an individual who possessed each characteristic. There were five main rival characteristics that provoke jealousy. These included social dominance, physical attractiveness, seductive behaviors, physical dominance, and social status. Males reported being more jealous when a rival was high in social dominance, physical dominance, and social status. In contrast, females were more jealous when the rival was high in physical attractiveness. Similar findings have been obtained across a number of different cultures (Buss et al., 2000) and even for aspects of body build that are specifically related to high male versus female mate value (Dijkstra & Buunk, 2001). For example, in men a high shoulder-to-hip ratio (wide shoulders and narrow hips) is associated with physical success. In women, a low waist-to-hip ratio (a narrow waist and wide hips) is associated with fertility. As would be expected by a consideration of mate value, studies show that women are more jealous of rivals with low (compared to high) waist-to-hip ratios and men are more jealous of rivals with high (compared to low) shoulder-to-hip ratios (see Figure 6.5).

Self-Evaluation Maintenance Model of Jealousy

To understand the self-evaluation maintenance model of jealousy, we must first examine its basis. Tesser (1988) came up with a general self-evaluation maintenance model (**SEM model**) by way of investigating how people seek and desire to maintain a positive evaluation of the self. Though Tesser did not specifically examine jealousy, subsequent scientists did so and theorized that the main determinant of jealousy is the extent to which a rival threatens an individual's self-evaluation in areas of psychological importance to the individual (DeSteno & Salovey, 1995, 1996b; Salovey, 1991; Salovey & Rothman, 1991). Tesser's general theory assumes that much of the activity of maintaining a positive evaluation of the self is played out in social interaction with people who are generally similar to the self. That is, we tend not to compare ourselves with individuals from entirely foreign cultures, distant generations, or of unusual social status (e.g., dead presidents and foreign royalty have very little bearing on our self-evaluation).

The two types of social interaction that are critical in SEM are **reflective processes** and **comparison processes.** Both occur (most importantly for jealousy) when we are exposed to

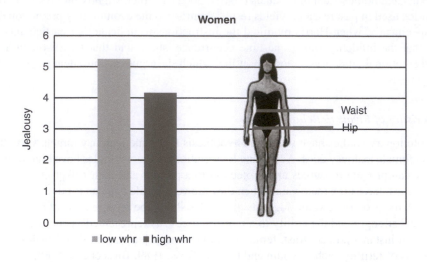

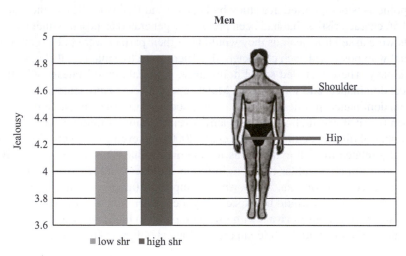

Figure 6.5 Jealousy as a function of a rival's waist-to-hip ratio (WHR) in women and shoulder-to-hip ratio
(SHR) in men. The standard errors were virtually the same for all ratings and varied between
0.26 and 0.29. Adapted from Dijkstra and Buunk (2001).

someone who is superior to us. Reflection occurs (as in something is "reflected off" someone on
to us) when someone we are close to is superior to us in a way that is not threatening to our self-
concept. Here, we "bask in the reflected glory" of that person's achievements or qualities and
feel great about ourselves (Cialdini et al., 1976). There are also situations, however, in which
the superior achievements and qualities of close others are in domains that matter very much
to our self-concept. In these situations, we engage mostly in comparison processes and feel
bad about ourselves. For example, perhaps your older brother or sister made excellent grades
in school and, because academic achievement is important to you, your worse grades made
you feel inadequate. No reflection occurs at all, only an unflattering comparison that leads to a
failure to hold onto a good feeling about the self.

What do people do when a comparison makes them feel bad? Because there is a need to maintain positive self-evaluation, the negative feelings caused by unflattering comparisons motivate behaviors intended to improve self-evaluation in some way. Some of those behaviors involve creating distance in the relationship to the close other (e.g., Tesser & Campbell, 1982), distorting one's beliefs about the other in order to see that person as worse than the self (e.g., Tesser & Campbell, 1982), distorting one's beliefs about oneself in order to see the self as better (e.g., Salovey & Rodin, 1988; Tesser, Campbell, & Smith, 1984), or even by interfering in some way with the successful performance of the close other (e.g., Tesser & Smith, 1980). All such activities serve to restore a positive evaluation of the self.

The SEM model can be used to explain any number of human behaviors. But for our purposes, an understanding of self-evaluative maintenance can help us better understand jealousy. One of the first observations we may make in light of SEM is that jealousy is not an either/or state. That is, people feel jealous to different degrees, and the intensity is due to the degree of threat that they perceive (Bringle, 1991). An individual will feel threatened most acutely by, and therefore be most jealous of, rivals who excel in domains that are of the utmost importance to that individual's self-definition (Salovey, 1991; Salovey & Rothman, 1991). So, jealousy is determined as much, or more, by the comparison between the jealous individual and the rival rather than objective features of the rival (or even the partner's expressed interest in the rival).

To test the hypothesis that the strongest jealousy is experienced when the rival excels in domains of importance to the self-definition of the jealous person, DeSteno and Salovey (1996a) assessed the degree to which intelligence, athleticism, and popularity were important to the self-concepts of their experimental participants. Then, participants read scenarios in which their partner flirted with another individual of the opposite sex (this study was of heterosexual jealousy). In each scenario the rival was described as excelling in one of the three domains of interest. Participants then rated how jealous they would be if their partner had flirted with that particular rival.

Individuals were much more jealous if the flirting situation happened with a rival who excelled in an area of specific importance to their self-concept. Interestingly, in a second study, DeSteno and Salovey also asked about the extent to which participants would like each rival, based on the provided description, in the event that the jealousy-provoking situation had not occurred. Without the flirting situation, participants actually preferred the rivals who excelled in the domain of importance to their self-concept. This is probably not surprising because similarity often predicts liking (e.g., Stroebe et al., 1971).

Function of Jealousy

What is the function of this very preoccupying and distressing emotion? Is there any function? When we realize that there is a rival for the attention of a significant other, of course, our relationships can be damaged because in the very extreme cases, we might act out the jealousy in destructive ways. But, by the same token, as many people have noted, a little jealousy may be good for the relationship. Why? Because it makes the partners consider the importance of the relationship and because it may motivate reparations and improvements in the relationship (Buss, 2000). This basic effect is even shown in babies. When they feel that their relationship with their mother is threatened by a rival, they consistently direct their attention at their mother and try to get closer to her (Hart et al., 2004).

In sum, although the social comparison emotions of envy and jealousy may be painful because they involve comparison to a greater or lesser degree, they may also motivate improvements to ourselves and our relationships by pointing out ways in which things might be made better and by setting new, higher standards of attainment or fulfillment.

Summary

- Self-conscious emotions rely on the cognitive abilities involved in having a sense of self and on self-reflection and evaluation. Some of those emotions require an ability to make comparisons between standards, morals, and ideals on the one hand, and on the other, actual behaviors and experiences in which the self is involved.
- Negative self-evaluations resulting from an individual's perceiving her behavior as unacceptable are experienced as guilt, whereas negative self-evaluations resulting from an individual's deeming herself bad or unworthy are experienced as shame.
- Embarrassment is distinct from shame in that it involves a focus on the self presented to an audience rather than the entire self and in that it is experienced as a sense of fluster and mortification arising from social awkwardness and a perceived loss of esteem in the eyes of others.
- Pride and hubris result from a positive self-evaluation, with pride involving an experience of having done something well, and hubris resulting from an overall self-satisfaction that can be seen as narcissistic arrogance.
- Self-evaluative emotions emerge from an ability to compare the attributes of the self to those of another person. The resulting emotions, depending on situational factors, are envy or jealousy. Envy involves just two persons, and jealousy involves three.
- These emotions all have some positive functions, particularly with regard to social relationships. Jealousy may signal that work on a significant relationship is needed, and guilt may lead people to make amends in a particular situation and avoid moral failures in the future. Benign envy may motivate emulation or the attempt to better oneself. Thus, although many self-conscious emotions may be painful, they may be seen as necessary over the long run for the smooth functioning of complex social systems.

Learning Links

1. Hear an interview with Dr. Jessica Tracy, an expert on the study of self-conscious emotions. https://www.youtube.com/watch?v=N9YKsv_ukTQ
2. Watch a TED talk on primate psychology, including an analysis of jealousy, by Dr. Laurie Santos. https://www.ted.com/speakers/laurie_santos
3. Experience this animation of an embarrassing moment. https://www.youtube.com/watch?v=B4NfStkDz50

References

Amodio, D. M., Devine, P. G., & Harmon-Jones, E. (2007). A dynamic model of guilt implications for motivation and self-regulation in the context of prejudice. *Psychological Science, 18*(6), 524–530. doi:10.1111/j.1467–9280.2007.01933.x.

Ausubel, D. P. (1955). Relationships between shame and guilt in the socializing process. *Psychological Review, 62*(5), 378. doi:10.1037/h0042534.

Bagozzi, R. P., Gopinath, M., & Nyer, P. U. (1999). The role of emotions in marketing. *Journal of the Academy of Marketing Science, 27*(2), 184–206. doi:10.1177/0092070399272005.

Belsky, J., Domitrovich, C., & Crnic, K. (1997). Temperament and parenting antecedents of individual differences in three-year-old boys' pride and shame reactions. *Child Development, 68*(3), 456–466. doi:10.2307/1131671.

Berndsen, M., van der Pligt, J., Doosje, B., & Manstead, A. (2004). Guilt and regret: The determining role of interpersonal and intrapersonal harm. *Cognition and Emotion, 18*(1), 55–70. doi:10.1080/02699930244000435.

Bertram, B. C. (1975). Social factors influencing reproduction in wild lions. *Journal of Zoology, 177*(4), 463–482. doi:10.1111/j.1469–7998.1975.tb02246.x.

Bringle, R. G. (1991). Psychosocial aspects of jealousy: A transactional model. In P. Salovey (Ed.), *The Psychology of Jealousy and Envy* (pp. 103–131). New York: Guilford Press.

Bushman, B. J., & Baumeister, R. F. (1998). Threatened egotism, narcissism, self-esteem, and direct and displaced aggression: Does self-love or self-hate lead to violence? *Journal of Personality and Social Psychology, 75*(1), 219. doi:10.1037/0022–3514.75.1.219.

Buss, A. H. (1980). *Self-consciousness and social anxiety.* San Francisco, CA: W. H. Freeman.

Buss, D. M. (1989). Sex differences in human mate preferences: Evolutionary hypotheses tested in 37 cultures. *Behavioral and Brain Sciences, 12*(1), 1–14. doi:10.1017/s0140525x00023992.

Buss, D. M. (1995). Evolutionary psychology: A new paradigm for psychological science. *Psychological Inquiry, 6*(1), 1–30. OR Buss, D. M. (1995). Psychological sex differences: Origins through sexual selection. *American Psychologist, 50*(3), 164–168 doi:10.1037/0003–066x.50.3.164.

Buss, D. M. (2000). *The dangerous passion: Why jealousy is as necessary as love and sex.* New York: Simon and Schuster. doi:10.5860/choice.37–6552.

Buss, D. M., Larsen, R. J., Westen, D., & Semmelroth, J. (1992). Sex differences in jealousy: Evolution, physiology, and psychology. *Psychological Science, 3*(4), 251–255. doi:10.1111/j.1467–9280.1992.tb00038.x.

Buss, D. M., Shackelford, T. K., Choe, J., Buunk, B. P., & Dijkstra, P. (2000). Distress about mating rivals. *Personal Relationships, 7*(3), 235–243. doi:10.1111/j.1475–6811.2000.tb00014.x.

Buss, D. M., Shackelford, T. K., Kirkpatrick, L. A., Choe, J. C., Lim, H. K., Hasegawa, M., . . . Bennett, K. (1999). Jealousy and the nature of beliefs about infidelity: Tests of competing hypotheses about sex differences in the United States, Korea, and Japan. *Personal Relationships, 6*(1), 125–150. doi:10.1111/j.1475–6811.1999.tb00215.x.

Cheng, J. T., Tracy, J. L., & Henrich, J. (2010). Pride, personality, and the evolutionary foundations of human social status. *Evolution and Human Behavior, 31*(5), 334–347. doi:10.1016/j.evolhumbehav.2010.02.004.

Cialdini, R., Levy, A., Herman, P., Kozlowski, L., & Petty, R. (1976). Elastic shifts of opinion: Determinants of direction and durability. *Journal of Personality and Social Psychology, 34*(4), 663–672. doi:10.1037/0022–3514.34.4.663.

Cryder, C. E., Springer, S., & Morewedge, C. K. (2012). Guilty feelings, targeted actions. *Personality and Social Psychology Bulletin, 38*(5), 607–618. doi:10.1177/0146167211435796.

Daly, M., & Wilson, M. (1983). *Sex, evolution and behavior*. Boston, MA: Wadsworth. doi:10.2307/2064296.

Daly, M., Wilson, M., & Weghorst, S. J. (1982). Male sexual jealousy. *Ethology and Sociobiology, 3*(1), 11–27. doi:10.1016/0162–3095(82)90027–9.

De Hooge, I. E., Zeelenberg, M., & Breugelmans, S. M. (2007). Moral sentiments and cooperation: Differential influences of shame and guilt. *Cognition and Emotion, 21*(5), 1025–1042. doi:10.1080/02699930600980874.

De Jong, P. J. (1999). Communicative and remedial effects of social blushing. *Journal of Nonverbal Behavior, 23*(3), 197–217. doi:10.1023/a:1021352926675.

de Rivera, J. (1977). *A structural theory of emotions*. New York: International Universities Press.

DeSteno, D., Bartlett, M. Y., Braverman, J., & Salovey, P. (2002). Sex differences in jealousy: Evolutionary mechanism or artifact of measurement? *Journal of Personality and Social Psychology, 83*(5), 1103. doi:10.1037/0022–3514.83.5.1103.

DeSteno, D. A., & Salovey, P. (1995). Jealousy and envy. In A. S. R. Manstead, M. Hewstone, S. T. Fiske, M. A. Hogg, H. T. Reis & G. R. Semin (Eds.), *The Blackwell encyclopedia of social psychology* (pp. 342–343). Oxford, MA: Blackwell.

DeSteno, D. A., & Salovey, P. (1996a). Evolutionary origins of sex differences in jealousy? Questioning the "fitness" of the model. *Psychological Science, 7*(6), 367–372. doi:10.1111/j.1467–9280.1996.tb00391.x.

DeSteno, D. A., & Salovey, P. (1996b). Jealousy and the characteristics of one's rival: A self-evaluation maintenance perspective. *Personality and Social Psychology Bulletin, 22*(9), 920–932. doi:10.1177/0146167296229006.

DeSteno, D., Valdesolo, P., & Bartlett, M. Y. (2006). Jealousy and the threatened self: Getting to the heart of the green-eyed monster. *Journal of Personality and Social Psychology, 91*(4), 626. doi:10.1037/0022–3514.91.4.626.

Dienstbier, R. A. (1984). The role of emotion in moral socialization. In C. E. Izard, J. Kegan, & R. B. Zajonc (Eds.), *Emotions, cognition, and behavior* (p. 484–514). New York: Cambridge University Press.

Dijkstra, P., & Buunk, B. P. (2001). Sex differences in the jealousy-evoking nature of a rival's body build. *Evolution and Human Behavior, 22*(5), 335–341. doi:10.1016/S1090–5138(01)00070–8.

Dijkstra, P., & Buunk, B. P. (2002). Sex differences in the jealousy-evoking effect of rival characteristics. *European Journal of Social Psychology, 32*(6), 829–852. doi:10.1002/ejsp.125.

Feinberg, M., Willer, R., Stellar, J., & Keltner, D. (2012). The virtues of gossip: Reputational information sharing as prosocial behavior. *Journal of Personality and Social Psychology, 102*(5), 1015. doi:10.1037/a0026650.

Ferguson, T. J., Stegge, H., & Damhuis, I. (1991). Children's understanding of guilt and shame. *Child Development, 62*(4), 827–839. doi:10.1111/j.1467–8624.1991.tb01572.x.

Fischer, A. H., & Manstead, A. S. (2008). Social functions of emotion. *Handbook of Emotions, 3*, 456–468.

Fischer, K., & Tangney, J. (1995). *Self conscious emotions: Shame, guilt, embarrassment, and pride*. Nova York: Guilford. doi:10.1002/0470013494.ch26.

Fredrickson, B. L. (2001). The role of positive emotions in positive psychology: The broaden-and-build theory of positive emotions. *American Psychologist, 56*(3), 218. doi:10.1037/0003–066x.56.3.218.

Frijda, N. H., Kuipers, P., & Ter Schure, E. (1989). Relations among emotion, appraisal, and emotional action readiness. *Journal of Personality and Social Psychology, 57*(2), 212. doi:10.1037/0022–3514.57.2.212.

Giner-Sorolla, R. (2001). Guilty pleasures and grim necessities: Affective attitudes in dilemmas of self-control. *Journal of Personality and Social Psychology, 80*(2), 206. doi:10.1037/0022–3514.80.2.206.

Gross, E., & Stone, G. P. (1964). Embarrassment and the analysis of role requirements. *American Journal of Sociology, 70*(1), 1–15. doi:10.1086/223733.

Haidt, J. (2003). The moral emotions. *Handbook of Affective Sciences, 11*, 852–870.

Harris, C. R. (2002). Sexual and romantic jealousy in heterosexual and homosexual adults. *Psychological Science, 13*(1), 7–12. doi:10.1111/1467–9280.00402.

Harris, C. R. (2003). Factors associated with jealousy over real and imagined infidelity: An examination of the social-cognitive and evolutionary psychology perspectives. *Psychology of Women Quarterly, 27*(4), 319–329. doi:10.1111/1471–6402.00112.

Harris, C. R., & Christenfeld, N. (1996). Gender, jealousy, and reason. *Psychological Science, 7*(6), 364–366. doi:10.1111/j.1467–9280.1996.tb00390.x.

Harris, P. L. (1989). *Children and emotion: The development of psychological understanding*. Cambridge, MA: Basil Blackwell.

Hart, D., & Karmel, M. P. (1996). Self-awareness and self-knowledge in humans, apes, and monkeys. In A. Russon, K. Bard, & S. Taylor Parker, *Reaching into Thought: The Minds of the Great Apes* (pp. 325–347). Cambridge, UK: Cambridge University Press.

Hart, S. L., Carrington, H. A., Tronick, E. Z., & Carroll, S. R. (2004). When infants lose exclusive maternal attention: Is it jealousy? *Infancy*, *6*(1), 57–78. doi:10.1207/s15327078in0601_3.

Harter, S. (1999). *The construction of the self: A developmental perspective*. New York: Guilford Press. doi:10.5860/choice.37–1226.

Heider, F. (1958). *The psychology of interpersonal relations*. New York: Wiley. doi:10.1037/10628–000.

Herrald, M. M., & Tomaka, J. (2002). Patterns of emotion-specific appraisal, coping, and cardiovascular reactivity during an ongoing emotional episode. *Journal of Personality and Social Psychology*, *83*(2), 434. doi:10.1037/0022–3514.83.2.434.

Hrdy, S. B. (1979). Infanticide among animals: A review, classification, and examination of the implications for the reproductive strategies of females. *Ethology and Sociobiology*, *1*(1), 13–40. doi:10.1016/0162–3095(79)90004–9.

Izard, C. E., Ackerman, B. P., & Schultz, D. (1999). Independent emotions and consciousness: Self-consciousness and dependent emotions. In J. A. Singer & P. Singer (Eds.), *At play in the fields of consciousness: Essays in honor of Jerome L. Singer* (pp. 83–102). Mahwah, NJ: Lawrence Erlbaum Associates.

Joireman, J. (2004). Empathy and the self-absorption paradox II: Self-rumination and self-reflection as mediators between shame, guilt, and empathy. *Self and Identity*, *3*(3), 225–238. doi:10.1080/13576500444000038.

Keltner, D. (1995). Signs of appeasement: Evidence for the distinct displays of embarrassment, amusement, and shame. *Journal of Personality and Social Psychology*, *68*(3), 441. doi:10.1037/0022–3514.68.3.441.

Keltner, D., Young, R. C., & Buswell, B. N. (1997). Appeasement in human emotion, social practice, and personality. *Aggressive Behavior*, *23*(5), 359–374. doi:10.1002/(sici)1098–2337(1997)23:5 <359::aid-ab5>3.0.co;2-d.

Kemeny, M. E., Gruenewald, T. L., & Dickerson, S. S. (2004). Shame as the emotional response to threat to the social self: Implications for behavior, physiology, and health. *Psychological Inquiry*, *15*(2), 153–160.

Leary, M. R., Britt, T. W., Cutlip, W. D., & Templeton, J. L. (1992). Social blushing. *Psychological Bulletin*, *112*(3), 446. doi: 10.1037/0033-2909.112.3.446.

Leary, M. R., Landel, J. L., & Patton, K. M. (1996). The motivated expression of embarrassment following a self-presentational predicament. *Journal of Personality*, *64*(3), 619–636. doi:10.1111/j.1467–6494.1996. tb00524.x.

Lewis, H. B. (1971). *Shame and guilt in neurosis*. New York: Int. Univ. Press.

Lewis, M. (1992). *Shame: The exposed self*. New York: The Free Press.

Lewis. M. (1993). Self-conscious emotions: Embarrassment, pride, shame, and guilt. In M. Lewis & J. M. Haviland (Eds.), *Handbook of emotions* (pp. 353–364). New York: Guilford.

Lewis, M. (1995). Embarrassment: The emotion of self-exposure and evaluation. In J. P. Tangney & K. W. Fischer (Eds.), *Self-conscious emotions: The psychology of shame, guilt, embarrassment, and pride* (pp. 198–218). New York: Guilford.

Lewis, M. (2000a). The emergence of human emotions. In M. Lewis & J. M. Haviland-Jones (Eds.), *Handbook of Emotions* (2nd ed., pp. 265–280). New York: Guilford Press.

Lewis, M. (2000b). Self-conscious emotions: Embarrassment, pride, shame, and guilt. In M. Lewis & J. M. Haviland-Jones (Eds.), *Handbook of emotions* (2nd ed., pp. 623–636). New York: Guilford Press.

Lewis, M., Alessandri, S. M., & Sullivan, M. W. (1992). Differences in shame and pride as a function of children's gender and task difficulty. *Child Development*, *63*, 630–638. doi:10.2307/1131351.

Lewis, M., & Brooks-Gunn, J. (1979). Toward a theory of social cognition: The development of self. *New Directions for Child and Adolescent Development*, *1979*(4), 1–20. doi:10.1002/cd.23219790403.

Lewis, M., & Ramsay, D. (2002). Cortisol response to embarrassment and shame. *Child Development*, *73*(4), 1034–1045. doi:10.1111/1467–8624.00455.

Lewis, M., Sullivan, M. W., Stanger, C., & Weiss, M. (1989). Self-development and self-conscious emotions. *Child Development*, *60*(1), 146–156. doi:10.2307/1131080.

Lindsay-Hartz, J. (1984). Contrasting experiences of shame and guilt. *American Behavioral Scientist*, *27*, 689–704. doi:10.1177/000276484027006003.

Lindsay-Hartz, J., De Rivera, J., & Mascolo, M. F. (1995). *Differentiating guilt and shame and their effects on motivation*. In J. Tangney and K.W. Fischer (Eds.), *Self-conscious emotions: The psychology of guilt, shame and embarrassment* (pp. 274–300). New York, NY: Guilford Press

Miller, R. S. (1996). *Embarrassment: Poise and peril in everyday life*. New York: Guilford Press. doi:10.5860/choice.34–3593.

Miller, R. S. (2004). Emotion as adaptive interpersonal communication: The case of embarrassment. In L. Z. Tiedens & C. W. Leach (Eds.), *The social life of emotions* (pp. 87–105). Cambridge: Cambridge University Press.

Miller, R. S., & Leary, M. R. (1992). Social sources and interactive functions of emotion: The case of embarrassment. In M. Clark (Ed.), *Review of' personality and social psychology* (Vol. 14, pp. 202–221). Newbury Park, CA: Sage.

Morf, C. C., & Rhodewalt, F. (2001). Unraveling the paradoxes of narcissism: A dynamic self-regulatory processing model. *Psychological Inquiry, 12*(4), 177–196. doi:10.1207/s15327965pli1204_1.

Mussweiler, T., Rüter, K., & Epstude, K. (2004). The ups and downs of social comparison: Mechanisms of assimilation and contrast. *Journal of Personality and Social Psychology, 87*, 832–844. doi:10.1037/0022–3514.87.6.832.

Neu, J. (1980). Jealous thoughts. In R. Rorty (Ed.), *Explaining emotions* (pp. 425–463). Berkeley, CA: University of California Press.

Niedenthal, P. M., & Brauer, M. (2012). Social functionality of human emotion. *Annual Review of Psychology, 63*, 259–285.

Niedenthal, P. M., Tangney, J. P., & Gavanski, I. (1994). "If only I weren't" versus "If only I hadn't": Distinguishing shame and guilt in counterfactual thinking. *Journal of Personality and Social Psychology, 67*(4), 585. Doi:10.1037/0022–3514.67.4.585.

Parrott, W. G. (1991). The emotional experiences of envy and jealousy. In P. Salovey (Ed.), *The psychology of jealousy and envy* (pp. 3–30). New York: The Guilford Press.

Parrott, W. G., Sabini, J., & Silver, M. (1988). The roles of self-esteem and social interaction in embarrassment. *Personality and Social Psychology Bulletin, 14*(1), 191–202. doi:10.1177/0146167288141019.

Parrott, W. G., & Smith, R. H. (1993). Distinguishing the experiences of envy and jealousy. *Journal of Personality and Social Psychology, 64*(6), 906. doi:10.1037/0022–3514.64.6.906.

Plutchik, R. (1980). *Emotion: A psychoevolutionary synthesis*. New York, NY: Harper & Row.

Rawls, J. (1971). *A theory of justice*. Cambridge, MA: Harvard University, Belknap Press.

Rhodewalt, F., Madrian, J. C., & Cheney, S. (1998). Narcissism, self-knowledge organization, and emotional reactivity: The effect of daily experiences on self-esteem and affect. *Personality and Social Psychology Bulletin, 24*(1), 75–87. doi:10.1177/0146167298241006.

Roese, N. J., & Olson, J. M. (Eds.). (1995). *What might have been: The social psychology of counterfactual thinking*. New York, NY: Psychology Press.

Russon, A. E., & Galdikas, B. M. (1993). Imitation in free-ranging rehabilitant orangutans (Pongo pygmaeus). *Journal of Comparative Psychology, 107*(2), 147. doi:10.1037/0735–7036.107.2.147.

Sabini, J., Siepmann, M., Stein, J., & Meyerowitz, M. (2000). Who is embarrassed by what? *Cognition & Emotion, 14*(2), 213–240. doi:10.1080/026999300378941.

Sabini, J., & Silver, M. (1982). *Moralities of everyday life* (pp. 43–4). Oxford: Oxford University Press.

Salovey, P. (Ed.). (1991). *The psychology of jealousy and envy*. New York: Guilford Press. doi:10.5860/choice.29–0604.

Salovey, P., & Rodin, J. (1984). Some antecedents and consequences of social-comparison jealousy. *Journal of Personality and Social Psychology, 47*(4), 780. doi:10.1037/0022–3514.47.4.780.

Salovey, P., & Rodin, J. (1986). The differentiation of social-comparison jealousy and romantic jealousy. *Journal of Personality and Social Psychology, 50*(6), 1100. doi:10.1037/0022–3514.50.6.1100.

Salovey, P., & Rodin, J. (1988). Coping with envy and jealousy. *Journal of Social and Clinical Psychology, 7*(1), 15–33. doi:10.1521/jscp.1988.7.1.15.

Salovey, P., & Rothman, A. (1991). Envy and jealousy: Self and society. In P. Salovey (Ed.), *The psychology of jealousy and envy* (pp. 271–286). New York: Guilford Press.

Schaubroeck, J., & Lam, S. S. (2004). Comparing lots before and after: Promotion rejectees' invidious reactions to promotees. *Organizational Behavior and Human Decision Processes, 94*(1), 33–47. doi:10.1016/j.obhdp.2004.01.001.

Scheff, T. J. (1988). Shame and conformity: The deference-emotion system. *American Sociological Review*, *53*(3), 395–406. doi:10.2307/2095647.

Scheff, T. J. (1990). *Microsociology: Discourse, Emotion, and Social Structure*. Chicago and London: The University of Chicago Press.

Scherer, K. R. (2001). Appraisal considered as a process of multilevel sequential checking. *Appraisal Processes in Emotion: Theory, Methods, Research*, *92*, 120.

Schoeck, H. (1969). *Envy: A theory of social behavior*. New York: Harcourt, Brace, and World.

Semin, G. R., & Manstead, A. S. R. (1982). The social implications of embarrassment displays and restitution behaviour. *European Journal of Social Psychology*, *12*(4), 367–377. doi:10.1002/ejsp.2420120404.

Silfver, M., Helkama, K., Lönnqvist, J. E., & Verkasalo, M. (2008). The relation between value priorities and proneness to guilt, shame, and empathy. *Motivation and Emotion*, *32*(2), 69–80. doi:10.1007/s11031-008-9084-2.

Silver, M., & Sabini, J. (1978). The perceptions of envy. *Social Psychology*, *41*(2), 105–111. doi:10.2307/3033570.

Smith, R. H., & Kim, S. H. (2007). Comprehending envy. *Psychological Bulletin*, *133*(1), 46. doi:10.1037/0033-2909.133.1.46.

Smith, R. H., Kim, S. H., & Parrott, W. G. (1988). Envy and jealousy: Semantic problems and experiential distinctions. *Personality and Social Psychology Bulletin*, *14*(2), 401–409. doi:10.1177/0146167288142017.

Smith, R. H., Parrott, W. G., Ozer, D., & Moniz, A. (1994). Subjective injustice and inferiority as predictors of hostile and depressive feelings in envy. *Personality and Social Psychology Bulletin*, *20*(6), 705–711. doi:10.1177/0146167294206008.

Stipek, D., Recchia, S., & McClintic, S, & Lewis, M. (1992). Self-evaluation in young children. *Monographs of the Society for Research in Child Development*, *57*, 1–84. doi:10.2307/1166190.

Stroebe, W., Insko, C. A., Thompson, V. D., & Layton, B. D. (1971). Effects of physical attractiveness, attitude similarity, and sex on various aspects of interpersonal attraction. *Journal of Personality and Social Psychology*, *18*(1), 79. doi:10.1037/h0030710.

Symons, D. (1979). *The evolution of human sexuality*. New York: Oxford University Press.

Tangney, J. P. (1990). Assessing individual differences in proneness to shame and guilt: Development of the self-conscious affect and attribution inventory. *Journal of Personality and Social Psychology*, *59*(1), 102. doi:10.1037/0022-3514.59.1.102.

Tangney, J. P. (1991). Moral affect: The good, the bad, and the ugly. *Journal of Personality and Social Psychology*, *61*(4), 598. doi:10.1037/0022-3514.61.4.598.

Tangney, J. P. (1992). Situational determinants of shame and guilt in young adulthood. *Personality and Social Psychology Bulletin*, *18*(2), 199–206. doi:10.1177/0146167292182011.

Tangney, J. P. (1999). The self-conscious emotions: Shame, guilt, embarrassment and pride. In T. Dagleish & M. Power (Eds.), *Handbook of cognition and emotion* (pp. 541–568). Chichester, UK: Wiley. doi:10.1002/0470013494.ch26.

Tangney, J. P. (2002). Self-conscious emotions: The self as a moral guide. In A. Tesser, D. A. Stapel & J. V. Wood (Eds.), *Self and motivation: Emerging psychological perspectives* (pp. 97–117). Washington, DC: American Psychological Press.

Tangney, J. P., & Dearing, R. L. (2002). *Shame and guilt*. New York: Guilford Press. doi:10.4135/9781412950664.n388.

Tangney, J. P., & Fischer, K. W. (Eds.). (1995). *Self-conscious emotions*. New York: Guilford Press.

Tangney, J. P., & Tracy, J. (2012). Self-conscious emotions. In M. Leary & J. P. Tangney (Eds.) *Handbook of self and identity* (2nd ed., pp. 446–478). New York: Guilford Press. doi:10.1177/0146167206290212.

Taylor, G. (1985). *Pride, shame, and guilt: Emotions of self-assessment*. Oxford: Clarendon Press.

Taylor, G. (1988). Envy and jealousy: Emotions and vices. *Midwest Studies in Philosophy*, *13*(1), 233–249. doi:10.1111/j.1475-4975.1988.tb00124.x.

Tesser, A. (1988). Toward a self-evaluation maintenance model of social behavior. *Advances in Experimental Social Psychology*, *21*(181–228). doi:10.1016/s0065-2601(08)60227-0.

Tesser, A., & Campbell, J. (1982). Self-evaluation maintenance and the perception of friends and strangers. *Journal of Personality*, *50*(3), 261–279. doi:10.1111/j.1467-6494.1982.tb00750.x.

Tesser, A., Campbell, J., & Smith, M. (1984). Friendship choice and performance: Self-evaluation maintenance in children. *Journal of Personality and Social Psychology*, *46*(3), 561–574. doi:10.1037/0022-3514.46.3.561.

Tesser, A., & Smith, J. (1980). Some effects of task relevance and friendship on helping: You don't always help the one you like. *Journal of Experimental Social Psychology*, *16*(6), 582–590. doi:10.1016/0022–1031(80)90060–8.

Tracy, J. L., Cheng, J. T., Martens, J. P., & Robins, R. W. (2011). The affective core of narcissism: Inflated by pride, deflated by shame. In W. K. Campbell & J. Miller (Eds.), *Handbook of narcissism and narcissistic personality disorder* (pp. 330–343). New York: Wiley.

Tracy, J. L., & Matsumoto, D. (2008). The spontaneous expression of pride and shame: Evidence for biologically innate nonverbal displays. *Proceedings of the National Academy of Sciences*, *105*(33), 11655–11660. doi:10.1073/pnas.0802686105.

Tracy, J. L., & Robins, R. W. (2004a). Putting the self into self-conscious emotions: A theoretical model. *Psychological Inquiry*, *15*(2), 103–125. doi:10.1207/s15327965pli1502_01.

Tracy, J. L., & Robins, R. W. (2004b). Show your pride: Evidence for a discrete emotion expression. *Psychological Science*, *15*(3), 194–197. doi:10.1111/j.0956–7976.2004.01503008.x.

Tracy, J. L., & Robins, R. W. (2006). Appraisal antecedents of shame and guilt: Support for a theoretical model. *Personality and Social Psychology Bulletin*, *32*(10), 1339–1351. doi:10.1177/0146167206290212.

Tracy, J. L., & Robins, R. W. (2007). Emerging insights into the nature and function of pride. *Current Directions in Psychological Science*, *16*(3), 147–150. doi:10.1111/j.1467–8721.2007.00493.x.

Tracy, J. L., & Robins, R. W. (2008). The nonverbal expression of pride: Evidence for cross-cultural recognition. *Journal of Personality and Social Psychology*, *94*(3), 516. doi:10.1037/0022–3514.94.3.516.

Tracy, J. L., & Robins, R. W. (2014). Conceptual and empirical strengths of the authentic/hubristic model of pride. *Emotion*, *14*(1), 33–37. doi:10.1037/a0034490.

Tracy, J. L., Robins, R. W., & Schriber, R. A. (2009). Development of a FACS-verified set of basic and self-conscious emotion expressions. *Emotion*, *9*(4), 554. doi:10.1037/a0015766.

Tracy, J. L., Shariff, A. F., Zhao, W., & Henrich, J. (2013). Cross-cultural evidence that the nonverbal expression of pride is an automatic status signal. *Journal of Experimental Psychology: General*, *142*(1), 163. doi:10.1037/a0028412.

Tracy, J. L., Weidman, A. C., Cheng, J. T., & Martens, J. P. (2014). Pride: The fundamental emotion of success, power, and status. In M. Tugade, L. Shiota & L. Kriby (Eds.), *Handbook of positive emotions* (pp. 294–310). New York: Guildford.

Van de Ven, N., Zeelenberg, M., & Pieters, R. (2009). Leveling up and down: The experiences of benign and malicious envy. *Emotion*, *9*(3), 419. doi:10.1037/a0015669.

Van de Ven, N., Zeelenberg, M., & Pieters, R. (2011). Why envy outperforms admiration. *Personality and Social Psychology Bulletin*, *37*(6), 784–795. doi:10.1177/0146167211400421.

Van de Ven, N., Zeelenberg, M., & Pieters, R. (2012). Appraisal patterns of envy and related emotions. *Motivation and Emotion*, *36*(2), 195–204. doi:10.1007/s11031–011–9235–8.

Verbeke, W., Belschak, F., & Bagozzi, R. P. (2004). The adaptive consequences of pride in personal selling. *Journal of the Academy of Marketing Science*, *32*(4), 386–402. doi:10.1177/0092070304267105.

Weiner, B. (1985). An attributional theory of achievement motivation and emotion. *Psychological Review*, *92*(4), 548. doi:10.1037/0033–295x.92.4.548.

Wells, G. L., & Gavanski, I. (1989). Mental simulation of causality. *Journal of Personality and Social Psychology*, *56*(2), 161. doi:10.1037/0022–3514.56.2.161.

Wicker, F. W., Payne, G. C., & Morgan, R. D. (1983). Participant descriptions of guilt and shame. *Motivation and Emotion*, *7*(1), 25–39. doi:10.1007/bf00992963.

Williams, L. A., & DeSteno, D. (2009). Pride adaptive social emotion or seventh sin? *Psychological Science*, *20*(3), 284–288. doi:10.1111/j.1467–9280.2009.02292.x.

Yang, M. L., Yang, C. C., & Chiou, W. B. (2010). When guilt leads to other orientation and shame leads to egocentric self-focus: Effects of differential priming of negative affects on perspective taking. *Social Behavior and Personality: An International Journal*, *38*(5), 605–614. doi:10.2224/sbp.2010.38.5.605.

Zemack-Rugar, Y., Bettman, J. R., & Fitzsimons, G. J. (2007). The effects of nonconsciously priming emotion concepts on behavior. *Journal of Personality and Social Psychology*, *93*(6), 927. doi:10.1037/0022–3514.93.6.927.

7 Happiness

Contents at a Glance

Representations of happiness are all around us. Our phones have smiley faces and positive, excited, or contented emojis. Smiling models look out at us from the covers of magazines. TV game shows feature people jumping up and down with glee over their good fortune.

Given the pervasiveness of happiness in popular culture, it's no surprise that we tend to use the idea of happiness to explain our decisions. For example, you might explain that you got a puppy because you thought the puppy would make you happy. You also might use the idea of happiness to refuse a night out at a sad movie (because it might make you feel unhappy) or to decline a boring job (because it might not be fun enough).

Some people say that happiness has become a modern obsession: too discussed, sought after, and worried about. Why are people obsessed with happiness? Do people try to achieve happiness because it feels good in and of itself, or because there are bigger benefits associated with happiness? One of the reasons people around the world are interested in happiness is that positive emotions seem to be associated with positive outcomes. As we shall see, happier people tend to be healthier, more productive, and more attractive to others. In this chapter, we'll start by explaining what happiness is and then document its benefits. Then we will discuss how and why people have trouble predicting and creating their own happiness. Finally, we will explore the causes of happiness, including research that supports the idea of a genetic predisposition to experiencing happiness with oneself and the world, with one's life circumstances, and with details of one's daily activities.

What Is Happiness?

Recent online headlines ask, "Can Social Media Make Us Happy?" and offer up "16 Ways to Create Happiness at Work." To even understand those headlines, we need a definition of happiness. In musing about this topic, a researcher who has been studying happiness for a long time, Martin Seligman (2004), wrote, "More words have been penned about defining happiness than about almost any other philosophical question" (p. 15). Still, there seems to be some scientific consensus that happiness means having positive emotions that are linked to a feeling of doing well in the world. For instance, Veenhoven (2000) defines happiness as "the degree to which someone evaluates positively the overall quality of his or her present life as a whole" (p. 267). In a more quantitative way, Linley and Joseph (2004) define happiness as

> the sum of life satisfaction (the positive evaluation of one's life as a whole), plus positive affect (the experience of positive emotions within any given time period), minus negative affect (the experience of negative emotions within any given time period). (p. 32)

Implicit in both of these definitions is the idea that happiness derives not from an objective assessment of how one is doing in the world, but rather from a subjective one. Thus happiness is often referred to in the psychological literature as subjective well-being (SWB).

In this chapter we endorse Lyubomirsky, King, and Diener's (2005) claim that a person's self-report of happiness is derived from the extent to which he or she experiences positive emotions in everyday life. In other words, when people say they are "happy," it is because they tend to be in a positive state much of the time. They take pleasure in their daily life. So, if you say you are happy, you are recognizing that you are experiencing mostly positive feelings.

Note that happiness is different from psychological well-being, which is defined as a person's perception of being engaged with and able to manage the challenges of life (Keyes, Shmotkin, & Ryff, 2002, p. 1007). The two types of well-being—psychological and subjective—are distinct, but research on the two occasionally overlaps (Ryan & Deci, 2001; Waterman, 1993) The two lines of inquiry have their roots in ancient Greece, in the philosophical traditions of hedonism and eudaimonia (Figure 7.1).

Hedonism is associated with subjective well-being. A philosophy of hedonism was likely first articulated by Aristippus, but is most often associated with Epicurus. According to the hedonistic tradition, happiness is the sum of momentary pleasures. Epicurus expanded on this notion, arguing that happiness is the sum of momentary pleasures plus pleasures of life as a

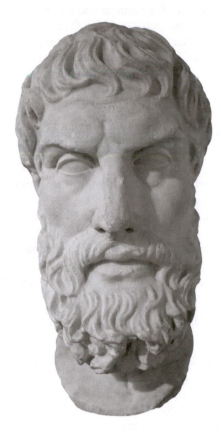

Figure 7.1 With regard to happiness, Aristotle (left) and Epicurus (right) had slightly different preoccupations. Aristotle developed the idea of eudaimonia, which is similar to self-realization, whereas Epicurus is associated with the idea of hedonism, something that college students are familiar with.

whole. This is similar to Diener's concept of life satisfaction (2006) and Kahneman and colleagues' (Kahneman et al., 2010) recent theory of hedonic happiness.

Research into psychological well-being is rooted in the philosophical tradition of eudaimonia, which is concerned with the realization of one's daimon, or true self. According to Aristotle, eudaimonia is a state of self-realization that is nurtured by virtuous activities that express our values, personal expressiveness, fulfillment, and meaning. This state of self-realization is similar to the modern concept of psychological well-being.

Kahneman (2011) divides the concept of happiness into experienced happiness and remembered happiness. He argues that each of us is made up of two selves that track our quality of life and report on it when asked. The **experiencing self**, according to Kahneman, is the self who lives in the moment and feels happy because of the details of life in the present. The **remembering self** is the self that takes stock of one's past life, manages the story of one's life, keeps score, and is happy about the narrative. To understand the distinction between the experiencing self and the remembering self, imagine a visit to the doctor's office. The doctor could ask you, "Does it hurt when I push right here?" How do you know? The experiencing self feels something at that moment and reports on the pain that the push generated. The doctor could also ask, "How have you been?" In that case, you need to draw on your remembering self, who assesses your life in the recent past and produces a general score: "I am doing pretty well."

Another example of the distinction between the experiencing and the remembering self is found in reports of parenthood. Parents in the midst of raising children sometimes report low levels of happiness. For example, many studies of mothers have shown that they experience more negative emotions and fewer positive ones during the day than nonparents (Hansen, 2012; White & Dolan, 2009; cf. Deaton & Stone, 2014). This is probably because caring for children involves sacrifice, worry, stress, and exhaustion. However, when evaluating their life as a whole, parents very often report that raising children generates the highest possible satisfaction in life. This means that although the experiencing self does not rate happiness high at individual moments, the remembering self offers a different, far more positive assessment.

Keep this distinction in mind the next time you are at a party, travel to another country, or lie on the beach with friends. Ask yourself, "Am I doing this for my remembering self or my experiencing self?" If your primary motivation is to generate pictures that you can post on social media, then you are doing it for your remembering self. If you are lost in the pleasures of the moment, then you are doing it for your experiencing self.

What Does Happiness Do?

Beyond feeling good, happiness offers some other hefty benefits. Over many decades, research on happiness has documented correlations between happiness and a number of positive outcomes, such as success (having a good job and making money), love (having close and fulfilling relationships), and good mental and physical health. These correlations might make you think that success, love, and health actually make people happy. Indeed, there is some support for that causal interpretation. However, research also supports the opposite idea—that happiness actually causes success, love, and good health. What's more, sometimes the effect of happiness on success, love, and good health is stronger than the effect of success, love, and good health on happiness. After summarizing the correlations between happiness and its benefits, Lyubomirsky and colleagues (2005) reviewed longitudinal studies (in which happiness is measured long before the outcome variable of success, love, or health) and experimental studies (in which happy feelings are directly manipulated). The experimental studies were important because they allowed the researchers to draw conclusions about causation. Their analysis showed that happiness does indeed cause success, love, and good health.

As evidence of this causal direction, Roberts, Caspi, and Moffitt (2003) conducted a longitudinal study that showed that positive affect at age 18 predicted better work outcomes at age 26. For instance, the happier participants were at 18, the greater financial independence and work autonomy they had achieved eight years later. Happiness is also associated with other types of work-related success such as better job performance and lower rates of burnout (Staw & Barsade, 1993). In the realm of love, longitudinal studies of happiness and marriage have consistently shown that single people who are happier are more likely to get married in subsequent years (Lucas et al., 2003; Marks & Fleming, 1999). Also, happy people have a range of positive health outcomes later in life, including suffering fewer health-related symptoms (Graham, Eggers, & Sukhtankar, 2004) and experiencing a lower incidence of stroke (Ostir, Markides, Peek, & Goodwin, 2001). Happier people therefore tend to live longer (Danner, Snowdon, & Friesen, 2001). The connection between happiness and health, furthermore, has been documented across the globe (Pressman, Gallagher, & Lopez, 2013).

How Does Happiness Do That?

When scientists study relationships between two factors, they don't just want to know how they are related (that is, the direction of causality)—they also want to know how the relationship came about in the first place. In psychology, when we study how a phenomenon occurs, we say we are studying the **mechanism** of the phenomenon. In examining how happiness causes success, love, and good health, scientists have proposed at least three mechanisms.

One mechanistic account relies on the broaden-and-build model, discussed in Chapter 4. According to this model, happiness and other positive feelings are signals to the organism that everything is safe in the environment. This safety signal triggers exploration, learning, and even creativity, with the result that the individual expands his or her repertoire of knowledge and behavior (Fredrickson, 2001). The resource building that occurs during periods of happiness is related to achieving success in work and relationships.

The second mechanism has to do with the signals that people give out when they are happy, such as smiles (Whalen et al., 1998) and even odors (de Groot et al., 2015). These signals stimulate the reward centers of other people's brains and make them feel happy too. If being around happy people feels good, then happier people will be more successful at attracting mates, maintaining relationships, and working with others.

The final mechanism, which may largely account for the relationship between happiness and health, has to do with the biology of happiness. Being in a state of happiness involves the production of good hormones, a sort of positive biochemical stew that creates a resilient and healthy bodily condition (Fredrickson, 2009; Steptoe, Wardle, & Marmot, 2005; Wager, Scott, & Zubieta, 2007).

Now that you know about some of the benefits of happiness, you might be ready to go find it in life. The problem is, most people, perhaps you included, are not experts at predicting what will actually make them happy.

Do You Really Know What Makes You Happy?

You've probably rolled your eyes at a friend's choices, thinking to yourself, "She's kidding herself, that's not going to make her happy." But have you ever stopped and wondered whether perhaps your friend might think the same thing about your choices? Do you really know what makes you happy? You probably think you do. But, as is often the case in science, the whole story is much more complex than you might think at first.

Consider two things that many people would consider sure-fire sources of happiness: having tons of money and living in a sunny climate. It seems intuitively obvious that money and sunshine would make a person happy. In other words, our intuition tells us the following:

- money → happiness
- sunshine → happiness

But when we look closely at these examples, we see that our intuitions about what makes us happy are not always supported by science. Although there is a folk saying that holds that "Money can't buy happiness," people's behavior shows that they do not believe that folk saying. Most people sure do behave as if they believe that money buys happiness: they work long hours to earn more money and they buy lottery tickets against all odds.

The reality is graphed in Figure 7.2. Happiness initially increases as income increases, but this relationship tapers off at about $75,000 per household. That is, adding income beyond $75,000 does not add significantly more positive emotions to one's life, nor does income beyond $75,000 eliminate negative emotions such as sadness, stress, or worry.

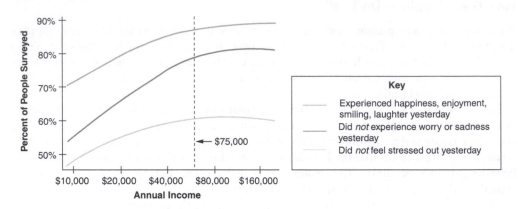

Figure 7.2 After about $75,000, increasing income is not associated with increases in happiness or decreases in stress and worry. Adapted from Kahneman and Deaton (2010).

Here's another illustration of the weak positive effects of money on happiness: over the last 50 years, average personal income has tripled, yet, over the same period of time, surveys rating levels of happiness show no change. These same relations have been observed all over the world (Easterlin et al., 2010). Such findings indicate that after basic needs are met, increasing income and material things does not necessarily increase the preponderance of positive emotions in one's life. It might all come down to what money can buy. If it can buy you security or the opportunity to give your life more meaning through education or contribution, then, yes, perhaps money can buy happiness.

Now let's look at the idea that living in a sunny climate would make you happy. Many scientists have tested the hypothesis that weather directly affects mood, but in all these studies they have documented only a small effect of weather on mood, or no effect at all. It turns out that people in Michigan are just as happy as people in Arizona (Keller et al., 2005). However, it is true that the amount of sunlight is often positively related to mood—that is, that more sunlight causes positive affect (Kööts, Realo, & Allik, 2011). This could occur because the production of serotonin, a neurochemical that is associated with positive feelings, increases with increased light (Lambert et al., 2002). Another finding is that any small effect of weather on mood only occurs for people who spend a significant amount of time outdoors in the weather itself (Keller et al., 2005; Kööts et al., 2011). Of course, there are likely *indirect* effects of weather: for example, people might be happy that the weather is good, perhaps because they can write about it on social media.

Research has documented many more disconnects between our beliefs about what makes us happy and the reality of what actually makes us happy. What is wrong with us? Why aren't our predictions and beliefs correct? In the next section, we'll investigate what limitations we have in predicting and controlling our happiness, and we'll then conclude by summarizing what science has revealed about what does cause happiness.

Affective Forecasting

The limitations that affect our ability to make judgments about happiness include decision-making biases and an inability to take account of how other aspects of our behavior regularly influence our emotions. These limitations in turn affect the extent to which we can control our own happiness.

Scientists use the term **affective forecasting** to refer to the process by which people generate predictions about the emotional effects of future life events (Wilson & Gilbert, 2003). Studies of affective forecasting have revealed a number of illusions about emotions. These studies also tell us about the consequences of the illusions for the pursuit of happiness. As you will see in the following sections, the bottom line is that people are not good affective forecasters.

Impact Bias

We are all familiar with how optical illusions can convince us, for instance, that two circles are the same size even though they're not. Research has demonstrated several examples of emotional illusions as well. If you've ever had your heart broken, you may have been convinced that you would never get over it. But you did. Your initial prediction was subject to **impact bias**, or the tendency to exaggerate the strength and duration of anticipated or future emotional reactions (Gilbert, Driver-Linn, & Wilson, 2002). For example, impact bias might cause you to imagine your life after being hired or fired or finding or losing love as more different than it actually turns out to be. In one study of impact bias, students were asked to predict how happy or unhappy they would be if their dorm assignments were fulfilled or not. Later, after they had received their housing and lived in it, their happiness was measured again. Results showed that students significantly overestimated their level of happiness for a good assignment and underestimated their level of unhappiness for a bad assignment compared to the eventual reality of the impact of the housing assignment (Dunn, Wilson, & Gilbert, 2003). Other research shows that people overestimate how unhappy they would be several months after a romantic breakup, university professors overestimate how unhappy they would be five years after being denied tenure, and women overestimate how unhappy they would be if they received an unwanted result on a pregnancy test (e.g., Mellers & McGraw, 2001).

Impact bias can be explained in part by a phenomenon known as **focalism**, in which people focus on one element in their lives to the expense of others (Wilson, Meyers, & Gilbert, 2001). Even when you experience something with strong emotional implications, many other aspects of your life go on as before. However, when you think about the emotional impact of a single event, focalism causes you to focus on the event itself and forget all the other parts of your life that cause emotions and affect your happiness. You get married to the love of your life, but your job is still annoying. You get fired from your dream job, but your family stays the same.

In an interesting study of focalism, Schkade and Kahneman (1998) asked undergraduate students at universities in the Midwest and in California to report how happy they were and to estimate how happy students were at other universities. As you can guess from the preceding paragraphs, students in the two regions did not differ in average happiness levels. Although students thought that they were happier than the typical student, all students thought that people in California were, on average, happier than people in the Midwest. We already know they were wrong, but why? It turns out that the participants believed that the weather in California makes people in California happier than in the Midwest. In other words, students believe that California weather makes people happy (which does not receive empirical support), and because they focus almost exclusively on the weather, they believe that people in California are happy (which also does not receive empirical support). Thus, sometimes people just focus too much on the weather!

Memory Bias

Another limitation on our predictions about our future emotions is **memory bias**, which causes people to base their affective forecasts on memories of similar experiences in the past.

There are several types of memory bias. One type is caused by **emotion-congruent retrieval**, in which people remember past events or features of past events not as they actually happened, but with the same emotional tone as the state they are currently in (Bower, 1981). For example, if you are sad when you are trying to decide whether to go sailing, you are likely to recall past sailing experiences that were disappointing (maybe the weather was very bad one time or you lost a sailing race another time). Calling up sad memories might then lead you to decide not to go sailing, even though you might very well enjoy it, if only you would give it a chance. This is an example of how poor affective forecasting can cause you to miss out on potential sources of happiness. (See Chapter 8 for a full discussion of emotion-congruent retrieval.)

A second memory bias is described by the **peak–end rule**, which states that people tend to recall their emotions in a way that neglects the duration of the event that caused the emotions and is summarized by an average of the most intense emotion and the emotional intensity at the very end of the event or time period (hence, "peak–end rule"). In a classic demonstration of this bias, Kahneman and his colleagues had experimental participants experience two different events in the laboratory (Kahneman et al., 1993). All participants put their hand in very cold water for 60 seconds (event A). They also put their hand in very cold water for 60 seconds followed by mildly cold water for an additional 30 seconds (event B). Because both events were unpleasant, it would make sense to assume that when asked later a participant would say that event B was a more unpleasant experience than event A. However, participants actually rated event A as more unpleasant than event B. This means that how they were feeling at the end of the experience (in event A the end of the experience was still the impression of very cold water) determined their memory for how the experience felt. The same results have been found when patients' estimates of the discomfort of colonoscopy were studied, and these are illustrated in Figure 7.3 (Redelmeier & Kahneman, 1996).

There are many other examples of biases that lead to errors of affective forecasting, such as the fact that we sometimes base our decisions on simple sayings such as "Variety is the spice of life!" We wish to preserve choice and variety, despite the fact that research shows that we are often more satisfied with routine and fewer choices (Iyengar & Lepper, 2000).

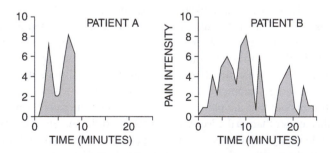

Figure 7.3 The peak–end rule says that people judge the emotional experience of an event by averaging the most intense moment with their feelings at the end of the event. This is illustrated in the report of pain by two patients. Redelmeier and Kahneman asked participants to report on their pain after the procedure. They found that even though Patient B suffered for twice as long, he or she remembered the pain as less intense than Patient A did, apparently because it had a gentler ending. From Redelmeier & Kahneman (1996).

Hedonic Adaptation

Another problem for seeking happiness is that when something does bring us happiness, over time we get used to it. Why don't we stay happy? Why aren't you as happy today as you were the day you graduated high school or as sad as you were on the day your grandmother died? One reason is that you adapt to whatever life sends your way. The term **hedonic adaptation** refers to people's tendency to habituate to the impact of repeated emotional experiences.

In a famous study of the emotional impacts of winning the lottery and of suffering a debilitating accident, Brickman, Campbell, and Janoff-Bulman (1978) documented hedonic adaptation to important positive and negative events. People tend to think that someone who wins a huge lottery will be happy for life and that someone who becomes a paraplegic as the result of a traumatic accident will be depressed for life. However, that is not the case. The emotions of people who experienced these two types of events are graphed in Figure 7.4. Over time, lottery winners' happiness returns to a lower level, no different from people who did not win the lottery. In the same way, people's unhappiness at suffering a traumatic accident also lessens. As a famous researcher in this field said,

> It's like eating pancakes: the first pancake is delicious, the second one is good, the third okay. By the fifth pancake, you're at a point where an infinite number more will not satisfy you to any greater degree. But no one stops earning money or striving for more money after they reach $50,000.

Scientists generally believe that hedonic adaptation is adaptive for human survival (Frederick & Loewenstein, 1999). This reasoning is based on the idea that our emotional reactions constitute useful information about the environment. For example, the fact that you are afraid when standing on the edge of a cliff is important information; it tells you what to do—step

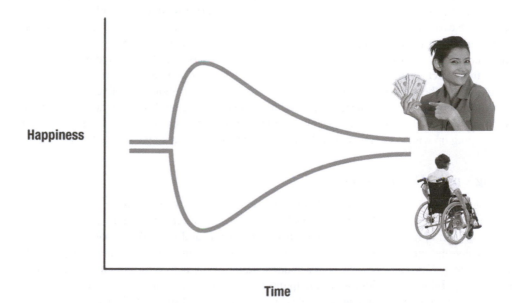

Time

Figure 7.4 After winning the lottery or experiencing a traumatic accident, people's reports of happiness changed in the ways you might expect. But over time their happiness returns to the level it was at before the event.

away from the edge! If people's emotions did not diminish over time, they would be less able to distinguish between objects and events that were more important (offering new information) or less important (offering already known information) to their survival. Indeed, if people did not experience hedonic adaptation, they would get overwhelmed and exhausted by their elevated emotions and lose the ability to detect important changes in their environment. So, just as you can dive into a cold swimming pool and then feel less cold after a minute, you can adapt to new levels of joy, fear, and other emotions. This in part explains why more money and great weather slowly lose their ability to affect our happiness over time. Life happens around those things.

Social Comparison

Social comparison is yet another way that we sabotage our affective forecasting. If you look at photos of athletes standing on Olympic podiums, you'll see that the bronze medalists often look happier than the silver medalists (Medvec, Madey, & Gilovich, 1995). You might think that the silver medalist would look happier—after all, silver medalists are better off in an absolute way, because the silver medal is a higher achievement than the bronze. However, it turns out our satisfaction—our happiness—doesn't depend only on absolutes. It depends on comparisons. Because the bronze medalist is comparing herself to someone who didn't get on the podium, she is happier than the silver medalist, who is comparing herself to the gold-medal winner.

Studies of social comparison have demonstrated the relativity of happiness in many ways. Wheeler and Miyake (1992) tracked the social comparisons made by a group of students for two weeks. Some students made comparisons upward—comparing themselves to others who made better grades, had better social skills, better looks, more money, etc. Others made downward comparisons—comparing themselves to others who had worse grades, less money, and so forth. The results were quite straightforward: upward comparisons consistently caused negative feelings; downward comparisons resulted in positive feelings.

The problem with the inevitability of social comparison is that, as we try to become happy, we put ourselves in situations in which we make upward social comparisons quite frequently. For instance, when people earn more money, they use it to do things they think bring happiness, such as buying bigger houses and going on fancier vacations. The move into a new social environment will put them in contact with many people who have more than them. Boyce, Brown, and Moore (2010) showed this effect when they looked at 80,000 observations of people's income and happiness. They found that the relative rank of an individual's income—that is, how they are doing compared to others in the social environment—predicted the individual's general life satisfaction. And this relationship was much stronger than the relationship between the actual income and life satisfaction. Thus, keeping up with the Joneses truly does undermine happiness. And yet people keep doing it.

Cutting Up the Happiness Pie

As we've just seen, we don't always know what makes us happy. Our affective forecasts are poor, due to both cognitive biases and a lack of insight into the fact that adaptation and social comparison can blunt emotional outcomes over time. So what does make us happy? This isn't just an academic question. Knowing what makes us happy can actually make us happier. As Tal Ben Shahar (2007) argues, "A better understanding of the nature of happiness—and, most important, applying certain ideas—can help most people in most situations become happier."

Scientists have shown that your happiness is actually caused by several factors: genes, life circumstances (the fact that you were born male or live in Minneapolis), and the small details of your day-to-day life (the music you are listening to, the lunch you just had with a friend). Research has provided estimates for those influences, as shown in the pie chart in Figure 7.5. In the following sections, we look into this research in more detail.

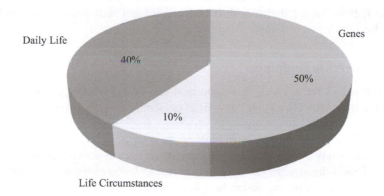

Figure 7.5 Research suggests that about 50 percent of your happiness is determined by your genes, 10 percent by life circumstances such as demographic factors (sex, age, geographic location), and the rest—a full 40 percent—by the details of your daily life, such as how you get to work, who you hang out with, and whether or not you stop to smell the roses. Based on Lyubomirsky, Sheldon, and Schkade (2005).

Biology

Are some people just born happier than others? Is there such thing as a sunny disposition? Research in behavioral genetics does indeed support the idea that our happiness is in part due to our genes (Lykken & Tellegen, 1996; Nes et al., 2006). By some estimates, 50 percent of our happiness can be explained by our genetic material (Lyubomirsky, 2007). This might mean that the biological factors that are responsible for personality traits are also related to our experiences of pleasure and pain, happiness and unhappiness (Weiss, Bates, & Luciano, 2008). This does not mean that our happiness levels are fixed, however. In the same way that a person's weight and cholesterol levels, which both have a biological basis, can be altered by diet and exercise, our levels of happiness, though affected by biology, can change in response to other factors.

Life Circumstances

Life circumstances include demographic factors (sex, age, and geographic location) as well as life status variables (such as socioeconomic status). Suppose you hear about a particular person who has a good job, makes enough money, is in good health, and is married. You might be tempted to think that person must be happy. But in fact, you wouldn't really know anything about that person's level of happiness. Still, we continue to make assumptions about people's happiness all the time based on life circumstances. For instance, you might imagine Sandra, a 55-year-old housecleaner living in Michigan, to be less happy than Claire, a 35-year-old architect living in San Francisco. If you don't think you do make such assumptions, then ask yourself which person you would choose to be if you had the choice—Claire or Sandra? Most people would choose Claire. Yet life circumstances determine happiness far less than you may think. Scientists estimate that 10 percent of the variability in people's levels of happiness is explained by differences in life circumstances such as income, geographic location, and socioeconomic status.

Daily Life

What about daily life? Scientists estimate that the remaining 40 percent of our happiness is explained by occurrences in our daily life, meaning the concerts we go to, the people we put ourselves around, the details of our jobs, and what we choose to have for dinner. For example, you are probably happier having dinner with friends in pleasant surroundings than walking in to take an exam for which you feel unprepared.

Behaviors That Increase Happiness

What we have learned so far suggests that happiness can be cultivated by making the right choices about daily life. After all, as you know from personal experience, positive feelings are often generated by our immediate surroundings.

Research tells us that, indeed, we can learn to integrate activities that increase our happiness, just like we can learn to play the piano. What are some of the occurrences under our control that make us happier? That is the topic of extensive recent research and of the next section.

In writing about techniques for increasing happiness, Seligman (2011) wrote:

> From the Buddha to modern pop psychology, there have been at least two hundred endeavors proposed that allegedly do this. Which—if any—of these really produce lasting increases in well-being, which are temporary boosts, and which are just bogus?

Here we survey some of the behaviors that seem to cause happiness, sometimes even in lasting ways. These include (but are not limited to):

- Gratitude
- Savoring
- Mindfulness
- Positive relationships
- Generosity and helping

Gratitude

Gratitude has been defined as a state marked by a sense of wonder, thankfulness, and appreciation for life that can be expressed toward other people, as well as toward impersonal (nature) or nonhuman entities (God) (Emmons & Shelton, 2002). In a number of studies, researchers have investigated the effects of asking people to stop and reflect on those things for which they are most grateful (Emmons & Crumpler, 2000; Emmons & McCullough, 2003; Lyubomirsky, Sheldon, & Schkade, 2005; Seligman et al., 2005). The details of the studies differ, but the results are always the same: counting your blessings on a regular basis makes you happier and more content with life.

In two separate studies Emmons and McCullough (2003) found that people who were randomly assigned to list five things they were grateful for—either weekly or daily—showed significant improvements in psychological, social, and physical well-being as compared to control groups. People asked to list five good things that occurred each week reported not only better mood, but increased alertness, energy, enthusiasm, and more optimism for the future. Social well-being also improved, with people in the gratitude group feeling more helpful and more connected to others. Finally, physical well-being improved, with people in the gratitude group reporting both fewer physical complaints (headaches, stomachache, congestion) and increased exercise as compared to the control groups.

Why is gratitude so effective? To understand why, we need to take a moment to think about the ways that the human mind has evolved over hundreds of thousands of years to be adaptive in environments very different from today. Certain tendencies that may have increased survival in the past may be detrimental to individual well-being in the present. Thus these tendencies partially explain the increased rates of chronic stress so prevalent in today's affluent, industrialized societies. Two such tendencies include the **negativity bias** (see, for example, Baumeister et al., 2001) whereby we focus our attention more on the negative than the positive, and the nature of our brain's seeking system, which makes us more sensitive to moving ahead and acquiring more than in relishing the fruits of our labors. In the past, people who continually wanted more—more food, a warmer house, a safer environment for their children—fared better than those who were content to settle with what they had. As the descendants of these nonstop seekers, we have brains that are flooded with dopamine more when working toward a goal than when actually achieving it (Ikemoto & Panksepp, 1999; O'Doherty et al., 2002). The practice of gratitude may be effective in increasing happiness in part because it specifically counteracts negative bias and our brains' seeking system. Some businesses are taking advantage of the effects of gratitude by developing apps to promote gratitude practice. (for example, Munson et al., 2010).

Savoring

Think of a time when you walked instead of drove somewhere and you passed through a pleasant park. How fast did you walk? Actually, you strolled. You took the time to savor your surroundings. You paid attention to them. Hopefully you didn't look at your phone or even think about something else at the same time. Why? Because you wanted to savor the moment. You know instinctively that by focusing your attention on your walk you can extend the enjoyment and milk it for more.

On a neurological level, pleasure can be thought of as a "continuous low-level activation of reward circuits" (Fredrickson, 2009). It is true that focused attention increases the total pleasure derived from an experience. People told to focus on eating chocolate reported more pleasure than those who were distracted (LeBel & Dube, 2001). The ability to savor the positive experiences in your life is one of the most important ingredients of happiness. People who savor and live in the present are better off on a variety of measures. Researchers describe **savoring** as the capacity to attend to the joys and pleasures of experience. Note then that savoring refers to the *capacity* to attend to the joys and pleasures of experience. That suggests that the ability to savor is something we can develop, a skill that can be learned.

In a series of studies, researchers showed the relationship between savoring and happiness by turning the relationship around and seeing whether lack of savoring food in a fast food restaurant is associated with less pleasure (House, DeVoe, & Zhong, 2013). In a first study, the researchers looked at the number of fast food signals (the presence of fast food restaurants and signs) in a person's environment (by using their ZIP code) and related these to reports of positive affect and pleasure. The number of fast food restaurants in the neighborhood was indeed negatively related to savoring even after other factors were controlled for. This means that when people are cued to be impatient and rush over pleasant experiences such as eating, they feel less happy. Further laboratory studies also confirmed this pattern of results.

Mindfulness

Mindfulness is another behavior that can increase your level of happiness. The term **mindfulness** refers to the awareness that arises from paying attention to the present moment, on purpose and without judgment (Kabat-Zinn, 2003). By directing attention to immediate experience, you can gain insight into how your mind responds to the environment. This makes it possible to see thoughts and emotions as mental events instead of facts. This understanding then allows you to gradually abandon mental habits that encourage stress, reactivity, anxiety, and depression.

There are now a substantial number of studies of adults demonstrating beneficial effects of mindfulness practice on a broad range of physical and mental health factors; on social and emotional well-being; and on cognitive capacities such as learning, memory, and attention (Grossman et al., 2004; Keng, Smoski, & Robins, 2011). Brain imaging studies have shown that these behavioral changes are reflected in reliable changes in brain structure and functioning as a result of mindfulness practice (Brefczynski-Lewis et al., 2007; Cahn & Polich, 2006; Weare, 2013). Davidson and Lutz (2008), for instance, showed increased blood flow to and thickening of areas in the cerebral cortex associated with attention and emotional integration in people practicing mindfulness. Results are particularly strong with experienced meditators, but have also been found with people participating in eight-week mindfulness meditation training programs, with increased gray-matter density in brain areas associated with learning and memory and decreased gray-matter density in brain areas associated with anxiety and stress.

Due to the impact of the empirical research base, mindfulness is now practiced by personnel in over 200 hospitals and medical centers worldwide, and is being used in universities such as Harvard and Oxford in fields as diverse as medicine, business, and law. It is now officially recognized by the National Institutes of Health (NIH) in the United States and the National Institute of Clinical Excellence (NICE) in the United Kingdom. It is so effective in treating depression that the NIH now *mandates* mindfulness training for people with recurrent episodes of major depression.

Mindfulness-based programs involve a variety of exercises, which include:

- **Body scan meditation**: concentrating intentionally on each part of the body with varying degrees of breath of attention
- **Sitting meditation**: focusing attention intentionally on one's breathing while in a sitting position
- **Walking meditation** walking while focusing attention intentionally on the physical sensations that are produced

Positive Relationships

Of all the things that affect happiness, relationships with others seem to be the most significant factor (Reis & Gable, 2003). Hundreds of studies have shown that people who have a network of close, supportive relationships are personally happier and healthier than people lacking such a network (Baumgardner & Crothers, 2009). The quality of our social relationships has been found to be one of the most important factors in predicting not only psychological health, but our physical health as well (Cohen, 2004).

Diener and Biswas-Diener (2008) conducted a study on the effects of relationships using experience-sampling techniques. Participants rated their levels of introversion and extroversion before the study started (because it could be that only extroverts feel happy when with others). Throughout the study they rated their feelings on a scale of 0 (no positive feelings) to 6 (extremely intense positive feelings) at different times during the day. Results showed that both introverts and extroverts had more positive emotions when they were with other people compared to when they were alone. Kahneman et al. (2004) found similar results when they asked over 1000 female participants about their happiness. The participants were least happy at times of the day when they were alone (commuting to work, using the computer) and happiest at times when they were with others (socializing, eating).

Diener and Seligman (2002) screened college students for their level of happiness and then selected the "very happy" people to study in fine detail. These researchers observed that every single one of them had excellent social relationships. People who were less happy did not always have excellent relationships. Quantity and, more importantly, quality of friendships correlate positively with happiness, and perceived loneliness is robustly linked to depression.

Of course, the findings reviewed here do not mean we always want to be with people. However, it seems that when we are with others and have the knowledge that we can be because our social connections are strong, we are generally happier. Clearly, teaching people social skills has more benefits than you might have realized!

Generosity and Helping

Earlier in this chapter we discussed research showing that money does not buy happiness. It turns out that is not entirely true. Money can buy happiness when it is used in the right way. How? By spending it on other people!

Developmental Detail

The Act of Giving Makes Toddlers Feel Happy Too!

When adults give money away, it makes them happy, happier even than when they receive it (Aknin et al., 2013)! What about children? You might think that children are selfish little things who are worried mostly about keeping resources for themselves. Scientists Aknin, Hamlin, and Dunn (2012) thought maybe not. They looked back over a number of studies that they had conducted on the social behavior of toddlers. In all of the studies, the toddlers had played a game with toys that did or did not involve the act of giving. In most of the past studies, the toddler either gave a toy to a puppet and the puppet responded positively, or the toddler played with a toy that produced an appealing sound that a puppet had taught them to activate and the puppet responded positively. Trained coders watched the videotapes of the toddlers playing these two games, remaining blind to which game they were playing, and coded the toddlers' faces on 7-point scales of expressed happiness. Findings showed that even though they were all having a good time, the toddlers who gave the puppet a toy expressed the most happiness (see panel A of the figure).

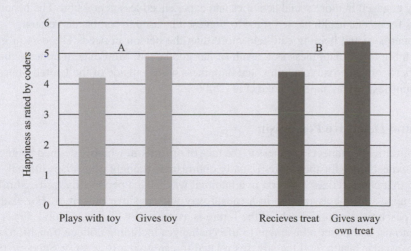

The experimenters then did a new study. This time, toddlers got treats of crackers such as Teddy Grahams and gave them away under conditions in which the giving was or was not personally costly to do so. Specifically, each child first met several puppets that were said to love getting treats, and they observed the experimenter giving each one a treat. The toddlers were then introduced to a new puppet and found out that it also loved treats. Under conditions in which treats seemed to be scarce, the toddlers received treats and could also give treats to the new puppet. Coding of the toddlers' facial expressions during different parts of the experimental paradigm showed that giving away treats made them most happy (panel B of the figure), and this happiness was not caused by the puppet's reaction of gratefulness so much as the act of giving itself.

Dunn, Aknin, and Norton (2008) gave people envelopes with either $5 or $20 and told them either to spend it on themselves before 5 p.m. that day or spend it on someone else. Later that day, the researchers recontacted the participants and asked them how they were feeling. People who spent the money on others reported higher levels of well-being than those who spent it on themselves, regardless of the amount. The pleasure of giving money to others can also be detected in the brain. In another study, participants who were in a functional magnetic resonance imaging (fMRI) scanner either saw transfers of money to a charity (presented on a computer screen) or were given the opportunity to choose to transfer the money to a charity. Both types of giving money activated pleasure centers of the brain (Harbaugh, Mayr, & Burghart, 2007).

Of course, there are many ways to be generous and helpful, and most all of them bring happiness. Schwartz (1999), for example, conducted a study to examine the effects of peer telephone support on multiple sclerosis (MS) patients. Their sample included 72 women with MS. Five women from the sample were selected as peer supporters, trained in active and compassionate listening techniques. The women then called each patient once a month and had a 15-minute conversation. Results showed that 15 minutes of peer support per month had beneficial effects on patient well-being. But more interestingly, results showed that the people who were doing the helping benefited the most. The five peer supporters reported increased satisfaction, self-efficacy, and feelings of mastery. They engaged in more social activities and experienced less depression. The benefits of helping others for mental health has led some to suggest it be used to combat depression.

In sum, generosity and helping can help more than the person in need. The person giving seems to get a big jolt of happiness as a result of her good deed. Moreover, it appears that the relationship between generosity, helping, and happiness holds outside of the United States and reaches to countries such as Japan (Otake et al., 2006).

Optimism and Defensive Pessimism

Most people intuitively connect happiness to the idea of **optimism**, which is defined by generalized positive expectations for the future. Usually optimism is thought of as dispositional—that is, something that characterizes a person in a habitual way (like a personality trait). Similar to happiness, it appears to be associated in a causal way with positive outcomes. For example, compared to pessimism, optimism about the future is associated with better mood, fewer psychiatric symptoms, and better adjustment to life challenges including college transition, pregnancy, cardiovascular health, and the stresses related to caregiving (Carver & Scheier, 1999).

However, optimism is not always a good thing. There are contradictory findings on the relationship between optimism and health (Segerstrom, 2005): sometimes optimism is associated with positive outcomes and sometimes more negative ones. One hypothesis, the disappointment hypothesis, suggests that optimism can make people vulnerable to substantial distress when faced with undeniable or uncontrollable negative outcomes (such as a diagnosis). Some research finds support for this idea (Sieber et al., 1992). A second hypothesis that has also received some empirical support is the engagement hypothesis (Segerstrom, 2001). This hypothesis says that when faced with a difficult situation, optimistic people keep trying to deal with it, whereas more pessimistic people give up. Sometimes it is not a bad idea to give up. Giving up can be physiologically protective because the negative effects of the difficult situation are avoided.

Optimism also plays a complex role in decision making. In general people make unrealistically optimistic predictions about the future, especially their own future (Lench & Ditto, 2008). This is called the **optimism bias**, and it does have some benefits (Sharot, 2011). For instance, unrealistic optimism seems to protect people from becoming depressed (Taylor & Brown, 1988). However, there are also downsides. The optimism bias sometimes results in bad decision making. These include engaging in risky behaviors such as smoking and speeding, and also the failure to plan for the future such as getting vaccinations and saving for retirement (Brewer et al., 2007; Jackson & Aiken, 2000; Madrian & Shea, 2001). In other words, assuming that everything is rosy sometimes prevents people from preparing appropriately or from paying attention to relevant statistics.

Conversely, pessimism can be useful, at least for certain people. Some individuals who are not dispositionally optimistic have been called **defensive pessimists**. Rather than predicting the best about their future (for example, performance on an upcoming exam) the way an optimist would, defensive pessimists tend to set low goals ("I am not going to do very well") and think through alternative plans and outcomes in anticipation of failure. Setting low expectations works well for these people because it motivates them to work hard, all the while protecting themselves against the possibility of disappointment (Norem & Cantor, 1986; Showers, 1992). When defensive

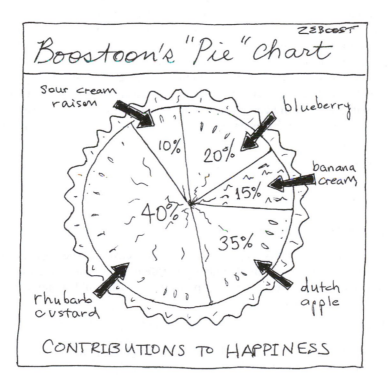

pessimists are prevented from using this defensive way of thinking, they actually perform worse (Norem & Illingworth, 1993). Thus, telling some people to be positive and optimistic before they are confronted with difficult circumstances is not the best way to help them do their best!

A consideration of optimism and defensive pessimism helps to put in perspective the meaning of the findings reported in this chapter. Positive feelings may be good for the body and good for relationships. However, for some people, there are times when negative emotions or states are temporarily beneficial. As we learned in Chapter 4, negative emotions have important functions too.

Summary

People have been talking about happiness for centuries. The French philosopher, theologian, and mathematician Blaise Pascal, in the seventeenth century, said

> All men seek happiness. This is without exception. Whatever different means they employ, they all tend to this end. The cause of some going to war, and of others avoiding it, is the same desire in both, attended with different views. The will never takes the least step but to this object. This is the motive of every action of every man, even of those who hang themselves.

If Pascal was right, then this chapter should have convinced you of why people seek happiness.

- First, happiness is associated with many positive outcomes, including better work, relationships, and health. Although in the past people have thought that good work, good relationships, and good health caused happiness, the reverse causality is at least as strong—in other words, happiness influences all of those positive outcomes.
- People think they know a lot about what will bring them happiness, but they are often wrong. In fact, people are poor affective forecasters. People think that emotion-eliciting events will have more intense and longer impact than they actually do. And people have trouble remembering the emotional impact of past events, so they do a poor job of using their own memory to make affective forecasts.
- Furthermore, people do not seem to know that they experience hedonic adaptation, or the tendency to habituate to things that brought them happiness initially. Comparing with others also tends to reduce the effects of certain things, such as wealth, on our happiness.
- Although our genes and life circumstances do play a role in how happy we are, details of our daily lives do too. Scientists have found that engaging in the following behaviors can bring us more happiness:
  - Gratitude
  - Savoring
  - Mindfulness
  - Positive relationships
  - Generosity and helping
- As we've seen throughout this chapter, happiness, subjective well-being, and psychological well-being are complex, but this shouldn't dissuade us from continuing to research them further. Indeed, as Pascal and others have pointed out, what could be more important?

Learning Links

1. Explore a website that tracks in real time the average happiness expressed on Twitter. http://hedonometer.org/index.html

2. View a chart that shows the average happiness of 82 jobs. http://www.wsj.com/articles/SB1 0001424052748703466704575489790936423402

3. Watch a TED talk by Dr. Nataly Kogan, who created happier.com, a site (https://www.happier.com) where you post your happy thoughts/moments and can share them with friends or everyone. https://www.youtube.com/watch?time_continue=917&v=tKaCN0-kpVE

4. See Frans de Waal's TED talk on the moral behavior of animals (relating to generosity and positive feelings). https://www.ted.com/talks/frans_de_waal_do_animals_have_morals?language=en

References

Aknin, L. B., Barrington-Leigh, C. P., Dunn, E. W., Helliwell, J. F., Burns, J., Biswas-Diener, R., . . . Norton, M. I. (2013). Prosocial spending and well-being: Cross-cultural evidence for a psychological universal. *Journal of Personality and Social Psychology, 104*(4), 635–652. doi:10.1037/a0031578.

Aknin, L. B., Hamlin, J. K., & Dunn, E. W. (2012). Giving leads to happiness in young children. *PLoS One, 7*(6), e39211. doi:10.1371/journal.pone.0039211.

Baumeister, R. F., Bratslavsky, E., Finkenauer, C., & Vohs, K. D. (2001). Bad is stronger than good. *Review of General Psychology, 5*(4), 323. doi:10.1037/1089–2680.5.4.323.

Baumgardner, S. R., & Crothers, M. K. (2009). *Positive psychology*. Upper Saddle River, NJ: Prentice Hall/Pearson Education.

Ben-Shahar, T. (2007). *Happier: Learn the secrets to daily joy and lasting fulfillment* (pp. 7). McGraw-Hill Companies. doi:10.1036/0071492399.

Bower, G. H. (1981). Mood and memory. *American Psychologist, 36*(2), 129–148. doi:10.1037/0003–066x.36.2.129.

Boyce, C. J., Brown, G. D., & Moore, S. C. (2010). Money and happiness rank of income, not income, affects life satisfaction. *Psychological Science, 21*(4), 471–475. doi:10.1177/0956797610362671.

Brefczynski-Lewis, J. A., Lutz, A., Schaefer, H. S., Levinson, D. B., & Davidson, R. J. (2007). Neural correlates of attentional expertise in long-term meditation practitioners. *Proceedings of the National Academy of Sciences, 104*(27), 11483–11488. doi:10.1073/pnas.0606552104.

Brewer, N. T., Chapman, G. B., Gibbons, F. X., Gerrard, M., McCaul, K. D., & Weinstein, N. D. (2007). Meta-analysis of the relationship between risk perception and health behavior: The example of vaccination. *Health Psychology, 26*(2), 136. doi:10.1037/0278–6133.26.2.136.

Brickman, P., Coates, D., & Janoff-Bulman, R. (1978). Lottery winners and accident victims: Is happiness relative? *Journal of Personality and Social Psychology, 36*(8), 917–927. doi:10.1037/0022–3514.36.8.917.

Cahn, B. R., & Polich, J. (2006). Meditation states and traits: EEG, ERP, and neuroimaging studies. *Psychological Bulletin, 132*(2), 180. doi:10.1037/0033–2909.132.2.180.

Carver, C. S., & Scheier, M. F. (1999). Themes and issues in the self-regulation of behavior. In R. S. Wyer Jr. (Ed.), *Perspectives on behavioral self-regulation: Advances in social cognition* (Vol. XII, pp. 1–105). Mahwah, NJ: Lawrence Erlbaum Associates Publishers.

Cohen, S. (2004). Social relationships and health. *American Psychologist, 59*(8), 676. doi:10.1037/0003–066x.59.8.676.

Danner, D. D., Snowdon, D. A., & Friesen, W. V. (2001). Positive emotions in early life and longevity: Findings from the nun study. *Journal of Personality and Social Psychology, 80*(5), 804. doi:10.1037/0022–3514.80.5.804.

Davidson, R. J., & Lutz, A. (2008). Buddha's brain: Neuroplasticity and meditation. *IEEE Signal Processing Magazine, 25*(1), 176. doi:10.1109/msp.2008.4431873.

de Groot, J. H., Smeets, M. A., Rowson, M. J., Bulsing, P. J., Blonk, C. G., Wilkinson, J. E., & Semin, G. R. (2015). A sniff of happiness. *Psychological Science, 26*, 0956797614566318. doi:10.1177/0956797614566318.

Deaton, A., & Stone, A. A. (2014). Evaluative and hedonic wellbeing among those with and without children at home. *Proceedings of the National Academy of Sciences, 111*(4), 1328–1333. doi:10.1073/pnas.1311600111.

Diener, E. (2006). Guidelines for national indicators of subjective well-being and ill-being. *Applied Research in Quality of Life, 1*(2), 151–157. doi:10.1007/s11482–006–9007-x.

Diener, E., & Biswas-Diener, R. (2008). *Rethinking happiness: The science of psychological wealth*. Malden, MA: Blackwell Publishing.

Diener, E., & Seligman, M. E. (2002). Very happy people. *Psychological Science, 13*(1), 81–84. doi:10.1111/1467–9280.00415.

Dunn, E. W., Aknin, L. B., & Norton, M. I. (2008). Spending money on others promotes happiness. *Science, 319*(5870), 1687–1688. doi:10.1126/science.1150952.

Dunn, E. W., Wilson, T. D., & Gilbert, D. T. (2003). Location, location, location: The misprediction of satisfaction in housing lotteries. *Personality and Social Psychology Bulletin, 29*(11), 1421–1432. doi:10.1177/0146167203256867.

Easterlin, R. A., McVey, L. A., Switek, M., Sawangfa, O., & Zweig, J. S. (2010). The happiness–income paradox revisited. *Proceedings of the National Academy of Sciences, 107*(52), 22463–22468. doi:10.1073/pnas.1015962107.

Emmons, R. A., & Crumpler, C. A. (2000). Gratitude as a human strength: Appraising the evidence. *Journal of Social and Clinical Psychology, 19*(1), 56–69. doi:10.1521/jscp.2000.19.1.56.

Emmons, R. A., & McCullough, M. E. (2003). Counting blessings versus burdens: An experimental investigation of gratitude and subjective well-being in daily life. *Journal of Personality and Social Psychology, 84*(2), 377. doi:10.1037//0022–3514.84.2.377.

Emmons, R. A., & Shelton, C. M. (2002). Gratitude and the science of positive psychology. *Handbook of Positive Psychology, 18*, 459–471.

Frederick, S., & Loewenstein, G. (1999). Hedonic adaptation. In D. Kahneman, E. Diener & N. Schwarz (Eds.), *Well being: The foundations of hedonic psychology* (pp. 302–329). New York: Russell Sage Foundation.

Fredrickson, B. L. (2001). The role of positive emotions in positive psychology: The broaden-and-build theory of positive emotions. *American Psychologist, 56*(3), 218. doi:10.1037/0003–066x.56.3.218.

Fredrickson, B. L. (2009). *Positivity*. New York, NY: Crown Publishers. doi:10.1080/17439760903157109.

Gilbert, D. T., Driver-Linn, E., & Wilson, T. D. (2002). The trouble with Vronsky: Impact bias in the forecasting of future affective states. In L. Feldman Barrett, & P. Salovey (Eds), *The wisdom in feeling: Psychological processes in emotional intelligence.* (pp. 114–143). New York, NY: Guilford Press

Graham, C., Eggers, A., & Sukhtankar, S. (2004). Does happiness pay? An exploration based on panel data from Russia. *Journal of Economic Behavior & Organization, 55*(3), 319–342. doi:10.1016/s0167–2681(04)00047–2.

Grossman, P., Niemann, L., Schmidt, S., & Walach, H. (2004). Mindfulness-based stress reduction and health benefits: A meta-analysis. *Journal of Psychosomatic Research, 57*(1), 35–43. doi:10.1016/s0022-3999(03)00573-7.

Hansen, T. (2012). Parenthood and happiness: A review of folk theories versus empirical evidence. *Social Indicators Research, 108*(1), 29–64. doi:10.1007/s11205–011–9865-y.

Harbaugh, W. T., Mayr, U., & Burghart, D. R. (2007). Neural responses to taxation and voluntary giving reveal motives for charitable donations. *Science, 316*(5831), 1622–1625. doi:10.1126/science.1140738.

House, J., DeVoe, S. E., & Zhong, C. B. (2013). Too impatient to smell the roses: Exposure to fast food impedes happiness. *Social Psychological and Personality Science, 41*, 534–541. doi:10.1177/1948550613511498.

Ikemoto, S., & Panksepp, J. (1999). The role of nucleus accumbens dopamine in motivated behavior: A unifying interpretation with special reference to reward-seeking. *Brain Research Reviews, 31*(1), 6–41. doi:10.1016/s0165–0173(99)00023–5.

Iyengar, S. S., & Lepper, M. R. (2000). When choice is demotivating: Can one desire too much of a good thing? *Journal of Personality and Social Psychology, 79*(6), 995. doi:10.1037/0022–3514.79.6.995.

Jackson, K. M., & Aiken, L. S. (2000). A psychosocial model of sun protection and sunbathing in young women: The impact of health beliefs, attitudes, norms, and self-efficacy for sun protection. *Health Psychology, 19*(5), 469. doi:10.1037/0278–6133.19.5.469.

Kabat-Zinn, J. (2003). Mindfulness-based interventions in context: Past, present, and future. *Clinical Psychology: Science and Practice, 10*(2), 144–156. doi:10.1093/clipsy/bpg016.

Kahneman, D. (2011). *Thinking, fast and slow*. London: Macmillan. doi:10.1007/s00362–013–0533-y.

Kahneman, D., & Deaton, A. (2010). High income improves evaluation of life but not emotional well-being. *Proceedings of the National Academy of Sciences*, *107*(38), 16489–16493. doi:10.1073/pnas.1011492107.

Kahneman, D., Fredrickson, B. L., Schreiber, C. A., & Redelmeier, D. A. (1993). When more pain is preferred to less: Adding a better end. *Psychological Science*, *4*(6), 401–405. doi:10.1111/j.1467–9280.1993.tb00589.x.

Kahneman, D., Krueger, A. B., Schkade, D. A., Schwarz, N., & Stone, A. A. (2004). A survey method for characterizing daily life experience: The day reconstruction method. *Science*, *306*(5702), 1776–1780. doi:10.1126/science.1103572.

Kahneman, D., Schkade, D. A., Fischler, C., Krueger, A. B., & Krilla, A. (2010). The structure of well-being in two cities: Life satisfaction and experienced happiness in Columbus, Ohio; and Rennes, France. *International Differences in Well-Being*, *1*(9), 16–34. doi:10.1093/acprof:oso/9780199732739.003.0002.

Keller, M. C., Fredrickson, B. L., Ybarra, O., Côté, S., Johnson, K., Mikels, J., . . . Wager, T. (2005). A warm heart and a clear head the contingent effects of weather on mood and cognition. *Psychological Science*, *16*(9), 724–731. doi:10.1111/j.1467–9280.2005.01602.x.

Keng, S. L., Smoski, M. J., & Robins, C. J. (2011). Effects of mindfulness on psychological health: A review of empirical studies. *Clinical Psychology Review*, *31*(6), 1041–1056. doi:10.1016/j.cpr.2011.04.006.

Keyes, C. L., Shmotkin, D., & Ryff, C. D. (2002). Optimizing well-being: The empirical encounter of two traditions. *Journal of Personality and Social Psychology*, *82*(6), 1007. doi:10.1037/0022–3514.82.6.1007.

Kööts, L., Realo, A., & Allik, J. (2011). The influence of the weather on affective experience: An experience sampling study. *Journal of Individual Differences*, *32*(2), 74–84. doi:10.1027/1614-0001/a000037.

Lambert, G. W., Reid, C., Kaye, D. M., Jennings, G. L., & Esler, M. D. (2002). Effect of sunlight and season on serotonin turnover in the brain. *The Lancet*, *360*(9348), 1840–1842. doi:10.1016/s0140–6736(02)11737–5.

LeBel, J. L., & Dube, L. (2001, June). The impact of sensory knowledge and attentional focus on pleasure and on behavioral responses to hedonic stimuli. Paper presented at the 13th annual American Psychological Society Convention, Toronto, Ontario, Canada.

Lench, H. C., & Ditto, P. H. (2008). Automatic optimism: Biased use of base rate information for positive and negative events. *Journal of Experimental Social Psychology*, *44*(3), 631–639. doi:10.1016/j.jesp.2007.02.011.

Linley, P. A., & Joseph, S. (2004). Toward a theoretical foundation for positive psychology in practice. In P. A. Linley & S. Joseph (Eds), *Positive psychology in practice* (pp. 713–731). Hoboken, NJ: Wiley.

Lucas, R. E., Clark, A. E., Georgellis, Y., & Diener, E. (2003). Reexamining adaptation and the set point model of happiness: Reactions to changes in marital status. *Journal of Personality and Social Psychology*, *84*(3), 527. doi:10.1037/0022–3514.84.3.527.

Lykken, D., & Tellegen, A. (1996). Happiness is a stochastic phenomenon. *Psychological Science*, *7*(3), 186–189. doi:10.1111/j.1467–9280.1996.tb00355.x.

Lyubomirsky, S. (2007). *The how of happiness: A new approach to getting the life you want*. New York, NY: Penguin. doi:10.1007/s10902–010–9200–3.

Lyubomirsky, S., King, L., & Diener, E. (2005). The benefits of frequent positive affect: Does happiness lead to success? *Psychological Bulletin*, *131*(6), 803. doi:10.1037/0033–2909.131.6.803.

Lyubomirsky, S., Sheldon, K. M., & Schkade, D. (2005). Pursuing happiness: The architecture of sustainable change. *Review of General Psychology*, *9*(2), 111. doi:10.1037/1089–2680.9.2.111.

Madrian, B., & Shea, D. (2001). The power of suggestion: An analysis of 401(k) inertia in 401(k) participation and savings behavior. *Quarterly Journal of Economics*, *116*(4), 18–116. doi:10.1162/003355301753265543.

Marks, G. N., & Fleming, N. (1999). Influences and consequences of well-being among Australian young people: 1980–1995. *Social Indicators Research*, *46*(3), 301–323. doi:10.1023/a:1006928507272.

Medvec, V. H., Madey, S. F., & Gilovich, T. (1995). When less is more: Counterfactual thinking and satisfaction among Olympic medalists. *Journal of Personality and Social Psychology*, *69*(4), 603. doi:10.1037/0022–3514.69.4.603.

Mellers, B. A., & McGraw, A. P. (2001). Anticipated emotions as guides to choice. *Current Directions in Psychological Science*, *10*(6), 210–214. doi:10.1111/1467–8721.00151.

Munson, S. A., Lauterbach, D., Newman, M. W., & Resnick, P. (2010). Happier together: Integrating a wellness application into a social network site. In T. Ploug, P. Hasle & H. Oinas-Kukkonen (Eds.), *Persuasive Technology* (pp. 27–39). Berlin Heidelberg: Springer. doi:10.1007/978–3–642–13226–1_5.

Nes, R. B., Røysamb, E., Tambs, K., Harris, J. R., & Reichborn-Kjennerud, T. (2006). Subjective well-being: Genetic and environmental contributions to stability and change. *Psychological Medicine*, *36*(7), 1033–1042. doi:10.1017/s0033291706007409.

Norem, J. K., & Cantor, N. (1986). Defensive pessimism: Harnessing anxiety as motivation. *Journal of Personality and Social Psychology*, *51*(6), 1208–1217. doi:10.1037/0022–3514.51.6.1208.

Norem, J. K., & Illingworth, K. S. (1993). Strategy-dependent effects of reflecting on self and tasks: Some implications of optimism and defensive pessimism. *Journal of Personality and Social Psychology*, *65*(4), 822. doi:10.1037/0022–3514.65.4.822.

O'Doherty, J. P., Deichmann, R., Critchley, H. D., & Dolan, R. J. (2002). Neural responses during anticipation of a primary taste reward. *Neuron*, *33*(5), 815–826. doi:10.1016/s0896–6273(02)00603–7.

Ostir, G. V., Markides, K. S., Peek, M. K., & Goodwin, J. S. (2001). The association between emotional well-being and the incidence of stroke in older adults. *Psychosomatic Medicine*, *63*(2), 210–215. doi:10.1097/00006842–200103000–00003.

Otake, K., Shimai, S., Tanaka-Matsumi, J., Otsui, K., & Fredrickson, B. L. (2006). Happy people become happier through kindness: A counting kindnesses intervention. *Journal of Happiness Studies*, *7*(3), 361–375. doi:10.1007/s10902–005–3650-z.

Pressman, S. D., Gallagher, M. W., & Lopez, S. J. (2013). Is the emotion-health connection a "first-world problem"? *Psychological Science*, *24*(4), 544–549. doi:10.1177/0956797612457382

Redelmeier, D. A., & Kahneman, D. (1996). Patients' memories of painful medical treatments: Real-time and retrospective evaluations of two minimally invasive procedures. *Pain*, *66*(1), 3–8. doi:10.1016/0304–3959(96)02994–6.

Reis, H. T., & Gable, S. L. (2003). Toward a positive psychology of relationships. In C.L.M. Keyes and J. Haidt (Eds.), *Flourishing: The positive person and the good life* (pp.129–159). Washington DC: American Psychological Association. doi:10.1037/10594–006.

Roberts, B. W., Caspi, A., & Moffitt, T. E. (2003). Work experiences and personality development in young adulthood. *Journal of Personality and Social Psychology*, *84*(3), 582. doi:10.1037/0022–3514.84.3.582.

Ryan, R. M., & Deci, E. L. (2001). On happiness and human potentials: A review of research on hedonic and eudaimonic well-being. *Annual Review of Psychology*, *52*(1), 141–166. doi:10.1146/annurev.psych.52.1.141.

Schkade, D. A., & Kahneman, D. (1998). Does living in California make people happy? A focusing illusion in judgments of life satisfaction. *Psychological Science*, *9*(5), 340–346. doi:10.1111/1467–9280.00066.

Schwartz, S. H. (1999). A theory of cultural values and some implications for work. *Applied Psychology*, *48*(1), 23–47. doi:10.1080/026999499377655.

Segerstrom, S. C. (2001). Optimism and attentional bias for negative and positive stimuli. *Personality and Social Psychology Bulletin*, *27*(10), 1334–1343. doi:10.1177/01461672012710009.

Segerstrom, S. C. (2005). Optimism and immunity: Do positive thoughts always lead to positive effects? *Brain, Behavior, and Immunity*, *19*(3), 195–200. doi:10.1016/j.bbi.2004.08.003.

Seligman, M. E. (2004). *Authentic happiness: Using the new positive psychology to realize your potential for lasting fulfillment*. New York, NY: Simon and Schuster. doi:10.1176/appi.ajp.161.5.936.

Seligman, M. E. (2011). *Learned optimism: How to change your mind and your life*. New York, NY: Vintage.

Seligman, M. E., Steen, T. A., Park, N., & Peterson, C. (2005). Positive psychology progress: Empirical validation of interventions. *American Psychologist*, *60*(5), 410. doi:10.1037/0003–066x.60.5.410.

Sharot, T. (2011). The optimism bias. *Current Biology*, *21*(23), R941–R945. doi:10.1016/j.cub.2011.10.030.

Showers, C. (1992). Compartmentalization of positive and negative self-knowledge: Keeping bad apples out of the bunch. *Journal of Personality and Social Psychology*, *62*(6), 1036. doi:10.1037/0022–3514.62.6.1036.

Sieber, W. J., Rodin, J., Larson, L., Ortega, S., Cummings, N., Levy, S., . . . Herberman, R. (1992). Modulation of human natural killer cell activity by exposure to uncontrollable stress. *Brain, Behavior, and Immunity*, *6*(2), 141–156. doi:10.1016/0889–1591(92)90014-f.

Staw, B. M., & Barsade, S. G. (1993). Affect and managerial performance: A test of the sadder-but-wiser vs. happier-and-smarter hypotheses. *Administrative Science Quarterly, 38*(2), 304–331. doi:10.2307/2393415.

Steptoe, A., Wardle, J., & Marmot, M. (2005). Positive affect and health-related neuroendocrine, cardiovascular, and inflammatory processes. *Proceedings of the National Academy of Sciences of the United States of America, 102*(18), 6508–6512. doi:10.1073/pnas.0409174102.

Taylor, S. E., & Brown, J. D. (1988). Illusion and well-being: A social psychological perspective on mental health. *Psychological Bulletin, 103*(2), 193. doi:10.1037//0033–2909.103.2.193.

Veenhoven, R. (2000). Freedom and happiness: A comparative study in forty-four nations in the early 1990s. In E. Diener & E. Suh (Eds.), *Culture and Subjective Well-Being* (pp. 257–288). Cambridge, MA: MIT Press. doi:10.1186/s13612–014–0017–4.

Wager, T. D., Scott, D. J., & Zubieta, J. K. (2007). Placebo effects on human μ-opioid activity during pain. *Proceedings of the National Academy of Sciences, 104*(26), 11056–11061. doi:10.1073/pnas.0702413104.

Waterman, A. S. (1993). Two conceptions of happiness: Contrasts of personal expressiveness (eudaimonia) and hedonic enjoyment. *Journal of Personality and Social Psychology, 64*(4), 678. doi:10.1037/0022–3514.64.4.678.

Weare, K. (2013). Developing mindfulness with children and young people: A review of the evidence and policy context. *Journal of Children's Services, 8*(2), 141–153. doi:10.1108/jcs-12–2012–0014.

Weiss, A., Bates, T. C., & Luciano, M. (2008). Happiness is a personal (ity) thing: The genetics of personality and well-being in a representative sample. *Psychological Science, 19*(3), 205–210. doi:10.1111/j.1467–9280.2008.02068.x.

Whalen, P. J., Rauch, S. L., Etcoff, N. L., McInerney, S. C., Lee, M. B., & Jenike, M. A. (1998). Masked presentations of emotional facial expressions modulate amygdala activity without explicit knowledge. *The Journal of Neuroscience, 18*(1), 411–418.

Wheeler, L., & Miyake, K. (1992). Social comparison in everyday life. *Journal of Personality and Social Psychology, 62*(5), 760. doi:10.1037/0022–3514.62.5.760.

White, M. P., & Dolan, P. (2009). Accounting for the richness of daily activities. *Psychological Science, 20*(8), 1000–1008. doi:10.1111/j.1467–9280.2009.02392.x.

Wilson, T. D., & Gilbert, D. T. (2003). Affective forecasting. *Advances in Experimental Social Psychology, 35*, 345–411. doi:10.1016/s0065–2601(03)01006–2.

Wilson, T. D., Meyers, J., & Gilbert, D. T. (2001). Lessons from the past: Do people learn from experience that emotional reactions are short-lived? *Personality and Social Psychology Bulletin, 27*(12), 1648–1661. doi:10.1177/01461672012712008.

8   Emotion and Cognition

Try to recall a recent time you felt angry. Maybe some traffic-related incident set you off: you were driving around a parking lot, looking for a space, and when you finally found one and signaled to take it, someone in a silver BMW sped into the spot. Did that anger persist? Later, driving home, were you irritated with other drivers? "All of them, they are so incompetent behind the wheel," you may have muttered to no one in particular, honking at an older woman whom you judged to be taking much too much time to turn left. At home, maybe you noticed that your roommate left dirty dishes stacked in the sink. What a pig. You were going to go to a party with him over the weekend, but now you think you won't. It would probably be a bad party, anyway . . .

Does this sound familiar? Your attention, perception, memory, judgment, and decisions are all affected by your emotional state. In this chapter we will explore how and why emotional states influence the way individuals perceive, remember, evaluate, and make decisions.

Notice that when we say emotions can influence cognition, we imply that emotions are separate from mental processes such as memory. But are emotion and cognition really two distinct processes? Maybe emotions are a type of cognition. Or maybe emotions do not come about without cognition. In either case, how can we say that emotions influence cognition? The question of whether emotion is distinct from cognition is one that has been debated in philosophy for centuries and more recently in psychology. For some theorists, emotion and cognition refer to two independent systems in the brain (Descartes, 1644; Zajonc, 1980, 1984). According to this view, emotions can occur prior to cognition, are independent of cognitive processes, and can influence their course (Zajonc, 1980). For others, cognition precedes emotion and is a necessary condition for the occurrence of emotion (Lazarus, 1982). Specifically, in this second view, emotions arise from cognitive appraisals of a situation (see Chapter 1). If emotion is dependent upon cognition, then the assertion that emotions can influence cognition is actually less meaningful. It would mean that emotions influence cognition, and that is not a very interesting hypothesis. The issue of how to define emotion and cognition is unresolved. We can't answer whether emotion and cognition are independent and, if so, which one occurs first. Probably it is accurate to say that emotion and cognition are, at the very least, interdependent (Storbeck & Clore, 2007). Cognitive processes may alter emotion (for example, cognitive reappraisal can affect which emotion is experienced), and emotion can influence, or regulate, cognitive processes in the many ways we describe in the present chapter.

We start by introducing models of how emotions are represented in our cognitive system. In particular, we briefly describe and compare two general classes of models of how emotion knowledge is stored and structured in our cognitive system: the associative network models of emotion and the embodied simulation models. Then we see how and when these models account for emotion-cognition interactions.

Mental Representation of Emotion Knowledge

We store information in memory so that we can perform mental tasks, ranging from the recognition of a particular object to complex reasoning and decision making. In cognitive psychology, the dominant models of memory have been the **associative network models** (Anderson, 1983; Collins & Loftus, 1975). According to those models, memory can be thought of as a web of semantic concepts that describe objects and events. The basic unit of thought is the proposition. An object or event is recorded in memory by a group of descriptive propositions. For example, when we perceive a dog, information about the dog is first taken in by the brain's modality systems, such as the visual, auditory, and sometimes emotion systems. These systems are responsible for seeing, hearing, and having feelings about the dog. In the brain, the sensory information is then summarized and stored as a "node" or a "unit" of information that can be thought of like a neuron. The node might store the word "DOG," and that word is then linked to nodes that stand for other features of most dogs such as "BARKING," "FURRY," and "SCARY." Later, when you think back on a dog, what is extracted from memory and used to make inferences about the dog or other dogs are these words—that is, a label for the concept "DOG" as well as words that stand for features of typical dogs.

In associative network models, nodes are connected to other nodes by associative links. The associative links are made through experience. The links also preserve something about the strength of connection between the two propositions. When one node is excited by exposure to an idea or an object (i.e., a particular dog), other nodes that are linked to it by association are activated through a process called **spreading activation** (Collins & Loftus, 1975; McNamara, 1992). This model thus predicts that when you are exposed to an example of a particular category (such as "beach"), other related thoughts (such as "cook-out") are easy to retrieve from memory. The full set of nodes and their linkages in the associative network constitute a person's memory (there are also competing accounts of how pieces of information influence each other in the conceptual system, e.g., Neely, 1991). According to this model, an idea can "come to mind" or enter consciousness such that you are aware of the thought when the corresponding node is activated above a particular threshold.

Bower (1981, 1991) added emotion concepts to the network models of memory. He suggested we have nodes that stand for what we believe about emotional states, just as we have nodes for what we know about dogs or beaches (Ingram, 1984; Niedenthal, Setterlund, & Jones, 1994; Teasdale, 1983, for related models). Notice that we are talking here about how our minds represent what we know about emotion and not about emotions themselves. Bower initially proposed that our experience of emotion is organized by the five basic emotions: anger, disgust, fear, happiness, and sadness. In his model, each emotion node is linked by associative pathways to nodes that represent propositions about the emotion, including what we know about the subjective feeling, about facial expressions, and objects and events that produced the emotion. Each emotion node is also linked to autobiographical memories during which the emotion was experienced. Figure 8.1 illustrates a schematic representation of part of the associative network of emotion.

When an emotion node—for example, the unit that represents "happiness"—is excited above some threshold because one is experiencing this emotion, activation spreads throughout the network to associated information. The excitatory links are represented by the solid lines in Figure 8.1. Propositions about physical reactions, expressive behaviors, emotion-related events, and personal memories are thereby excited and may enter the individual's consciousness. For instance, when one is feeling happiness, the material in memory related to happiness becomes activated. As a consequence, one may experience a heightened accessibility to the words and

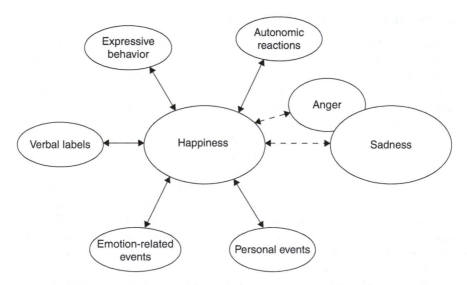

Figure 8.1 Associative network model of emotion. The node for happiness is linked by associative links to personal events, emotion-related events, verbal labels, and other bodily manifestations of the emotion. There are inhibitory links between the happiness node and representations of other emotions, such as sadness, that are inconsistent or incongruent with it. From Bower (1981).

memories associated with happiness, as well as a description of how it feels. In some versions of this model, the nodes that represent "opposite" states, such as happiness and sadness, are connected by inhibitory links such that the activation of one emotion node leads to the inhibition of the other one (Bower, 1981). The inhibitory links are represented by dotted lines in Figure 8.1. For instance, activating happiness is expected to inhibit the activation of sadness.

Notice that in associative network models, objects and events that we encounter are first experienced in our perceptual systems (e.g., vision, audition). But then, the experience is extracted and stored in an abstract form such as a word that stands for the proposition about the event (Fodor, 1975; Newell & Simon, 1972; Pylyshyn, 1984). We say that a word is an abstract representation of the concept because it does not preserve anything about the experience of the object or event it refers to. Words are arbitrarily assigned to objects; this is shown by the fact that different languages have different words for the same objects, events, and experiences. The implication for emotions is that what people know about emotions—what is stored in the conceptual system—is disconnected from their bodily experience of emotion.

Embodied simulation models are a different way to describe how emotions are stored in memory (e.g., Niedenthal, 2007). In these models, our knowledge is not separate from sensory and motor systems and some knowledge is not stored in an abstract form (Barsalou, 2008; Wilson, 2002). So although there may be an abstract system of words about tools, furniture, songs, and emotional faces, such knowledge is also (or perhaps primarily) stored in memory as the initial sensory-motor brain states that occurred during experience. This means that remembering an object or event involves reactivating some of the brain's sensory-motor states that occurred when the perceiver actually encountered the object or experienced the event (Barsalou, 1999, 2008). For example, when recalling information, such as describing a particular dog to a friend, traces of direct perceptual and motor experiences with that dog are brought to mind, perhaps re-creating the bark of that dog or reconstructing the feelings that the dog tends to create in us.

An embodied simulation model is particularly useful for describing how emotional information is stored in the conceptual system (Niedenthal et al., 2005; Winkielman, Niedenthal, & Oberman, 2008). You might notice that when you think about a particularly sad experience, you partly reproduce the sad feelings. Maybe you don't become terribly sad, but you re-experience enough of the sadness so that you can make judgments and predictions about what would happen if you or someone else were in that situation again. To use the same example as earlier, the concept of a dog is the set of sensory, motor, and affective states associated with the experience of dog: the sight of four legs, the sound of a bark, the feel of the fur, and a feeling of pleasure (or fear). These sensory-motor states in the brain are captured by sets of neurons in modality-specific sensory, motor, or affective systems (see Figure 8.2, left). Thinking of an object or idea then involves partial reactivation of the neurons in modality-specific (sensory, motor, and affective) systems (Figure 8.2, right). This means that understanding the emotional meaning of an object or event involves the partial reactivation of posture, expression, and feelings associated with this emotion (Niedenthal, 2007; Winkielman & Kavanagh, 2013).

We now see that embodied simulation models predict that understanding the meaning of an emotion word (such as "distress") or facial expression of emotion (such as a disgusted one) is based on a re-experience of the corresponding emotion in the self rather than just an abstract conceptualization as described in associative network models. Niedenthal, Winkielman, Mondillon, and Vermeulen (2009) tested the prediction about the understanding of word meaning. In their studies, participants were presented emotional words (e.g., concrete nouns, such as SUN or SLUG, or abstract words, such as FOUL and JOYFUL). Some participants were asked whether each word was written in capital letters or not (a perceptual task), whereas others were asked whether or not the word had an emotional meaning. During the study, the activation of participants' facial muscles was measured using electromyography (EMG). When participants were trying to figure out if a word had an emotional meaning but not when they made judgments

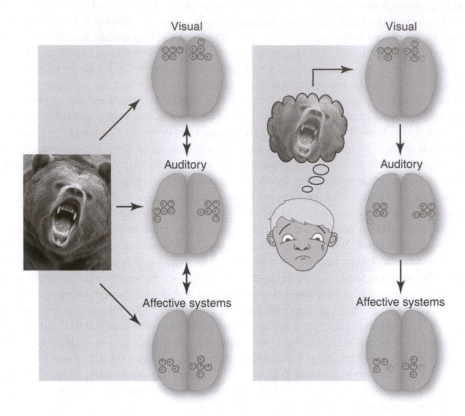

Figure 8.2 (Left) Activation of populations of neurons on visual, auditory, and affective systems upon perception of the snarling bear. (Right) Later, when remembering the appearance of the bear, parts of the original states of the visual system are reinstated. These then can act to reactivate the parts of the states that were originally active in the other systems. From Niedenthal (2007).

of letter case, they automatically made the corresponding emotional expression on their faces, thus showing they were re-creating the emotion in themselves as a part of the very process by which they could judge that the word had an emotional meaning.

The associative network models of emotion and the embodied simulation models of emotion representation in the cognitive system are the two main ways of modeling how what we know and see about emotion comes to mind and are used to help people navigate the world. The models make different claims about how emotion information is taken in through our senses, is stored in memory, and is retrieved for use. We will refer to both models in examining how emotions influence cognitive processes.

Emotion Shapes Perception

You might have the commonsense belief that when someone is in a specific emotional state, she sees objects and events in her life differently than when she is in another emotional state. The belief is that your friend, cat, and university campus all look beautiful when you are happy, but quite drab or lackluster when you are sad. Common sense aside, there is substantial experimental evidence that shows that emotion shapes perception by influencing the things we pay attention to in the environment and what and how things are actually perceived.

Our environments are complex and contain a huge amount of information. We cannot attend to all of the information because the scope of our attention is limited. Attention is a cluster of processes that involve the abilities to focus selectively on a particular object, sustain focus, and shift the focus at will. Imagine that a good-looking person is approaching you with a smile on her face. If you are attending to her face, you will think of her as friendly and prepare yourself to act friendly in return. However, if your attention is directed to the aggressive dog that she is walking, you might instead feel anxious and act decidedly unfriendly. Research on attention has shown that emotion can influence both the objects we attend to (i.e., the smiling face vs. the threatening dog) as well as the breadth of our attention scope (i.e., whether we pay attention to one of the two stimuli or to both).

Emotional Objects Capture Attention

Objects with emotional significance attract our attention. You might have experienced this when, out of a sea of students walking across campus, your attention is automatically attracted by the presence of someone you like very much or someone you dislike. How did this happen? It appears that you start to have an emotional reaction to something very quickly (Schupp et al., 2003), sometimes before you are even consciously aware of the object or event that caused it (Pasley, Mayes, & Schultz, 2004; Rotteveel et al., 2001; Williams et al., 2004). Then, you automatically direct attention to it, probably because it is so important to you (Compton, 2003). As a result, you are more likely to become conscious of the presence of the object and of its location in your environment, and you are thus ready to act adaptively (Yang, Zald, & Blake, 2007).

Emotional objects attract attention, whether they cause positive feelings such as joy (Becker & Leinenger, 2011; Williams et al., 2005) or negative reactions such as fear (Frischen, Eastwood, & Smilek, 2008). However, objects that represent a threat and that elicit fear or anxiety are particularly good at capturing attention (Fenske & Eastwood, 2003). The capture of attention by threatening objects is a robust effect. It has been observed in many different attention tasks (e.g., attentional blink, Stroop task; Pratto & John, 1991; dot probe task, Fox et al., 2001; MacLeod, Mathews, & Tata, 1986) and with a variety of objects, including human and schematic faces, images of objects, and words. For instance, people detect threatening faces more rapidly than friendly ones in a crowd of neutral faces (Hansen & Hansen, 1988; Öhman, Lundqvist, & Esteves, 2001; Figure 8.3 illustrates examples of displays used in these studies),

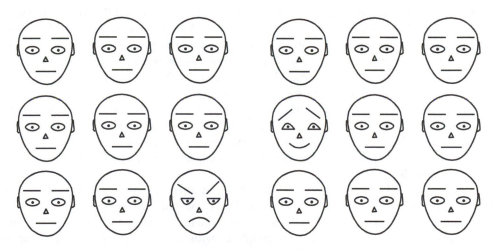

Figure 8.3 Two examples of 3 × 3 displays used by Öhman and colleagues, one presenting a threatening face among neutral faces (left display) and one presenting a friendly face among neutral ones (right display). From Öhman, Lundqvist, & Esteves (2001).

and you are faster at detecting a snake among flowers than a flower among snakes (Öhman, Flykt, & Esteves, 2001).

Objects that cause emotional reactions capture attention very quickly, even in conditions in which our attention resources are limited, such as when our attention is diverted by distracting objects that are irrelevant to what we are doing. For instance, we make more efficient eye movements toward fearful faces than toward neutral faces, even when the faces are presented as briefly as 20 milliseconds on a computer screen (Bannerman, Milders, & Sahraie, 2010), and we are able to detect fearful faces more rapidly than neutral or happy faces when the faces are presented in conditions that make them very difficult to see at all (Milders et al., 2006; Yang, Zald, & Blake, 2007).

Once we allocate our attention to an emotional object, we tend to keep attending to it. We have a lot of trouble disengaging our attention from a threatening object and moving it to attend to something else (Fox et al., 2001; Fox, Russo & Dutton, 2002). Thus, not only is your attention likely to be attracted by an aggressive dog, but you will have trouble shifting attention to something else that is more pleasant to look at! Furthermore, people are even more likely to pay attention to threating things when they are already in a state of anxiety or fear (Bar-Haim et al., 2007; Fox, Russo, & Dutton, 2002; LoBue, 2014; MacLeod, Mathews, & Tata, 1986).

The fact that threatening objects demand our attention has been interpreted as consistent with evolutionary theory (LeDoux, 1996; Öhman, Flykt, & Esteves, 2001). According to this view, emotional reactions to threatening stimuli were selected in the human species over evolution in order to assure survival. This does not mean that these effects are restricted to objects that could have recurrently posed a threat over evolution of human beings (e.g., snakes, spiders, angry faces). Neutral objects (neutral faces or geometrical shapes) can also capture attention the same way if people learned, even during a short laboratory session, to associate these neutral stimuli with fear (Milders et al., 2006; Theeuwes, Schmidt, & Belopolsky, 2014).

Emotion Influences the Scope of Attention

Emotions not only affect what we attend to, but also the scope of our attention (e.g., Fredrickson & Branigan, 2005). As we saw in Chapter 4, when in a positive emotional state, people's attentional scope or focus seems to become more broad, or global, than when in more neutral states of no particularly strong emotion (Fredrickson & Branigan, 2005; Gasper & Clore, 2002). But other states also influence attention. Long ago, a scientist proposed that **drive states**, by which he meant high-arousal unpleasant states, narrow the scope of attention, making people more focused on the cues (information) relevant to that state (Easterbrook, 1959). This effect was described in terms of a cue-utilization hypothesis, which stated that stimuli that are threatening increase an individual's arousal level. This makes the individual's attentional scope restricted to central cues at the expense of peripheral cues.

Since the original attention-narrowing hypothesis was proposed, studies have shown that the narrowing of attention can be caused by such negative experiences as experimenter-exerted stress (Chajut & Algom, 2003), threat of electric shock (Wachtel, 1968), simulated danger (Weltman & Egstrom, 1966), and exposure to facial expressions of negative emotions (Fenske & Eastwood, 2003).

One of the applied implications of this narrowing of attention in highly aroused states is a phenomenon called **weapon focus** (Loftus, Loftus, & Messo, 1987). We have learned that threatening stimuli tend to capture and hold people's attention and that this is especially true when people are in a threatened state. When people are witnesses to a crime involving a weapon, they are in a highly aroused state and the weapon tends to capture their attention. Furthermore, the scope of their attention narrows so that the person cannot take in other information. Weapon focus specifically refers to a decrease in memory for details of the perpetrator of a crime by an eyewitness because of this narrowing of attention to just the weapon. In an example study, participants watched a video of a mock crime scene in which a weapon was either highly visible or mostly hidden from view. Memory for details of the perpetrator of the crime was later measured and self-reports of arousal were also obtained. Findings showed that participants in the highly visible condition recalled significantly less detail of the perpetrator (Kramer, Buckhout, & Eugenio, 1990).

As the weapon focus phenomenon seems to demonstrate, the influences of emotion on the scope of attention may be less due to the valence of the emotion experienced and more to its arousal or motivational intensity (i.e., "the urge to act"; Gable & Harmon-Jones, 2010, p. 211). Harmon-Jones and colleagues observed that emotional states of a high level of motivational intensity (e.g., desire or disgust) narrow attentional focus compared to a neutral state. In contrast, emotional states of a low level of motivational intensity, whatever their valence (e.g., amusement or sadness), broaden the scope of attention (Gable & Harmon-Jones, 2008, 2010; see for a review, see Harmon-Jones, Gable, & Price, 2012).

Emotion-Congruent Word and Face Processing

Once you have turned your attention to something emotional, you can then use the perceptual systems of your body and brain to take in the information. You very rapidly make certain acts of categorization. The associative network models of emotion predict an **emotion-congruence hypothesis** for these acts of categorization. The emotion-congruence prediction is that objects and events that have the same emotional significance as the current emotion state of the individual can be classified by that individual with greater efficiency than neutral or emotion-incongruent objects. By "efficiency" we mean that less perceptual information from the object is required before it is categorized. Less perceptual information is needed for an emotionally congruent event or object because the nodes for representing the object have already been pre-activated by the current emotional state (Gerrig & Bower, 1982). Therefore, when you feel sad, you should more readily classify the sad song played on the radio or the name of that depressing painting because those ideas are already activated to some degree in memory by your emotional state.

How do scientists study these very rapid acts of categorization? One way is by looking at how quickly people can decide that a string of letters forms a word (for example, BACON) or does not (for example, BUPLE), which is called a **lexical decision task**. In one study using this task, participants were faster at correctly identifying strings of letters as words when the word meaning matched their current affective state than when it mismatched (Niedenthal & Setterlund, 1994). So, for instance, compared to sad participants, happy participants could more quickly indicate that the letter string GLEE was a word. Similar results were found with another task called a word-naming task (Niedenthal, Halberstadt, & Setterlund, 1997). In this study, participants who had been put into a sad, a neutral, or a happy state with the use of classical music had to say aloud words presented on a computer screen as fast as possible. People in happy states could name words with happy meanings faster than people in sad or neutral states (see Figure 8.4). And people in sad states could name words with sad meanings faster than people in happy or neutral states. Interestingly, happiness did not facilitate word naming for words with meanings related to the emotion of love, and sadness did not facilitate the naming of words related to anger. These findings mean that emotion affects the perception of words that have meanings that are categorically related to this emotion. The positive emotion of happiness did not make all positive words easier to perceive, and the negative emotion of sadness did not make it easier to perceive all negative words. Other studies have reported similar findings for the perceptual processing of facial expression of emotion (Niedenthal et al., 2000).

Now we know that emotions affect how information in the world gets categorized. Once the information gets in, it can be committed to memory. How do emotions affect memory?

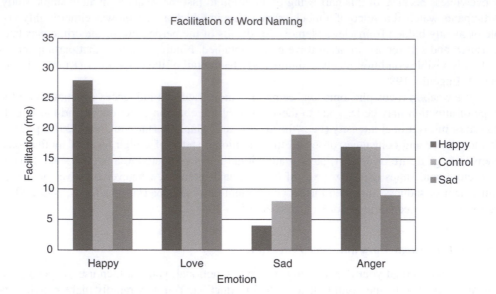

Figure 8.4 Facilitation (in milliseconds) in naming words that are synonyms with happy, love, sad, and anger compared to neutral words by participants in happy, sad, and neutral states. From Niedenthal, Halberstadt, & Setterlund (1997).

Emotion Influences Memory

Memory is a set of mental processes that elaborate, store, and retrieve experiences and ideas from the past. But memory does not work like taking a photograph and then finding it in a carefully labeled photo album on your computer. Rather, memory is an active and constructive process, meaning that where you are, who you are, and what you want or care about all affect how you record and retrieve memories (Schacter, 1999). Emotion plays an important role in this construction. It can influence not only what we remember, but also how and when we are most likely to retrieve certain memories.

Memory for Emotional Events

One of the oldest, and probably most common, empirical observations in the area of emotion and memory is that events and objects that arouse emotions are later more easily recalled than neutral events and objects (Cahill & McGaugh, 1995; Houston et al., 2013). For instance, if you see a bicycle accident you will later have better memory for that event than for a banal event that also involves a bicycle. Better recall of emotional information is also accompanied by impaired recall of nonemotional aspects of the same event or the context in which it occurred, as we saw for the weapon focus effect. To return to the bicycle accident, because attention is limited, although you will have excellent memory for the central features of the accident, you will also have particularly poor memory for peripheral features of the event such as the color of a car in the background (Christianson & Loftus, 1991; Christianson et al., 1991; Kensinger, Garoff-Eaton, & Schacter, 2007). Researchers have shown that we also have better memory for information that is related to the gist, or general theme, of emotional events (e.g., "a bicycle accident") than for details unrelated to the gist. The memory for gist occurs because information related to the central theme is better integrated and more easily retrieved (Adolphs, Denburg, & Tranel, 2001). Even peripheral information that is associated with the gist of the event will be easier to remember than peripheral information that is not associated with the gist (Kensinger, Garoff-Eaton, Schacter, 2007).

Developmental Detail

Aging Brains Are More Positive than Negative

Aging is associated with a decline in cognitive performance, in particular in attention and memory. However, this decrement is not as general as you might think. Research suggests that late adulthood is associated with increasing attention to and recall of pleasant versus unpleasant information (Charles, Mather, & Carstensen, 2003). This is called the **positivity effect**. There is a positivity effect in the use of visual attention, for example: old people tend to pay more attention to positive than to negative information, as illustrated in the figure (and see, for a meta-analysis on the positivity effects, Reed, Chan, & Mikels, 2014). Compared to young adults who tend to have better recall for negative information, older adults also recall more positive than negative memories.

It appears that, as people age, they become more aware of the limitation of their time left in life. Such awareness leads them to expose themselves to positive information more than negative (Charles, Mather, & Carstensen, 2003). Recent findings provide evidence that the shift to focusing on positive

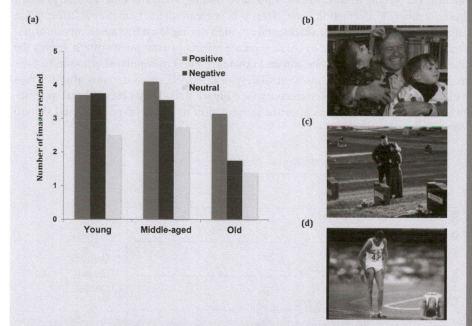

Number of images correctly recalled (out of 32) as a function of the age of the participants (young = 18–29; middle = 41–53; old = 65–80) and of the valence of the images in the Charles, Mather, and Carstensen (2003) study. The figure includes examples of positive (b), negative (c), and neutral images (d). Results indicate that older participants recall proportionally more positive images than younger participants.

material is a motivated (either conscious or unconscious) one (Kennedy, Mather, & Carstensen, 2004). When older adults are constrained to pay attention to specific aspects of the information (e.g., they have to evaluate the valence of the stimuli or to generate sentences containing the name of the stimulus), the positivity effect is reduced and they recall the same amount of negative and positive information as younger people (Kalenzaga et al., 2016). In other words, it is possible to interfere with the strategic nature of the positivity effect by interfering with the motivated preference to focus on the positive and avoid the negative. But then, who would want to?

What about positive versus negative events? Are they equally easy to remember? Some research has shown that people remember negative information better than positive information (e.g., D'Argembeau & Van der Linden, 2005; Kensinger, Addis, & Atapattu, 2011; Kensinger, Garoff-Eaton, & Schacter, 2007). This might be because negative objects and events on average require more action and adaptation than positive objects and events. The negative is just more important for our safety and survival. But negative objects and events also typically generate more physiological arousal (Schmidt, Patnaik, & Kensinger, 2011). So it might be the level of arousal, not the negativity of the stimuli, that accounts for improved memory. People are simply better able to recall high-arousal compared to low-arousal information (Mather, 2007).

The conundrum in coming to conclusions from these studies is that emotion is usually caused by the to-be-remembered information itself. Thus it is unclear whether emotional information is always more memorable or whether incidental emotion during learning causes any information to be more memorable. In order to try to separate effects of emotional stimuli versus the emotions they produce on memory, Nielson and Powless (2007) manipulated emotion in their participants by showing them film clips immediately or at 10, 30, or 45 minutes after the participants had committed some words to memory (see Figure 8.5). They observed that an emotional induction occurring 30 minutes after the presentation of the to-be-remembered stimuli

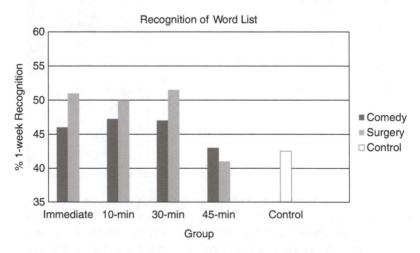

Figure 8.5 Mean recognition of neutral words after one week as a function of type of movie watched (positive: comedy vs. negative: surgery) and the delay between the presentation of the word list and the movie. From Nielson and Powless (2007).

still enhanced recall of these words one week later (no effect was observed when the emotional clip was presented 45 minutes after the word list). These results confirm that emotion makes information more memorable not only during learning, but also throughout the process of committing the information to memory (see also, Phelps, 2006; Sharot & Yonelinas, 2008).

In addition to enhanced memory for emotional events, there are two other ways in which emotions influence memory. These are called mood-congruent memory and mood-state–dependent memory.

Mood-Congruent Memory

Take a moment and try to remember events of the previous weeks of your life. If you are in a happy mood, you will probably recall events during which or about which you were happy. In contrast, if you are feeling sad, you will probably recall sad events (Snyder & White, 1982). **Mood-congruent memory** is the tendency for individuals in a particular emotional state, or a mood, to retrieve information from memory that has the same emotional or affective tone. This derives easily from the associative network models of emotions that we learned about earlier in the chapter (Bower, 1981). The idea is that an emotional state excites the relevant emotion node in memory. Excitation then spreads throughout the network and brings to mind memories associated with the emotion.

Mood-congruent memory has been observed with a variety of ways of inducing emotional states, such as music (Eich, Macaulay, & Ryan, 1994), hypnosis (Bower, Gilligan, & Monteiro, 1981), the guided recall of personal events (Fiedler & Stroehm, 1986), odors (Ehrlichman & Halpern, 1988), and naturally occurring emotional states (Mayer et al., 1992). In a study of mood-congruent memory, experimenters put their participants in different emotional states using music (Halberstadt, Niedenthal, & Kushner, 1995). Then, the experimenters read *homophones* (words that sound alike but that have different spellings and meanings) to the participants and asked them to write down the word. Because the homophones were not spelled the same way, it was clear, from how the participant spelled the word exactly, which meaning they had retrieved from memory. The homophones of interest had one emotional (mourning) and one neutral meaning (morning; see Table 8.1). As predicted, the word meanings that were brought to mind by the participants were influenced by their current emotional state. Sad participants were more likely, for instance, to write down the word "mourning," whereas happy participants were more likely to write down the word "morning" (see also Nygaard & Lunders, 2002).

Table 8.1 Examples of pairs of happy and sad homophones. The emotional word is in italics. From Halberstadt, Niedenthal, & Kushner (1995).

Happy	*Sad*
bridal-bridle	*banned*-band
dear-deer	*bored*-board
heal-heel	*die*-dye
hymn-him	*fined*-find
medal-metal	*missed*-mist
peace-piece	*mourning*-morning
presents-presence	*pain*-pane
pride-pried	*poor*-pore
rose-rows	
sweet-suite	
won-one	

Interestingly, when emotional state guides memory retrieval, it can lead people to recall things that did not actually happen but are nonetheless congruent in tone with their emotional state. That is, people are also likely to *falsely* recall information that is congruent with their emotional state but that was never experienced or learned (Knott & Thorley, 2014; Ruci, Tomes, & Zelenski, 2009).

Mood-State–Dependent Memory

Mood-state–dependent memory is a phenomenon characterized by better retrieval during a specific emotional state of any information that was learned during that same state, compared to a different emotional state. The information can be neutral in meaning itself; the important factor is the match between the state at encoding and at recall. For example, if you are feeling happy when you study for a particular class, you will have better memory for the material if you are also in a good mood during the exam.

How does this work? Well, when you learn or do something during a specific mood, elements of the learned information or experience are stored in memory along with information about your mood state. The mood state can therefore cue the stored information at a later time. Mood-state–dependent memory is also best understood by thinking about the associative network model of emotion. When a mood is experienced, the node in memory for that state becomes activated. In turn, the node spreads activation to associated memories. These memories include information that has been learned previously during that exact state. In this way, memories that have been encoded in a specific affective state become easier to retrieve during the same affective state versus a different one.

Mood-state–dependent recall is more robust if the to-be-learned information is generated by the participant rather than furnished by the experimenter. If someone asks you to say the first word that comes to mind when she gives you a target word, you would be generating the information. If you are in a good mood, you will later recall your associations better in a good mood than in a bad mood. If the experimenter gives you both the target word and an association, the mood-state–dependent recall effect will be far less strong (Mayer & Salovey, 1988).

The same is true for retrieval of the stored information. Mood-state–dependent memory is more likely in free recall, where participants are instructed to produce what they remember, than in **recognition tasks**, where the participant is instructed to distinguish between old and new (never seen before and thus not committed to memory) material provided by the experimenter (Eich, 1995; Eich & Metcalfe, 1989; see also Bower, 1981). Why is this so? In a recognition task, the old words are learned during the original viewing. Thus, these words provide cues for the retrieval of the information. As a result, people use their mood state as retrieval cues very little. In contrast, in free recall tasks, participants are asked to simply generate previously learned items. Because no other cues are provided, participants rely much more on their emotional state for recall (Eich & Metcalfe, 1989; Kanayama, Sato, & Ohira, 2008).

As you might have expected, emotions influence processes of memory. People tend to recall emotional material better than neutral material from memory. In addition, specific emotions such as sadness tend to bring to mind memories that are also sad. Finally, emotional states serve as cognitive contexts for memory. As such, they can later cue any information that has been committed to memory during an emotional state, making it easier to retrieve said information during a matching emotional state.

Judgment and Decision Making

At the beginning of this chapter, you learned that emotions influence what information is attended to and how events and objects are perceived and remembered. In this final section, you will learn how emotion influences people's judgments and decisions. Recently this issue has received considerable attention from researchers in psychology (Lerner, Li, Valdesolo, & Kassam, 2015) and in related fields such as behavioral economics (Rick & Loewenstein, 2008) and neuroscience (Phelps, Lempert, & Sokol-Hessner, 2014). This interest is illustrated by the increasing number of papers published yearly, which more than doubled between 2006 and 2013 (Lerner et al., 2015).

First, what is the distinction between judgment and decision making? For psychologists, judgment refers to an evaluation of some aspects of a situation such as how good, likely, or important it is. Decision making involves the choice between multiple options (Blanchette & Richards, 2010). Obviously, these two mental processes are related. For example, judgments (or evaluations) of the different options available to a decision maker should at least in part determine the choice that is made. It is a natural progression, therefore, to discuss first the role of emotion in judgment and then its influences in decision making, or choice behavior.

Emotion and Judgment

Mood-Congruent Judgment

You might have noticed that some activities seem aversive to you when you feel sad, whereas the same activities are experienced as exciting when you feel happy. Such changes in evaluation illustrate one of the most robust findings in the literature on affect and cognition: **mood-congruent judgment**. This effect refers to the fact that people tend to make judgments that are congruent with their current emotional state. In a classic study of mood-congruent judgments of probability, Johnson and Tversky (1983) put participants in a negative state by having them read a short, rather depressing text. They were then asked to make probability judgments about the likelihood that different types of emotional events would occur. Compared to participants in a more neutral state, individuals who were in a negative state later estimated that negative events (diseases, hazards, and violence) were more likely to occur in general. In contrast, participants in a positive affective state were more optimistic in their risk estimates than neutral participants. People also make mood-congruent judgments about sensory experiences (Winkielman, Berridge, & Wilbarger, 2005), other people (Esses & Zanna, 1995; Innes-Ker & Niedenthal, 2002), and even about themselves (Sedikides, 1995; Wright & Mischel, 1982).

Although the term "mood" congruence is often used to talk about how emotions influence judgments, even fleeting and perhaps unconscious feelings can similarly influence judgment. For instance, in one study participants saw on a computer screen brief flashes of images of a person smiling or else making a face of real disgust. Immediately after the first image, a second image of a novel cartoon character appeared on the screen in the same location for a longer time. The initial face was effectively masked by the cartoon character so that it could not be consciously seen. After a number of trials in which one type of emotional face (happy or disgusted) was paired with the cartoon character, participants rated their overall impression of the cartoon on a series of personality attributes. When the disgust face was repeatedly paired with the cartoon, participants made more negative judgments of the character than when the happy face was repeatedly paired with the character (Niedenthal, 1990; see also Anderson, Siegel, White, & Barrett, 2012).

Whereas initial demonstrations of mood-congruent judgment focused on the influence of broadly positive or negative moods on judgments about positive and negative objects and events (hence the term mood-congruent judgment), subsequent research showed that discrete emotions had emotion-specific influences on judgment (Lerner & Keltner, 2001). In one study, participants in whom sadness had been experimentally induced judged the likelihood of sad events (e.g., "Of the 60,000 orphans in Romania, how many are malnourished due to food shortages?") as higher than angry events (e.g., "Of the 2,000,000 people in the United States who will buy a used car this year, how many will intentionally be sold a 'lemon' by a dishonest car dealer?"), whereas the reverse was true for participants in whom anger had been induced (DeSteno et al., 2000).

Explanations of the Mood-Congruent Judgment

A way to understand how mood-congruent judgment works is to see it as a specific case of mood-congruent memory. Perhaps the emotional state you are in makes memories related to the judgment easier to bring to mind. In other words, sad things seem more likely to you when you are sad because sad events are so easy to bring to mind. Another model, the **affect-as-information** model, explains mood-congruent judgment in a different way (Greifeneder, Bless & Pham, 2011).

The affect-as-information model holds that individuals use their affective state (which includes the information that their affective state activates in memory) as relevant information when making evaluative judgments (Clore & Huntsinger, 2007; Schwarz, 1990; Schwarz & Clore, 1983). Sometimes feelings are at the heart of the judgment; feeling good about someone and liking him or her are likely related. Have you ever changed your opinion of someone's attractiveness after you got to know him or her? If you came to like the personality behind the face, you may have consequently judged the face as more attractive than you had in your original assessment. However, we may also use our feelings as *heuristics*, or simple "tricks" for making an efficient judgment, even if our feelings are not the best or only information we have for making the judgment. For instance, if the evaluation task is complex because there is a lot of information about the target, or if one does not want to invest in the judgment task, one may ask "How do I feel about it?" If the answer is that one feels good, the judgment will be positive, whereas it will be negative in case of a negative affective state. You can probably think of a movie or song you used to judge positively back in high school. Chances are that your initial positive judgment arose from the affective state you were experiencing during your initial exposure. There's a lot of information to take in during a feature-length film, and it can necessitate a lot of effort to come to a carefully considered evaluation. So we often rely on the heuristic of our feelings. If you enjoyed the company with whom you saw the film, you may still have a fondness for it, independent of the complex attributes of the film that might deem it worthy of esteem. Importantly, according to this model, the use of affect as information is reduced when individuals realize that their emotions have nothing to do with the object of judgment at hand. If they know that they are happy or sad due to another event in their life, then that emotion will no longer be taken into account and no longer influence judgment (Hirt et al., 1997; Lantermann & Otto, 1996; Schwarz & Clore, 1983)

The associative network models do not predict these correction processes. Moreover, the few studies directly testing the mood-memory against the affect-as-information explanations of mood-congruent judgment seem to favor affect-as-information. For instance, DeSteno and colleagues (2000) observed that the effects of induced emotional states on likelihood judgments were guided by participants' perception of the world (an indicator of the informational value of their emotion), but not by autobiographical congruent memories (as would be expected on the basis of an associative network model).

Beyond Congruency: The Unique Role of Discrete Emotions

Other results are more difficult to interpret in terms of mood congruency. For instance, Lerner and Keltner (2001) observed that anger and fear, two negative affective states, had differential impact on risk estimations, whereas angry and happy participants did not differ from each other. Fear appears to make participants overestimate risk, whereas anger and happiness make participants underestimate risk. Lerner and Keltner proposed an Appraisal Tendency Framework

(Lerner & Keltner, 2000, 2001) in which they apply the appraisal theories of emotions (see Chapter 1) to explain the effects of specific emotions on judgment and decision making. According to this framework, the appraisals associated with different discrete emotions lead to predictable effects on evaluation of the current state of the situation. For instance, anger (and happiness) is associated with the appraisal of future events as under individual control, whereas fear is associated with the appraisal of future events as under situational control. As a result, angry (and happy) individuals estimate risks as less likely than scared individuals (Lerner & Keltner, 2001; see Figure 8.6).

Lerner and Tiedens (2006) proposed that appraisals could be considered part of the associative network that contains emotion nodes. As a result, activating one emotion node would also activate the related appraisals. Alternatively, appraisals can be considered part of the information provided by the emotion. For instance, experiencing fear would inform the organism that the situation is problematic, but also that the situation is uncertain and not under control.

Emotion and Processing Strategies

In addition to direct effects on the content of people's thought, emotion has been found to play a role in our information-processing strategies, including how energetically we acquire and use information. The idea that emotions are related to cognitive strategies was initially suggested by research showing that happy people are often more efficient in performing tasks that require the use of broad categories and elimination of superfluous details (Isen & Means, 1983). Their efficiency results from their using simpler ways of processing information.

Imagine that you receive a message that is intended to influence your opinion about a particular political policy. You may examine carefully the arguments that are presented in the message in order to evaluate their strength and relevance so that you can form your opinion, a process that requires time and cognitive resources. Alternatively, you can form your opinion by relying on simple heuristic cues, like the perceived degree of expertise of the author of the message. As we've already discussed, simple rules of thumb that involve forming an opinion without paying attention to detailed information are called heuristics. Research shows

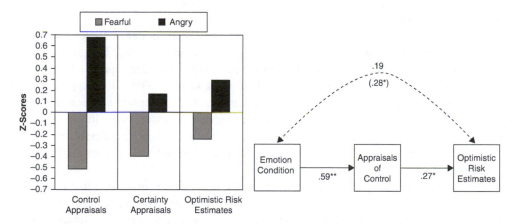

Figure 8.6 Left: Impact of fear and anger on cognitive appraisals (the higher the value, the more control or certainty) and on risk estimates (the higher the value, the more optimistic the risk estimate). Right: appraisals of control mediate the impact of emotion on risk estimate. The direct effect of emotion condition on optimistic risk estimates (dotted line, $\beta = .28$) is significant, but it turns to nonsignificance ($\beta = .19$) when the appraisals of control that are influenced by emotion are statistically controlled. From Lerner & Keltner (2001).

that people who are feeling happy are less likely to be influenced by the arguments contained in a persuasive message and more influenced by heuristics than are people in sad states (e.g., Bohner et al., 1992; Schwarz, Bless, & Bohner, 1991). In fact, happiness increases reliance on generalized knowledge such as stereotypes (Bless et al., 1996; Bless & Fiedler, 1995; Boden-hausen, Kramer, &Süsser, 1994), whereas sadness leads people to be more sensitive to detailed information (Bless & Fiedler, 1995; Forgas, 2013) and to rely less on heuristics in judgment (Krauth-Gruber & Ric, 2000).

Two main kinds of explanations have been offered for these results: the hedonic and the informational approaches. According to the hedonic view (Isen, 1987), individuals will seek to experience or maintain a positive affective state. When individuals are already in a posi-tive affective state, they will avoid engaging in any task that could alter their current affective state (Carlson, Charlin, & Miller, 1988). As a result, they do not engage in careful information processing and rely on heuristics that allow them to preserve their current affective state. In contrast, individuals in most negative states are happy to try to change what they are feeling. They are likely to process the incoming information in a careful manner in order to find a way to change their current affective state.

Informational models explain these effects by totally different processes. Informational mod-els like the affect-as-information model make the basic assumption that affective states inform us about the state of the environment. Because a positive affective state informs us that the environment is secure and that no action is needed to make things right, there is no need to engage in careful processing of the incoming information, unless this would be required by other situational demands (Bless et al., 1990). As a result, when happy, we should naturally tend to engage in heuristic processing of information and/or to rely on general knowledge struc-tures (Bless et al., 1996). In contrast, a negative affective state (like sadness) indicates that the environment is problematic, that we should thus invest resources in information processing in order to resolve the problem. This motivation leads us to process incoming information care-fully, paying attention to details, and to avoid the use of a heuristic strategy, as it could have detrimental consequences (Forgas, 2013). Extensions of this model propose that our emotions are even used to evaluate the content of one's current thoughts. The idea is that positive emo-tions serve to validate—and negative emotions serve to invalidate—what we are thinking at the moment (Clore & Huntsinger, 2007).

As was the case for mood-congruent judgment, other research has demonstrated that not all negative emotions are the same. For instance, in contrast with sadness, which is typically associ-ated with careful processing, anger and disgust have been found to lead to superficial processing of social information (Small & Lerner, 2008; Tiedens & Linton, 2001). The Appraisal Ten-dency Framework (Lerner & Keltner, 2001; Lerner et al., 2015) described earlier again offers an explanation for these results. Because anger and disgust are associated with the appraisal tendency of certainty, they lead people to evaluate the situation as being predictable and there-fore to rely more on heuristic judgmental devices than they would if they were fearful or sad (Han, Lerner, & Keltner, 2007).

It appears that emotions can exert two types of effects on judgment. One is that judgments seem to be emotionally congruent in many cases such that when you are feeling a particular emotion, your judgments reflect that emotion, often in a very specific way. In addition, ways of processing information, or judgmental strategies, are also affected by emotions such that some positive emotions make the use of superficial or efficient strategies more likely, and sadness and perhaps other negative emotions make a more systematic strategy (one in which you consider all relevant information) the strategy of choice. Judgments feed into our decisions, as we see in the next section.

Emotion and Decision Making

A decision involves a choice among multiple alternatives. Each of the alternatives is associated with some degree of desirability determined by the expected outcome, also called its "utility" or its "value" (Phelps, Lempert, & Sokol-Hessner, 2014). If the expected outcome of a particular alternative is positive, then that alternative has high utility or value. Although there are exceptions, people usually make choices in ways that maximize utility. The utility of different choice options can be due to the extent to which they cause positive (vs. negative) emotion. For instance, the act of buying a lottery ticket may have high value because it is associated with imagining the happiness caused by the ability to buy your parents a new house or yourself a new car (Slovic et al., 2007). Having a drink of alcohol at a party might be associated with the fear of being involved in an accident and eventually the guilt that would be associated with your misconduct (Bjälkebring, Västfjäll, Svenson, & Slovic, 2015) and thus have negative utility. Expected emotions enter the decision process of a "rational" decision maker (Figure 8.7) (Loewenstein et al., 2001).

The idea that expected emotions guide decisions is also called the **somatic marker hypothesis** (Damasio, 1994). The name refers to the idea that options are "marked" by a particular emotional expectation stored in memory. In the somatic marker hypothesis, when making decisions, people create embodied simulations of the possible choice outcomes. Expected emotions then guide decisions either consciously or unconsciously (Damasio, 1994). In a classic demonstration of this, Bechara et al. (1996) had participants play a game in which they chose cards one at a time presented in four decks. Each card was associated with a value in terms of gain or loss. Two decks had cards that were overall beneficial (more gain than loss), whereas the two others were disadvantageous for the participant (less gain than loss). After a number of trials, participants learned to choose the advantageous decks to select their card. Interestingly, before

Figure 8.7 Many situations in everyday life require making a decision between alternatives. Research demonstrates that emotion is often used as a guide to make this decision more efficient.

they could consciously indicate that these decks were more advantageous, their physiological emotional reactions indicated that they were able to discern the "good" decks from the "bad" ones, with the amplitude of skin conductance reactions becoming greater when selecting a card from the bad deck. Exploring further this hypothesis, Bechara and colleagues also observed that patients who did not exhibit differential physiological reactions to the two types of decks due to bilateral damage of the ventromedial prefrontal cortex did not learn to select the "good" deck. These results suggest that emotional reactions (even nonconscious) can sometimes help people make good decisions.

Emotion also enters the decision processes at other stages. As we learned about emotion and judgment, the evaluation of an outcome can be influenced by emotions that have been aroused by factors unrelated to the choices in the decision. For instance, being happy can make you underestimate risk estimates and overestimate the positivity of an outcome, thereby influencing your choice (Winkielman, Berridge, & Wilbarger, 2005). Similarly, the presentation of fearful faces before a gambling task leads people to be more cautious (Schulreich, Gerhardt, & Heekeren, 2015). Emotion can also make us value specific properties of an outcome that fit the motivational implications of our emotional state. For instance, people who are feeling sad are more in favor of the imposition of a tax law when the tax supposedly solves "sad" but not "angering" problems, and the reverse is true for people who are feeling angry (DeSteno et al., 2004).

Such processes can paradoxically lead happy people to avoid risk (Blanchette & Richards, 2010). As already mentioned, happiness is a positive state that people are motivated to maintain

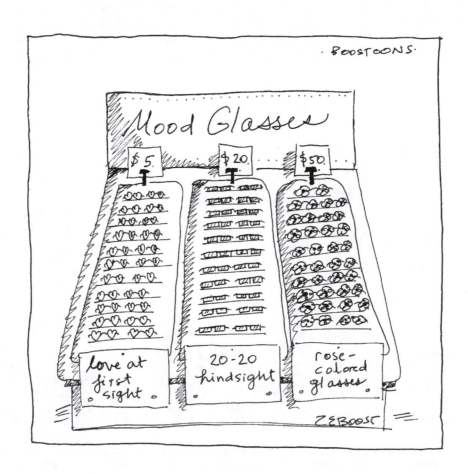

(Nygren et al., 1996). Therefore, when people perceive the consequences of a decision as risky, such as involving the loss of money, happiness should lead them to avoid the risk, which they see as threatening for their well-being. In other words, those who feel happy are less prone to engage in risky choices. These effects can be due to the current state of the individual, but also to the expected emotion (potential negative consequences) that could alter the current state. Indeed, the expected outcome might influence the current emotional state of the individual, making, say, a happy person feel guilty as she anticipates an outcome, and in turn modifying how she will perceive the situation and to which information she will pay attention (Lerner et al., 2015).

Thus, as can be seen from this example, decision making is a complex, multiprocess phenomenon for which we possess now strong evidence of the important role of emotion (Hsee, Hastie, & Chen, 2008; Lerner et al., 2015; Loewenstein et al., 2001; Winkielman, Knutson, Paulus, & Trujillo, 2007). However, it remains clear that the whole process of decision making, as well as the precise role of emotions in each of the processes involved, is far from being fully understood.

Summary

- Though it's unclear whether emotion and cognition are separate mental processes, we can still examine the interaction between emotion and other mental faculties, like perception, memory, evaluation, and decision making.
- The associative network models of memory, which theorize that perception of an object or event excites associated nodes through spreading activation, posit a distinction between our conceptual system and our bodily experience of emotion. Embodied simulation models, in contrast, claim that our sensory and affective systems are simultaneously activated upon perception, and thus when we access a memory, we re-experience the initial emotion.
- Emotional objects capture and hold our attention, and our emotions determine how broad or narrow our attentional focus might be.
- High-arousal experiences are more easily recalled than neutral events and objects, and negative information tends to generate more arousal, thus being easier to recall. But it's unclear whether emotional information is always more memorable or whether incidental emotion during learning causes information to be more memorable. We tend to recall information from memory that has the same emotional or affective tone as the mood we're currently experiencing.
- Our judgments, too, are influenced by our moods and/or by our discrete emotions. We use our feelings as heuristics to make quick appraisals, and thus we may be more efficient—but not more thoughtful or considered—in processing new information when we're experiencing positive affective states.
- In making decisions, we evaluate the utility of the expected emotion, but we're also influenced by our current emotional state.

Learning Links

1. Read about a study of patients with amnesia that finds that the emotion tied to a memory lingers in the mind even after the memory is gone. http://www.npr.org/templates/story/story.php?storyId=125869707
2. Listen to a round-table discussion of emotion, cognition, and consciousness. http://www.npr.org/templates/story/story.php?storyId=1461612
3. Read a very interesting article relating emotion and cognition to computer systems. https://www.infoq.com/articles/emotion-cognition

References

Adolphs, R., Denburg, N. L., & Tranel, D. (2001). The amygdala's role in long-term declarative memory for gist and detail. *Behavioral Neuroscience, 115*(5), 983. doi:10.1037/0735–7044.115.5.983.

Anderson, E., Siegel, E., White, D., & Barrett, L. F. (2012). Out of sight but not out of mind: Unseen affective faces influence evaluations and social impressions. *Emotion, 12*(6), 1210. doi:10.1037/a0027514.

Anderson, J. R. (1983). A spreading activation theory of memory. *Journal of Verbal Learning and Verbal Behavior, 22*(3), 261–295. doi:10.1016/b978–1–4832–1446–7.50016–9.

Bannerman, R. L., Milders, M., & Sahraie, A. (2010). Attentional bias to brief threat-related faces revealed by saccadic eye movements. *Emotion, 10*(5), 733. doi:10.1037/a0019354.

Bar-Haim, Y., Lamy, D., Pergamin, L., Bakermans-Kranenburg, M. J., & Van Ijzendoorn, M. H. (2007). Threat-related attentional bias in anxious and nonanxious individuals: A meta-analytic study. *Psychological Bulletin, 133*(1), 1. doi:10.1037/0033–2909.133.1.1.

Barsalou, L. W. (1999). Perceptions of perceptual symbols. *Behavioral and Brain Sciences, 22*(04), 637–660. doi:10.1017/s0140525x99532147.

Barsalou, L. W. (2008). Grounded cognition. *Annual Review of Psychology, 59*, 617–645. doi:10.1146/annurev.psych.59.103006.093639.

Bechara, A., Tranel, D., Damasio, H., & Damasio, A. R. (1996). Failure to respond autonomically to anticipated future outcomes following damage to prefrontal cortex. *Cerebral Cortex, 6*(2), 215–225. doi:10.1093/cercor/6.2.215.

Becker, M. W., & Leininger, M. (2011). Attentional selection is biased toward mood-congruent stimuli. *Emotion, 11*(5), 1248. doi:10.1037/a0023524.

Bjälkebring, P., Västfjäll, D., Svenson, O., & Slovic, P. (2015). Regulation of experienced and anticipated regret in daily decision making. *Emotion, 16*(3), 381–386. doi:10.1037/a0039861.

Blanchette, I., & Richards, A. (2010). The influence of affect on higher level cognition: A review of research on interpretation, judgement, decision making and reasoning. *Cognition & Emotion, 24*(4), 561–595. doi:10.1080/02699930903132496.

Bless, H., Bohner, G., Schwarz, N., & Strack, F. (1990). Mood and persuasion a cognitive response analysis. *Personality and Social Psychology Bulletin, 16*(2), 331–345. doi:10.1177/0146167290162013.

Bless, H., Clore, G. L., Schwarz, N., Golisano, V., Rabe, C., & Wölk, M. (1996). Mood and the use of scripts: Does a happy mood really lead to mindlessness? *Journal of Personality and Social Psychology, 71*(4), 665. doi:10.1037//0022–3514.71.4.665.

Bless, H., & Fiedler, K. (1995). Affective states and the influence of activated general knowledge. *Personality and Social Psychology Bulletin, 21*(7), 766–778. doi:10.1177/0146167295217010.

Bodenhausen, G. V., Kramer, G. P., & Süsser, K. (1994). Happiness and stereotypic thinking in social judgment. *Journal of Personality and Social Psychology, 66*(4), 621. doi:10.1037/0022–3514.66.4.621.

Bohner, G., Crow, K., Erb, H. P., & Schwarz, N. (1992). Affect and persuasion: Mood effects on the processing of message content and context cues and on subsequent behaviour. *European Journal of Social Psychology, 22*(6), 511–530. doi:10.1002/ejsp.2420220602.

Bower, G. H. (1981). Mood and memory. *American Psychologist, 36*(2), 129. doi:10.1037/0003–066X.36.2.129.

Bower, G. H. (1991). Mood congruity of social judgments. In J. Forgas (Ed.), *Emotion and social judgments* (pp. 31–53). Oxford, England: Pergamon Press.

Bower, G. H., Gilligan, S. G., & Monteiro, K. P. (1981). Selectivity of learning caused by affective states. *Journal of Experimental Psychology: General, 110*(4), 451. doi:10.1037/0096–3445.110.4.451.

Cahill, L., & McGaugh, J. L. (1995). A novel demonstration of enhanced memory associated with emotional arousal. *Consciousness and Cognition, 4*(4), 410–421. doi:10.1006/ccog.1995.1048.

Carlson, M., Charlin, V., & Miller, N. (1988). Positive mood and helping behavior: A test of six hypotheses. *Journal of Personality and Social Psychology, 55*(2), 211. doi:10.1037/0022–3514.55.2.211.

Chajut, E., & Algom, D. (2003). Selective attention improves under stress: Implications for theories of social cognition. *Journal of Personality and Social Psychology, 85*(2), 231. doi:10.1037/0022–3514.85.2.231.

Charles, S. T., Mather, M., & Carstensen, L. L. (2003). Aging and emotional memory: The forgettable nature of negative images for older adults. *Journal of Experimental Psychology: General, 132*(2), 310–324. doi:10.1037/0096–3445.132.2.310.

Christianson, S. Å., & Loftus, E. F. (1991). Remembering emotional events: The fate of detailed information. *Cognition & Emotion, 5*(2), 81–108. doi:10.1080/02699939108411027.

Christianson, S. Å., Loftus, E. F., Hoffman, H., & Loftus, G. R. (1991). Eye fixations and memory for emotional events. *Journal of Experimental Psychology: Learning, Memory, and Cognition*, *17*(4), 693. doi:10.1037//0278–7393.17.4.693.

Clore, G. L., & Huntsinger, J. R. (2007). How emotions inform judgment and regulate thought. *Trends in Cognitive Sciences*, *11*(9), 393–399. doi:10.1016/j.tics.2007.08.005.

Collins, A. M., & Loftus, E. F. (1975). A spreading-activation theory of semantic processing. *Psychological Review*, *82*(6), 407. doi:10.1016/b978–1–4832–1446–7.50015–7.

Compton, R. J. (2003). The Interface between Emotion and Attention: A Review of Evidence from Psychology and Neuroscience. *Behavioral and Cognitive Neuroscience Reviews*, *2*(2), 115–129. doi:10.11 77/1534582303002002003.

D'Argembeau, A., & Van der Linden, M. (2005). Influence of emotion on memory for temporal information. *Emotion*, *5*(4), 503–507. doi:10.1037/1528-3542.5.4.503.

Damasio, A. R. (1994). *Descartes error: Emotion, reason, and the human brain*. New York: Putnam.

Descartes, R. (1644/1988). The passions of the soul. In J. Cottingham, R. Stoothoff & D. Murdoch (Eds.), *Selected philosophical writings of René Descartes* (pp. 218–238). Cambridge: Cambridge University Press.

DeSteno, D., Petty, R. E., Rucker, D. D., Wegener, D. T., & Braverman, J. (2004). Discrete emotions and persuasion: The role of emotion-induced expectancies. *Journal of Personality and Social Psychology*, *86*(1), 43. doi:10.1037/0022–3514.86.1.43.

DeSteno, D., Petty, R. E., Wegener, D. T., & Rucker, D. D. (2000). Beyond valence in the perception of likelihood: The role of emotion specificity. *Journal of Personality and Social Psychology*, 78(3), 397. doi:10.1037/0022–3514.78.3.397.

Easterbrook, J. A. (1959). The effect of emotion on cue utilization and the organization of behavior. *Psychological Review*, *66*(3), 183. doi:10.1037/h0047707.

Ehrlichman, H., & Halpern, J. N. (1988). Affect and memory: Effects of pleasant and unpleasant odors on retrieval of happy and unhappy memories. *Journal of Personality and Social Psychology*, *55*(5), 769. doi:10.1037/0022–3514.55.5.769.

Eich, E. (1995). Searching for mood dependent memory. *Psychological Science*, *6*(2), 67–75. doi:10.1111/j.1467–9280.1995.tb00309.x.

Eich, E., Macaulay, D., & Ryan, L. (1994). Mood dependent memory for events of the personal past. *Journal of Experimental Psychology: General*, *123*(2), 201. doi:10.1037/0096–3445.123.2.201.

Eich, E., & Metcalfe, J. (1989). Mood dependent memory for internal versus external events. *Journal of Experimental Psychology: Learning, Memory, and Cognition*, *15*(3), 443. doi:10.1037/0278–7393.15.3.443.

Esses, V. M., & Zanna, M. P. (1995). Mood and the expression of ethnic stereotypes. *Journal of Personality and Social Psychology*, *69*(6), 1052. doi:10.1037//0022–3514.69.6.1052.

Fenske, M. J., & Eastwood, J. D. (2003). Modulation of focused attention by faces expressing emotion: Evidence from flanker tasks. *Emotion*, *3*(4), 327. doi:10.1037/1528–3542.3.4.327.

Fiedler, K., & Stroehm, W. (1986). What kind of mood influences what kind of memory: The role of arousal and information structure. *Memory & Cognition*, *14*(2), 181–188. doi:10.3758/bf03198378.

Fodor, J. A. (1975). *The language of thought* (Vol. 5). Cambridge, MA: Harvard University Press.

Forgas, J. P. (2013). Don't worry, be sad! On the cognitive, motivational, and interpersonal benefits of negative mood. *Current Directions in Psychological Science*, *22*(3), 225–232. doi:10.1177/0963721412474458.

Fox, E., Russo, R., Bowles, R., & Dutton, K. (2001). Do threatening stimuli draw or hold visual attention in subclinical anxiety? *Journal of Experimental Psychology: General*, *130*(4), 681. doi:10.1037//0096–3445.130.4.681.

Fox, E., Russo, R., & Dutton, K. (2002). Attentional bias for threat: Evidence for delayed disengagement from emotional faces. *Cognition & Emotion*, *16*(3), 355–379. doi:10.1080/02699930143000527.

Fredrickson, B. L., & Branigan, C. (2005). Positive emotions broaden the scope of attention and thought-action repertoires. *Cognition & Emotion*, *19*(3), 313–332. doi:10.1080/02699930441000238.

Frischen, A., Eastwood, J. D., & Smilek, D. (2008). Visual search for faces with emotional expressions. *Psychological Bulletin*, *134*(5), 662. doi:10.1037/0033–2909.134.5.662.

Gable, P. A., & Harmon-Jones, E. (2008). Approach-motivated positive affect reduces breadth of attention. *Psychological Science*, *19*(5), 476–482. doi:10.1111/j.1467–9280.2008.02112.x.

Gable, P. A., & Harmon-Jones, E. (2010). The blues broaden, but the nasty narrows attentional consequences of negative affects low and high in motivational intensity. *Psychological Science. 21*(2), 211–215. doi:10.1177/0956797609359622.

Gasper, K., & Clore, G. L. (2002). Attending to the big picture: Mood and global versus local processing of visual information. *Psychological Science, 13*(1), 34–40. doi:10.1111/1467–9280.00406.

Gerrig, R. J., & Bower, G. H. (1982). Emotional influences on word recognition. *Bulletin of the Psychonomic Society, 19*(4), 197–200. doi:10.3758/bf03330231.

Greifeneder, R., Bless, H., & Pham, M. T. (2011). When do people rely on affective and cognitive feelings in judgment? A review. *Personality and Social Psychology Review, 15*(2), 107–141. doi:10.1177/1088868310367640.

Halberstadt, J. B., Niedenthal, P. M., & Kushner, J. (1995). Resolution of lexical ambiguity by emotional state. *Psychological Science, 6*(5), 278–282. doi:10.1111/j.1467–9280.1995.tb00511.x.

Han, S., Lerner, J. S., & Keltner, D. (2007). Feelings and consumer decision making: The appraisal-tendency framework. *Journal of Consumer Psychology, 17*(3), 158–168. doi:10.1016/s1057–7408(07)70023–2.

Hansen, C. H., & Hansen, R. D. (1988). Finding the face in the crowd: An anger superiority effect. *Journal of Personality and Social Psychology, 54*(6), 917. doi:10.1037//0022–3514.54.6.917.

Harmon-Jones, E., Gable, P., & Price, T. F. (2012). The influence of affective states varying in motivational intensity on cognitive scope. *Frontiers in Integrative Neuroscience, 6*, 1–5. doi:10.3389/fnint.2012.00073.

Hirt, E. R., Levine, G. M., McDonald, H. E., Melton, R. J., & Martin, L. L. (1997). The role of mood in quantitative and qualitative aspects of performance: Single or multiple mechanisms? *Journal of Experimental Social Psychology, 33*(6), 602–629. doi:10.1006/jesp.1997.1335.

Houston, K. A., Clifford, B. R., Phillips, L. H., & Memon, A. (2013). The emotional eyewitness: The effects of emotion on specific aspects of eyewitness recall and recognition performance. *Emotion, 13*(1), 118. doi:10.1037/a0029220.

Hsee, C. K., Hastie, R., & Chen, J. (2008). Hedonomics: Bridging decision research with happiness research. *Perspectives on Psychological Science, 3*(3), 224–243. doi:10.1111/j.1745–6924.2008.00076.x.

Ingram, R. E. (1984). Toward an information-processing analysis of depression. *Cognitive Therapy and Research, 8*(5), 443–477. doi:10.1007/bf01173284.

Innes-Ker, Å., & Niedenthal, P. M. (2002). Emotion concepts and emotional states in social judgment and categorization. *Journal of Personality and Social Psychology, 83*(4), 804. doi:10.1037/0022–3514.83.4.804.

Isen, A. M. (1987). Positive affect, cognitive processes, and social behavior. In L. Berkowitz (Ed.), *Advances in experimental social psychology* (Vol. 20, pp. 203–253). New York: Academic Press.

Isen, A. M., & Means, B. (1983). The influence of positive affect on decision-making strategy. *Social Cognition, 2*(1), 18–31. doi:10.1521/soco.1983.2.1.18.

Johnson, E. J., & Tversky, A. (1983). Affect, generalization, and the perception of risk. *Journal of Personality and Social Psychology, 45*(1), 20. doi:10.1037/0022–3514.45.1.20.

Kalenzaga, S., Lamidey, V., Ergis, A. M., Clarys, D., & Piolino, P. (2016). The positivity bias in aging: Motivation or degradation? *Emotion, 16*(5), 602–610. doi:10.1037/emo0000170.

Kanayama, N., Sato, A., & Ohira, H. (2008). Dissociative experience and mood-dependent memory. *Cognition and Emotion, 22*(5), 881–896. doi:10.1080/02699930701541674.

Kennedy, Q., Mather, M., & Carstensen, L. L. (2004). The role of motivation in the age-related positivity effect in autobiographical memory. *Psychological Science, 15*(3), 208–214. doi:10.1111/j.0956–7976.2004.01503011.x.

Kensinger, E. A., Addis, D. R., & Atapattu, R. K. (2011). Amygdala activity at encoding corresponds with memory vividness and with memory for select episodic details. *Neuropsychologia, 49*(4), 663–673. doi:10.1016/j.neuropsychologia.2011.01.017.

Kensinger, E. A., Garoff-Eaton, R. J., & Schacter, D. L. (2007). Effects of emotion on memory specificity: Memory trade-offs elicited by negative visually arousing stimuli. *Journal of Memory and Language, 56*(4), 575–591. doi:10.1016/j.jml.2006.05.004.

Knott, L. M., & Thorley, C. (2014). Mood-congruent false memories persist over time. *Cognition & Emotion, 28*(5), 903–912. doi.org/10.1080/02699931.2013.860016.

Kramer, T. H., Buckhout, R., & Eugenio, P. (1990). Weapon focus, arousal, and eyewitness memory: Attention must be paid. *Law and Human Behavior, 14*(2), 167. doi:10.1007/bf01062971.

Krauth-Gruber, S., & Ric, F. (2000). Affect and stereotypic thinking: A test of the mood-and-general-knowledge model. *Personality and Social Psychology Bulletin, 26*(12), 1587–1597. doi:10.1177/01461672002612012.

Lantermann, E. D., & Otto, J. H. (1996). Correction of effects of memory valence and emotionality on content and style of judgements. *Cognition and Emotion, 10*, 505–527. doi:10.1080/026999396380132.

Lazarus, R. S. (1982). Thoughts on the relations between emotion and cognition. *American Psychologist, 37*(9), 1019. doi:10.1037/0003–066x.37.9.1019.

LeDoux, J. E., 1996. *The emotional brain.* New York: Simon and Schuster.

Lerner, J. S., Li, Y., Valdesolo, P., & Kassam, K. S. (2015). Emotion and decision making. *Psychology, 66*, 33–1. doi:10.1093/acprof:oso/9780199659890.001.0001.

Lerner, J. S., & Keltner, D. (2000). Beyond valence: Toward a model of emotion-specific influences on judgement and choice. *Cognition & Emotion, 14*(4), 473–493. doi:10.1080/026999300402763.

Lerner, J. S., & Keltner, D. (2001). Fear, anger, and risk. *Journal of Personality and Social Psychology, 81*(1), 146. doi:10.1037/0022–3514.81.1.146.

Lerner, J. S., & Tiedens, L. Z. (2006). Portrait of the angry decision maker: How appraisal tendencies shape anger's influence on cognition. *Journal of Behavioral Decision Making, 19*(2), 115–137. doi:10.1002/bdm.515.

LoBue, V. (2014). Deconstructing the snake: The relative roles of perception, cognition, and emotion on threat detection. *Emotion, 14*(4), 701. doi:10.1037/a0035898.

Loewenstein, G. F., Weber, E. U., Hsee, C. K., & Welch, N. (2001). Risk as feelings. *Psychological Bulletin, 127*(2), 267. doi:10.1037/0033–2909.127.2.267.

Loftus, E. F., Loftus, G. R., & Messo, J. (1987). Some facts about "weapon focus." *Law and Human Behavior, 11*(1), 55. doi:10.1007/bf01044839.

MacLeod, C., Mathews, A., & Tata, P. (1986). Attentional bias in emotional disorders. *Journal of Abnormal Psychology, 95*(1), 15. doi:10.1037//0021–843x.95.1.15.

Mather, M. (2007). Emotional arousal and memory binding: An object-based framework. *Perspectives on Psychological Science, 2*(1), 33–52. doi:10.1111/j.1745–6916.2007.00028.x.

Mayer, J. D., Gaschke, Y. N., Braverman, D. L., & Evans, T. W. (1992). Mood-congruent judgment is a general effect. *Journal of Personality and Social Psychology, 63*(1), 119. doi:10.1037/0022–3514.63.1.119.

Mayer, J. D., & Salovey, P. (1988). Personality moderates the interaction of mood and cognition. In K. Fiedler & J. Forgas (Eds.), *Affect, cognition and social behavior* (pp. 87–99). Gottingen, Germany: Hogrefe. doi:10.1016/j.paid.2011.01.016.

McNamara, T. P. (1992). Theories of priming: I. Associative distance and lag. *Journal of Experimental Psychology: Learning, Memory, and Cognition, 18*(6), 1173. doi:10.1037//0278–7393.18.6.1173.

Milders, M., Sahraie, A., Logan, S., & Donnellon, N. (2006). Awareness of faces is modulated by their emotional meaning. *Emotion, 6*(1), 10. doi:10.1037/1528–3542.6.1.10.

Neely, J. H. (1991). Semantic priming effects in visual word recognition: A selective review of current findings and theories. In D. Besner & G. W. Humphreys (Eds.), *Basic processes in reading: Visual word recognition, 11*, 264–336.

Newell, A., & Simon, H. A. (1972). *Human problem solving.* Englewood Cliffs, NJ: Prentice-Hall.

Niedenthal, P. M. (1990). Implicit perception of affective information. *Journal of Experimental Social Psychology, 26*(6), 505–527. doi:10.1016/0022–1031(90)90053-O.

Niedenthal, P. M. (2007). Embodying emotion. *Science, 316*(5827), 1002–1005. doi:10.1126/science.1136930.

Niedenthal, P. M., Barsalou, L. W., Winkielman, P., Krauth-Gruber, S., & Ric, F. (2005). Embodiment in attitudes, social perception, and emotion. *Personality and Social Psychology Review, 9*(3), 184–211. doi:10.1207/s15327957pspr0903_1.

Niedenthal, P. M., Halberstadt, J. B., Margolin, J., & Innes-Ker, Å. H. (2000). Emotional state and the detection of change in facial expression of emotion. *European Journal of Social Psychology, 30*(2), 211–222. doi:10.1002/(sici)1099–0992(200003/04)30:2<211::aid-ejsp988>3.0.co;2–3.

Niedenthal, P. M., Halberstadt, J. B., & Setterlund, M. B. (1997). Being happy and seeing "happy": Emotional state mediates visual word recognition. *Cognition and Emotion, 11*, 403–432. doi:10.1080/026999397379863.

Niedenthal, P. M., & Setterlund, M. B. (1994). Emotion congruence in perception. *Personality and Social Psychology Bulletin, 20*(4), 401–411. doi:10.1177/0146167294204007.

Niedenthal, P. M., Setterlund, M. B., & Jones, D. E. (1994). Emotional organization of perceptual memory. In P. Niedenthal & S. Kitayama (Eds.), *The heart's eye: Emotional infludences in perception and attention* (pp. 87–113). San Diego, CA: Academic Press. doi:10.1016/b978-0-12-410560-7.50011-9.

Niedenthal, P. M., Winkielman, P., Mondillon, L., & Vermeulen, N. (2009). Embodiment of emotion concepts. *Journal of Personality and Social Psychology*, *96*(6), 1120. doi:10.1037/a0015574.

Nielson, K. A., & Powless, M. (2007). Positive and negative sources of emotional arousal enhance long-term word-list retention when induced as long as 30 min after learning. *Neurobiology of Learning and Memory*, *88*, 40–47. doi:10.1016/j.nlm.2007.03.005.

Nygaard, L. C., & Lunders, E. R. (2002). Resolution of lexical ambiguity by emotional tone of voice. *Memory & Cognition*, *30*(4), 583–593. doi:10.3758/bf03194959.

Nygren, T. E., Isen, A. M., Taylor, P. J., & Dulin, J. (1996). The influence of positive affect on the decision rule in risk situations: Focus on outcome (and especially avoidance of loss) rather than probability. *Organizational Behavior and Human Decision Processes*, *66*(1), 59–72. doi:10.1006/obhd.1996.0038.

Öhman, A., Flykt, A., & Esteves, F. (2001). Emotion drives attention: Detecting the snake in the grass. *Journal of Experimental Psychology: General*, *130*(3), 466. doi:10.1037//0096-3445.130.3.466.

Öhman, A., Lundqvist, D., & Esteves, F. (2001). The face in the crowd revisited: A threat advantage with schematic stimuli. *Journal of Personality and Social Psychology*, *80*(3), 381. doi:10.1037//0022-3514.80.3.381.

Pasley, B. N., Mayes, L. C., & Schultz, R. T. (2004). Subcortical discrimination of unperceived objects during binocular rivalry. *Neuron*, *42*(1), 163–172. doi:10.1016/s0896-6273(04)00155-2.

Phelps, E. A. (2006). Emotion and cognition: Insights from studies of the human amygdala. *Annual Review of Psychology*, *57*, 27–53. doi:10.1146/annurev.psych.56.091103.070234.

Phelps, E. A., Lempert, K. M., & Sokol-Hessner, P. (2014). Emotion and decision making: Multiple modulatory neural circuits. *Annual Review of Neuroscience*, *37*, 263–287. doi:10.1146/annurev-neuro-071013-014119.

Pratto, F., & John, O. P. (1991). Automatic vigilance: The attention-grabbing power of negative social information. *Journal of Personality and Social Psychology*, *61*, 380–391. doi:10.1037/0022-3514.61.3.380.

Pylyshyn, Z. W. (1984). *Computation and cognition*. Cambridge, MA: MIT press.

Reed, A. E., Chan, L., & Mikels, J. A. (2014). Meta-analysis of the age-related positivity effect: Age differences in preferences for positive over negative information. *Psychology and Aging*, *29*(1), 1–15. doi:10.1037/a0035194.

Rick, S., & Loewenstein, G. (2008). The role of emotion in economic behavior. In M. Lewis, J. M. Haviland-Jones & L. F. Barrett (Eds.), *Handbook of emotions* (3rd ed., pp. 138–156). New York: Guilford Press. doi:10.2139/ssrn.954862.

Rotteveel, M., de Groot, P., Geutskens, A., & Phaf, R. H. (2001). Stronger suboptimal than optimal affective priming? *Emotion*, *1*(4), 348. doi:10.1037//1528-3542.1.4.348.

Ruci, L., Tomes, J. L., & Zelenski, J. M. (2009). Mood-congruent false memories in the DRM paradigm. *Cognition and Emotion*, *23*(6), 1153–1165. doi:10.1080/02699930802355420.

Schacter, D. L. (1999). The seven sins of memory: Insights from psychology and cognitive neuroscience. *American Psychologist*, *54*(3), 182. doi:10.1037/0003-066x.54.3.182.

Schmidt, K., Patnaik, P., & Kensinger, E. A. (2011). Emotion's influence on memory for spatial and temporal context. *Cognition and Emotion*, *25*(2), 229–243. doi:10.1080/02699931.2010.483123.

Schulreich, S., Gerhardt, H., & Heekeren, H. R. (2016). Incidental fear cues increase monetary loss aversion. *Emotion*, *16*(3), 402–412. doi:10.1037/emo0000124.

Schupp, H. T., Junghöfer, M., Weike, A. I., & Hamm, A. O. (2003). Attention and emotion: An ERP analysis of facilitated emotional stimulus processing. *Neuroreport*, *14*(8), 1107–1110. doi:10.1097/00001756-200306110-00002.

Schwarz, N. (1990). *Feelings as information: Informational and motivational functions of affective states*. New York: Guilford Press.

Schwarz, N., Bless, H., & Bohner, G. (1991). Mood and persuasion: Affective states influence the processing of persuasive communications. *Advances in Experimental Social Psychology*, *24*, 161–199. doi:10.1016/s0065-2601(08)60329-9.

Schwarz, N., & Clore, G. L. (1983). Mood, misattribution, and judgments of well-being: Informative and directive functions of affective states. *Journal of Personality and Social Psychology*, *45*(3), 513. doi:10.1037/0022-3514.45.3.513.

Sedikides, C. (1995). Central and peripheral self-conceptions are differentially influenced by mood: Tests of the differential sensitivity hypothesis. *Journal of Personality and Social Psychology*, *69*(4), 759. doi:10.1037//0022–3514.69.4.759.

Sharot, T., & Yonelinas, A. P. (2008). Differential time-dependent effects of emotion on recollective experience and memory for contextual information. *Cognition*, *106*(1), 538–547. doi:10.1016/j.cognition.2007.03.002.

Slovic, P., Finucane, M. L., Peters, E., & MacGregor, D. G. (2007). The affect heuristic. *European Journal of Operational Research*, *177*(3), 1333–1352. doi:10.4135/9781412956253.n9.

Small, D. A., & Lerner, J. S. (2008). Emotional policy: Personal sadness and anger shape judgments about a welfare case. *Political Psychology*, *29*(2), 149–168. doi:10.1111/j.1467–9221.2008.00621.x.

Snyder, M., & White, P. (1982). Moods and memories: Elation, depression, and the remembering of the events of one's life. *Journal of Personality*, *50*(2), 149–167. doi:10.1111/j.1467–6494.1982.tb01020.x.

Storbeck, J., & Clore, G. L. (2007). On the interdependence of cognition and emotion. *Cognition and Emotion*, *21*(6), 1212–1237. doi:10.1080/02699930701438020.

Teasdale, J. D. (1983). Negative thinking in depression: Cause, effect, or reciprocal relationship? *Advances in Behaviour Research and Therapy*, *5*(1), 3–25. doi:10.1016/0146–6402(83)90013–9.

Theeuwes, J., Schmidt, L. J., & Belopolsky, A. V. (2014). Attentional capture by signals of threat. *Journal of Vision*, *14*(10), 321–321. doi:10.1167/14.10.321.

Tiedens, L. Z., & Linton, S. (2001). Judgment under emotional certainty and uncertainty: The effects of specific emotions on information processing. *Journal of Personality and Social Psychology*, *81*(6), 973. doi:10.1037/0022–3514.81.6.973.

Wachtel, P. L. (1968). Anxiety, attention, and coping with threat. *Journal of Abnormal Psychology*, *73*(2), 137. doi:10.1037/h0020118.

Weltman, G., & Egstrom, G. H. (1966). Perceptual narrowing in novice divers. *Human Factors: The Journal of the Human Factors and Ergonomics Society*, *8*(6), 499–506. doi:10.1177/001872086600800604.

Williams, M., Moss, S., Bradshaw, J., & Mattingley, J. (2005). Look at me, I'm smiling: Visual search for threatening and nonthreatening facial expressions. *Visual Cognition*, *12*(1), 29–50. doi:10.1080/13506280444000193.

Williams, M. A., Morris, A. P., McGlone, F., Abbott, D. F., & Mattingley, J. B. (2004). Amygdala responses to fearful and happy facial expressions under conditions of binocular suppression. *The Journal of Neuroscience*, *24*(12), 2898–2904. doi:10.1523/jneurosci.4977–03.2004.

Wilson, M. (2002). Six views of embodied cognition. *Psychonomic Bulletin & Review*, *9*(4), 625–636. doi:10.3758/bf03196322.

Winkielman, P., Berridge, K. C., & Wilbarger, J. L. (2005). Unconscious affective reactions to masked happy versus angry faces influence consumption behavior and judgments of value. *Personality and Social Psychology Bulletin*, *31*(1), 121–135. doi:10.1177/0146167204271309.

Winkielman, P. & Kavanagh, L (2013). The embodied perspective on emotion-cognition interactions. In M.D. Robinson, E.R. Watkins, & E. Harmon-Jones (Eds.), Handbook of cognition and emotion (pp 213–230). New York, NY: Guilford.

Winkielman, P., Knutson, B., Paulus, M.P. & Trujillo, J.T. (2007). Affective influence on decisions: Moving towards the core mechanisms. Review of General Psychology, 11, 179–192.

Winkielman, P., Niedenthal, P., & Oberman, L. (2008). The embodied emotional mind. In G. R. Semin & E. R. Smith (Eds.), *Embodied grounding: Social, cognitive, affective, and neuroscientific approaches* (pp. 263-288). New York: Cambridge University Press.

Wright, J., & Mischel, W. (1982). Influence of affect on cognitive social learning person variables. *Journal of Personality and Social Psychology*, *43*(5), 901. doi:10.1037/0022–3514.43.5.901.

Yang, E., Zald, D. H., & Blake, R. (2007). Fearful expressions gain preferential access to awareness during continuous flash suppression. *Emotion*, *7*(4), 882. doi:10.1037/1528–3542.7.4.882.

Zajonc, R. B. (1980). Feeling and thinking: Preferences need no inferences. *American Psychologist*, *35*(2), 151. doi:10.1037/0003–066x.35.2.151.

Zajonc, R. B. (1984). On the primacy of affect. *American Psychologist*, *39*, 117–123. doi:10.1037//0003–066x.39.2.117.

9   Emotion Regulation

Contents at a Glance

Some people really love to speak in public, but most people find the experience terrifying, at least the first time they try it. Even standing up in front of a class of 15 other university students can cause butterflies in your stomach, sweaty palms, and a desire to run away. If you let your emotions carry you away (or "hijack" you, Goleman, 1995), you might even jump up and sprint from the room in fright. Like a cartoon character, you might run into the distance until all your classmates could see was a little puff of smoke.

But most of the time, whether it is in a high school debate or a presentation of a scientific experiment in a university class, you actually have to follow through. To do so effectively, you have to "redirect the spontaneous flow" of your emotions (Koole, 2009). In the case of public speaking, you might breathe deeply, bite the inside of your cheek, or even visualize everyone in the audience in their underwear. In everyday life, we also fight back tears, feign or exaggerate joy, and redirect our anger at someone else by kicking the garbage can or slamming the door. All of these tactics are used to regulate emotions.

The term **emotion regulation** refers to the ways that individuals influence the intensity, duration, and type of emotions they experience and do not experience; the situations under which they experience a given emotion; and how and whether they eventually express those emotions (Gross, 1999, 2015). People sometimes regulate their feelings intentionally, as is revealed in statements such as, "I don't want to go to that movie because it will make me too sad" or "I am super angry at my friend; let's go eat ice cream!" (Ochsner & Gross, 2005, 2008; Tice & Bratslavsky, 2000). People also regulate their feelings involuntarily, such as when they spontaneously turn their head away to avoid looking at the scene of an automobile accident (Mauss, Bunge, & Gross, 2007).

We begin this chapter by discussing *why* people regulate their emotions. After considering these motives, we go on to consider *how* people do so. Our examples illustrate a number of ways that people regulate their emotion, which we will call **emotion regulation strategies**. By "strategies" we do not mean to imply that the various processes of emotion regulation are intentional. We have already seen that emotion regulation can be automatic. Rather, by "strategies" we mean that the way of regulating emotion is consistent with the opportunities, capacities, and goals of the individual at that time. Indeed, the emotion regulation strategies that we describe can affect different components of the emotion, including its cognitive, physiological, behavioral-expressive, and experiential aspects. Finally, we evaluate the consequences of emotion regulation. Although there might be a goal for managing one's emotions, there might be costs for doing so. These costs can include negative effects on memory, personal relationships, and health.

Motives for Regulating Emotions

There are a number of reasons to want to alter the expression or experience of emotion (Koole, 2009). All of them start from the idea that the current emotional state is somehow "undesirable." What makes an emotion undesirable and thus subject to regulation? One reason an emotion might be undesirable is due to its negative hedonic tone—that is, its psychological unpleasantness. If you try to regulate your emotions because you want to feel better, you are being driven by a state of **hedonic motivation** (Larsen, 2000). Hedonic motivation is what inspires you to say that you want to go to a comedy club tonight because you are feeling down. Feeling bad and wanting to feel good is also related to other, more destructive emotion regulation behaviors, such as gambling (Dickerson, 1991) and drinking (Sayette, 1993).

Sometimes your emotional state feels just fine, but you know that it will not serve you well in performing a particular task. For instance, it is probably not very useful to you to be in a silly mood as you go into a lecture hall to take an organic chemistry exam. If you try to regulate your emotions because you believe certain emotions are appropriate (and others inappropriate) to the tasks you need to perform, you are being driven by a state of **instrumental motivation** (Erber, Wegner, & Therriault, 1996; Parrott, 1993). In illustrative studies, participants tried to ramp up their fear (Tamir & Ford, 2009) and their anger (Tamir, Mitchell, & Gross, 2008) when participants considered these emotions helpful. For example, in the study by Tamir and colleagues (2008), participants chose to engage in activities that would make them feel anger before playing a computer game that involved confrontation with enemies but not before playing a computer game that involved building an empire (Figure 9.1).

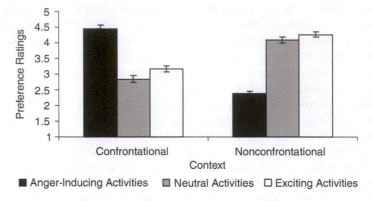

Figure 9.1 Participants' preferences for anger-inducing, neutral, and exciting activities when they anticipated performing confrontational versus nonconfrontational activities. From Tamir, Mitchell, & Gross (2008).

What people want to feel or to express is also determined by concerns involving the expected interpersonal consequences of displaying certain emotions. Individuals may regulate their emotions to serve **prosocial motives**, that is, in order to protect the feelings of others. For example, concealing your feelings of romantic interest in the partner of your best friend is a good idea, at least if you want to maintain best friend status with that person.

Self-protection motives may also underlie emotion regulation. Individuals may suppress their emotions or feign an emotion in order to protect their personal safety or to elicit helpful reactions from others. For example, an employee might try to control both the experience and expression of anger in front of her employer in order to avoid negative consequences in the workplace. Or she may feign embarrassment in order to be forgiven for an error that she has committed.

Finally, an **impression management motive**, or the fear of being judged negatively by others because of expressing an inappropriate emotion, often underlies emotion regulation. The motivation to avoid being evaluated unfavorably by others is based on knowledge of norms that prescribe what emotions are appropriate in a particular context (Fischer et al., 2004; Manstead & Fischer, 2000). Emotion norms not only prescribe outward emotional displays, but also the very feeling that can be experienced in a given situation (Hochschild, 1983). Display rules specify the emotional expressions appropriate to a specific situation, and feeling rules prescribe the feelings one should experience according to social and cultural conventions. As an example of display rules, employees working in the service sector are sometimes expected to "serve with a smile"—that is, to display positive emotions and to inhibit negative ones in order to increase customer satisfaction (Grandey, 2000).

Now that we know why individuals are motivated to control their emotions, we can ask *how* they do it. As we discuss in the following section, individuals employ a variety of strategies that are more or less efficient in changing their emotions.

Emotion Regulation Strategies

One way to provide conceptual organization to emotion regulation strategies is to distinguish between the processes that occur before an emotion is experienced and after it is experienced (Gross, 1998, 1999; Gross & Thompson, 2007). Gross's process model of emotion regulation posits that we use different strategies at different points in our experience of emotion-eliciting situations. **Antecedent-focused** emotion regulation involves attempts to control or modify an emotion before it has even been elicited (because we know what is to come). **Response-focused**

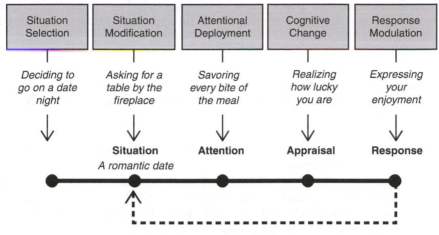

Figure 9.2 Gross's process model of emotion regulation, which highlights five families of emotion regulation that occur at different times (represented by the black line running from left to right) in the elicitation of an emotional response. Here we look at enhancing positive feelings. Adapted from Quoidbach, Mikolajczak, and Gross (2015).

regulation refers to the modification of the subjective, expressive, or physiological aspects of an emotion when the experience is already occurring.

When time is broken down this way, Gross identifies five families of emotion regulation strategies (as exemplified in Figure 9.2). Four of these are antecedent focused, and one is response focused. Let's start with the antecedent-focused families of emotion regulation strategies.

Antecedent-Focused Regulation Strategies

The first antecedent-focused strategy, **situation selection**, involves seeking out events or people that you know might evoke feelings that you do want to experience and avoiding those you know you don't want to experience. You can, for example, decide not to attend a party in order to avoid a particular person who usually makes you feel sad or angry. Alternatively, you can decide to go to a party where you will encounter people or events that you know will make you feel good.

Another antecedent-focused strategy, **situation modification**, involves trying to alter the features of a situation in order to modify its emotional impact. Asking a friend to keep his dog on a leash during a visit and asking a housemate to turn her music down are examples of modifying the situation.

A third antecedent-focused strategy, **attentional deployment**, allows you to affect the emotional impact of a situation by how you take in information in your environment. Attentional deployment occurs when individuals use selective attention to limit (or enhance) their exposure to the emotionally evocative aspects of an event (Gross & Thompson, 2007). For instance, when you are watching a horror film, you might avert your gaze from a bloody hand or a scary-looking zombie to look at a neutral part of the image. The strategic use of attention has also been shown to decrease various kinds of negative affective experience, including bad mood (Rusting, 1998), angry feelings (Gerin et al., 2006), and even stress (Bennett et al., 2007).

Fourth, individuals can also modify how they think about a situation in order to increase or to decrease the occurrence of specific emotions (**cognitive change**). For instance, you might start to get upset about not having been acknowledged by a neighbor, which seems to you to be intentional ignoring. However, the fact that the neighbor did not say hello could be interpreted as due to chronic impoliteness (directed at everyone), as due to her preoccupation with personal problems, or even as due to her poor eyesight. If you reappraised the situation as being due to one of these causes, you would feel differently about the apparent slight of failing to say hello.

Response-Focused Strategies

The family of response-focused regulation strategies consists of strategies that people employ once an emotion has already been elicited. These strategies involve attempts to modify an emotion's specific subjective, physiological, and expressive components. One such strategy, the **regulation of expressive behavior**, involves the suppression or amplification of facial expressions of emotion in particular, but also bodily and vocal displays of emotion, which might, in turn, modulate emotional experience.

Psychologists have identified additional response-focused regulation strategies. The **regulation of physiological arousal** is affected by medication such as tranquilizers, which decrease muscle tension, or by beta-blockers, which inhibit the adrenergic beta-receptors, thereby reducing sympathetic arousal. Beta-blockers are frequently used in the treatment of hypertension, but also for fighting stage fright and exam nerves. Other drugs that affect muscle tension and/or physiological arousal include alcoholic beverages, coffee, marijuana, and cigarettes. College students believe that alcohol use can enhance their mood, and they use it to this end (Merrill & Read, 2010). The regulation of physiological arousal may also be achieved more positively through self-induced muscle relaxation and biofeedback or through exercising (Thayer, Newman, & McClain, 1994).

Another response-focused regulation strategy, the **regulation of experience**, involves focused concentration on, or suppression of, intense thoughts that accompany feelings. The first, often called **rumination**, consists of consciously drawing attention to (especially) negative thoughts and feelings with the goal of making sense of them, and thus reducing their unpleasant impact. Rumination has primarily been studied in the context of psychopathological symptoms such as anxiety and depression, and has been found to worsen the depressive symptoms especially when they occur in an intrusive way (Aldao, Nolen-Hoeksema, & Schweizer, 2010; Nolen-Hoeksema & Morrow, 1993). The second, the conscious suppression of emotional thoughts, is illustrated by the familiar experience of trying not to think of a former lover in order not to feel bad. As discussed later in this chapter, **emotional thought suppression** may produce ironic effects similar to those produced by thought suppression in general (Wegner, 1994). That is, it may paradoxically facilitate the return of the suppressed emotions.

A third response-focused regulation strategy is emotional disclosure, or the so-called **social sharing of emotions**. Immediately following intense positive or negative emotional experiences, people are inclined to talk about their feelings to others, which, in turn, may influence their emotions.

In the rest of this chapter, we discuss in detail the efficacy of four commonly studied emotion regulation strategies: cognitive reappraisal, expressive suppression, emotional thought suppression, and emotional disclosure. We discuss whether each strategy works to modify one or all aspects of emotion and also whether each strategy has any hidden costs to the individual, including to their interpersonal relationships and to their health.

Cognitive Reappraisal

Much of our behavior is intentional, so in our daily lives we usually know what is going to happen to us next. We also know how we are likely to respond emotionally to upcoming events. Because we can make these emotional predictions, we can use the cognitive change strategy of reappraisal to change how we think about an upcoming situation in order to modify its emotional impact. People often use reappraisal to think about a negative event in less emotional terms, thereby dampening their negative emotions (Giuliani & Gross, 2009). The intensity of negative feelings of sadness (Ochsner et al., 2004) and anger (Stemmler, 1997) has been shown to be diminished by cognitive reappraisal. Studies also show that college students can successfully reduce feelings of worry and stress about an upcoming exam by thinking of the situation in a more detached or positive way, for example, by interpreting the exam situation as an occasion to show what they know (a challenge) rather than the possible revelation of their ignorance (Tomaka et al., 1997).

Positive experiences can also be reappraised in ways that regulate positive feelings as well. Trying to alter your feelings and expressions of amusement is probably something you are very familiar with. You might be able to recall a time when you and someone with whom you tend to be very silly—perhaps a friend or sibling—were on your way to a very serious event, such as a religious service. You might have started your emotion regulation before you even got there, maybe in the car. Participants in a study of the use of reappraisal to control amusement saw a number of moderately amusing film clips. Before each clip started, participants were told to look at the film and to increase their amusement through reappraisal or to decrease their amusement through reappraisal. (Initial instructions told participants how to use reappraisal to generate more and less amusement.) During the films, participants' facial expressions and vocalizations, as well as physiological responses such as blood pressure, heart rate, and galvanic skin response, were measured. Participants also reported their experienced amusement after seeing each clip.

The findings of this study show that reappraisal allowed participants to successfully modify many aspects of their emotional responses in the intended direction (see Figure 9.3). Other studies have also demonstrated that reappraisal of negative emotion-eliciting stimuli modulates the

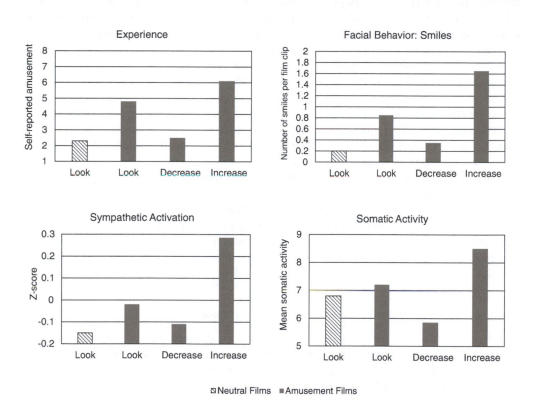

Figure 9.3 After viewing each film clip, participants rated how amused they felt during the film. While viewing films, participants' facial expressions were videotaped. These expressions were later coded for smiles. Sympathetic activation of the cardiovascular system was assessed by creating a composite of finger pulse amplitude, finger pulse transit time, ear pulse transit time, and finger temperature. Somatic activity was measured by using an electric device attached to the participants' chair that sent electrical signals proportional to overall body movement. Adapted from Giuliani, McRae, & Gross (2008).

experiential, behavioral, physiological, and neural components of emotion as intended (Gross, 1998; Ochsner et al., 2004). This suggests that reappraisal is a successful strategy for modifying many components of emotion.

Taken together, research on reappraisal suggests that this emotion regulation strategy is successful in reducing both negative and positive emotional experience, expression, and physiological arousal (Gross, 2002). Furthermore, reappraisal does not consume cognitive resources in that it does not impair memory.

Suppression of Expressive Behavior

You have probably had the experience of being in a full-blown state of hilarity, when suddenly you are forced to inhibit your feelings of amusement, perhaps because you are in a place where laughter is inappropriate. In this case, you might work hard to clamp down on your outward expression of mirth. The voluntary inhibition of the facial and bodily expression of emotion, known as **expressive suppression**, is a highly studied, response-focused emotion regulation strategy. In many studies of expressive suppression, experimental participants are exposed to emotion-inducing films or slides, and are instructed to suppress their overt emotional reactions when they occur. Control condition participants receive no regulation instructions. Participants' facial expressions are filmed (or activation of their facial muscles are assessed with methods of electromyography [EMG]), their physiological responses are recorded, and their self-reports of subjective feelings are collected. Measuring multiple components of emotion allows us to see whether people do a good job at modifying their expression of emotion and whether or not that suppression also affects other parts of the emotional response.

Gross and Levenson (1997) had participants watch three films—one sad, one amusing, and one neutral. Some were instructed to suppress facial expressions, whereas others were given no specific instructions. Participants who tried to suppress their expression of emotion during the emotional films did so to a significant degree compared to those with no suppression instructions. However, suppressors were still more expressive during emotion-arousing films than during the neutral film. This and other findings indicate that although people can suppress expression, they do not do so completely (Richards & Gross, 1999). Importantly, suppression was also associated with increased sympathetic arousal, which suggests that trying to prevent displays of emotions takes some effort. Other studies have replicated the increase in sympathetic arousal during expressive suppression (Demaree et al., 2006). Furthermore, suppressors reported feeling less amused when watching a funny film, but did not feel less sad watching a sad film compared to no-suppressors. In another study, the suppression of expressions of disgust during the viewing of films showing surgical amputations did not decrease the subjective experience of disgust (Gross & Levenson, 1993).

Comparing Reappraisal and Expressive Suppression

Cognitive reappraisal seems to be an emotion regulation strategy that alters many components of emotion. By contrast, expressive suppression seems to work mostly on the outward display of emotion, which is often the intention of the person trying to regulate his or her emotion. However, there may be different hidden costs to the two strategies.

Cognitive Consequences of Expressive Suppression and Cognitive Reappraisal

The suppression of emotion-expressive behavior is a deliberate and effortful act that not only changes outward appearance and bodily arousal, but also influences individuals' cognitive functioning. The suppression of emotional expression in response to emotion-inducing images has been found to impair memory for information encountered during the suppression period, suggesting that suppression is cognitively taxing. Suppressors also reported being less confident than nonsuppressors in their capacity to memorize image information, indicating that they were aware of their memory impairment (Richards & Gross, 1999, 2000).

Reappraisal does not seem to have the same cognitive cost. In studies that compared the two types of emotion regulation, reappraisal did not impair the recall of verbal information that was presented together with emotion-eliciting events (Richards & Gross, 2000). Similar results were found in a more complex interactive situation where married couples were asked to discuss a relationship conflict with the instruction either to reappraise the situation in positive terms or to suppress any emotional expression (Richards, Butler, & Gross, 2003). Again, suppression did impair memory for the verbal content of the conversation, whereas reappraisal did not.

The memory impairment in suppressors may thus be due to reduced cognitive and attentional resources imposed by suppression. The instruction to conceal one's feelings draws attention to the internal aspects of the self and reduces attentional resources for encoding the external event. Furthermore, suppression heightens self-monitoring—that is, it increases the suppressors' concern as to whether they are successfully concealing their feelings. ("Do I show anything?" or "I must try to keep my face still.") This language-based monitoring impedes the encoding of verbal information, which explains why suppression impairs verbal memory more than any other type of memory (Richards & Gross, 2000). By contrast, reappraisal is cognitively inexpensive, as it does not involve constant self-monitoring: once the situation is reappraised in nonemotional terms, it does not require further self-regulatory efforts and leaves attentional and cognitive resources intact for the processing of information.

Emotion regulation strategies thus differ in their cognitive consequences. Suppression impairs the recall of details of an emotional event, whereas reappraisal does not. This finding may have implications for individuals' social functioning. Those who conceal their feelings during a social encounter are prone to forget details of what has been said, which could influence the way they perceive and evaluate the people with whom they interact.

Social Consequences of Expressive Suppression and Cognitive Reappraisal

As we have seen, expressive suppression leads to changes in self-focus and self-monitoring and produces an attentional shift away from the situation to internal aspects of the self. But these cognitive effects are not the only consequences of expressive suppression. Expressive suppression also has social consequences. For example, it is reasonable to suspect that suppression distracts attention away from the interaction partner. Suppression may impair the suppressor's responsiveness in a social encounter—that is, it may impair appropriate contingent responses and impede the coordination with the interaction partner. Furthermore, expressive suppression conceals the feelings, social motives, and behavioral intentions of an individual. In a study showing the social costs of expressive suppression, researchers had some participants regulate their emotional reactions to viewing an upsetting film and others reappraise the film to control their emotions while they engaged in an interaction with a partner. Compared to control participants, who had received no instructions, participants who suppressed could reduce their expression of emotion, but at the cost of being less responsible and more distracted in interaction with their partner (Figure 9.4; Butler et al., 2003). Furthermore, the partners of individuals who were suppressing their emotions were found to have higher blood pressure during the interaction, indicating that interacting with someone who was suppressing their emotions was stressful. Similar social costs have also been observed in real-world contexts such as young adults transitioning to college and dealing with emotional events of that challenge with expressive suppression versus other emotion regulations strategies (Srivastava et al., 2009)

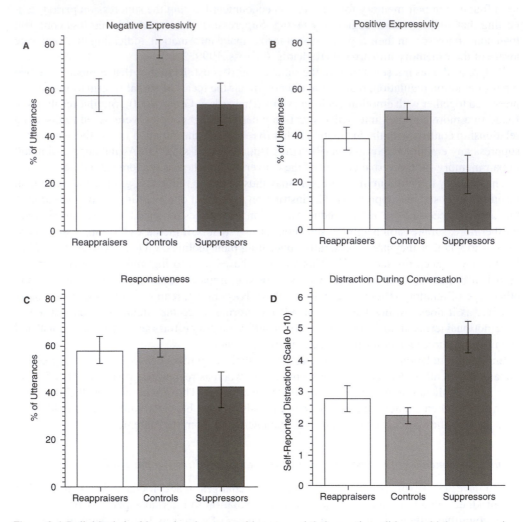

Figure 9.4 Individuals in this study who were told to conceal their emotions did a good job at expressing their displays of emotion. This came with the cost of being distracted and not very responsive to their interaction partner. From Butler et al. (2003).

Additional support for the detrimental effects of suppression on social relationships comes from research on marital interactions. Low expressiveness in married couples has been found to be associated with negative feelings and reduced marital satisfaction in both spouses (Gottman & Levenson, 1986), whereas responsive listening (as indicated by attention to and comprehension of the partner) has been found to be beneficial for marital satisfaction (Pasupathi et al., 1999).

Of course, as we have noted previously in this chapter, concealing one's feelings, and in particular one's negative feelings, during social exchange can also have positive social consequences because it protects others' feelings and prevents interpersonal conflict. Whether expressive suppression is beneficial or detrimental depends on the specific emotions that are concealed, on the situation in which the suppression occurs, and on the frequency with which the emotions are suppressed. Suppression may also be desirable in situations in which interpersonal distance is required, such as in interactions with a superior. Hiding one's feelings may be beneficial when it is used as a temporary tool that allows the individual to conform to personal needs and social demands in a given context. Chronic suppression, however, may put existing relationships at risk and hinder the development of new ones. It may also perpetuate the feelings one is concealing. For example, suppression of the anger caused by recurrent, unfair, and insolent remarks of a colleague will prevent the colleague from realizing the harmful impact of his or her remarks; instead of correcting the behavior by apologizing, he or she may persist in it, which will further enflame the anger and cause a deterioration of the relationship.

To conclude, expressive suppression has physiological as well as cognitive and social costs. Note, however, that these negative effects of expressive suppression seem to be specific to Western cultures in which the overt emotion expression is valued. The same negative effects were not replicated in Asian cultures in which emotional control is prescribed (Butler, Lee, & Gross, 2007), and research using electrocortical responding has suggested that people from East Asian cultures can effectively down-regulate emotional processing when engaging in expressive suppression (Murata, Moser, & Kitayama, 2012).

In Western culture, however, reappraisal does appear to be a more efficient emotion regulation strategy, with more adaptive consequences for the individual. A meta-analysis that compared the effectiveness of three emotion regulation strategies (attentional deployment, cognitive change, and response modulation) confirmed these findings. Distracting oneself or reinterpreting the emotion-eliciting situation was found to be the most efficient ways to prevent unwanted emotions. Expressive suppression was efficient in modifying individuals' expressive behavior but proved to negatively affect their physiological responding while leaving their feelings unchanged (Webb, Miles, & Sheeran, 2012). It should be noted, however, that despite its benefits, reappraisal is not the preferred strategy in every context. For example, reappraisal is more likely to be chosen over distraction when the situation elicits a low-intensity negative emotion (Sheppes et al., 2011) and when the expectation of repeated exposure to an emotion-eliciting stimulus leads to a longer-term regulation goal (Sheppes et al., 2014).

Emotional Thought Suppression

So far we have focused on how people regulate their emotions when they are faced with, or potentially faced with, an emotion-eliciting object or event. However, people's own thoughts can also cause them to experience both positive and negative emotions that they want to control. Thinking about an impending event such as a final exam can be very anxiety provoking, for example. The **suppression of unwanted thoughts** is quite common. People try not to think of cigarettes when they want to stop smoking, and try not to think of food when they want to lose weight. In the same way, people try to regulate their emotions by suppressing thoughts that elicit unwanted pleasant, painful, or unpleasant feelings. Unfortunately, although common, this emotion regulation strategy is not very effective. Attempts to banish unwanted thoughts from one's mind may paradoxically increase the frequency with which these thoughts come to mind.

Rebound of Suppressed Thoughts

The ironic and counterproductive effect of the active suppression of an unwanted thought is called the **rebound effect**. The rebound effect was first demonstrated in a classic experiment by a psychologist named Daniel Wegner (Figure 9.5). Participants who had been taught to report on their stream of consciousness were told to report their thoughts into a tape recorder and to also avoid thinking about a white bear. Other participants did not receive the white bear instruction. Later, when again reporting on their stream of consciousness without avoiding thoughts of

Figure 9.5 Daniel Wegner got the idea of studying suppression of thoughts of a white bear from a story in which Dostoevsky, the Russian novelist, challenges his brother not to think of a white bear.

a white bear, the white bear thought came to mind much more for individuals who had earlier suppressed the thought than for individuals who had not (Wegner et al., 1987). Why do suppressed thoughts come back to mind after suppression? And, even more importantly for the present concerns, is there also a rebound after suppression of emotionally arousing thoughts?

According to Wegner's model of mental control (Wegner, 1994), thought suppression involves two processes. The first is an **automatic monitoring process**, which is effortless and involuntary, and which functions outside of conscious awareness. It requires no cognitive resources. The second is a **controlled operating process**, which is conscious, intentional, and requires cognitive resources. The monitoring process searches mental content for instances of the unwanted thought. Each time it detects the presence of the to-be-suppressed unwanted thought, the operating process is then activated with the goal to seek out other so-called **distracter** thoughts that capture conscious attention and serve to keep the unwanted thought out of mind.

Wegner's model of mental control proposes different explanations for the rebound of suppressed thoughts. The **association explanation** holds that the distracter thoughts that are used to replace the unwanted thought become strongly associated with the unwanted thought. Distracters then serve as memory cues that prompt the unwanted thought whenever they come to mind or appear in the environment. This explains why rebound effects are stronger when the suppression and subsequent expression periods take place in the same physical or emotional environment (Wegner et al., 1991; Wenzlaff, Wegner, & Klein, 1991).

A second explanation of the rebound effect is the **accessibility explanation**. It holds that suppression increases the accessibility of the to-be-suppressed thoughts because the automatic monitoring process continues to search for the unwanted thought even when suppression is no longer required. Thus suppression increases the likelihood that the previously suppressed thought rebounds, without being cued by a distracter (Macrae et al., 1994; Page, Locke, & Trio, 2005).

The final explanation, the **cognitive load explanation**, says that the rebound effect is more likely when cognitive resources are reduced due to a concurrent task, time pressure, or stress. Cognitive load undermines the cognitively costly operating process, and so the monitoring processes find even more instances of the unwanted thoughts. This is because under cognitive load, the monitoring process continues to search for the to-be-suppressed thought. However, because the operating process is no longer able to replace the thought with distracters, the unwanted thought will become even more accessible (Reich & Mather, 2008; Wenzlaff & Wegner, 2000).

Emotional Rebound

Studies have shown suppression of emotions and emotional thoughts does not cause the classic thought rebound. For example, suppression of emotional arousing thoughts such as thoughts of a fatal car accident (Muris et al., 1992) or a desired ex-lover (Wegner & Gold, 1995) does not lead to rebound. Suppression seems thus to be quite efficient in banishing emotional thoughts from people's minds, at least when their cognitive resources are not taxed otherwise.

The absence of an emotional rebound may be due to people's prior experience with controlling intrusive emotional thoughts. In everyday life, thought suppression is certainly more common for emotional than for neutral thoughts. People may therefore have a greater variety of distracters they normally use to avoid their emotional thoughts. Furthermore, the presence of emotion-relevant distracters may redirect attention away from the emotional thoughts and reduce their rebound. For example, suppression of disgust was found to facilitate avoidance of disgust-related images when they were presented together with images representing cleanliness but not when they were paired with neutral, disgust-irrelevant images (Vogt & De Houwer, 2014).

One might then ask whether the suppression of emotional thoughts also prevents the individual from experiencing the undesirable emotions. Several studies suggest that the inhibition of emotional thoughts may calm the mind but not the body. Physiological arousal was found to increase after suppression of emotionally arousing thoughts in response to an emotionally upsetting film about work accidents (Koriat et al., 1972), sexually arousing slides of nude women (Martin, 1964), or sexually arousing topics (Wegner et al., 1990).

Does this mean that the more one tries to put a past relationship out of mind, the more one will be disturbed by unpleasant bodily arousal? Indeed, participants who were previously asked to suppress thoughts of a still desired ex-lover thought and talked less about him or her afterwards but showed an increased electrodermal response, suggesting a physiological rebound (Wegner & Gold, 1995). But what happens when feelings are suppressed in more complex interaction situations? Imagine that you plan to get together with a friend because you need to talk to her about your recent relationship problems. When you arrive at the agreed-upon time and place, you find that your friend has brought along an acquaintance of hers whom you do not know. There is no way to talk about your problems, and so you half-heartedly engage in a discussion of a new film. You might feel especially aroused because you have to avoid thinking about what you really want to discuss. Mendes et al. (2003) found that participants who had to suppress thoughts about emotional topics exhibited greater physiological arousal compared to baseline arousal and to the nonemotional suppressors, as shown in Figure 9.6.

The suppression of emotionally exciting thoughts may thus be counterproductive because even though it diminishes the frequency of the to-be suppressed thoughts, it causes people to become bodily aroused the few times the suppressed thought returns to mind. A gradual confrontation with the unwanted emotional thought may be a remedy against the physiological rebound. Accepting rather than avoiding the unwanted emotional thought facilitates habituation and reduces the other concomitant emotional responses (i.e., bodily arousal) over the course of time. This helps the individual to face the unwanted emotional thought and to process and re-evaluate its emotional content in order to render it supportable (Wegner, 1989).

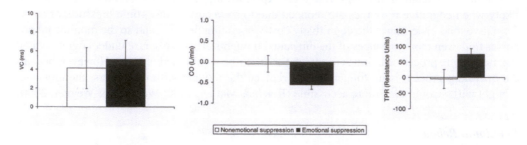

Figure 9.6 Cardiovascular reactivity comparing emotional suppression and nonemotional suppression conditions. VC = ventricular contractility, CO = cardiac output, TPR = peripheral resistance. Results show that suppression is related to higher and not lower cardiovascular activity. From Mendes et al. (2003).

Social Sharing of Emotions

Within the psychoanalytic tradition (Bucci, 1995; Freud, 1920/2005) the accumulation of non-expressed emotions is associated with mental and physical disorders. The verbalization of traumatic events and the associated emotions are considered beneficial for the individual. Common sense also holds that it is helpful and good to talk about one's emotions and feelings because it makes one feel better. In addition to emotional recovery, revealing one's feelings to others is considered to be beneficial for physical and psychological health and for people's social relationships (Zech, 1999). Let's see if the research supports this idea.

Initial studies of the **social sharing** of emotion were mainly concerned with its quantitative aspects, such as what emotional events people share, when, how often, and with whom (Luminet et al., 2000; Rimé et al., 1998). Across studies and methods, the vast majority of participants reported having engaged in social sharing, usually on the very day of the emotional event. The frequency of social sharing is positively correlated with the intensity of the emotional experience, indicating that people are more inclined to talk about intense and disturbing emotional episodes. Talking about one's emotion also does not vary substantially with age, sex, and culture (Rimé et al., 1998; Rimé et al., 1992). But does talking about their emotions make people really feel better? We'll investigate that question next.

Social Sharing and Emotional Recovery

Most people not only talk to other people about their emotions, but they also believe that sharing their emotions with someone is relieving (Zech, 1999). However, there is no empirical evidence for this **expression discharge hypothesis**, which posits that social sharing of emotion contributes to emotional recovery (Rimé, 2009).

Typically, there is no significant relationship between social sharing and emotional recovery, indicating that recalling and talking about an emotional event does not decrease its emotional impact, at least in the short term (Finkenauer & Rimé, 1998a; Rimé, 2009). On the contrary, social sharing has been found to reactivate the shared emotion. That is, talking about a past emotional event was found to reinstigate concomitant mental images, bodily sensations, and subjective feelings. However, the disclosure of negative emotional episodes was not perceived as unpleasant or painful but as useful and beneficial (Zech & Rimé, 2005). People tolerate re-experiencing negative emotions during social sharing because it satisfies socioaffective needs and facilitates a cognitive reappraisal of the emotional event (for a review, see Rimé, 2009).

Emotionally upsetting events are globally distressing and may induce feelings of helplessness; insecurity; and the need for comfort, proximity, and support. Talking about an upsetting past experience was found to provide important subjective benefits to participants. Social sharing was perceived as meaningful, helpful, and relieving because it made them feel understood and comforted and allowed people to understand themselves more clearly (Zech & Rimé, 2005). Self-reported motives for spontaneous social sharing were also mainly linked to need for support, comfort, consolation, and bonding (Wetzer, Zeelenberg, & Pieters, 2005).

Assimilation and Accommodation

Emotions—in particular, negative ones—may challenge people's belief about the world and lead them to see the world as unfair, unsafe, or out of control. People's willingness to talk about emotional events is not only motivated by a desire to feel better, but also by a need to understand the meaning of the emotional event and to adapt to it. By verbalizing and putting their emotional experience into words, people distance themselves from the emotional experience, which enables them to reprocess the emotional information and to restore the threatened beliefs about the world. This working through the emotional experience allows people to integrate the emotional event in their existing emotional schemas and scripts (**assimilation**) or to modify them (**accommodation**) in order to adjust to a new reality, especially in the case of a major emotional life event (Horowitz, 1976/1992). This cognitive mode of social sharing contributes to overcoming a negative emotional episode (Figure 9.7).

Figure 9.7 Social sharing of emotion helps people recover from emotional events to the extent that sharing helps the person work through the experience and come to understand the world in a new, more realistic, light.

Developmental Detail

Older Adults Regulate Emotions Better Than You Do!

The ways that people regulate their emotions continue to evolve across their life span (Charles & Carstensen, 2007). Studies now show that compared to younger people, older people dedicate more resources to using emotion regulation techniques that promote positive experiences. This is probably why older adults self-report higher, not lower, levels of well-being than younger adults (Urry & Gross, 2010). The process model of emotion regulation that you learned about in this chapter (see Figure 9.3) holds that emotion regulation can occur at any one of five points in time: situation selection, situation modification, attentional deployment, cognitive reappraisal, or response modulation after the emotion is being experienced. As people age, they start to use some of these strategies less, and others more, in managing their emotions. For example, older adults become less likely than younger adults to rely on the expressive suppression of a full-blown emotion, probably because it is quite resource demanding.

As you learned in the last chapter on cognition and emotion, older adults also start to focus more on things that make them happy and avoid focusing attention on things that make them sad. This is only the beginning. Older adults also become more strategic about situation selection. Research shows that as they age, adults increasing rely on smaller, closer-knit social support networks as a resource. The more constrained networks seem to help older adults predict how they will feel in situations and thereby be more effective than younger adults at avoiding toxic social situations. In addition, older adults experience and perceive less anger in interpersonal situations (Charles & Carstensen, 2008) and in general benefit more than younger adults from the avoidance of interpersonal confrontations in the first place (Charles, Piazza, Luong, & Almeida, 2009). When it comes to emotion regulation, then, it appears that older adults are truly wiser!

Do people get less happy with age? That is not what the research shows. Older adults do a better job than younger ones in making sure they have positive social experiences.

Several experimental studies have indeed shown that talking with a "challenging" listener who behaves in an emotionally detached way and expresses alternative views of the disclosed emotional episode is more beneficial in terms of less intrusive thoughts, psychological distress, and physiological arousal compared to a "validating" listener who empathetically agrees with the narrator's reactions and feelings (Lepore et al., 2004; Nils & Rimé, 2012). However, a validating listener is perceived as more friendly, empathic, and similar (Lepore et al., 2004) and makes narrators feel less lonely (Nils & Rimé, 2012), and is thus more solicited in the first place.

Although talking to someone about one's emotion does not result in immediate emotional recovery, it provides short-term socioaffective benefits and is beneficial in the long term because it enables people to reappraise the emotional event in a more positive way.

Finally, studies on the consequences of written disclosure of emotion have shown that writing about stressful or traumatic episodes is beneficial for people's physical and mental health (Pennebaker & Beall, 1986; for a review see Frattaroli, 2006). This raises the question of the health implications of emotion regulation.

Emotion Regulation and Health

Emotion regulation is commonly considered central to and even necessary for mental and physical health. Emotional dysregulation is held to be responsible for clinical problems such as eating disorders, alcohol abuse, and anxiety and mood disorders, in particular depression (for a review, see Gross & Muñoz, 1995). In correlation studies, chronic emotional suppression (as compared to reappraisal) has been found to be associated with more self-reported depressive symptoms, lower life satisfaction, weaker self-esteem, and lower overall well-being (Gross & John, 2003). Several studies have explored the relationship between cognitive emotion regulation strategies and measures of depression and anxiety (Garnefski, Kraaij, & Spinhoven, 2001; Garnefski et al., 2002). The following "maladaptive" cognitive regulation strategies are positively related to depression and anxiety:

* **Rumination:** Recurrent thinking about negative feelings
* **Catastrophizing:** Explicitly emphasizing the negativity of the event
* **Self-blame:** Blaming oneself for what has happened
* **Other blame:** Blaming others for what has happened

The following more adaptive strategies are negatively related to anxiety and depression:

* **Positive reappraisal:** Interpretation of a negative event in a positive way in terms of personal growth
* **Positive refocus:** Thinking about pleasant, joyful things that distract from the negative event
* **Putting into perspective:** Emphasizing the relativity of the event compared to other events
* **Acceptance:** Accepting and resigning to what has happened
* **Refocus on planning:** Thinking about the steps necessary to deal with the negative event

Another cognitive regulation strategy that has positive consequences for depression and cardiovascular health is **self-distancing** (Kross, Ayduk, & Mischel, 2005). Rather than inhibiting an emotion or thought, an individual takes a self-distanced (observer's perspective), as opposed to a self-immersed (own perspective), point of view when thinking about an emotional experience. The self-distanced perspective leads people to reconstrue experiences rather than recount them and reduces blood pressure reactivity (Ayduk & Kross, 2008), facilitates coping, and is effective for reducing depressive symptoms including rumination (Kross & Ayduk, 2009).

In addition to psychological problems and mood disorders, emotion dysregulation can cause somatic illness. It has been shown quite consistently that avoidance, inhibition, suppression, and holding back of negative emotions have deleterious consequences for physical health and can lower self-reported life satisfaction (Finkenauer & Rimé, 1998b). Chronic emotion inhibition may even increase the risk of cancer and accelerate cancer progression (Gross, 1989; Kune et al., 1991), as well as cardiovascular and immune-related diseases (Mund & Mitte, 2012).

The adverse effects of emotion inhibition may be due to the increased sympathetic nervous system activation that it produces. According to Pennebaker and colleagues' **inhibition theory**, the conscious effort to inhibit one's emotional thoughts, feelings, and emotion-related behavior generates physiological arousal (Pennebaker, 1989; Pennebaker & Beall, 1986; Pennebaker, Hughes, & O'Heeron, 1987). Chronic inhibition produces cumulative physiological arousal and increase the likelihood of stress-related psychological and physical health problems. Another mechanism through which emotional suppression affects health is its selective inhibitory effect on immune functioning (Petrie, Booth, & Davison, 1995; Petrie, Booth, & Pennebaker, 1998). In particular, cumulative sympathetic arousal may produce changes in gene expression that increases the vulnerability for inflammation-related diseases (i.e., heart diseases, neurodegenerative disease, and some types of cancer) and viral infections (Cole, 2009). Disclosure of stressful, traumatic events, by the same token, appears to enhance immune functioning (Esterling et al., 1994; Pennebaker, Kiecolt-Glaser, & Glaser, 1988) and to reduce the risk of cardiovascular disease (Frattaroli, 2006). Emotion regulation through reappraisal was also linked to lower cardiovascular disease risk (Appleton & Kubzansky, 2014).

Of course, based on what we have learned about emotion regulation and health, we should not infer that the less we inhibit or the more often we express our emotions, the healthier we are. As Gross and Muñoz have noted, "It is the ability to flexibly adjust the way one regulates one's emotions to environmental exigencies that is related to . . . health, not how often one regulates one's emotions" (Gross & Muñoz, 1995, p. 160). This reasoning is consistent with research showing that the ability to flexibly enhance and suppress the expression of emotions, depending on situational demands, predicts long-term reductions in distress (Bonanno et al., 2004).

Cultural and Individual Differences

We started this chapter with the idea that emotions are subjected to regulation efforts when the person having the emotion regards the state as undesirable (Mesquita, de Leersnyder, & Albert, 2014). The definition of "undesirable," of course, varies with cultural context (Mesquita & Leu, 2007; Tsai, Knutson, & Fung, 2006). We have already seen that different cultures also have different display rules governing which emotions can be expressed to others in public settings (Rychlowska et al., 2015). Thus, although the basics of emotion regulation strategies might be the same across cultures, the frequency of use and the contexts for the regulation strategies vary.

For example, the expression of one's emotion is more likely to cause social disruptions in some East Asian cultures (Kim & Sherman, 2007). Unsurprisingly, then, expressive suppression appears to be a more common emotion regulation strategy among East Asians than among Westerners (Gross & John, 2003; Murata, Moser, & Kitayama, 2012; Tsai & Levenson, 1997). Furthermore, the costs of emotion suppression seem to be lower for those who value expressive suppression compared to people who do not (Butler, Lee, & Gross, 2007). Westerners tend to disclose distress and ask for support more than East Asians. In fact, asking for emotional support is viewed by East Asians as stressful because it puts pressure on the harmony in their relationships (Kim, Sherman, & Taylor, 2008; Taylor et al., 2007).

There are also stable individual differences within cultures in the use of emotion regulation strategies. In particular, stable tendencies to reappraise situations and to engage in expressive suppression have been observed (Gross & John, 2003). Some people, called reappraisers, tend to work on their emotions before events occur, thus modifying their expression, experience, and even the content of their social sharing of emotion with some success. The results of a number of experiments demonstrate that reappraisal decreases the expressive and subjective aspects of emotion in negative emotion-eliciting contexts, without many cognitive, physiological, or interpersonal costs (John & Gross, 2004). In contrast, habitual suppressors mostly engage in effortful modification of the display of what they are already feeling. Some of the cognitive and social costs of using these strategies are experienced in a more chronic way by individuals who habitually use suppression instead of reappraisal to regulate their emotions.

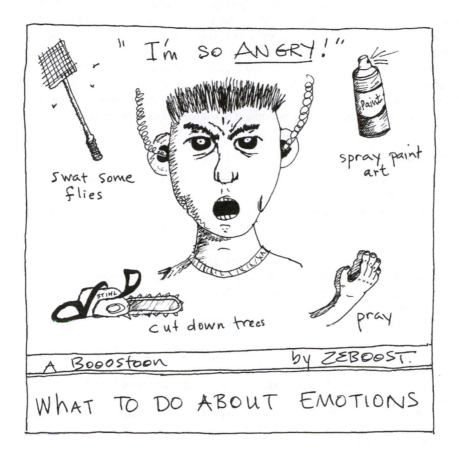

Summary

- Although emotions have evolved for their adaptive value, they are not always desirable because they may be inconsistent with social norms for a given situation, or because they can cause physical or psychological suffering. Individuals may therefore regularly attempt to inhibit or reduce emotions that are painful and/or inappropriate and to generate or enhance emotions that are pleasant and/or socially desirable.
- Individuals have at their disposal a wide variety of emotion regulation strategies, some of which occur before and some of which occur after an emotion is actually experienced.

- A comparison of the strategies of cognitive reappraisal and of suppression of expressive behavior, feelings, and thoughts suggests that these two means of emotion regulation have different affective, physiological, cognitive, and social consequences.
- Reappraisal of an emotional situation is more effective than avoiding, inhibiting, and suppressing emotional responses. Reappraisal may diminish the subjective experience and the expressive aspects of an emotion without impairing memory, indicating that reappraisal is not cognitively taxing.
- Expressive suppression can decrease behavioral displays of emotion. However, it is associated with increases in sympathetic activation in both the suppressor and the interaction partner, and at the same time it impairs memory for information encountered during suppression. Thus, suppression can be a physiologically, cognitively, and socially costly strategy.
- The suppression of emotionally exciting thoughts may be possible but sometimes counterproductive because it causes people to become bodily aroused when the suppressed thought returns to mind.
- The social sharing of emotion may, under certain conditions, facilitate emotional adjustment in the long term and can promote psychological and physical health.
- Each of these strategies must be evaluated in terms of cultural values and cultural fit. The expression and suppression of emotion are not valued equally across cultures.

Learning Links

1. A talk by emotion regulation expert Dr. James Gross. https://www.youtube.com/watch?v=9n5MqKLitWo
2. An Angry Birds video about controlling emotions. https://www.youtube.com/watch?v=pFkRbUKy19g&list=PLd5JFRsnPq7H5QrhdikqO_3muc-a4FUd8
3. A review article on the relationship between mindfulness meditation and emotion regulation. http://www.hindawi.com/journals/bmri/2015/670724/
4. A video showing an experiment about toddlers using emotion information to control their emotions. https://www.youtube.com/watch?v=7FC4qRD1vn8

References

Aldao, A., Nolen-Hoeksema, S., & Schweizer, S. (2010). Emotion-regulation strategies across psychopathology: A meta-analytic review. *Clinical Psychology Review*, *30*(2), 217–237. doi:10.1016/j.cpr.2009.11.004.

Appleton, A. A., & Kubzansky, L. D. (2014). Emotion regulation and cardiovascular disease risk. In J. J. Gross (Ed.), *Handbook of emotion regulation* (2nd ed., pp. 596–612). New York: Guilford.

Ayduk, Ö., & Kross, E. (2008). Enhancing the pace of recovery self-distanced analysis of negative experiences reduces blood pressure reactivity. *Psychological Science*, *19*(3), 229–231. doi:10.1111/j.1467–9280.2008.02073.x.

Bennett, P., Phelps, C., Brain, K., Hood, K., & Gray, J. (2007). A randomized controlled trial of a brief self-help coping intervention designed to reduce distress when awaiting genetic risk information. *Journal of Psychosomatic Research*, *63*(1), 59–64. doi:10.1016/j.jpsychores.2007.01.016.

Bonanno, G. A., Papa, A., Lalande, K., Westphal, M., & Coifman, K. (2004). The importance of being flexible: The ability to both enhance and suppress emotional expression predicts long-term adjustment. *Psychological Science*, *15*(7), 482–487. doi:10.1111/j.0956–7976.2004.00705.x.

Bucci, W. (1995). The power of the narrative: A multiple code account. In J. Pennebaker (Ed.), *Emotion, disclosure, and health* (pp. 93–122). Washington, DC: American Psychological Association.

Butler, E. A., Egloff, B., Wilhelm, F. H., Smith, N. C., Erickson, E. A., & Gross, J. J. (2003). The social consequences of expressive suppression. *Emotion*, *3*(1), 48–67. doi:10.1037/1528–3542.3.1.48.

Butler, E. A., Lee, T. L., & Gross, J. J. (2007). Emotion regulation and culture: Are the social consequences of emotion suppression culture-specific? *Emotion*, *7*(1), 30–48. doi:10.1037/1528–3542.7.1.30.

Charles, S. T., & Carstensen, L. L. (2008). Unpleasant situations elicit different emotional responses in younger and older adults. *Psychology and Aging, 23*(3), 495–504. doi:10.1037/a0013284.

Charles, S. T., Piazza, J. R., Luong, G., & Almeida, D. M. (2009). Now you see it, now you don't: Age differences in affective reactivity to social tensions. *Psychology and Aging, 24*(3), 645–653. doi:10.1037/a0016673.

Cole, S. W. (2009). Social regulation of human gene expression. *Current Directions in Psychological Science, 18*(3), 132–137. doi:10.1111/j.1467–8721.2009.01623.x.

Demaree, H. A., Schmeichel, B. J., Robinson, J. L., Pu, J., Everhart, D. E., & Berntson, G. G. (2006). Up-and down-regulating facial disgust: Affective, vagal, sympathetic, and respiratory consequences. *Biological Psychology, 71*(1), 90–99. doi:10.1016/j.biopsycho.2005.02.006.

Dickerson, M. (1991). Internal and external determinants of persistent gambling: Implications for treatment. In N. Heather, W. R. Miller & J. Greeley (Eds.), *Self-control and the addictive behaviors* (pp. 317–338). Botany, Australia: MacMillan.

Erber, R., Wegner, D. M., & Therriault, N. (1996). On being cool and collected: Mood regulation in anticipation of social interaction. *Journal of Personality and Social Psychology, 70*(4), 757. doi:10.1037/0022–3514.70.4.757.

Esterling, B. A., Antoni, M. H., Fletcher, M. A., Margulies, S., & Schneiderman, N. (1994). Emotional disclosure through writing or speaking modulates latent Epstein-Barr virus antibody titers. *Journal of Consulting and Clinical Psychology, 62*(1), 130–140. doi:10.1037/0022–006X.62.1.130.

Finkenauer, C., & Rimé, B. (1998a). Socially shared emotional experiences vs. emotional experiences kept secret: Differential characteristics and consequences. *Journal of Social and Clinical Psychology, 17*(3), 295–318. doi:10.1521/jscp.1998.17.3.295.

Finkenauer, C., & Rimé, B. (1998b). Keeping emotional memories secret: Health and subjective well-being when emotions are not shared. *Journal of Health Psychology, 3*(1), 47–58. doi:10.1177/135910539800300104.

Fischer, A. H., Manstead, A. S. R., Evers, C., Timmers, M., & Valk, G. (2004). Motives and norms underlying emotion regulation. In P. Philippot & R. S. Feldman (Eds.), *The regulation of emotion* (pp. 187–210). Mahwah, NJ: Erlbaum.

Frattaroli, J. (2006). Experimental disclosure and its moderators: A meta-analysis. *Psychological Bulletin, 132*(6), 823–865. doi:10.1037/0033–2909.132.6.823.

Freud (1920/2005). *A general introduction to psychoanalysis.* New York, NY: Horace Liveright.

Garnefski, N., Kraaij, V., & Spinhoven, P. (2001). Negative life events, cognitive emotion regulation and emotional problems. *Personality and Individual Differences, 30*(8), 1311–1327. doi:10.1016/S0191–8869(00)00113–6.

Garnefski, N., Van Den Kommer, T., Kraaij, V., Teerds, J., Legerstee, J., & Onstein, E. (2002). The relationship between cognitive emotion regulation strategies and emotional problems: Comparison between a clinical and a non-clinical sample. *European Journal of Personality, 16*(5), 403–420. doi:10.1002/per.458.

Gerin, W., Davidson, K. W., Christenfeld, N. J., Goyal, T., & Schwartz, J. E. (2006). The role of angry rumination and distraction in blood pressure recovery from emotional arousal. *Psychosomatic Medicine, 68*(1), 64–72. doi:10.1097/01.psy.0000195747.12404.aa.

Giuliani, N. R., & Gross, J. J. (2009). Reappraisal. In D. Sander & K. Scherer (Eds.), *Oxford companion to the affective sciences* (pp. 329–330). New York: Oxford University Press.

Giuliani, N. R., McRae, K., & Gross, J. J. (2008). The up-and down-regulation of amusement: Experiential, behavioral, and autonomic consequences. *Emotion, 8*(5), 714–719. doi:10.1037/a0013236.

Goleman, D. (1995). *Emotional intelligence: Why it can matter more than IQ.* New York: Bantam Books.

Gottman, J. M., & Levenson, R. W. (1986). Assessing the role of emotion in marriage. *Behavioral Assessment, 8*(1), 31–48.

Grandey, A. A. (2000). Emotional regulation in the workplace: A new way to conceptualize emotional labor. *Journal of Occupational Health Psychology, 5*(1), 95–110. doi:10.1037/1076–8998.5.1.95.

Gross, J. J. (1989). Emotional expression in cancer onset and progression. *Social Science & Medicine, 28*(12), 1239–1248. doi:10.1016/0277–9536(89)90342–0.

Gross, J. J. (1998). Antecedent- and response-focused emotion regulation: Divergent consequences for experience, expression, and physiology. *Journal of Personality and Social Psychology, 74*(1), 224. doi:10.1037/0022–3514.74.1.224.

Gross, J. J. (1999). Emotion regulation: Past, present, future. *Cognition & Emotion, 13*(5), 551–573. doi:10.1080/026999399379186.

Gross, J. J. (2002). Emotion regulation: Affective, cognitive, and social consequences. *Psychophysiology, 39*(3), 281–291. doi:10.1017/S0048577201393198.

Gross, J. J. (2015). Emotion regulation: Current status and future prospects. *Psychological Inquiry, 26*(1), 1–26. doi:10.1080/1047840X.2014.940781.

Gross, J. J., & John, O. P. (2003). Individual differences in two emotion regulation processes: Implications for affect, relationships, and well-being. *Journal of Personality and Social Psychology, 85*(2), 348–362. doi:10.1037/0022–3514.85.2.348.

Gross, J. J., & Levenson, R. W. (1993). Emotional suppression: Physiology, self-report, and expressive behavior. *Journal of Personality and Social Psychology, 64*(6), 970–986. doi:10.1037/0022–3514.64.6.970.

Gross, J. J., & Levenson, R. W. (1997). Hiding feelings: The acute effects of inhibiting negative and positive emotion. *Journal of Abnormal Psychology, 106*(1), 95–103. doi:10.1037/0021–843X.106.1.95.

Gross, J. J., & Muñoz, R. F. (1995). Emotion regulation and mental health. *Clinical Psychology: Science and Practice, 2*(2), 151–164. doi:10.1111/j.1468–2850.1995.tb00036.x.

Gross, J. J., & Thompson, R. A. (2007). Emotion regulation: Conceptual foundations. In J. J. Gross (Ed.), *Handbook of emotion regulation* (pp. 3–24). New York: Guilford Press.

Hochschild, A. (1983). *The managed heart: Commercialization of human feeling*. Berkeley, CA: University of California Press.

Horowitz, M. J. (1976/1992). *Stress response syndromes*. Northvale, NJ York: Jason Aronson.

John, O. P., & Gross, J. J. (2004). Healthy and unhealthy emotion regulation: Personality processes, individual differences, and life span development. *Journal of Personality, 72*(6), 1301–1334. doi:10.1111/j.1467–6494.2004.00298.x.

Kim, H. S., & Sherman, D. K. (2007). " Express yourself": Culture and the effect of self-expression on choice. *Journal of Personality and Social Psychology, 92*(1), 1–11. doi:10.1037/0022–3514.92.1.1.

Kim, H. S., Sherman, D. K., & Taylor, S. E. (2008). Culture and social support. *American Psychologist, 63*(6), 518–526. doi:10.1037/0003–066X.

Koole, S. L. (2009). The psychology of emotion regulation: An integrative review. *Cognition and Emotion, 23*(1), 4–41. doi:10.1080/02699930802619031.

Koriat, A., Melkman, R., Averill, J. R., & Lazarus, R. S. (1972). The self-control of emotional reactions to a stressful film. *Journal of Personality, 40*(4), 601–619. doi:10.1111/j.1467–6494.1972.tb00083.x.

Kross, E., & Ayduk, Ö. (2009). Boundary conditions and buffering effects: Does depressive symptomology moderate the effectiveness of distanced-analysis for facilitating adaptive self-reflection? *Journal of Research in Personality, 43*(5), 923–927. doi:10.1016/j.jrp.2009.04.004.

Kross, E., Ayduk, O., & Mischel, W. (2005). When asking "why" does not hurt distinguishing rumination from reflective processing of negative emotions. *Psychological Science, 16*(9), 709–715. doi:10.1111/j.1467–9280.2005.01600.x.

Kune, G. A., Kune, S., Watson, L. F., & Bahnson, C. B. (1991). Personality as a risk factor in large bowel cancer: Data from the Melbourne colorectal cancer study. *Psychological Medicine, 21*(1), 29–41. doi:10.1017/S0033291700014628.

Larsen, R. J. (2000). Toward a science of mood regulation. *Psychological Inquiry, 11*(3), 129–141. doi:10.1207/S15327965PLI1103_01.

Lepore, S. J., Fernandez-Berrocal, P., Ragan, J., & Ramos, N. (2004). It's not that bad: Social challenges to emotional disclosure enhance adjustment to stress. *Anxiety, Stress & Coping, 17*(4), 341–361. doi:10.1080/10615800412331318625.

Luminet IV, O., Bouts, P., Delie, F., Manstead, A. S., & Rimé, B. (2000). Social sharing of emotion following exposure to a negatively valenced situation. *Cognition & Emotion, 14*(5), 661–688. doi:10.1080/02699930050117666.

Macrae, C. N., Bodenhausen, G. V., Milne, A. B., & Jetten, J. (1994). Out of mind but back in sight: Stereotypes on the rebound. *Journal of Personality and Social Psychology, 67*(5), 808–817. doi:10.1037/0022–3514.67.5.808.

Manstead, A. S. R., & Fischer, A. H. (2000). Emotion regulation in full. *Psychological Inquiry, 11*(3), 188–191.

Martin, B. (1964). Expression and inhibition of sex motive arousal in college males. *The Journal of Abnormal and Social Psychology, 68*(3), 307–312. doi:10.1037/h0039866.

Mauss, I. B., Bunge, S. A., & Gross, J. J. (2007). Automatic emotion regulation. *Social and Personality Psychology Compass*, *1*(1), 146–167. doi:10.1111/j.1751–9004.2007.00005.x.

Mendes, W. B., Reis, H. T., Seery, M. D., & Blascovich, J. (2003). Cardiovascular correlates of emotional expression and suppression: Do content and gender context matter? *Journal of Personality and Social Psychology*, *84*(4), 771–792. doi:10.1037/0022–3514.84.4.771.

Merrill, J. E., & Read, J. P. (2010). Motivational pathways to unique types of alcohol consequences. *Psychology of Addictive Behaviors*, *24*(4), 705–711. doi:10.1037/a0020135.

Mesquita, B., & Leu, J. (2007). The cultural psychology of emotion. In S. Kitayama & D. Cohen (Eds.), *Handbook of cultural psychology* (pp. 734–759). New York: Guilford Press.

Mesquita, de Leersnyder, & Albert (2014). The cultural regulation of emotions. In J. J. Gross (Ed.), *Handbook of Emotion Regulation* (2nd ed., pp. 284-304). New York, NY: Guilford Press.

Mund, M., & Mitte, K. (2012). The costs of repression: A meta-analysis on the relation between repressive coping and somatic diseases. *Health Psychology*, *31*(5), 640–649. doi:10.1037/a0026257.

Murata, A., Moser, J. S., & Kitayama, S. (2012). Culture shapes electrocortical responses during emotion suppression. *Social Cognitive and Affective Neuroscience*, *8*(5), 595–601. doi:10.1093/scan/nss036.

Muris, P., Merckelbach, H., van den Hout, M., & de Jong, P. (1992). Suppression of emotional and neutral material. *Behaviour Research and Therapy*, *30*(6), 639–642. doi:10.1016/0005–7967(92)90009–6.

Nils, F., & Rimé, B. (2012). Beyond the myth of venting: Social sharing modes determine the benefits of emotional disclosure. *European Journal of Social Psychology*, *42*(6), 672–681. doi:10.1002/ejsp.1880.

Nolen-Hoeksema, S., & Morrow, J. (1993). Effects of rumination and distraction on naturally occurring depressed mood. *Cognition & Emotion*, *7*(6), 561–570. doi:10.1080/02699939308409206.

Ochsner, K. N., & Gross, J. J. (2005). The cognitive control of emotion. *Trends in Cognitive Sciences*, *9*(5), 242–249. doi:10.1016/j.tics.2005.03.010.

Ochsner, K. N., & Gross, J. J. (2008). Cognitive emotion regulation insights from social cognitive and affective neuroscience. *Current Directions in Psychological Science*, *17*(2), 153–158. doi:10.1111/j.1467–8721.2008.00566.x.

Ochsner, K. N., Ray, R. D., Cooper, J. C., Robertson, E. R., Chopra, S., Gabrieli, J. D., & Gross, J. J. (2004). For better or for worse: Neural systems supporting the cognitive down-and up-regulation of negative emotion. *Neuroimage*, *23*(2), 483–499. doi:10.1016/j.neuroimage.2004.06.030.

Page, A. C., Locke, V., & Trio, M. (2005). An online measure of thought suppression. *Journal of Personality and Social Psychology*, *88*(3), 421–431. doi:10.1037/0022–3514.88.3.421.

Parrott, W. G. (1993). Beyond hedonism: Motives for inhibiting good moods and for maintaining bad moods. In D. M. Wegner & J. W. Pennebaker (Eds.), *Handbook of mental control* (pp. 278–305). Upper Saddle River, NJ: Prentice Hall.

Pasupathi, M., Carstensen, L. L., Levenson, R. W., & Gottman, J. M. (1999). Responsive listening in long-married couples: A psycholinguistic perspective. *Journal of Nonverbal Behavior*, *23*(2), 173–193.

Pennebaker, J. W. (1989). Confession, inhibition, and disease. In L. Berkowitz (Ed.), *Advances in experimental social psychology* (Vol. 22, pp. 211–244). Sand Diego, CA: Academic Press.

Pennebaker, J. W., & Beall, S. K. (1986). Confronting a traumatic event: Toward an understanding of inhibition and disease. *Journal of Abnormal Psychology*, *95*(3), 274–281. doi:10.1037/0021–843X.95.3.274.

Pennebaker, J. W., Hughes, C. F., & O'Heeron, R. C. (1987). The psychophysiology of confession: Linking inhibitory and psychosomatic processes. *Journal of Personality and Social Psychology*, *52*(4), 781–793. doi:10.1037/0022–3514.52.4.781.

Pennebaker, J. W., Kiecolt-Glaser, J. K., & Glaser, R. (1988). Disclosure of traumas and immune function: Health implications for psychotherapy. *Journal of Consulting and Clinical Psychology*, *56*(2), 239–245. doi:10.1037/0022–006X.56.2.239.

Petrie, K. J., Booth, R. J., & Davison, K. P. (1995). Repression, disclosure, and immune function: Recent findings and methodological issues. In J. W. Pennebaker (Ed.), *Emotion, disclosure, and health* (pp. 223–237). Washington, DC: American Psychological Association.

Petrie, K. J., Booth, R. J., & Pennebaker, J. W. (1998). The immunological effects of thought suppression. *Journal of Personality and Social Psychology*, *75*(5), 1264–1272. doi:10.1037/0022–3514.75.5.1264.

Quoidbach, J., Mikolajczak, M., & Gross, J. J. (2015). Positive interventions: An emotion regulation perspective. *Psychological Bulletin*, *141*(3), 655–693. doi:10.1037/a0038648.

Reich, D. A., & Mather, R. D. (2008). Busy perceivers and ineffective suppression goals: A critical role for distracter thoughts. *Personality and Social Psychology Bulletin, 34*(5), 706–718. doi:10.1177/0146167207313732.

Richards, J. M., Butler, E. A., & Gross, J. J. (2003). Emotion regulation in romantic relationships: The cognitive consequences of concealing feelings. *Journal of Social and Personal Relationships, 20*(5), 599–620. doi:10.1177/02654075030205002.

Richards, J. M., & Gross, J. J. (1999). Composure at any cost? The cognitive consequences of emotion suppression. *Personality and Social Psychology Bulletin, 25*(8), 1033–1044. doi:10.1177/01461672992511010.

Richards, J. M., & Gross, J. J. (2000). Emotion regulation and memory: The cognitive costs of keeping one's cool. *Journal of Personality and Social Psychology, 79*(3), 410–424. doi:10.1037/0022–3514.79.3.410.

Rimé, B. (2009). Emotion elicits the social sharing of emotion: Theory and empirical review. *Emotion Review, 1*(1), 60–85. doi:10.1177/1754073908097189.

Rimé, B., Finkenauer, C., Luminet, O., Zech, E., & Philippot, P. (1998). Social sharing of emotion: New evidence and new questions. *European Review of Social Psychology, 9*(1), 145–189. doi:10.1080/14792779843000072.

Rimé, B., Philippot, P., Boca, S., & Mesquita, B. (1992). Long-lasting cognitive and social consequences of emotion: Social sharing and rumination. *European Review of Social Psychology, 3*(1), 225–258. doi:10.1080/14792779243000078.

Rusting, C. L. (1998). Personality, mood, and cognitive processing of emotional information: Three conceptual frameworks. *Psychological Bulletin, 124*(2), 165–196. doi:10.1037/0033–2909.124.2.165.

Rychlowska, M., Miyamoto, Y., Matsumoto, D., Hess, U., Gilboa-Schechtman, E., Kamble, S., . . . Niedenthal, P. M. (2015). Heterogeneity of long-history migration explains cultural differences in reports of emotional expressivity and the functions of smiles. *Proceedings of the National Academy of Sciences, 112*(19), E2429–E2436. doi:10.1073/pnas.1413661112.

Sayette, M. A. (1993). An appraisal-disruption model of alcohol's effects on stress responses in social drinkers. *Psychological Bulletin, 114*(3), 459–476. doi:10.1037/0033–2909.114.3.459.

Sheppes, G., Scheibe, S., Suri, G., & Gross, J. J. (2011). Emotion regulation choice. *Psychological Science, 22*(11), 1391–1396. doi:10.1177/ 0956797611418350.

Sheppes, G., Scheibe, S., Suri, G., Radu, P., Blechert, J., & Gross, J. J. (2014). Emotion regulation choice: A conceptual framework and supporting evidence. *Journal of Experimental Psychology: General, 143*(1), 163–181. doi:10.1037/a0030831.

Srivastava, S., Tamir, M., McGonigal, K. M., John, O. P., & Gross, J. J. (2009). The social costs of emotional suppression: A prospective study of the transition to college. *Journal of Personality and Social Psychology, 96*(4), 883–897. doi:10.1037/a0014755.

Stemmler, G. (1997). Selective activation of traits: Boundary conditions for the activation of anger. *Personality and Individual Differences, 22*(2), 213–233. doi:10.1016/S0191–8869(96)00189–4.

Tamir, M., & Ford, B. Q. (2009). Choosing to be afraid: Preferences for fear as a function of goal pursuit. *Emotion, 9*(4), 488–497. doi:10.1037/a0015882.

Tamir, M., Mitchell, C., & Gross, J. J. (2008). Hedonic and instrumental motives in anger regulation. *Psychological Science, 19*(4), 324–328. doi:10.1111/j.1467–9280.2008.02088.x.

Taylor, S. E., Welch, W. T., Kim, H. S., & Sherman, D. K. (2007). Cultural differences in the impact of social support on psychological and biological stress responses. *Psychological Science, 18*(9), 831–837. doi:10.1111/j.1467–9280.2007.01987.x.

Thayer, R. E., Newman, J. R., & McClain, T. M. (1994). Self-regulation of mood: Strategies for changing a bad mood, raising energy, and reducing tension. *Journal of Personality and Social Psychology, 67*(5), 910–925. doi:10.1037/0022–3514.67.5.910.

Tice, D. M., & Bratslavsky, E. (2000). Giving in to feel good: The place of emotion regulation in the context of general self-control. *Psychological Inquiry, 11*(3), 149–159. doi:10.1207/S15327965PLI1103_03.

Tomaka, J., Blascovich, J., Kibler, J., & Ernst, J. M. (1997). Cognitive and physiological antecedents of threat and challenge appraisal. *Journal of Personality and Social Psychology, 73*(1), 63–72. doi:10.1037/0022–3514.73.1.63.

Tsai, J. L., & Levenson, R. W. (1997). Cultural influences on emotional responding Chinese American and European American dating couples during interpersonal conflict. *Journal of Cross-Cultural Psychology, 28*(5), 600–625. doi:10.1177/0022022197285006.

Tsai, J. L., Knutson, B., & Fung, H. H. (2006). Cultural variation in affect valuation. *Journal of Personality and Social Psychology*, *90*(2), 288–307. doi:10.1037/0022–3514.90.2.288.

Urry, H. L., & Gross, J. J. (2010). Emotion regulation in older age. *Current Directions in Psychological Science*, *19*(6), 352–357. doi:10.1177/0963721410388395.

Vogt, J., & De Houwer, J. (2014). Emotion regulation meets emotional attention: The influence of emotion suppression on emotional attention depends on the nature of the distracters. *Emotion*, *14*(5), 840–845. doi:10.1037/a0037399.

Webb, T. L., Miles, E., & Sheeran, P. (2012). Dealing with feeling: A meta-analysis of the effectiveness of strategies derived from the process model of emotion regulation. *Psychological Bulletin*, *138*(4), 775–808. doi:10.1037/a0027600.

Wegner, D. M. (1989). *White bears and other unwanted thoughts*. New York: Viking/Penguin. doi:10.5860/choice.27–2392.

Wegner, D. M. (1994). Ironic processes of mental control. *Psychological Review*, *101*(1), 34–52. doi:10.1037/0033–295X.101.1.34.

Wegner, D. M., & Gold, D. B. (1995). Fanning old flames: Emotional and cognitive effects of suppressing thoughts of a past relationship. *Journal of Personality and Social Psychology*, *68*(5), 782–792. doi:10.1037/0022–3514.68.5.782.

Wegner, D. M., Schneider, D. J., Carter, S. R., & White, T. L. (1987). Paradoxical effects of thought suppression. *Journal of Personality and Social Psychology*, *53*(1), 5–13. doi:10.1037/0022–3514.53.1.5.

Wegner, D. M., Schneider, D. J., Knutson, B., & McMahon, S. R. (1991). Polluting the stream of consciousness: The effect of thought suppression on the mind's environment. *Cognitive Therapy and Research*, *15*(2), 141–152. doi:10.1007/bf01173204.

Wegner, D. M., Shortt, J. W., Blake, A. W., & Page, M. S. (1990). The suppression of exciting thoughts. *Journal of Personality and Social Psychology*, *58*(3), 409–418. doi:10.1037/0022–3514.58.3.409.

Wenzlaff, R. M., & Wegner, D. M. (2000). Thought suppression. *Annual Review of Psychology*, *51*(1), 59–91. doi:10.1146/annurev.psych.51.1.59.

Wenzlaff, R. M., Wegner, D. M., & Klein, S. B. (1991). The role of thought suppression in the bonding of thought and mood. *Journal of Personality and Social Psychology*, *60*(4), 500–508. doi:10.1037/0022–3514.60.4.500.

Wetzer, I. M., Zeelenberg, M., & Pieters, R. (2005). *Motivations for socially sharing emotions: Why being specific matters*. Manuscript submitted for publication. Tilburg University, NL: Department of Psychology.

Zech, E., (1999). Is it really helpful to verbalize one's emotions? *Gedrag en Gezondheid, 27*, 23–47.

Zech, E., & Rimé, B. (2005). Is talking about an emotional experience helpful? Effects on emotional recovery and perceived benefits. *Clinical Psychology & Psychotherapy*, *12*(4), 270–287. doi:10.1002/cpp.460.

10 Emotion and Group Processes

Contents at a Glance

Imagine watching the final soccer match of the World Cup. Do you think you would feel the same way if you were in a stadium with 80,000 other people as you would if you were alone in front of your television screen (Figure 10.1)? Probably not. Just like people's coordinated actions in the "wave" cheer, emotion can ripple across a group as if it was a single organism. Of course, even if you were watching the game on television, your emotions would be determined

Figure 10.1 These people are all watching the same soccer game. Will their emotions be exactly the same, and if not, how will they be different?

in part by the teams who were competing and their outcomes. If one of the teams represented your country, your emotions might be stronger than if neither team represented your country. And suppose your team won and you went out with a number of friends, all from your country. How would you feel if you saw a group of people from the country of the losing team? Which emotions would your group feel and express toward the other group and why? Emotions are more than events that happen in your mind and body; they are experiences that are shared in interaction between two people or many people.

There are at least two important ways in which emotions can be called group processes. First, there is the idea that emotions can be shared—and shaped—in groups, such as the group of people in the stadium. These are group emotions. Second, there is the idea that individuals can feel emotions because other members of their group have experienced or have caused an emotional event. Examples might be feeling pride because members of your swim team broke record times at a state tournament or shame because people from your religious group engaged in racist acts. These are emotions on behalf of the group. Of course, although group emotions and emotions on behalf of the group may seem to be separate, they are in fact intertwined in daily life. Furthermore, both emotion phenomena are of importance because they often occur in situations in which two groups are interacting. An understanding of emotion and group processes can help explain, and generate potential solutions for, group conflict in which emotions play an integral role. It is indeed in intergroup contexts that we generally have the unpleasant experience of observing the most intense anger, hatred, or fear among individuals.

Group Emotions

Group emotions occur in and are shared within a collective of interacting individuals at a moment in time, as when a small group becomes energized with excitement and joy (Barsade, 2002; Bartel & Saavedra, 2000; Kelly & Barsade, 2001) or a crowd becomes gripped by fear or galvanized into anger (Hatfield, Cacioppo, & Rapson, 1994; Le Bon, 1895). Our emotions are affected by the emotions of the people around us in several ways (Parkinson, 1996; Parkinson, Fischer, & Manstead, 2005). First, other people influence our understanding of what we are feeling and of the cause of our feelings in situations in which we are not sure (Schachter & Singer, 1962). Second, our expressions of emotion and the intensity of our emotion are also affected by the mere presence of other people because they serve as receivers of our emotional communications and amplifiers of our expressions. As we saw in Chapter 5, we are more likely to smile when someone is around to see us, and especially if that other person is our friend (Hess, Banse, & Kappas, 1995).

An interest in group emotions has been around for a long time. Gustave Le Bon, who was a French anthropologist, studied crowds and crowd behavior. His observations led him to propose that groups provide contexts for intense and contagious emotional experiences (Le Bon, 1895/1963). Although the study of group emotions all but disappeared for many decades, the pendulum swung back, and there is renewed interest in the topic (e.g., see for recent reviews, Collins et al., 2013; Niedenthal & Brauer, 2012). Still, the very concept of group emotion remains problematic because there exists no clear, consensual means to define and measure it (Kuppens & Yzerbyt, 2014). First, what about the size of the group? Do groups of 4 people and groups of 4000 people share emotions in the same way? There are also conceptual problems with the measurement of group emotion itself. Calculating the mean of the self-reported emotion of everyone in the group, the "average level" of emotion, does not say anything about whether there is a shared emotion because the average level does not tell us anything about the variability of the emotional experience within the group. It could be that some group members feel very strongly one way and that other members do not feel much of that emotion at all. The variability of group members' emotions is thus important for being able to characterize the emotion or even say that it defines the group at all (George, 1990).

Researchers have come to agree that high homogeneity in the emotions experienced by members of a given group is a good indicator of the existence of a group emotion because it suggests that the whole group is experiencing a similar state. Following this reasoning, we usually conclude that groups of people experience group emotions when the members' evaluations of their own emotional state are highly consistent within groups or tend to converge over time (George, 1990; Sy, Côté, & Saavedra, 2005; Totterdell et al., 1998).

Although the "group" part of group emotions poses some conceptual difficulties, the "emotion" part of group emotion does not seem to differ fundamentally in its definition from the one presented in Chapter 1. That is, most researchers use the same emotion categories, and study the same psychological processes, as do researchers who study individual emotions. Thus, for now and as long as no other evidence is offered for the uniqueness of group emotions, the group can be seen as another source of (individual) emotion or a modulator of the intensity or expression of individual emotion. For instance, group emotions may be both more intense and longer lasting than emotions at the individual level.

In the next section, we describe how emotions arise and spread through the group. It is obvious that emotions can be induced in the members of a group if they are exposed to the same eliciting event at the same time (say, for instance, the victory or defeat of your favorite football team or a natural disaster). However, it is far less obvious how group processes intensify and maintain these emotions. We will discover how research has explained the spread of emotion in a group.

Emotional Contagion

Emotional contagion is defined as "the tendency to 'catch' another person's emotions (his or her emotional appraisals, subjective feelings, expressions, patterned physiological processes, action tendencies, and instrumental behaviors)" (Hatfield, Cacioppo, & Rapson, 1992, p. 153). The contagion of emotion can occur without any intention or awareness of transmitting or catching of the emotion. Hatfield and her colleagues (Hatfield, Cacioppo, & Rapson, 1992, 1994; Hatfield, Cacioppo, & Rapson, 1993) have placed specific emphasis on what they have called "primitive emotional contagion," which is especially relevant for group emotions, and which they have defined as "the tendency to automatically mimic and synchronize movements, expressions, postures, and vocalizations with those of another person and, consequently, to converge emotionally" (Hatfield, Cacioppo, & Rapson, 1992, pp. 153–154). Emotional contagion is important from an evolutionary perspective because it could serve as the basic process on which perspective taking and empathy are built (De Waal, 2012). Consistent with this view, the similarity in emotional responding strengthens social bonds within the group (Anderson, Keltner, & John, 2003), especially when the members of the group experience positive emotions (Knight & Eisenkraft, 2015). As we shall see later, it may also cause collective action that is supposed to be of first importance for survival of social species, like human beings (Nakahashi & Ohtsuki, 2015).

Emotional contagion is probably familiar to you, as well as to people working in marketing and advertising, as evidenced by the canned laughter that is so often used in television shows and commercials. Canned laughter is intended to provoke the audience's mirth, a positive affective state, and ultimately a positive attitude toward the series or the product, and it seems to work (Bush et al., 1989). Emotion contagion has also been demonstrated in actual interactions between group members. For instance, Barsade (2002) had participants take part in a negotiation task. Each group of three to five members included a confederate trained to express either a positive (frequent smiles) or a negative affective state (no smile at all). In addition, the confederate was trained to convey high energy (he spoke rapidly, had a strong tone of voice) or low energy (he spoke very slowly with a low voice tone). The behavior of the participants was videotaped and then evaluated by independent judges who rated their mood. Results indicated that participants of these groups tend to experience the same affective state as the confederate, independently of the level of energy conveyed (Neumann, Seibt, & Strack, 2001; Sy, Côté, & Saavedra, 2005).

Although emotional contagion has been mainly studied in the laboratory, it has also been observed in the field (Totterdell et al., 1998). For example, as part of a larger study of health outcomes, scientists analyzed the influences of our real-world social networks on our longer lasting moods (such as depression and happiness) over a 20-year period. The research findings, depicted in Figure 10.2, showed that moods are transferred through social networks with people who have close social relationships experiencing similar emotional states (Fowler & Christakis, 2008). Now that we interact through social media, you might also wonder whether emotional contagion can occur when we are not face to face but in virtual contact with our social networks. Using a controversial method (because the ethics of influencing social media came into question), Kramer, Guillory, and Hancock (2014) conducted a study involving more than 650,000 unknowing Facebook users. In the study, the researchers either slightly reduced the positive or slightly reduced the negative content in people's newsfeeds. Facebook users' emotional states were influenced by this manipulation such that when positive posts were reduced, people themselves produced fewer positive posts and more negative posts, and when negative expressions were reduced, the opposite pattern was observed.

As you can guess, we are not all equally susceptible to emotional contagion. There seem to exist individual differences in the readiness to catch others' emotions. Components of temperament such as our tendency to approach or withdraw, our distractibility and attention span, and the intensity of our emotional responses are related to susceptibility (Eisenberg et al., 1991). Other individual differences such as gender, early experience, and personality characteristics also contribute to our susceptibility to emotional contagion. Indeed, one researcher constructed the Emotional Contagion Scale to assess this variability across people (Doherty, 1997). There are also cultural differences in emotional contagion due to cultural differences in conformity and values about adhering to group norms (Ilies, Wagner, & Morgeson, 2007).

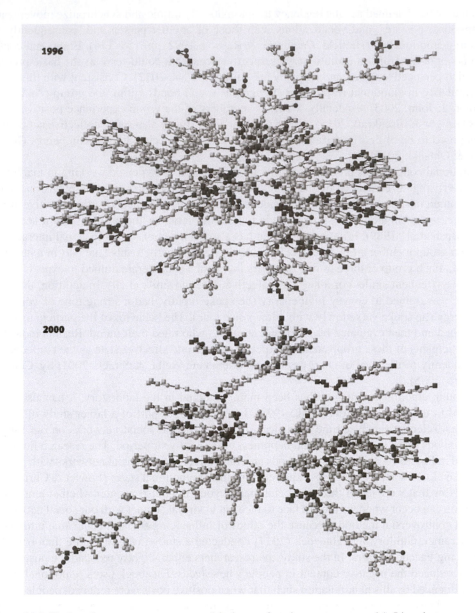

Figure 10.2 Each node represents one person (circles are female, squares are male). Lines between nodes
indicate relationship (black for siblings, red for friends and spouses). Node color denotes
average happiness of one person and all directly connected members of their network, with
blue shades indicating least happy and yellow shades indicating most happy (shades of green
are intermediate). The colors are not randomly distributed, but cluster together at a rate much
higher than chance. From Fowler & Christakis (2008).

Explanations of Emotional Contagion

How do emotions propagate throughout a group? The explanations run the gamut from
relying on basic principles of learning theory to more complex psychological phenomena
such as empathy. We organize the explanations according to whether they suggest that the

mechanisms underlying emotional contagion are automatic (in the sense of happening unconsciously, effortlessly, and without intention) or due to controlled processes (in the sense of
processes that are engaged consciously, effortfully, and with intention). Suggesting that emotional contagion happens automatically rather than in a more intentional way implies that
different processes would be necessary to change or counteract the contagion if it were undesirable or destructive. Because some of the explanations offered for emotional contagion
have already been discussed in Chapter 5's discussion of facial expression, they will only be
briefly mentioned in this chapter.

Automatic Processes of Contagion

LEARNING

One way to think of emotional contagion is that it is a learned response (Bandura, 1976). Generally, we learn that when other people express fear, something frightening happens in the
following seconds. Thus, fear and escape behavior can be automatically associated with your
perception of fear on the face of others. It may also be that reactions of others, for instance, in
a situation of high anxiety or of irritation, produce behavioral changes (agitation, rapid movements, noise) that irritate you. If learned over years, it is likely that as soon as the first signs of
these emotional states are detected in others, they will elicit the conditioned response in you.
However, it is also possible that the stimulus eliciting the emotion in the person observed has
no direct impact on the perceiver. For instance, individuals may learn that when other people
are happy, they act kindly and generously, which leads other people to feel positive feelings. As
a result, the individuals may automatically experience joy as soon as they detect the smallest
indicator of other people's happiness.

Developmental Detail

Babies Catch Emotions Too!

Catching emotions from other people starts early in life. Indeed, achieving
emotional synchrony, or having the physiology of your emotions sync up
with someone else's, is a basis for feeling empathy with that person (De
Waal, 2012). One of the earliest social bonds that an infant forges in her life
is with her mother. So if you anticipate that mothers and babies tend to catch
each other's emotions, you would guess right. The achievement of emotional
synchrony by mothers and infants has been observed in studies that tracked
cardiovascular (Waters, West, & Mendes, 2014) and hormonal indicators of
emotion (Williams et al., 2013).

In one such study, mothers of 12-month-old babies (without the baby
present) gave a five-minute speech in front of a critical (e.g., frowning,
shaking their heads) or supportive (e.g., smiling, nodding) audience. In
a control condition, a third group of mothers presented a speech alone

with no audience. After giving the speech, the mother and the baby were reunited while the mother answered a series of questions. Before and after the speech situation, cardiac reactivity of the mother and her baby were measured and their convergence was assessed. As expected, the cardiac reactivity of the mother varied as a consequence of the situation she had just experienced (negative vs. positive vs. control), with the negative situation producing the most stress. More importantly, and as can be seen in the figure, even though they were not present during the speech session, the baby's cardiac reactivity became synchronous with their mother's. Thus, babies whose mothers had performed in front of a critical audience got stressed too. In addition, the babies whose mothers had undergone the stress of giving a speech (irrespective of the type of audience) also tended to avoid contact with strangers in a subsequent experimental interaction. They showed social aftereffects of syncing with their mother!

How are emotions transferred from mother to baby and back? Facial expressions, touch, and emotional tone of voice all seem to be good candidates for emotional influence. Future research will identify the channels through which people make their emotions most contagious to others.

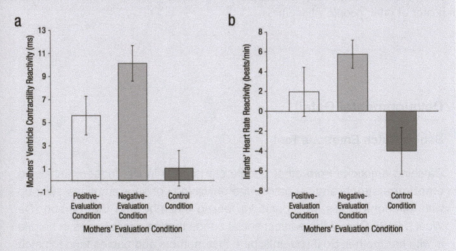

The emotional situation (positive vs. negative vs. control) produces a similar pattern of physiological responses in the mothers (a) and in their children (b) who were not aware of this situation.

IMITATION

Emotional contagion can also occur because we automatically imitate the facial expressions, postures, and vocal expressions of others, particularly those who are part of our own group, and this imitation activates a similar emotion in ourselves (Niedenthal, 2007; Niedenthal et al., 2005; Zajonc & Markus, 1984). More specifically, the observation of a person experiencing an emotion activates in perceivers the same sensory-motor states, that is, the same patterns of activation in the brain that are implicated in the production of the emotional response that is being observed. Furthermore, it is more likely that the state will be fully or partially shared if individuals are observing people with whom they want to empathize and have a close understanding, such as members of one's own group.

CO-ATTENTION

Co-attention, defined as the synchronization of attention with other people, is also an important cause of emotional contagion (Shteynberg et al., 2014). Attending to the same objects and events can lead people to have the same emotions because they spend more time thinking about the same cause of their feelings (Shteynberg, 2010). For example, in a study by Boothby, Clark, and Bargh (2014) participants were either together or alone when tasting chocolate. Even though participants were not permitted to talk to each other, they took greater pleasure in eating high-quality chocolate and less pleasure in eating poor-quality chocolate when sharing that experience with others compared to eating alone. It was as if the presence of other people affected the extent to which they focused on the cause of their pleasure and displeasure (Figure 10.3). This work suggests that the group, even in the absence of direct interaction or observation of each other, amplifies emotional reactions due to co-attention to the causes of emotion.

Figure 10.3 When people in a group all attend to the same emotion-eliciting object or event, their emotions tend to converge and amplify.

Intentional Processes of Contagion

COMMUNICATIVE IMITATION

Intentional acts also contribute to emotional contagion. For example, mimicry is not always automatic but is sometimes an intentional, communicative act that shows other people that we know how they feel and that we feel the same as they do (Buck et al., 1992; Fridlund, 1991). A relevant study showed that when an experimenter dropped a television monitor on his already injured finger and displayed pain, participants who could make eye contact with the experimenter tended to mimic his pain more than did people who could not make eye contact with the experimenter (Bavelas et al., 1986). It was as if the mimicry only occurred if the person expressing the emotion could actually see it. Moreover, participants' facial reactions to the experimenter's pain were unobtrusively videotaped and shown to another group of participants (observers). Observers judged that participants in the eye contact condition had a better understanding of how the experimenter felt and cared more about what happened compared with participants in the no-eye contact condition (see also Kraut & Johnston, 1979). Thus, emotional mimicry (and thus contagion) may be caused by emotional communication among individuals. And it may be propagated in a conscious and intentional way.

SOCIAL COMPARISON

Another controlled process that produces emotional contagion is social comparison (Wrightsman, 1960). Social psychologists have shown that in many domains of life people tend to compare themselves in order to evaluate their aptitudes, opinions, and feelings. Research suggests that, particularly in situations in which appropriate feelings are ambiguous, group members compare with each other and tend to interpret their feelings and emotional reactions as similar. As an example, in one study participants who had a five-minute wait in the presence of another participant, without talking to them, tended to converge emotionally with that other participant. The convergence happened specifically when the other participant was said to be participating in the same experiment as they were (Sullins, 1991).

EMPATHY

Finally, emotional contagion may also be due to **empathy**, which we define as the process by which an observer places herself in the place of another person (Davis, 2004; Kelly & Barsade, 2001). If you do a good job of empathizing, you should come to appraise the emotion-eliciting situation in the same manner and to experience it similarly to the one experienced by that person (Stocks et al., 2011). For example, think of watching an extremely sad movie in which the character's beloved dies just after she learns she is expecting his baby. If you put yourself in her shoes, you will start to feel the same emotional experience the actor is expressing, that is sadness, and even see events just as she sees them.

Given the state of our knowledge, it is fair to assume that the automatic and controlled processes that contribute to emotional contagion described so far probably work together. For instance, although you might automatically mimic someone else's smile, you might also intentionally accentuate your facial expression in order to communicate that her smile was received. You might also intentionally mask your smile if the situation calls for the expression of negative or neutral emotional expression. Relatedly, research by Neumann and Strack (2000) on emotional contagion caused by voices suggests that the observation of others' affective states has different effects as a result of automatic or of more controlled processes. In their studies, participants' moods were affected by the affective tone of the voice in messages they listened to. However, when the participants' attention was directed toward the emotional state of the speaker by asking them to adopt the perspective of the speaker and to think about how the person was feeling in the situation, they could imagine his or her emotion state as well as its source. In such conditions the tone of the voice altered emotion states of the participants in addition to their mood so that they matched the expressed emotion of the voice. Therefore, according to Neumann and Strack, there exists automatic contagion of mood, but the transfer of emotions among individuals requires additional cognitive resources directed to the appraisal of the observed person's situation.

Emotion on Behalf of a Group

When people identify as members of a group, they can experience emotions for or from the standpoint of the group (Branscombe & Doosje, 2004; Mackie, Devos, & Smith, 2000). Emotion on behalf of a group can be experienced when you are actually alone, so your experience is not that of a group emotion, but research has made it clear that the emotion is for the group and not for yourself (Doosje et al., 1998; Leach, Iyer, & Pedersen, 2006; Smith, 1993). For instance, Germans who were not even alive during World War II have experienced guilt on behalf of their country, a group of which they are undeniably members. Similarly, although they had not been involved in any acts against Indigenous Australians themselves, Australian participants in one study reported feeling guilt on behalf of their country for such acts, which had been committed in the past (McGarty et al., 2005).

The idea that emotions are determined by group membership has been around for a long time. Classic studies demonstrated that individuals feel pride or shame as a function of the success or failure, respectively, of their group. Cialdini and colleagues (1976) showed that American university students wear their university athletic apparel more frequently after a victory of their university team than after a loss. Individuals also use the pronoun "we" to describe a team victory more frequently than when describing a loss. We also feel good or bad on the team's behalf (Branscombe, Doosje, & McGarty, 2002; Hirt et al., 1992).

In a study that capitalized on a very emotional event, Belgian and Dutch university students completed a questionnaire within weeks of the September 11, 2001, terrorist attacks on New York and Washington, D.C. (Dumont et al., 2003). Participants were informed that the aim of the study was either to compare the emotional reactions of Europeans to Americans or the attitude of Arabs to Westerners toward the September 11 terrorist attacks. In this way, the participants were implicitly categorized as members of a different group than Americans in the first condition and in the same group as Americans (i.e., "Westerners") in the second condition. Participants in the second ("Westerners") condition reported more intense fear about the attacks and were more inclined to engage in fear-related behaviors (e.g., research of information on terrorist networks) than those in the second condition.

The extent to which a person feels emotions on behalf of the group depends upon how much she identifies with the group in the first place. In almost every study of emotions on behalf of the group, the feelings are strongest if group membership is important for the individual (Bizman et al., 2001; Gordijn et al., 2006; Iyer et al., 2004; Leach & Tiedens, 2004; Magee & Tiedens, 2006; Miller et al., 2004; van Zomeren, Postmes, & Spears, 2008). For example, in one study, Belgian students from the University of Louvain-La-Neuve (Belgium) were asked to participate in a study comparing their opinions with those of another group on an (alleged) unfair decision of the board of directors of another Belgian university (University of Ghent). In one condition, the participants were told that the study was comparing the opinion of students with those of professors on the decision. In this condition, participants were led to categorize themselves in the same group as the students whose university made the unfair decision (i.e., the group of Belgian students). In a second condition, students from the University of Louvain-La-Neuve learned their reactions were going to be compared with those of the students who were affected by this decision (students at the University of Ghent). Thus, in this condition, they were led to categorize themselves in a different group. As expected, the emotional reactions (in particular, anger) were stronger when the students categorized themselves in the same group as those who experienced the unfair decision at their university, and these reactions were particularly marked for those individuals who strongly identified with the group (as illustrated in Figure 10.4; Yzerbyt et al., 2003).

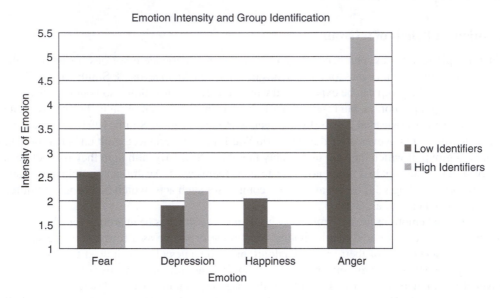

Figure 10.4   Belgian students at the University of Louvain-La-Neuve who were temporarily led to categorize themselves as Belgian students (and thus as in the same category as students of another university who underwent an unfair decision) felt even stronger feelings if their identification with Belgian students was high (grey line) versus low (black line).

Finally, because of the motivational component of emotion (see Chapter 1), emotions on behalf of a group emotion contribute to the emergence of **collective action**, defined as coordinated or synchronized efforts by an existing or spontaneous group leading to a single outcome or change (Wohl et al., 2011). In a demonstration of this idea, van Zomeren, Spears, Fischer, and Leach (2004) observed that the more anger college students experienced as a result of an increase in tuition fees that affected the whole group, the more they were willing to engage in collective action opposing the decision (see also Leonard et al., 2011). Going one step further, it appears that a correspondence between the emotion currently experienced by an individual and by the members of his or her group increases that individual's feeling of belonging to this group, as well as the willingness to engage in collective actions (Livingstone et al., 2011). Hence, recent research attests to the existence of collective emotions and to their power in both group processes and collective action.

In sum, events that concern a group, or members of a group to which you belong, can cause emotions in you. These emotions on behalf of your group are strongest if you are highly identified with the group and do not easily distance yourself from it. Emotions on behalf of the group can inspire you to take actions that you might not take in the absence of this important group experience.

Emotions about Other Groups

As mentioned in the introduction of this chapter, group emotions and emotions on behalf of the group can be states that are directed toward another group. Thus, interactions between members of two groups, intergroup settings, are those in which we observe the most intense anger, hatred, or fear. Just think of the last news report you watched or heard: how many defeats, mistreatments, murders, and attacks—all highly emotion-arousing situations—involved members of one group opposing those of other groups? Contact between groups thus provides context for intense emotion, which may drive behavior toward one's own group and other groups. In the remainder of this chapter, we explore ideas and research on prejudice and in intergroup behavior and illustrate the crucial role emotion plays in such intergroup dynamics.

Emotion as the Basis of Prejudice

Prejudice is typically conceptualized as a global negative attitude towards an out-group and can often be an emotion on behalf of one's group toward another group. Global negative feelings have been found to be a better predictor of people's attitudes toward social groups than are the content of their stereotypes (Jackson et al., 1996; Stangor, Sullivan, & Ford, 1991). For example, Jussim et al. (1995) told experimental participants that hypothetical people were members of either positive ("rock performers") or negative ("child abusers") social categories. They then asked the participants to rate the person's likely level of mental illness. The mental illness ratings were predicted by the participants' feelings about members of those categories and not by beliefs about the categories (i.e., stereotypes). Neuropsychological evidence provides further support for this view. Phelps and colleagues (2000) observed greater activity in the amygdala (a neural structure involved in emotional processing—see Chapter 8) when Caucasian participants looked at faces of unfamiliar African American people than when they saw faces of unfamiliar Caucasian American faces. More important here, activity in the amygdala was predictive of participants' prejudice toward African Americans.

What exactly is the relationship between prejudice and emotion? There are a few possibilities. First, prejudice may be partly determined by the individual's emotional reactions to the stereotypic beliefs about an out-group (Esses, Haddock, & Zanna, 1993). So, for example, if you have a stereotype of a group of people that is mainly negative (such as that they are arrogant, egocentric, and stingy), this stereotype will trigger negative feelings toward them, and the resulting emotion will constitute your overall prejudice toward that group. It is also possible that an individual's current emotional state increases the likelihood that emotion-congruent features of the stereotype come to mind (e.g., Bower, 1981; see Chapter 8). These aspects of the stereotype that come to mind determine the positivity (or negativity) of the stereotype content, at least for the moment (Esses & Zanna, 1995), and ultimately the individual's momentary prejudice toward the group. As an example, imagine that you are in a negative emotional state when you encounter members of a given group. According to this hypothesis, your current emotional state will influence your stereotype of the group such that it will be more negative in content. As a result, you should have more negative feelings and act in a discriminatory fashion toward members of the group.

Rather than focusing on generally negative feelings, some research has demonstrated that prejudice should be defined in terms of discrete emotions rather than in terms of general negativity toward the out-group. For instance, Cottrell and Neuberg (2005) observed that although their participants possessed equally negative feelings toward the groups African Americans, Asian Americans, and Native Americans, their specific negative emotions were very different. For example, they reported more fear of African Americans and more pity toward Native Americans (Figure 10.5). In turn, these specific emotions predicted attitudes toward policies

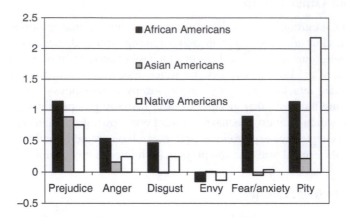

Figure 10.5 Level of prejudice and of specific emotions felt toward African Americans, Asian Americans, and Native Americans. The reported data represent the mean differences between the evaluation of the individuals' group (European Americans) on these dimensions and the three target out-groups (from Cottrell & Neuberg, 2005). Thus a high value indicates a greater evaluation of the out-group on this dimension with respect to the in-group.

relevant to the groups. One study showed that self-reported feelings of disgust toward gays and lesbians predicted attitudes toward gays rights policy, whereas anger toward Arab Muslims predicted attitudes toward homeland security policy (Cottrell, Richards, & Nichols, 2010; also, Tapias et al., 2007).

Other evidence of the role of discrete emotions in prejudice comes from studies showing that implicit prejudice toward out-groups is heightened when people are induced to experience an emotional state, at least when the induced emotion is consistent with the stereotype (and the threat) associated with the group (Dasgupta et al., 2009). For example, feeling angry, but not disgusted, increases negative prejudice towards Arabs. In contrast, disgust, but not anger, increases prejudice toward gays and lesbians.

Emotion and Intergroup Behavior

We have now seen that specific emotions towards out-groups predict prejudice and even attitudes toward public policy. Do emotions also influence intergroup behavior? One study showed that threats of unjust terrorist attacks elicited anger toward terrorists, and anger was specifically related to an intention to take aggressive action toward terrorists as well (Giner-Sorolla & Maitner, 2013). A meta-analysis that reviewed 57 different studies revealed that emotional reactions toward an out-group predict behavioral intentions, and do so beyond the content of stereotypical beliefs (Talaska, Fiske, & Chaiken, 2008).

Other studies have examined how emotions toward groups motivate specific behavioral responses in addition to intentions. One study conducted in England showed that when participants were led to think about the category "hoodie," which is associated with violence and other antisocial behavior in that context, they tended to feel anxiety. The anxiety in turn led them to increase the distance that they maintain from another person who they did not know (Wyer & Calvini, 2011; Wyer et al., 2010). In a similar study, researchers observed that skin conductance, usually interpreted as an arousal response, could predict how much physical distance Dutch participants placed between themselves and avatars of Moroccan appearance (Dotsch & Wigboldus, 2008). Masicampo, Barth, and Ambady (2014) found the same general effect for disgust. Participants in that study made harsher punishment judgment toward members of groups toward whom they felt disgust (e.g., hippies or obese people) when members of these groups engaged in misconduct related to disgust (e.g., being dirty, watching X-rated adult videos) but not when members of those groups engaged in misconduct unrelated to disgust (e.g., refusing to share lecture notes, making fun of others).

We have so far essentially discussed the role of anger and fear in intergroup relations, as these emotions seem to be at the heart of tragic relations between groups. However, similar findings have been observed with other emotions. For instance, Leach and colleagues (Leach, Iyer, & Pedersen, 2006) have found that having one's in-group unfairly advantaged may produce guilt toward the disadvantaged and anger toward in-group members that ultimately increase willingness to compensate the disadvantaged group (Iyer, Schmader & Lickel, 2007; Leach, Iyer, & Pedersen, 2006).

In sum, the research just reviewed emphasizes the role of emotion in intergroup relations. The relative failure to consider emotions in theories and research on prejudice for many years may help to explain why previous research generally observed weak relationships between the extent to which stereotypic content is negative and the degree of self-reported prejudice, on the one hand (e.g., Brigham, 1971; Jussim et al., 1995; Stangor, Sullivan, &Ford, 1991), and between prejudice and behavior, on the other hand (e.g., LaPiere, 1934). In all such work, prejudice was measured as a general antipathy to, or dislike of, the out-group. Clearly, it is something more complex than just dislike.

Models of Emotions and Intergroup Behavior

Emotion is an important component in prejudice and intergroup behavior, but exactly what role does emotion play? Three general models have been offered as explanation. These models all hold that prejudice should be considered a social emotion (Smith, 1993) that triggers specific behaviors toward out-group members. However, they differ on the processes at play in these effects, particularly the origin of the emotion and its consequences.

Intergroup Emotions Theory

Intergroup Emotions Theory (IET, Smith, 1993; see also Mackie, Devos, & Smith, 2000) posits that there are times when our group identity trumps our individual identity, and at such times, we tend to evaluate and interact with out-groups using group emotions. As we will explain, this theory combines **social identity theory** (Tajfel, 1982; Turner et al., 1987) with cognitive appraisals models of emotion (e.g., Smith & Ellsworth, 1985; see Chapter 1).

Based on principles of social identity theory, IET assumes that one's identity is partly determined by personal experiences and characteristics and partly by one's social category memberships. Depending on the situation, social category memberships are more or less salient. If no category membership is salient, you will think of yourself as a unique individual characterized by idiosyncratic properties and will act toward others on this basis. However, when one of your group memberships becomes salient (such as during the singing of a national anthem or at a sporting event), the related social identity will become temporarily central to your identity. You will perceive yourself as a member of the group, characterized by the attributes of the group. And your feelings and behavior toward others are more likely to be influenced by the meaning of your group membership. Why is that so?

According to appraisal theories of emotion, emotion arises from the evaluation (or appraisal) of the situation on various dimensions (see Chapter 1). For instance, you will experience fear *because* you evaluate the situation as negative and uncertain, and you feel you do not have the resources to cope with it. In contrast, if the situation is appraised as negative and under control, you will more probably experience anger. For appraisal theories, the self must be involved in the emotion-eliciting situation in order for the individual to experience an emotion. Smith and colleagues propose that, because social identity becomes an integral part of the self when social identity is salient, appraisal theories of emotion are applicable at the group level in such conditions. Therefore, events or situations in which appraisals elicit a specific emotion among members of the in-group should also affect other members of the group who are not directly confronted with the eliciting events. In such cases, individuals may experience emotions on behalf of their group as predicted by appraisal theories of emotions as well as the corresponding actions tendencies directed toward the out-group (see Table 10.1). These emotions will be the basis of the prejudice against the out-group. In this conception, prejudice is thus considered highly situation specific. It can, however, take the form of a more general attitude when based on the general stereotypical beliefs about the out-group (Smith, 1993). This prejudiced emotion will then in turn guide behavioral reaction toward the out-group members. For instance, if an individual who identifies strongly with his group believes that fellow in-group members are hindered in the attainment of a goal by out-group members, and he also believes that the in-group has sufficient resources to confront the out-group (the out-group is perceived as less powerful than the in-group), his prejudice will more likely reflect anger and he will be likely to engage in offensive behavior (e.g., aggression, discrimination) toward out-group members (see the first line in Table 10.1). In contrast, if the same person believes his group is unable to change the situation, for instance, because the opposing group is more powerful, the emotion felt is more likely to be anxiety or fear, which will trigger defensive behavior, like avoidance of out-group members.

Table 10.1 The table presents intergroup emotions, their likely cause, the behavioral tendencies triggered by these emotions, and the way they are likely to translate in intergroup behavior, according to the Intergroup Emotion Theory (Smith, 1993) and the Sociofunctional Model (Neuberg & Cottrell, 2002). The sequences of events predicted by these two theories are mixed in the same table as they are relatively similar, though based on different processes.

Emotion	Cause	Action Tendencies	Intergroup Behavior
Anger	Obstacle in goal attainment (e.g., by a powerless outgroup)	Approach to aggress and suppress the obstacle (i.e., move against)	Aggression; discrimination
Disgust	Contamination (e.g., by a low-status outgroup)	Rejection	Avoidance of outgroup members
Fear	Threat to group safety (e.g., by a powerful outgroup)	Escape the situation; protection	Avoidance of outgroup members
Guilt	Perception of one's own (group) unfairness	Reparation	Reconciliatory behavior
Sadness (pity)	Others in need; object of unfairness	Self-contemplation, reflection; apathy	Pro-social behavior

Sociofunctional Theory

Cottrell and Neuberg (2005) proposed a related model in which prejudice toward out-groups more directly reflects emotional reactions to the threat these groups are posing for the in-group. This model relies on two assumptions. The first assumption is that emotions serve individuals in the attainment of their basic human motives, which concern survival in order to reproduce (see Chapter 4). Anything that interferes with the individual's ability to satisfy these motives is considered a threat. The role of emotions is to activate the action program adapted to respond to this threat. The second assumption is that humans have evolved as a group-living species, and life in cooperative groups has higher survival and reproductive values than solitary life. Because group life facilitates access to resources as well as a successful management of threat, individuals are very concerned about group-level threats. Group-level threats concern both the resources of the group (e.g., physical safety, territory) and its social integrity (e.g., trust, social coordination, values). As in previously discussed theories, depending on the threat, different appraisals will be aroused that will activate the corresponding emotion and the associated action tendencies. For instance, a threat to group safety will elicit fear in individuals who will then feel a need to escape the threat, whereas if possessions are threatened by a group, individuals will experience anger and probably act aggressively toward members of the other group.

The model proposed by Cottrell and Neuberg thus shares many features with the IET. Both models assume that parts of a person's identity have to do with unique aspects of the person and other parts refer to group memberships, and that prejudice corresponds to specific differentiated emotions that lead to specific actions toward the out-group, depending on the appraisals of the situation. However, the sociofunctional model differs from the IET mainly in the fact that it emphasizes the evolutionary basis of prejudice and its link to intergroup conflict. In this perspective, prejudice and intergroup behaviors reflect basic processes that are present across time and culture.

Behaviors from Intergroup Affect and Stereotypes

Finally, the **BIAS** (Behaviors from Intergroup Affect and Stereotypes) map provides another theory of the relationships between emotions and behavioral tendencies toward group members (Cuddy, Fiske, & Glick, 2007). The BIAS map is an extension of the **Stereotype Content Model** (Fiske et al., 2002) of behavioral tendencies. The SCM assumes that the content of stereotypes about members of other groups is generally organized around two central dimensions: *competence* and *warmth*. Specific emotions felt by an individual toward a particular group are caused by her perceptions of the group on these two dimensions. If the group is appraised as warm (noncompetitive) and not competent (low status), this should produce feelings of sympathy and/ or pity. A group perceived as cold (competitive) and not competent should produce feelings of contempt and disgust. An appraisal of a group as cold and competent will produce envy and jealousy. Finally, groups appraised as competent and warm (generally in-groups) elicit admiration and pride (Figure 10.6). On this basis, the BIAS map proposes that emotions triggered by appraisals of a group's warmth and competence predict behavioral tendencies toward the group.

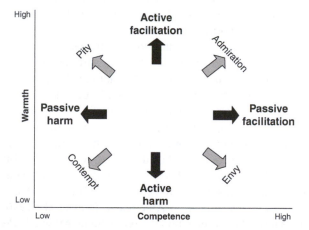

Figure 10.6 Schematic representation of the hypotheses of the BIAS map. The X- and Y-axis represent the competence and the warmth stereotype dimensions, respectively. The emotion elicited by the content of the stereotype is a function of these two dimensions (gray arrows), as are the behavioral tendencies (black bold arrows). From Cuddy, Fiske, and Glick (2007).

Cuddy and colleagues further distinguish two dimensions of intergroup behavior: the active/passive and the valence (facilitation/harm) dimensions. These two dimensions can be crossed to encompass a variety of intergroup behaviors (see Figure 10.6). Active facilitation refers to effortful positive behaviors toward the out-group (e.g., assisting or defending). Active harm refers to effortful negative behaviors toward the out-group (e.g., physical and verbal aggression). Passive facilitation refers to passive positive behaviors toward the out-group, such as cooperation; and passive harm refers to passive negative behavior toward this group (e.g., ignoring). Consistent with this model, Cuddy and colleagues (2007) found that admired groups (evaluated as warm and competent) activate active and passive facilitation, whereas hated groups activate active and passive harm. In addition, envied groups activate active harm but also passive facilitation, whereas pitied groups activate active facilitation and passive harm.

Similar to the other two theories of emotions and intergroup behavior, the BIAS map holds that prejudice should not be conceptualized as general antipathy toward out-group members. Rather, there are different kinds of prejudice characterized by different emotions toward the out-groups that lead to specific behavioral reactions. In contrast to the other theories, however, the SCM suggests that emotions toward a group are generally mixed—that is, both positive and negative emotions may be felt simultaneously toward a group, and that may lead, depending on the context, to different intergroup behavior.

Intergroup Contact and Emotions

We conclude this chapter by addressing the special situation in which members of different groups are in direct contact. Whereas intergroup contact can sometimes result in a more positive attitude toward the out-group (Pettigrew & Tropp, 2006), this situation is often associated with enhanced prejudice (e.g., Amir, 1969; Worchel, 1986). One main reason for this outcome is that intergroup contact increases anxiety among the individuals of the interacting groups (Islam & Hewstone, 1993; Stephan & Stephan, 1985). First, we will show how intergroup contact increases anxiety and then how anxiety may, in turn, deteriorate intergroup relations.

Intergroup contact increases anxiety for a variety of reasons (Stephan & Stephan, 1985). First, people may fear negative consequences of the contact for their sense of self-worth (being embarrassed) or for their security (being harmed physically). More simply, they may just anticipate negative evaluations by the out-group members or from members of their own group for having contact with an out-group member (i.e., a potential rival). For instance, behavior toward the out-group could be judged as either too friendly (they can be considered a traitor) or too discriminating, depending of the norms of their group.

What are the consequences of anxiety on intergroup attitude and behavior? One consequence is that anxiety can fuel prejudice. For instance, Amodio and Hamilton (2012) observed that Caucasian American students were more anxious when anticipating interacting with an African American student than anticipating an interaction with a Caucasian American student. Importantly, this anxiety led them to express more implicit prejudice toward black people in general. In another study on the relationship between British and Japanese nationals, Greenland and Brown (1999) found that intergroup categorization, favoritism toward the in-group, and negative affect toward the out-group were all predicted by intergroup anxiety. Intergroup anxiety is also found to be one of the best predictors of negative attitudes toward the out-group in relationships between various social groups: whites toward Native Canadians (Corenblum & Stephan, 2001), European Americans toward African Americans (Britt et al., 1996; see also Stephan et al., 2002), or teachers toward children with HIV (Greenland, Maser, & Prentice, 2001).

Anxiety can influence interaction in even more subtle ways. Because the individual is preoccupied with the situation, he may express fewer than expected positive emotions, or express serious or somewhat negative facial expressions of emotion, even without being aware of doing so.

Therefore, it is possible that in intergroup contact situations, individuals exhibit negative facial displays, triggered by either the situation (e.g., attempt to control one's responses) or by the mere presence of out-group members (e.g., Vanman et al., 1997). Out-group members may interpret these expressions, accurately or inaccurately, as an indicator of negative attitude toward their group. Of course, it could be that, at least if they are conscious of possible negative emotional expressions, individuals try to control and attenuate their expressions in order to look natural and avoid direct negative reactions from out-group members. But, in general, individuals fail at this because, as already mentioned, they are frequently unaware of their facial expressions (see Chapter 5). Moreover, even in situations in which they are conscious of potentially expressing negative emotions toward the out-group, their efforts to control these emotional expressions are likely to backfire and have unexpected negative consequences. For instance, Leyens et al. (2002) found that Caucasian Belgian participants who posed emotions for a photographer thought they did better when the photographer was a black African (out-group member) than when he was a Caucasian Belgian. In contrast, independent judges rated the performance of the "models" as better when the photographer (unbeknownst to the judges) was an in-group member than when he was an out-group member. These results suggest that people are far worse at controlling their emotional expressions (looking natural) than they think they are.

Paradoxically, intergroup contact may be even more problematic when perceived as being initiated by out-group members. Anxiety is associated with avoidance. Thus, contact initiated by members of the out-group can be considered a transgression of this norm. As a result, intergroup anxiety may amplify anger and offensive actions in order to protect the self and members of the in-group from the perceived threat posed by the contact. For instance, Van Zomeren, Fischer, and Spears (2007) found that offensive actions of students towards homeless people who initiate contact can be amplified by intergroup anxiety toward homeless people (as measured by a questionnaire) and that this relationship is mediated by feelings of anger.

Another negative consequence of anxiety in intergroup situations is that it increases the degree to which the out-group members appear similar to each other. These effects have been observed in the laboratory with artificial groups (Wilder & Shapiro, 1989a, 1989b) as well as in more naturalistic settings. As an example, Islam and Hewstone (1993) conducted a survey of Hindu and Muslim students in Bangladesh. The student participants answered a series of questions about quantitative (e.g., amount of contact with out-group members at college) as well as qualitative aspects of out-group contact (e.g., whether the contact was perceived as equal), intergroup aspects of contact (e.g., contact as individuals or members of one's group), and perceived out-group homogeneity. Moreover, the participants completed a questionnaire measuring their self-reported intergroup anxiety toward the other group (the intergroup anxiety scale, Stephan & Stephan, 1985). In this study, intergroup anxiety was negatively related to the number of intergroup contacts and to quality of intergroup contact, and was positively related to the level of intergroup (as opposed to interpersonal) contact. In turn, an increase in intergroup anxiety was associated with an increase in perceived out-group homogeneity as well as more negative attitudes toward the out-group.

By most accounts, the increase in perceived homogeneity is due to a reduced attention to inconsistent information. Anxiety reduced people's attentional focus (see Chapter 8). Because their attention is reduced, anxious people can easily notice information common to most out-group members, but they fail to integrate multiple inconsistencies between members of the out-group. As a result, they tend to have a homogenous impression of the out-group members and underestimate the differences between them. Such processes also cause problems of intergroup communication (e.g., Gudykunst & Shapiro, 1996; Stephan, Stephan, & Gudykunst, 1999). When anxiety exceeds some threshold, communication between groups becomes less effective because anxiety reduces one's attentional focus and leads people to process information in a simplistic manner. In sum, anxiety may lead individuals to exaggerate the similarities between members of out-groups and to treat their message superficially.

A first look at the effects of emotions on intergroup perception and intergroup relations may lead to a pessimistic view of the situation, but these results may also be considered in a more optimistic light. If we accept that prejudice is a main cause for the failure of intergroup relations, and if we acknowledge that prejudice is largely determined by emotions elicited by out-group members, then factors increasing positive affect toward the out-group, such as cooperation or observation of an out-group member being a victim of discrimination, can ultimately reduce prejudice and intergroup conflict. Consistent with this view, research shows that positive emotions sometimes mediate the link between intergroup contact and prejudice. In other words, intergroup contact results in positive emotions, and a reduction in prejudice follows (Miller, Smith, & Mackie, 2004; Tropp & Pettigrew, 2004). These positive emotions, in turn, increase individuals' willingness to engage in contact with out-group members (Esses & Dovidio, 2002). Moreover, recent research suggests that an increase in positive emotions could even be more powerful in these processes than a reduction of intergroup anxiety (Seger et al., in press).

Summary

- Emotions occur in and between members of social groups.
- Emotions that ripple through a collective of people, causing the members of the group to experience strongly homogeneous feelings, like a flash mob, are called group emotions.

- Group emotions are generated by a process called emotional contagion. Contagion itself is caused by learning, imitation of emotional expressions and behaviors, social comparison, and empathy.
- People can experience emotions on behalf of groups to which they belong. When a group to which they belong is made salient to them and they strongly identify with the group, their feelings on behalf of the group are particularly powerful.
- Specific emotions toward other groups can be conceptualized as prejudice. People's specific prejudicial feelings toward other groups are in part due to appraisals of the relationship between their own in-group and the out-group.
- Several theories, including Intergroup Emotions Theory, Sociofunctional theory, and the theory of Behaviors from Intergroup Affect and Stereotypes try to explain when, which, and why intergroup emotions are experienced in intergroup relations.
- When groups interact, their members often experience anxiety. Anxiety has many negative effects, including the tendency to make people think that the members of an out-group are very similar to each other and are basically "all the same."

Learning Links

1. Listen to a discussion of emotion in groups from a business school angle by Dr. Jochen Menges. https://www.youtube.com/watch?v=WT2WvKOE9Xg
2. Watch a TED talk by Dr. Nicholas Christakison on the hidden influence of our social networks. https://www.ted.com/talks/nicholas_christakis_the_hidden_influence_of_social_networks?language=en
3. Learn about emotional contagion. https://www.youtube.com/watch?v=HTFdMwCXpMw
4. Read a report on emotional contagion study on Facebook. http://www.forbes.com/forbes/welcome/?toURL=http://www.forbes.com/sites/gregorymcneal/2014/06/28/facebook-manipulated-user-news-feeds-to-create-emotionalcontagion/&refURL=&referrer=#79ca427c5fd8

References

Amir, Y. (1969). Contact hypothesis in ethnic relations. *Psychological Bulletin*, *71*(5), 319–342. doi:10.1037/h0027352.

Amodio, D. M., & Hamilton, H. K. (2012). Intergroup anxiety effects on implicit racial evaluation and stereotyping. *Emotion*, *12*(6), 1273–1280. doi:10.1037/a0029016.

Anderson, C., Keltner, D., & John, O. P. (2003). Emotional convergence between people over time. *Journal of Personality and Social Psychology*, *84*(5), 1054. doi:10.1037/0022–3514.84.5.1054.

Bandura, A. (1976). *Social learning theory*. Englewood Cliffs, NJ: Prentice-Hall.

Barsade, S. G. (2002). The ripple effect: Emotional contagion and its influence on group behavior. *Administrative Science Quarterly*, *47*(4), 644–675. doi:10.2307/3094912.

Bartel, C. A., & Saavedra, R. (2000). The collective construction of work group moods. *Administrative Science Quarterly*, *45*(2), 197–231. doi:10.2307/2667070.

Bavelas, J. B., Black, A., Lemery, C. R., & Mullett, J. (1986). "I show how you feel": Motor mimicry as a communicative act. *Journal of Personality and Social Psychology*, *50*(2), 322. doi:10.1037/0022–3514.50.2.322.

Bizman, A., Yinon, Y., & Krotman, S. (2001). Group-based emotional distress: An extension of self-discrepancy theory. *Personality and Social Psychology Bulletin*, *27*(10), 1291–1300. doi:10.1177/01461672012710005.

Boothby, E. J., Clark, M. S., & Bargh, J. A. (2014). Shared experiences are amplified. *Psychological Science*, *25*(12), 2209–2216. doi:10.1177/0956797614551162.

Bower, G. H. (1981). Mood and memory. *American Psychologist*, *36*(2), 129–148. doi:10.1037/0003–066X.36.2.129.

Branscombe, N. R., & Doosje, B. (2004). *Collective guilt: International perspectives*. Cambridge: Cambridge University Press. doi:10.1017/cbo9781139106931.002.

Branscombe, N. R., Doosje, B., & McGarty, C. (2002). Antecedents and consequences of collective guilt. In D. M. Mackie & E. R. Smith (Eds.), *From prejudice to intergroup relations: Differentiated reactions to social groups* (pp. 49–66). New York: Psychology Press.

Brigham, J. C. (1971). Ethnic stereotypes. *Psychological Bulletin*, *76*(1), 15–38. doi:10.1037/h0031446.

Britt, T. W., Bonieci, K. A., Vescio, T. K., Biernat, M., & Brown, L. M. (1996). Intergroup anxiety: A person× situation approach. *Personality and Social Psychology Bulletin*, *22*(11), 1177–1188. doi:10.1177/01461672962211008.

Buck, R., Losow, J. I., Murphy, M. M., & Costanzo, P. (1992). Social facilitation and inhibition of emotional expression and communication. *Journal of Personality and Social Psychology*, *63*(6), 962–968. doi:10.1037/0022–3514.63.6.962.

Bush, L. K., Barr, C. L., McHugo, G. J., & Lanzetta, J. T. (1989). The effects of facial control and facial mimicry on subjective reactions to comedy routines. *Motivation and Emotion*, *13*(1), 31–52. doi:10.1007/bf00995543.

Cialdini, R. B., Borden, R. J., Thorne, A., Walker, M. R., Freeman, S., & Sloan, L. R. (1976). Basking in reflected glory: Three (football) field studies. *Journal of Personality and Social Psychology*, *34*(3), 366. doi:10.1037/0022–3514.34.3.366.

Collins, A. L., Lawrence, S. A., Troth, A. C., & Jordan, P. J. (2013). Group affective tone: A review and future research directions. *Journal of Organizational Behavior*, *34*(S1), S43–S62. doi:10.1002/job.1887.

Corenblum, B., & Stephan, W. G. (2001). White fears and native apprehensions: An integrated threat theory approach to intergroup attitudes.*Canadian Journal of Behavioural Science/Revue canadienne des sciences du comportement*, *33*(4), 251–268. doi:10.1037/h0087147.

Cottrell, C. A., & Neuberg, S. L. (2005). Different emotional reactions to different groups: A sociofunctional threat-based approach to" prejudice". *Journal of Personality and Social Psychology*, *88*(5), 770–789. doi:10.1037/0022–3514.88.5.770.

Cottrell, C. A., Richards, D. A., & Nichols, A. L. (2010). Predicting policy attitudes from general prejudice versus specific intergroup emotions. *Journal of Experimental Social Psychology*, *46*(2), 247–254. doi:10.1016/j.jesp.2009.10.008.

Cuddy, A. J., Fiske, S. T., & Glick, P. (2007). The BIAS map: Behaviors from intergroup affect and stereotypes. *Journal of Personality and Social Psychology*, *92*(4), 631–648. doi:10.1037/0022–3514.92.4.631.

Dasgupta, N., DeSteno, D., Williams, L. A., & Hunsinger, M. (2009). Fanning the flames of prejudice: The influence of specific incidental emotions on implicit prejudice. *Emotion*, *9*(4), 585–591. doi:10.1037/a0015961.

Davis, M. H. (2004). Empathy: Negotiating the border between self and other. In L. Z. Tiedens & C. W. Leach (Eds.), *The social life of emotions* (pp. 19–42). Cambridge: Cambridge University Press.

De Waal, F. B. (2012). The antiquity of empathy. *Science*, *336*(6083), 874–876. doi:10.1126/science.1220999.

Doherty, R. W. (1997). The emotional contagion scale: A measure of individual differences. *Journal of Nonverbal Behavior*, *21*(2), 131–154. doi:10.1007/s10919–013–0166–9.

Doosje, B., Branscombe, N. R., Spears, R., & Manstead, A. S. (1998). Guilty by association: When one's group has a negative history. *Journal of Personality and Social Psychology*, *75*(4), 872–886. doi:10.1037/0022–3514.75.4.872.

Dotsch, R., & Wigboldus, D. H. (2008). Virtual prejudice. *Journal of Experimental Social Psychology*, *44*(4), 1194–1198. doi:10.1016/j.jesp.2008.03.003.

Dumont, M., Yzerbyt, V., Wigboldus, D., & Gordijn, E. H. (2003). Social categorization and fear reactions to the September 11th terrorist attacks. *Personality and Social Psychology Bulletin*, *29*(12), 1509–1520. doi:10.1177/0146167203256923.

Eisenberg, N., Fabes, R. A., Schaller, M., Miller, P., Carlo, G., Poulin, R., . . . Shell, R. (1991). Personality and socialization correlates of vicarious emotional responding. *Journal of Personality and Social Psychology*, *61*(3), 459. doi:10.1037/0022–3514.61.3.459.

Esses, V. M., & Dovidio, J. F. (2002). The role of emotions in determining willingness to engage in intergroup contact. *Personality and Social Psychology Bulletin*, *28*(9), 1202–1214. doi:10.1177/01461672022812006.

Esses, V. M., & Zanna, M. P. (1995). Mood and the expression of ethnic stereotypes. *Journal of Personality and Social Psychology*, *69*(6), 1052–1068. doi:10.1037/0022–3514.69.6.1052.

Esses, V. M., Haddock, G., & Zanna, M. P. (1993). Values, stereotypes, and emotions as determinants of intergroup attitudes. In D. M. Mackie & D. L. Hamilton (Eds.), *Affect, cognition, and stereotyping: Interactive processes in group perception* (pp. 137–166). San Diego, CA: Academic Press. doi:10.1016/b978–0–08–088579–7.50011–9.

Fiske, S. T., Cuddy, A. J., Glick, P., & Xu, J. (2002). A model of (often mixed) stereotype content: Competence and warmth respectively follow from perceived status and competition. *Journal of Personality and Social Psychology, 82*(6), 878–902. doi:10.1037/0022–3514.82.6.878.

Fowler, J. H., & Christakis, N. A. (2008). Dynamic spread of happiness in a large social network: Longitudinal analysis over 20 years in the Framingham Heart Study. *BMJ, 337*, a2338. doi:10.1136/bmj.a2338.

Fridlund, A. J. (1991). Sociality of solitary smiling: Potentiation by an implicit audience. *Journal of Personality and Social Psychology, 60*(2), 229. doi:10.1037/0022–3514.60.2.229.

George, J. M., & Bettenhausen, K. (1990). Understanding prosocial behavior, sales performance, and turnover: A group-level analysis in a service context. *Journal of Applied Psychology, 75*(6), 698. doi:10.1037/0021–9010.75.6.698.

Giner-Sorolla, R., & Maitner, A. T. (2013). Angry at the unjust, scared of the powerful emotional responses to terrorist threat. *Personality and social psychology bulletin, 39*(8), 1069–1082. doi:10.1177/0146167213490803.

Gordijn, E. H., Yzerbyt, V., Wigboldus, D., & Dumont, M. (2006). Emotional reactions to harmful intergroup behavior. *European Journal of Social Psychology, 36*(1), 15–30. doi:10.1002/ejsp.296.

Greenland, K., & Brown, R. (1999). Categorization and intergroup anxiety in contact between British and Japanese nationals. *European Journal of Social Psychology, 29*(4), 503–521. doi:10.1002/(SICI)1099–0992(199906)29:4<503::AID-EJSP941>3.0.CO;2-Y.

Gudykunst, W. B., & Shapiro, R. B. (1996). Communication in everyday interpersonal and intergroup encounters. *International Journal of Intercultural Relations, 20*(1), 19–45. doi:10.1016/0147–1767(96)00037–5.

Hatfield, E., Cacioppo, J. T., & Rapson, L. R. (1992). Primitive emotional contagion. In M. S. Clark (Ed.), *Review of personality and social psychology: Emotion and social behavior* (Vol. 14, pp. 151–177). Newbury Park, CA: Sage.

Hatfield, E., Cacioppo, J. T., & Rapson, R. L. (1993). Emotional contagion. *Current Directions in Psychological Science, 2*(3), 96–99. doi:10.1111/1467–8721.ep10770953.

Hatfield, E., Cacioppo, J. T., & Rapson, R. L. (1994). *Emotional contagion*. New York: Cambridge University Press.

Hess, U., Banse, R., & Kappas, A. (1995). The intensity of facial expression is determined by underlying affective state and social situation. *Journal of Personality and Social Psychology, 69*(2), 280. doi:10.1037/0022–3514.69.2.280.

Hirt, E. R., Zillmann, D., Erickson, G. A., & Kennedy, C. (1992). Costs and benefits of allegiance: Changes in fans' self-ascribed competencies after team victory versus defeat. *Journal of Personality and Social Psychology, 63*(5), 724. doi:10.1037/0022–3514.63.5.724.

Ilies, R., Wagner, D. T., & Morgeson, F. P. (2007). Explaining affective linkages in teams: Individual differences in susceptibility to contagion and individualism-collectivism. *Journal of Applied Psychology, 92*(4), 1140. doi:10.1037/0021–9010.92.4.1140.

Islam, M. R., & Hewstone, M. (1993). Dimensions of contact as predictors of intergroup anxiety, perceived out-group variability, and out-group attitude: An integrative model. *Personality and Social Psychology Bulletin, 19*(6), 700–710. doi:10.1177/0146167293196005.

Iyer, A., Leach, C. W., Pedersen, A. (2004). Racial wrongs and restitutions: the role of guilt and other group-based emotions. In N. Branscombe, & B, Doosje (Eds.), *Collective guilt: InternationalpPerspectives* (pp. 262–283). Cambridge: Cambridge University Press.

Iyer, A., Schmader, T., & Lickel, B. (2007). Why individuals protest the perceived transgressions of their country: The role of anger, shame, and guilt. *Personality and Social Psychology Bulletin, 33*(4), 572–587. doi:10.1177/0146167206297402.

Jackson, L. A., Hodge, C. N., Gerard, D. A., Ingram, J. M., Ervin, K. S., & Sheppard, L. A. (1996). Cognition, affect, and behavior in the prediction of group attitudes. *Personality and Social Psychology Bulletin, 22*(3), 306–316. doi:10.1177/0146167296223009.

Jussim, L., Nelson, T. E., Manis, M., & Soffin, S. (1995). Prejudice, stereotypes, and labeling effects: Sources of bias in person perception. *Journal of Personality and Social Psychology, 68*(2), 228–246. doi:10.1037/0022–3514.68.2.228.

Kelly, J. R., & Barsade, S. G. (2001). Mood and emotions in small groups and work teams. *Organizational Behavior and Human Decision Processes*, *86*(1), 99–130. doi:10.1006/obhd.2001.2974.

Knight, A. P., & Eisenkraft, N. (2015). Positive is usually good, negative is not always bad: The effects of group affect on social integration and task performance. *Journal of Applied Psychology*, *100*(4), 1214. doi:10.1037/apl0000006.

Kramer, A. D., Guillory, J. E., & Hancock, J. T. (2014). Experimental evidence of massive-scale emotional contagion through social networks. *Proceedings of the National Academy of Sciences*, *111*(24), 8788–8790. doi:10.1073/pnas.1320040111.

Kraut, R. E., & Johnston, R. E. (1979). Social and emotional messages of smiling: An ethological approach. *Journal of Personality and Social Psychology*, *37*(9), 1539–1553. doi:10.1037/0022–3514.37.9.1539.

Kuppens, T., & Yzerbyt, V. Y. (2014). When are emotions related to group-based appraisals? A comparison between group-based emotions and general group emotions. *Personality and Social Psychology Bulletin*, *40*, 1574–1588. doi:10.1177/0146167214551542.

LaPiere, R. T. (1934). Attitudes vs. actions. *Social Forces*, *13*(2), 230–237. doi:10.2307/2570339.

Le Bon, G. (1895/1963). *Psychologie des foules*. Paris: Presses Universitaires de France.

Leach, C. W., Iyer, A., & Pedersen, A. (2006). Anger and guilt about ingroup advantage explain the willingness for political action. *Personality and Social Psychology Bulletin*, *32*(9), 1232–1245. doi:10.1177/0146167206289729.

Leach, C. W., & Tiedens, L. Z. (2004). A world of emotions. In L. Z Tiedens & C. W. Leach (Eds.), *The social life of emotions* (pp 1–16). Cambridge: Cambridge University Press. doi:10.1017/CBO9780511819568.

Leonard, D. J., Moons, W. G., Mackie, D. M., & Smith, E. R. (2011). "We're mad as hell and we're not going to take it anymore": Anger self-stereotyping and collective action. *Group Processes & Intergroup Relations*, *14*(1), 99–111. doi:10.1177/1368430210373779.

Leyen, L. P., Demoulin, S., Désert, M., Vaes, J., & Philippot, P. (2002). Expressing emotions and decoding them: Ingroups and outgroups do not share the same advantages. In D. M. Mackie & E. R. Smith (Eds.), *From prejudice to intergroup emotions: Differentiated reactions to social groups* (pp. 139–151). New York: Psychology Press.

Livingstone, A. G., Spears, R., Manstead, A. S., Bruder, M., & Shepherd, L. (2011). We feel, therefore we are: Emotion as a basis for self-categorization and social action. *Emotion*, *11*(4), 754. doi:10.1037/a0023223.

Mackie, D. M., Devos, T., & Smith, E. R. (2000). Intergroup emotions: Explaining offensive action tendencies in an intergroup context. *Journal of Personality and Social Psychology*, *79*(4), 602–616. doi:10.1037/0022–3514.79.4.602.

Magee, J. C., & Tiedens, L. Z. (2006). Emotional ties that bind: The roles of valence and consistency of group emotion in inferences of cohesiveness and common fate. *Personality and Social Psychology Bulletin*, *32*(12), 1703–1715. doi:10.1177/0146167206292094.

Masicampo, E. J., Barth, M., & Ambady, N. (2014). Group-based discrimination in judgments of moral purity-related behaviors: Experimental and archival evidence. *Journal of Experimental Psychology: General*, *143*(6), 2135–2152. doi:10.1037/a0037831.

McGarty, C., Pedersen, A., Wayne Leach, C., Mansell, T., Waller, J., & Bliuc, A. M. (2005). Group-based guilt as a predictor of commitment to apology. *British Journal of Social Psychology*, *44*(4), 659–680. doi:10.1348/014466604X18974.

Miller, D. A., Smith, E. R., & Mackie, D. M. (2004). Effects of intergroup contact and political predispositions on prejudice: Role of intergroup emotions. *Group Processes & Intergroup Relations*, *7*(3), 221–237. doi:10.1177/1368430204046109.

Nakahashi, W., & Ohtsuki, H. (2015). When is emotional contagion adaptive? *Journal of Theoretical Biology*, *380*, 480–488. doi:10.1016/j.jtbi.2015.06.014.

Neuberg, S. L., & Cottrell, C. A. (2002). Intergroup emotions: A sociofunctional approach. In D. Mackie & E. R. Smith (Eds.), *From prejudice to intergroup emotions: Differentiated reactions to social groups* (pp. 265–283). New York: Psychology Press.

Neumann, R., Seibt, B., & Strack, F. (2001). The influence of mood on the intensity of emotional responses: Disentangling feeling and knowing. *Cognition & Emotion*, *15*(6), 725–747. doi:10.1080/02699930143000266.

Neumann, R., & Strack, F. (2000). " Mood contagion": The automatic transfer of mood between persons. *Journal of Personality and Social Psychology*, *79*(2), 211–223. doi:10.1037/0022–3514.79.2.211.

Niedenthal, P. M. (2007). Embodying emotion. *Science*, *316*(5827), 1002–1005. doi:10.1126/science.1136930.

Niedenthal, P. M., Barsalou, L. W., Winkielman, P., Krauth-Gruber, S., & Ric, F. (2005). Embodiment in attitudes, social perception, and emotion. *Personality and Social Psychology Review*, *9*(3), 184–211. doi:10.1207/s15327957pspr0903_1.

Niedenthal, P. M., & Brauer, M. (2012). Social functionality of human emotion. *Annual Review of Psychology*, *63*, 259–285. doi:10.1146/annurev.psych.121208.131605.

Parkinson, B. (1996). Emotions are social. *British Journal of Psychology*, *87*(4), 6. doi:10.1111/j.2044–8295.1996.tb02615.x.

Parkinson, B., Fischer, A. H., & Manstead, A. S. R. (2005). *Emotion in social relations*. New York: Psychology Press. doi: 11245/1.269963.

Pettigrew, T. F., & Tropp, L. R. (2006). A meta-analytic test of intergroup contact theory. *Journal of Personality and Social Psychology*, *90*(5), 751–783. doi: 0.1037/0022-3514.90.5.751.

Phelps, E. A., O'Connor, K. J., Cunningham, W. A., Funayama, E. S., Gatenby, J. C., Gore, J. C., & Banaji, M. R. (2000). Performance on indirect measures of race evaluation predicts amygdala activation. *Journal of Cognitive Neuroscience*, *12*(5), 729–738. doi:10.1162/089892900562552.

Schachter, S., & Singer, J. (1962). Cognitive, social, and physiological determinants of emotional state. *Psychological Review*, *69*(5), 379. doi:10.1037/h0046234.

Seger, C., Banerji, I., Park, S. H., Smith, E. R., & Mackie, D. (in press). Emotions as mediators of the effect of intergroup contact on prejudice. *Journal of Personality and Social Psychology*.

Shteynberg, G. (2010). A silent emergence of culture: The social tuning effect. *Journal of Personality and Social Psychology*, *99*(4), 683. doi:10.1037/a0019573.

Shteynberg, G., Hirsh, J. B., Galinsky, A. D., & Knight, A. P. (2014). Shared attention increases mood infusion. *Journal of Experimental Psychology: General*, *143*(1), 123. doi:10.1037/a0031549.

Smith, C. A., & Ellsworth, P. C. (1985). Patterns of cognitive appraisal in emotion. *Journal of Personality and Social Psychology*, *48*(4), 813–838. doi:10.1037/0022–3514.48.4.813.

Smith, E. R. (1993). Social identity and social emotions: Toward new conceptualization of prejudice. In D. M. Mackie & D. L. Hamilton (Eds.), *Affect, cognition, and stereotyping: Interactive group processes in group perception* (pp. 297–315). San Diego, CA: Academic Press.

Stangor, C., Sullivan, L. A., & Ford, T. E. (1991). Affective and cognitive determinants of prejudice. *Social Cognition*, *9*(4), 359–380. doi:10.1521/soco.1991.9.4.359.

Stephan, W. G., Boniecki, K. A., Ybarra, O., Bettencourt, A., Ervin, K. S., Jackson, L. A., . . . Renfro, C. L. (2002). The role of threats in the racial attitudes of Blacks and Whites. *Personality and Social Psychology Bulletin*, *28*(9), 1242–1254. doi:10.1177/01461672022812009.

Stephan, W. G., & Stephan, C. W. (1985). Intergroup anxiety. *Journal of Social Issues*, *41*(3), 157–175. doi:10.1111/j.1540–4560.1985.tb01134.x.

Stephan, W. G., Stephan, C. W., & Gudykunst, W. B. (1999). Anxiety in intergroup relations: A comparison of anxiety/uncertainty management theory and integrated threat theory. *International Journal of Intercultural Relations*, *23*(4), 613–628. doi:10.1016/S0147–1767(99)00012–7.

Stocks, E. L., Lishner, D. A., Waits, B. L., & Downum, E. M. (2011). I'm embarrassed for you: The effect of valuing and perspective taking on empathic embarrassment and empathic concern. *Journal of Applied Social Psychology*, *41*(1), 1–26. doi:10.1111/j.1559–1816.2010.00699.x.

Sullins, E. S. (1991). Emotional contagion revisited: Effects of social comparison and expressive style on mood convergence. *Personality and Social Psychology Bulletin*, *17*(2), 166–174. doi:10.1177/014616729101700208.

Sy, T., Côté, S., & Saavedra, R. (2005). The contagious leader: Impact of the leader's mood on the mood of group members, group affective tone, and group processes. *Journal of Applied Psychology*, *90*(2), 295. doi:10.1037/0021–9010.90.2.295.

Tajfel, H. (1982). Social psychology of intergroup relations. *Annual Review of Psychology*, *33*(1), 1–39. doi:10.1146/annurev.ps.33.020182.000245.

Talaska, C. A., Fiske, S. T., & Chaiken, S. (2008). Legitimating racial discrimination: Emotions, not beliefs, best predict discrimination in a meta-analysis. *Social Justice Research*, *21*(3), 263–296. doi:10.1007/s11211–008–0071–2.

Totterdell, P., Kellett, S., Teuchmann, K., & Briner, R. B. (1998). Evidence of mood linkage in work groups. *Journal of Personality and Social Psychology, 74*(6), 1504–1515. doi:10.1037/0022–3514.74.6.1504.

Tropp, L. R., & Pettigrew, T. F. (2004). Intergroup contact and the central role of affect in intergroup prejudice. In L.Z. Tiedens & C. W. Leach (Eds.),*The Social Life of Emotions* (pp, 246–269). Cambridge: Cambridge University Press. doi:10.1017/cbo9780511819568.014.

Turner, J. C., Hogg, M. A., Oakes, P. J., Reicher, S. D., & Wetherell, M. S. (1987). *Rediscovering the social group: A self-categorization theory*. Oxford: Blackwell.

Van Zomeren, M., Fischer, A. H., & Spears, R. (2007). Testing the limits of tolerance: How intergroup anxiety amplifies negative and offensive responses to out-group-initiated contact. *Personality and Social Psychology Bulletin, 33*(12), 1686–1699. doi:10.1177/0146167207307485.

van Zomeren, M., Postmes, T., & Spears, R. (2008). Toward an integrative social identity model of collective action: A quantitative research synthesis of three socio-psychological perspectives. *Psychological Bulletin, 134*(4), 504–535. doi:10.1037/0033–2909.134.4.504.

Van Zomeren, M., Spears, R., Fischer, A. H., & Leach, C. W. (2004). Put your money where your mouth is! Explaining collective action tendencies through group-based anger and group efficacy. *Journal of Personality and Social Psychology, 87*(5), 649–664. doi:10.1037/0022–3514.87.5.649.

Vanman, E. J., Paul, B. Y., Ito, T. A., & Miller, N. (1997). The modern face of prejudice and structural features that moderate the effect of cooperation on affect. *Journal of Personality and Social Psychology, 73*(5), 941–959. doi:10.1037/0022–3514.73.5.941.

Waters, S. F., West, T. V., & Mendes, W. B. (2014). Stress contagion physiological covariation between mothers and infants. *Psychological Science, 25*(4), 934–942. doi:10.1177/0956797613518352.

Wilder, D. A., & Shapiro, P. (1989a). Effects of anxiety on impression formation in a group context: An anxiety-assimilation hypothesis. *Journal of Experimental Social Psychology, 25*(6), 481–499. doi:10.1037/0022–3514.56.1.60.

Wilder, D. A., & Shapiro, P. N. (1989b). Role of competition-induced anxiety in limiting the beneficial impact of positive behavior by an out-group member. *Journal of Personality and Social Psychology, 56*(1), 60. doi:10.1037/0022–3514.56.1.60.

Williams, S. R., Cash, E., Daup, M., Geronimi, E. M., Sephton, S. E., & Woodruff-Borden, J. (2013). Exploring patterns in cortisol synchrony among anxious and nonanxious mother and child dyads: A preliminary study. *Biological Psychology, 93*(2), 287–295. doi:10.1016/j.biopsycho.2013.02.015.

Wohl, M. J., Giguère, B., Branscombe, N. R., & McVicar, D. N. (2011). One day we might be no more: Collective angst and protective action from potential distinctiveness loss. *European Journal of Social Psychology, 41*(3), 289–300. doi:10.1002/ejsp.773.

Worchel, S. (1986). The role of cooperation in reducing intergroup conflict. In S. Worchel & W. Austin (Eds.), *The psychology of intergroup relations* (pp. 288–304). Chicago, IL: Nelson-Hall.

Wrightsman Jr, L. S. (1960). Effects of waiting with others on changes in level of felt anxiety. *The Journal of Abnormal and Social Psychology, 61*(2), 216–222. doi:10.1037/h0040144.

Wyer, N. A., & Calvini, G. (2011). Don't sit so close to me: Unconsciously elicited affect automatically provokes social avoidance. *Emotion, 11*(5), 1230–1234. doi:10.1037/a0023981.

Wyer, N. A., Calvini, G., Nash, A., & Miles, N. (2010). Priming in interpersonal contexts: Implications for affect and behavior. *Personality and Social Psychology Bulletin, 36*(12), 1693–1705. doi:10.1177/0146167210386968.

Yzerbyt, V., Dumont, M., Wigboldus, D., & Gordijn, E. (2003). I feel for us: The impact of categorization and identification on emotions and action tendencies. *British Journal of Social Psychology, 42*(4), 533–549. doi:10.1348/014466603322595266.

Zajonc, R. B., & Markus, H. (1984). Affect and cognition: The hard interface. In C. Izard, J. Kagan & R. B. Zajonc (Eds.), *Emotions, cognition, and behavior* (pp. 73–102). Cambridge: Cambridge University Press.

11 Gender and Emotion

Contents at a Glance

American country-western music has produced thousands of songs about men and women and their emotions. What do those songs say? Even if you're not familiar with the country-western tradition, you might suspect that the songs mostly tell stories of women falling in love and losing control of their emotions, and of men putting on their hats, squaring their shoulders and their jaws, and riding into the sunset without looking back—perhaps going off to ride in the rodeo. If that is what you guessed, you would be relying on the stereotype that women are emotional and emotionally expressive and that men are stoic and tend to be overwhelmed by expressions of emotion by women. But then you might listen to the actual words of country-western songs sung by men and find that the men are having a whole lot of emotion. Very often in fact it is the man who is losing control of his emotions.

In Western culture, people generally believe that women are the more tender sex, with greater emotional insight and more fine-tuned emotional responsiveness, but also with a tendency toward emotional instability, or even hysteria. Meanwhile men, according to the stereotype, keep cool and maintain self-control.

Is this belief in the emotional woman and the unemotional man a reality or a myth? If it is a reality, how did this difference come about? In this chapter, we explore the complex relationship between gender and emotion. We first examine the content of stereotypic beliefs about men's and women's emotions. Then we turn to the question of whether emotional behavior is consistent or inconsistent with those stereotypes. In the last part of the chapter, we discuss how social roles, socialization history, and culture contribute to gender differences in emotions.

Before we proceed, we should stop to clarify our terminology. Very little of the research we report involved examination of differences in emotion processes as a function of biological sex. We use the term "gender" to refer to the classification of study participants as male versus female. In some cases, the participants labeled themselves as male or female. In others, the experimenter assigned a gender label. This classification system is based on a belief in the gender binary, the idea that all people can be categorized as either male or female. We now know that the possibilities exceed these categories. Indeed, some people see themselves as genderqueer, which means they don't fit clearly within the categories of male or female. The research on gender and emotion that we explore in this chapter has stemmed from the assumption of a gender binary, and so current nuance is not represented. We will refer to boys and girls and men and women as categories that were investigated and so assigned in past research, not as an endorsement of the gender binary for research on this or any other topic in psychology.

Stereotypes of Men's and Women's Emotions

The stereotype of women as emotional is not as simple as it sounds. In general terms, individuals understand "being emotional" as the tendency to respond too quickly (without control) and too much (too intensely) to emotion-eliciting events (Robinson & Johnson, 1997). But even when both men and women behave in a way that conveys strong emotion, they are not necessarily called "emotional." For example, people attribute a man's emotional reaction in response to an upsetting event (for example, his car has been stolen) to excusable situational factors (for example, he was about to leave on vacation in the car). In contrast, people attribute a woman's emotional reaction to the same upsetting event as due to her personality (for example, she is "hysterical"; Barrett & Bliss-Moreau, 2009; Brescoll & Uhlmann, 2008). In other words, given the same reaction to the same event, the man is not labeled "emotional," whereas the woman is (Fischer, 1993; Shields, 2002). Beyond this simple idea of the greater emotionality of women than men, there are other, more specific stereotypes about gender and emotion (Figure 11.1).

Figure 11.1 According to common stereotypes, women are overly emotional and men do not express their emotions much at all.

Emotion-Specific Stereotypes

Adults possess gender stereotypes about the typical experience and expression of specific emotions. Studies demonstrate that men and women believe that women experience and express most emotional states more frequently than men (Brody & Hall, 2008; Grossman & Wood, 1993). Happiness, embarrassment, surprise, sadness, fear, shame, and guilt are consistently found to be stereotypical female emotions. Meanwhile, people believe that men experience and express anger, contempt, and pride more often than women (Hess et al., 2000; Plant et al., 2000). Furthermore, stereotypes are stronger and more consensual regarding the *expression* of emotion than the *experience* of emotion (Fabes & Martin, 1991). That is, people appear to believe in stronger gender differences for what men and women display on their face, body, and voice than what men and women are feeling inside.

Similar emotion-specific gender stereotypes seem to be held by very young children, suggesting that the beliefs are learned early in development. In one study, three- to five-year-old adults and children were asked to say if gender-neutral puppies depicting happy, angry, fearful, and sad emotions were little boy or little girl puppies (Birnbaum, Nosanchuk, & Croll, 1980). Children as well as adults thought that the happy-, sad-, and fearful-looking puppies were female and that angry-looking puppies were males. In a similar study, boys and girls listened to scenarios about the anger- or sadness-inducing events (Brechet, 2013). For example, an anger scenario involved a main character (a child) trying to watch a video while another child keeps talking, making it impossible to hear. The main character had either a female or a male name. Participants then drew a face to depict the emotion felt by that character. Boys drew anger faces in response to anger-eliciting scenarios more often than did girls. Also the intensity of the facial expressions of anger was higher when the character had a male name rather than a female name (Figure 11.2).

a   *b*

Figure 11.2 Examples of drawings of girls and boys responding with anger. Whether the participant was a
girl or a boy, they drew boys' anger as more intense than girls' anger (Brechet, 2013).

Notice that the stereotypical female emotions of sadness, shame, fear, and guilt are emotions
that convey a certain amount of social vulnerability. For this reason, researchers sometimes
describe these as **powerless emotions**. The emotions of anger, pride, and contempt, stereotypi-
cally male emotions, all convey dominance. Sometimes these are called **powerful emotions**
(Timmers, Fischer, & Manstead, 2003; Zammuner, 2000). The terminology of powerless and
powerful is used to highlight the fact that gender stereotypes for emotions are linked to broader
societal expectations that women perform behaviors that reflect social sensitivity and men perform behaviors that reflect agency, or acting effectively on the world (Brody & Hall, 2010).

Context-Specific Stereotypes

The nature of the situation in which an emotion is experienced, particularly whether it involves a
focus on other people versus the self, also determines people's stereotypical beliefs about men's
and women's emotions (Brody & Hall, 2010). Johnson and Shulman (1988) had participants
try to imagine a male or female friend in several situations that elicited pleasant and unpleasant
emotions about other people (for example, being content while relaxing with friends or being
fearful about the health of a relative) and pleasant and unpleasant about the self (for example,
being proud after receiving the highest grade in the class or being envious of the superior grade
that someone else had received). Participants then evaluated the likelihood that the male or
female friend would experience and express those emotions. Participants judged the likelihood
of female friends expressing emotions directed toward other people as higher and of expressing
emotions about the self as lower than male friends. In contrast, male friends were judged to be
more likely to express emotions about the self and less likely to express emotions directed at
others compared to female friends. These findings underscore the fact that gender stereotypes
for emotion contain the broader belief that women should be concerned with and be responsive
to other people and that men should be concerned with achievement and self-promotion.

In a related study, a gender-neutral target person expressing pride over a personal success was
rated as more likely to be a man, whereas the target person expressing pride over another person's success was rated as more likely to be a woman (Stoppard & Grunchy, 1993). Furthermore,

women are expected to be more expressive in interpersonal, relationship-oriented situations, whereas men's expressivity is associated with achievement situations and with situations where their autonomy is challenged (Brody, 1997; Kelly & Hutson-Comeaux, 1999). Findings such as these indicate that stereotypical beliefs concerning emotional expression are differentially linked to gender depending on the specific situation in which a given emotion is expressed.

Prescriptive Norms

Stereotypes about men's and women's emotions not only describe what people believe about gender differences. Stereotypical beliefs also contain **prescriptive norms** that specify the emotional reactions that are socially acceptable for men and women. One norm that you might have encountered is that "boys don't cry." Another familiar norm dictates that women should be kinder and more modest than men (Heilman, 2001; Rudman, 1998). Women are supposed to convey kindness by smiling a lot, particularly at other people (Hess, Adams, & Kleck, 2005; LaFrance & Hecht, 2000).

Men and women are aware of these norms and feel pressure to conform to them. People generally believe that gender-stereotype–consistent emotions will be socially approved, whereas gender-stereotype–inconsistent emotions will be disapproved and sanctioned (Graham, Gentry, & Green, 1981; Stoppard & Grunchy, 1993). They know that there are societal norms and sanctions, even if they personally disagree with them. For example, women anticipate negative social consequences for expressions of anger and aggression and are concerned that the expression of such emotions will be detrimental to their social relations (Davis, LaRosa, & Foshee, 1992; Eagly & Steffen, 1986). In a study of four different cultures, Matsumoto and his colleagues found that women reported that they try to control their anger, contempt, and disgust more than men did; men reported that they try to control their fear and surprise more than women (Matsumoto et al., 1998).

Women seem to be right to worry about expressing anger because there are social and economic costs to this norm violation. In a series of studies, male and female participants saw video clips of men and women who expressed anger or sadness or neutral emotion in a professional context. They then rated the salary and status they believed the person deserved. Men who expressed anger were conferred higher status and salary than men who expressed sadness or neutral emotion. In contrast, women who expressed anger were conferred lower status and salary. In fact, on average, the highest salary was assigned to the men who expressed anger and the lowest salary to the women who expressed anger! As in other studies cited in this chapter, women's emotional reactions were also attributed to internal characteristics (for example, "she is an angry person"), whereas men's emotional reactions were attributed to the external circumstances that he experienced (Table 11.1; Brescoll & Uhlmann, 2008).

Interestingly, despite the pressure to behave in line with gender emotion stereotypes, emotion-stereotypic women are not actually more *liked*. Indeed, people report stronger negative attitudes toward emotional women than emotional men. The expression of powerless emotions by men seems to give them extra value, making them suitable for typical female roles without making them unsuitable for male roles (Fischer et al., 2004; Timmers, Fischer, & Manstead, 2003). Women more than men are thus confronted with a dilemma, because both their emotional expressions, often judged as excessive and exaggerated, and their emotional control may lead to negative evaluations (Hutson-Comeaux & Kelly, 2002; Kelly & Hutson-Comeaux, 2000).

In sum, there are strong and consistent gender stereotypes and prescriptive norms about emotions, some of which are quite context specific. Beliefs and rules are most consensual for the public expression of emotion: girls and women are expected to display many powerless emotions that convey the fact that they are socially engaged. Boys and men are supposed to express the more powerful emotions of anger, contempt, and pride. Do the actual emotional behaviors of males and females correspond to those norms and beliefs? This is the question we turn to next.

Table 11.1 Mean ratings of status salary and competence of male and female targets expressing anger and sadness. From Study 1 of Brescoll & Uhlmann (2008).

	Anger		Sadness	
	Male	*Female*	*Male*	*Female*
Status Conferral	6.47	3.75	4.05	5.02
Yearly Salary	$37,807	$23,464	$30,033	$28,970
Competence	7.55	5.44	5.79	6.17
External Attributions	7.72	5.80	6.57	6.94

Emotional Behavior of Men and Women

Feelings—or emotional experience—expressive displays, and emotion regulation are all aspects of our emotional lives. Which of any of these shows systematic differences by gender?

Developmental Detail

Pacifiers May Have Emotional Consequences for Boys

Should parents give their children pacifiers? Pacifier use by infants and children is a controversial topic, and the answer to that question varies depending on whom you ask. An emotion researcher may advise you to think twice. As you learned in earlier chapters, there is evidence that facial mimicry plays a causal role in decoding the facial expressions of others. This ability to understand the expression of others grounds emotional development. Because pacifiers occupy the muscles around the mouth, they likely disrupt facial mimicry. How, then, might pacifier use affect emotional development?

Niedenthal and colleagues (2012) hypothesized that pacifier use during critical periods in early childhood could pose an obstacle for emotional development. To test this hypothesis, they examined the relationship between facial mimicry and history of pacifier use in seven-year-olds and surveyed young adults on pacifier use, perspective taking, and emotional intelligence. Their findings show that the duration of pacifier use during infancy is associated with less spontaneous facial mimicry, less perspective taking, and lower emotional intelligence (all illustrated in the figure). However, none of these effects are observed in girls! The researchers hypothesize that the strong social norms that favor expressivity in girls likely play a role in this gender difference. According to another study conducted by Rychlowska and colleagues (2014), adults perceive both three-year-old boys and girls with pacifiers as less emotionally skilled and developed than the same boys and girls without pacifiers. Because girls are generally expected to be "emotional experts," however, their parents may go to extra lengths to emotionally stimulate them, thereby compensating for potential developmental consequences of the pacifier use. Social norms for boys, however, are typically that they should be unemotional. So, caretakers of boys are less likely to engage in compensatory behaviors, thus leaving them more vulnerable to the consequences of disrupted facial mimicry.

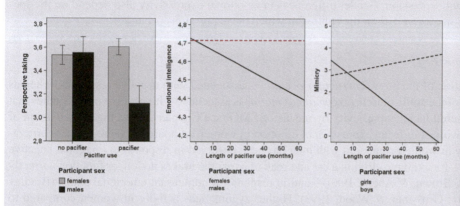

From Niedenthal et al (2012). Pacifier use is negatively related to the amount of automatic facial mimicry exhibited by boys, as well as their scores on perspective taking and emotion intelligence questionnaires.

Emotional Experience

Consistent with stereotypes, gender differences have been found in people's reports of the intensity of their emotions in general, in their reports of the experience of specific emotions, and in emotional experience in response to imagined/recalled emotional situations. Women report higher intensity of positive and negative affect than men (Fujita, Diener, & Sandvik, 1991). Women also report experiencing the positive emotions of joy, love, and affection, as well as the negative emotions of sadness, fear, anger, distress, embarrassment, shame, and guilt more intensely and more frequently than men (Brebner, 2003; Brody, 1999; Brody & Hall, 2000; Ferguson & Crowley, 1997; Ferguson, Eyre, & Ashbaker, 2000; Fischer & Manstead, 2000; Tangney, 1990). However, men report experiencing pride more frequently and more intensely than women (Brebner, 2003).

Women's more intense emotional experience may in part be due to their susceptibility to **emotional contagion**—that is, the tendency to automatically "catch" the emotions of others and to respond in an emotion-congruent way (Hatfield, Cacioppo, & Rapson, 1994). Women score higher than men on the Emotional Contagion Scale (see Chapter 10) and report being more susceptible than men to others' emotional expressions. That is, women more than men reported being cheered up when with happy people and feeling nervous when listening to a screaming child at the doctor's office (Doherty, 1997).

In self-reported emotional experience, as in stereotypical beliefs, gender differences are generally smaller than those found for emotional expression. Indeed, studies that directly compare emotional experience and expression often find fewer differences between men and women in emotional experience compared to overt emotional display, or else no difference in experience at all (Kring & Gordon, 1998; Wagner, Buck, & Winterbotham, 1993).

Emotional Expressiveness

Women's higher overall emotional expressivity has been shown across different measures of expressivity, including electromyography (EMG) recordings, observer ratings, and self-ratings of emotional expression. Gender differences in emotional expressivity also depend on the specific emotions, as well as on the context in which the expressions occur.

Facial Expressions

The activation of the brow (*corrugator occulis*) is associated with negative responses, whereas activation of the smile muscle (*zygomaticus major*) is associated with positive ones. Studies that have measured facial expressivity by means of EMG (see Chapter 2) find higher activation of muscles involved in facial expression of emotion in women compared to men. Higher corrugator activity in women compared with men has been observed in response to imagined negative situations—for example, driving a car and realizing that the brakes no longer function correctly (Schwartz, Brown, & Ahern, 1980)—and in response to unpleasant emotional slides (Bradley et al., 2001; Grossman & Wood, 1993). Higher zygomaticus activity in women compared to men has been observed in response to pleasant emotional images, especially those depicting family scenes and babies (Bradley et al., 2001).

Gender differences in emotional expressivity have also been observed in studies that compare men and women's facial displays in response to emotion-inducing images and films (Kring & Gordon, 1998; Wagner, Buck, & Winterbotham, 1993). For example, observers rated females' videotaped facial expressions induced by emotion-eliciting happy-, sad-, disgust-, anger-, and fear-evoking films as more expressive than males' facial expressions across all films, with the smallest sex difference for anger (Figure 11.3, Kring & Gordon, 1998).

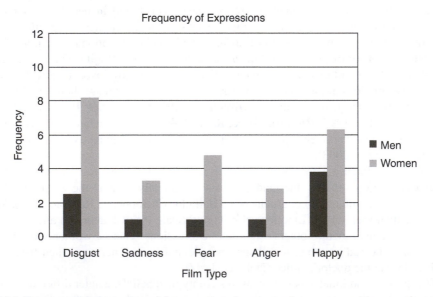

Figure 11.3 Frequency of expression of five emotions by men and women watching emotion-eliciting films. From Kring and Gordon (1998).

Women also tend to be more emotionally expressive in real social interactions. In conflictual marital exchanges, for example, women tend to express their emotions more, whereas men tend to react with so-called stonewalling—that is, with withdrawal from the situation, inhibited emotional display, and an avoidance of eye contact (Levenson, Carstensen, & Gottman, 1994). Hall and Friedman (1999) examined the nonverbal behavior of employees who were between 25 and 65 years of age. Employees' dyadic interactions were videotaped while they performed two standard tasks (i.e., a discussion about a nonwork-related topic, and a creativity task involving the construction of a tower). In their nonverbal behavior, women were also more emotionally expressive in this professional context.

Self-Reported Expressiveness

Women tend to describe themselves as more emotionally expressive than men. Studies that measure this use several self-report measures of emotion expressivity, including the Emotional Expressivity Scale (EES; Kring, Smith, & Neale, 1994), the Emotional Expressivity Questionnaire (EEQ; King & Emmons, 1990), and the Berkeley Expressivity Questionnaire (BEQ; Gross & John, 1995). On these questionnaires, which measure one's general predisposition to express emotions in most situations, women generally score higher than men (Kring & Gordon, 1998).

Women also report higher frequency and intensity of expressing specific emotions. In general, the gender differences in self-reported emotional expression parallel those of stereotypical beliefs. For instance, women report expressing happiness, love, sadness, and fear more intensely and with greater frequency than men, whereas men tend to report more intense and more frequent expressions of anger than women (Grossman & Wood, 1993). Male participants also report expressing contempt and pride more frequently and more intensely than female participants (Stapley & Haviland, 1989).

It is noteworthy that gender differences in expression of anger are complex. When situational information is provided, women sometimes report that they would express equal or even more anger than men (Frost & Averill, 1982). Differences are also found in the way that men and women express their anger. Men react physically by hitting and throwing objects and verbally by name calling, whereas women express their anger more by crying. Furthermore, men tend to express anger more toward males and strangers and when the target is the cause of their anger (such as expressing anger at a colleague for being late). Meanwhile, women express anger more toward others they are close to, whether male or female, who are not the cause of their anger. For example, they might express anger about unfair treatment by a superior to a friend (Kring, 2000; Timmers, Fischer, & Manstead, 1998).

Emotion Competences

As we learned in Chapter 4 on the functions of emotion, some people are particularly adept at understanding and acting on their own and others' emotions (for example, Mayer, Salovey, & Caruso, 2004; Salovey et al., 2003). Together, the capacities to perceive emotions accurately, use emotions and emotion knowledge effectively, and regulate emotions appropriately are called **emotional intelligence** (Salovey & Mayer, 1990). Women tend to score higher on measures of emotional intelligence than men (Brackett et al., 2006; Mirgain & Cordova, 2007). What is the specific evidence for women's greater emotion competence?

Sending and Reading Facial Expressions

Women might be more expressive overall than men, but how clear are the emotional signals they send? Is it easier for people, men and women, to interpret the facial expressions of women than men? What about women and men's ability to read other people's facial expressions?

Sending Accuracy

Studies generally show that women send clearer, more easily interpreted facial expressions than men (Hall, 1984; Rotter & Rotter, 1988). For instance, Buck and colleagues showed male and female undergraduates ("senders") pleasant, unpleasant, sexual, scenic, and unusual images with the instruction to describe their feelings and to rate the pleasantness of each one (Buck, Miller, & Caul, 1974). Senders' facial expressions were videotaped during the entire experiment, and their physiological reactions (skin conductance, heart rate) were measured continuously. Observers later watched each sender's videotaped facial expressions with no sound and made judgments about the sender's feelings toward each image. This method is called the **slide-viewing paradigm** (Buck et al., 1974). Observers were more accurate at guessing women's emotional reactions from their facial expressions, indicating that women were better at communicating their emotions than men.

One exception to this rule is the expression of anger. An illustrative study found that male participants' facial expressions while recalling past anger-provoking events were more easily interpreted as expressions of anger than were those of female participants (Coats & Feldman, 1996). This finding is consistent with the norm that women should not express anger.

Reading Accuracy

Research also shows that women are more accurate in reading the facial expressions of others (Hall & Matsumoto, 2004; Hampson, van Anders, & Mullin, 2006; Scholten et al., 2005). Thayer and Johnsen (2000), for example, found women to be more accurate in their recognition of happy, sad, angry, disgusted, fearful, surprised, and neutral emotional expressions. In another study, women were also faster at correctly identifying a variety of facial expressions as seen in Figure 11.4 (Vassallo, Cooper, & Douglas, 2009).

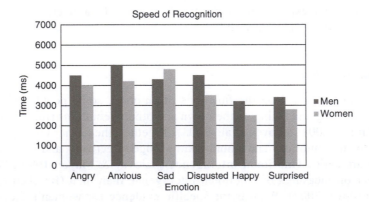

Figure 11.4 In a number of studies, women have been found to correctly identify facial expressions faster than men. From Vassallo, Cooper, and Douglas (2009).

A possible reason for women's accuracy in reading other people's facial expressions has to do with how they use visual attention to obtain information from a face. In one study, researchers used eye tracking to investigate precisely what women and men look at when they examine facial expressions (Vassallo, Cooper, & Douglas, 2009). Results showed that women looked more often at the eyes than men, and men more often at the nose and mouth than women while exploring the face. For a variety of reasons, attending more to the eyes may give women an advantage (either in speed or accuracy) in reading facial expressions (Niedenthal et al., 2010).

Emotion Knowledge

Are men "clueless" about their emotions and emotions in general? There is some empirical evidence to support this cliché. Starting at an early age, when tested for their understanding about which emotions occur in specific emotion-eliciting situations, girls compared to boys show superior understanding (Ontai & Thompson, 2002). Later in development, this pattern continues. Compared to men, women show greater emotional awareness, which is defined as the ability to report on and describe emotional reactions of the self and other people (Lane et al., 2000). Specifically, women are better able to predict their own emotional reactions and those of others in hypothetical scenarios (Barrett et al., 2000). An example of a hypothetical scenario is this: "You and your best friend are in the same line of work. There is a prize given annually to the best performance of the year. The two of you work hard to win the prize. One night the winner is announced—your friend." When women and men respond to the questions, "How would you feel?" and "How would the other person feel?" women usually give precise answers that involve more complex emotion understanding than men.

Overall, then, girls and women convey more nuance and accuracy in anticipating and understanding their and other's emotions in different contexts.

Emotion Regulation

What do males and females do about their emotions? Some evidence suggests that infant boys engage in less emotion regulation overall, especially less self-soothing, than do infant girls (Feldman, Brody, & Miller, 1980; Weinberg et al., 1999). This would leave boys to experience and express more irritation, tension, and distress than girls. Studies also find that girls use more effortful control strategies than boys (Else-Quest et al., 2006). These include cognitive strategies, such as changing the focus of attention and reappraisal, and also behavioral strategies, such as withdrawing from the emotional event and taking action to change it.

Adult males and females also show differences in what they do with and about their emotions. In fact, a meta-analysis by Tamres and colleagues (2002) revealed that in terms of 17 distinct regulation strategies, women used 11 of the 17 strategies more than men. In particular, with respect to the strategies we learned about in Chapter 9, women reported using distraction, reappraisal, and social support to manage their emotions more than did men. There are some exceptions. Research shows that men report that they "drink to cope" more than do women (Nolen-Hoeksema & Harrell, 2002; Park & Levenson, 2002). This appears to be related to men's overall greater tendency to engage in denial or avoidance of emotions. Moreover, women may not use alcohol to manage their emotions because they expect alcohol to interfere with rather than increase their ability to cope with stress and because they fear social sanctions against such behavior (Nolen-Hoeksema, 2004).

Although it is difficult to evaluate the significance of the gender differences we have reviewed in this section, it is apparent that the stereotypes that we hold about men and women, at least in Western culture, are represented to some degree in actual emotional experience, expression, and even the components of emotional intelligence. When such differences are observed, it is often the case that they shape and are shaped by processes in the brain. Using the neuroimaging methods described in Chapter 2, affective neuroscientists have explored how male and female brains process emotional information.

Neural Underpinnings of Emotion

The amygdala is involved in the neural circuitry that supports emotional responses (see Chapter 3). Many neuroimaging studies have measured the activation of the amygdala in men and women while they look at emotional stimuli. A meta-analysis of such studies revealed significant gender differences in amygdala reactivity (Stevens & Hamann, 2012). The difference depended upon the type of emotional stimulus, negative or positive, the participant was responding to. For negative images, left amygdala activation was higher in women. Women also showed higher activation in other neural regions such as the left thalamus, hypothalamus, left caudate, and medial prefrontal cortex (Figure 11.5 upper panel). For positive images, left amygdala activation was higher in men. Men also exhibited higher activation than women in the bilateral inferior frontal gyrus and right fusiform gyrus (Figure 11.5, lower panel). These findings mean that men and women respond more strongly to positive versus negative stimuli, respectively; they do not mean that men and women use different areas of the brain to process emotion.

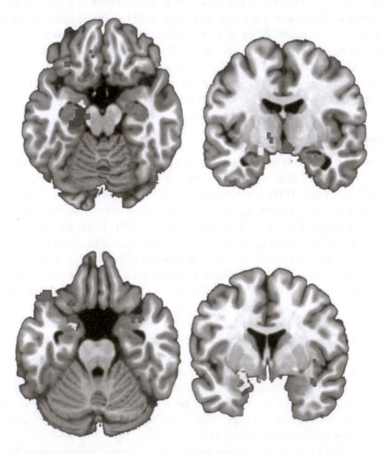

Figure 11.5 Brain regions that were significantly more activated in women than men when they were observing negative images (above). Brain regions that were significantly more activated in men than women when they were observing positive images (below). From Stevens & Hamann (2012).

Gender differences have also been found in the neural circuitry that is activated when women and men experience empathy (Schulte-Ruether et al., 2008). Women tend to score higher on self-report scales that measure empathic responding (Baron-Cohen & Wheelwright, 2004), and this may be due to the way they recruit empathic responses in the brain. In particular, the neuroimaging findings suggest that women more than men use their brains to reproduce in themselves the emotion they perceive in another person. Men engage in this neural resonance to a lesser degree; instead they recruit parts of the brain that help them think about what the person must be experiencing. This latter activity is sometimes called perspective taking. These findings suggest that women and men perform the task of being empathic in different ways.

In sum, different parts of men and women's brains are activated when they see emotional stimuli and when they are being empathic. It's important to remember that if males and females are taught, either implicitly (by merely being a member of society) or explicitly (being directed by parents or teachers) to pay attention—or not—to certain aspects of emotional behavior and to do certain things—or not—with their own emotional reactions, then variation in brain activation should be expected. A good scientific strategy is to explore both what goes on in the brain when men and women do things naturally and also what goes on in the brain when the scientist is sure that men and women are performing exactly the same task.

Origins of Gender Differences in Emotion

As we have seen, stereotypes about gender differences in the display and experience of emotions correspond rather well to observed gender differences in such behavior. Women report experiencing emotions more intensely and expressing them more and with greater frequency than men. This is particularly true for the so-called powerless emotions of sadness, fear, shame, and guilt, as well as socially desirable positive emotions such as empathy, sympathy, and love. Men, on the other hand, report expressing more powerful emotions such as anger, contempt, disgust, and pride. These findings seem to indicate that gender stereotypes mirror reality.

The correspondence between stereotype and actual behavior might not be surprising, because stereotypes shape reality insofar as they create expectations about men and women's emotional reaction. In this way, stereotypes can influence people's self-report of emotions and even their perceptions of other people's emotional behavior (Brody & Hall, 2000). We describe such effects and then propose broader theories of where gender differences might come from.

Stereotypes Create Differences

As we have seen, gender stereotypes function as social and cultural norms that prescribe how and when and by whom emotion can be expressed; stereotype-consistent emotional reactions are socially approved, whereas stereotype-inconsistent emotional behaviors lead to social disapproval, which may motivate individuals to behave in a stereotype-congruent way. Consequently, gender stereotypes may bias how people report on their own emotions, perceive emotions in others, and teach children about emotions.

Self-Reports of Emotion

The effect of gender stereotypes on self-reported emotions is strong when people provide global retrospective, or memory-based, reports of their emotions (Feldman Barrett et al., 1998; LaFrance & Banaji, 1992). But these differences may disappear when men and women report their emotions online. In a study by Feldman Barrett and colleagues (1998), for example, gender differences emerged in global retrospective self-reports of emotional experience, but not in online self-reports of momentary emotional experience. Consistent with the gender stereotype, women reported higher affect intensity and more happiness, sadness, and fear on global self-report scales than men. However, men and women did not differ in their momentary, online ratings of specific emotional reactions measured immediately after dyadic social interactions.

The lack of correspondence between global, retrospective reports and momentary reports of affective experience may be explained by a reconstruction and recollection bias. In order to provide a global summary of one's experience of sadness, fear, and so forth, individuals must retrieve, summarize, and integrate information about numerous prior emotional experiences. Because this is a difficult task, they may rely on stereotypical beliefs concerning the emotional reactions of men and women to produce their global account. Retrospective reports of previous emotional experiences are also biased by the individual's emotion knowledge. Indeed, women have been found to have more complex and differentiated general emotion knowledge than men. Not surprisingly, they also describe their own emotional experiences and those of others in a more differentiated and integrative way than men (Feldman Barrett et al., 2000).

Gender differences in global, retrospective ratings may thus be due to gender differences in emotional knowledge and to men and women's conformity to gender stereotypes rather than to differences in emotional experience and expression. In situations where no or few gender differences actually exist, memory-based reconstruction may create or enhance them.

Perception

Plant et al. (2000) examined effects of gender stereotypes on adults' perception of adult facial expressions of emotion. They showed their participants facial expressions of both men and women that were blends of both sadness and anger. An example of the morphed expressions can be seen in Figure 11.6. The same sad–angry expression displayed by a female was rated as sadder and less angry than when displayed by a male, suggesting that the facial expression was seen to send a different emotion depending upon the person's gender.

In another study, Plant, Kling, and Smith (2004) used identical expressions that consisted of morphed faces depicting a blend of sadness and anger. Posers' gender was manipulated by choosing male or female hairstyle and clothing. Results revealed gender-stereotype–consistent interpretation of the ambiguous sad–angry facial expressions. The same facial expression was judged as sadder and less angry when dressed up as a woman than when disguised as a man. The finding that people interpret ambiguous facial expressions by using gender stereotypes was also supported in a study that investigated the impact of a poser's gender and head position on

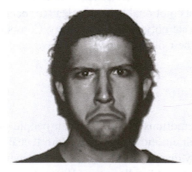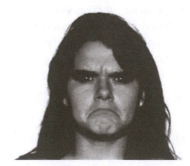

Figure 11.6 Blends of anger and sadness on male and female faces used in Plant et al. (2000).

perceived dominance (Mignault and Chaudhuri, 2003). Females' neutral faces were more likely perceived as expressing happiness and powerless emotions, including sadness, shame, guilt, regret, embarrassment, and respect, and as expressing less dominance. Males' neutral faces were more likely perceived as expressing anger and powerful "superiority" emotions, including contempt, pride, haughtiness, and self-assurance.

We have seen that stereotypes and norms can create social reality on the fly. There are also larger, more permanent, social realities that transmit and perpetuate gender stereotypes and norms for emotions. Gender differences in emotional experience, expression, and recognition have also been explained by the differential socialization of boys and girls, by the different social roles that men and women occupy in society, and by their cultural background. We discuss each of these possible determinants of sex differences in emotion in the next sections.

Socialization of Emotion

Gender differences in emotions can be explained by the socialization of girls and boys to behave in accordance with the societal stereotypes and norms. Consistent with the gender stereotype, girls are taught to express emotions that facilitate their relationships with other people. Girls tend to be taught to be nice, to be friendly, to smile, and not to behave aggressively and wildly. Boys, in contrast, tend to be taught to behave in a "manly" way—that is, to be strong and brave and to defend themselves, and not to express sadness, fear, pain, or other signs of weakness and vulnerability.

These norms are transmitted by parents and peers and by other socialization agents such as the school and the media. For example, boys and girls who behave in a gender-consistent masculine-competitive-aggressive and feminine-cooperative-friendly manner, respectively, have been found to be more popular and more liked among their peers than those who violated gender norms (Adler, Kless, & Adler, 1992). Furthermore, parents encourage their daughters to express feminine emotions and to inhibit the expression of anger and aggression and encourage their sons to express anger but otherwise to control the expression of their feelings (Birnbaum & Croll, 1984). More recent findings suggest that this is particularly true of fathers (Chaplin, Cole, & Zahn-Waxler, 2005).

Parental reactions to their sons and daughters are not only guided by gender stereotypes, but also by gender-related characteristics such as the child's temperament, language skills, and sociability (Brody, 2000; Brody & Hall, 2000). The child's temperament—that is, the child's innate reactivity to internal and external stimulation—may elicit different responses from parents and caretakers. Male infants tend to have a higher level of arousal than girls and to be more irritable, more startled, and less consolable than girls (Else-Quest, Hyde, Goldsmith, & Van Hulle, 2006). Boys' higher arousal and activity level may incite parents to teach them to inhibit the expression of their emotions and to control their feelings. Boys will thus become less expressive with age because they experience more socialization pressure to control their emotions that are perceived as *too* intense. Mothers have also been found to exaggerate their facial expressions when interacting with their sons, probably to get their attention and to regulate their behavior. In the long run, such behavior may prevent boys from learning to identify subtle emotional expressions and may thus explain males' inferior ability to read expressive cues to emotion.

Girls, by contrast, have better and earlier language skills, a more extensive emotion vocabulary, and are more responsive to others. They thus show stronger empathic responses than boys when faced with another person's pain, and they react more strongly to their mother's fearful facial displays. When interacting with their responsive and language-skilled girls, parents tend to express more positive emotions and to use more emotional language. Parents also tend to discuss emotions more with their daughters than with their sons (Adams et al., 1995; Fivush & Wang, 2005).

Boys and girls are socialized to conform to the culturally dominant gender stereotypes and to behave in accordance with their gender roles. However, a child's endorsement of gender stereotypes has been shown to depend on their *fathers'* implication in child-rearing and household tasks (Brody, 1997). The time fathers spend with their children is negatively correlated with the children's expression of gender-stereotypical emotions. Girls with more involved fathers express more competition, more aggression, more positive emotions, and less sadness compared to girls with less involved fathers. And boys with highly involved fathers express more affiliation, warmth, and fear and less competition, anger, and aggression.

In sum, socialization processes may determine gender differences in emotions to a great degree. If you anticipated that people pay attention to little girls when they cry and tell little boys to "suck it up," you anticipated correctly (Zeman et al., 1997).

Social Roles

Eagly's (1987) **Social Role Theory** explains gender differences in social behavior in terms of gender roles—that is, the social roles that men and women hold in society. Women's social roles involve child-rearing, domestic work, and caring professions (for example, nurses, teachers) that strongly determine the content of the female gender role. Men's social roles typically involve those of the provider and protector, and are related to more dominant, power-related positions in the family, as well as in professional life and in society. The different social roles of men and women create gender role expectations—that is, expectations concerning the appropriate behavior for men and women. Women are expected to possess communal qualities such as being friendly, being sensitive to the needs of others, being warm and nurturing, and behaving in an affiliative and relationship-oriented way. Men are expected to possess agentic qualities, including attributes such as independence, assertiveness, and instrumental competence. The enactment of their different social roles causes men and women to develop different skills (i.e., more or less sensitivity for others, more or less emotional responsiveness). According to the social role account, gender differences in emotions are thus due to men's and women's conformity with their gender role as well as to their different emotional skills, which cause them to behave differently.

Support for the social role interpretation comes from the observation of gender differences concerning the type and the nature of men and women's activities. Women occupy more caretaker roles with children and the elderly, and they provide more personal care and support, whereas men provide more technical and administrative help. Women, consequently, have more opportunities to practice emotion-related skills (Grossman & Wood, 1993). Similarly, studies examining gender stereotypes have found that the typical woman is judged as more likely to occupy the homemaker and caretaker role, which requires emotional sensitivity and expressivity, and thus to possess higher communal traits than the typical man. However, when men and women hold the same roles, no sex differences in the attribution of communal traits are observed (Eagly & Steffen, 1984).

The question of whether gender roles guide the expression of emotion was examined in a study by Kring and Gordon (1998). Participants were classified as masculine, feminine, or androgynous (i.e., neither masculine nor feminine, but, rather, having both qualities) on the basis of their score on the Bem Sex Role Inventory (Bem, 1979). Androgynous participants were those who endorsed a high number of both masculine-instrumental and feminine-expressive characteristics, feminine participants were those who scored high on feminine traits and low on masculine traits, and masculine participants were those who scored high on masculine traits and low on feminine traits. Results revealed that androgynous participants reported the highest dispositional expressivity on a self-report measure and were judged as the most expressive, whereas masculine participants were judged as the least expressive, with feminine participants falling in between.

A similar finding comes from a study that examined individuals' proneness to cry. Independent of their biological sex, masculine participants more than participants with a feminine gender identity tended to be reluctant to cry (Ross & Mirowsky, 1984). These findings suggest that gender role identity determines emotional behavior at least as much as, if not more than, their biological sex.

Emotion, Gender, and Culture

Most of the studies of gender and emotion that we have reviewed in this chapter were conducted in Western cultures (North America and Western Europe) and support a conclusion of overall greater female emotionality. Although gender differences in emotionality vary with the type of emotion, with the component of emotion, and with the measurement of emotional response and the social context, they are mainly characterized by differences in the extent to which men and women outwardly express or control their emotions. Studies that have examined gender and emotions across cultures have found gender differences to be more pronounced in Western cultures compared to, in particular, Asian cultures (Brody, 1997; Fischer & Manstead, 2000).

For example, gender differences in crying frequency and overall crying proneness also tend to be greater in Western countries compared to African and Asian countries (Vingerhoets & Becht, 1996; Vingerhoets & Scheirs, 2000). And women's greater tendency to report shame, fear, and nervousness in response to emotion-eliciting stories is more pronounced in European American samples than in Asian American and Asian samples (Copeland, Hwang, & Brody, 1996).

The impact of culture on gender differences in emotions may be explained by the different social roles that men and women occupy across cultures, by the relative status and power they hold in society, and by differences in values about social orientation. Fischer and Manstead (2000) tested the hypothesis that differences in cultural values and in the division of labor promote culture-specific patterns of sex differences in emotions. These researchers obtained three measures of culture:

- The actual division of labor as listed by the gender empowerment measure (GEM), which reports the extent to which women actively participate in economic and political life
- Gender role ideology (a measure of masculinity–femininity)
- A measure of individualism–collectivism (the degree to which the culture values individual achievement versus group harmony and interdependence, as discussed in the next chapter)

They then used the measures to predict self-reported intensity, duration, and nonverbal expression of seven emotions (joy, fear, anger, sadness, disgust, shame, guilt) of participants from 37 countries on five continents using a cross-cultural database.

Women in all countries reported experiencing emotions more intensely and for longer durations and expressing them more overtly than men. Unexpectedly, gender differences in emotional reactions were greater in countries with *less* traditional divisions of labor (high GEM) and with prevailing individualistic values (Western European countries, United States, Australia) than in more traditional, collectivistic countries (African, Asian, South American countries).

These findings suggest that gender differences in emotionality cannot be reduced to the traditional division of labor between men and women as suggested by Social Role Theory. To the contrary, the less traditional labor division in individualistic countries seems to be related to a need for gendered emotional differentiation.

One explanation for this unexpected finding is that the search for independence and autonomy that characterizes individualistic cultures threatens the basic human need for social relations. Thus, in order to establish a balance between the need for independence from others and the need for relatedness, men are socialized to become specialists in independence and women to become specialists in social relations. In particular, men are socialized to control their emotions, mainly those that threaten their independence, power, and status, whereas women are encouraged to express positive, other-directed emotions and powerless emotions that foster relations with others. Collectivistic cultures, which emphasize the search for interdependence with others and adjustment to others, are less in need of this gendered emotional differentiation. The dichotomy of the emotional woman and the unemotional man seems to be largely a "Western dichotomy" that cannot be generalized to collectivistic cultures (Fischer & Manstead, 2000).

Intersectionality

Intersectionality is an important new discipline that is reshaping psychologists' approach to gender studies. To understand the term, it's helpful to start by learning what it is *not*: it is not the study of the singular difference between categories of people, such as the difference between men and women regarding emotions. Rather, **intersectionality** is the study of the intersection between multiple ways of dividing people into social categories (Cole, 2009). For example, it appears that emotions are importantly determined not by simply being male or female, but also being male and female of particular ethnicities. In many cases, social categories such as "gender" contain subtypes (female and male in this case) that also differ, as we have seen in this chapter, in terms of power or status (Else-Quest & Hyde, 2016). The same is true for different subtypes under the category of "ethnicity."

The importance of attending both to gender and ethnicity in understanding emotion processes is illustrated in research by Durik and colleagues (Durik, Hyde, Marks, Roy, Anaya, & Schultz, 2006). Those researchers investigated gender stereotypes of emotions such as those that we learned about at the beginning of the chapter, largely replicating the work of Plant and colleagues (Plant et al., 2000). However, they collected data from four ethnic groups in the United States, including European Americans, African Americans, Hispanic Americans, and Asian Americans. Their particular interest was a comparison between European Americans' gender stereotypes for emotion and the gender stereotypes of each of the other three groups. The stereotype that women express and experience more powerless emotions than men was observed in all four ethnic groups. However, the European Americans' gender stereotypes were the most gender differentiated. These differences were most apparent in the emotions of pride and love. European Americans reported that men express more pride than women do, but African Americans reported that men and women did not differ in pride (Figure 11.7). Similarly, European Americans thought that women express much more love than men do, but the difference was smaller among Hispanic Americans and Asian Americans.

Although these findings do not examine the role of power and status in accounting for the ways in which intersections between categories refine more general gender differences, it is likely that future research will find that power and status differences between social categories importantly determine such fundamental social responses as emotions (Else-Quest & Hyde, 2016).

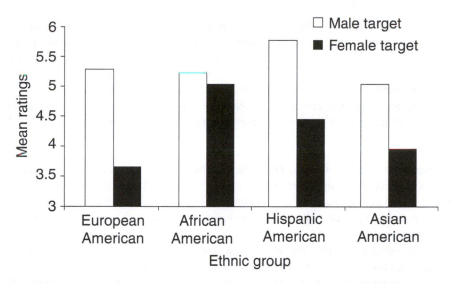

Figure 11.7 Mean ratings of the expression of pride among four ethnic groups in the United States. From Durik et al. (2006).

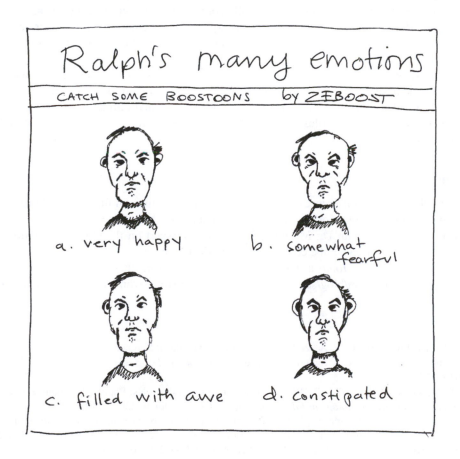

Summary

- Most extant research in the psychology of emotion has made the assumption of a gender binary and reports results of studies that categorize individuals exhaustively as male or female. Future research will certainly push the categories to be more inclusive of other possibilities.
- In the meantime, there are strong stereotypes according to which women express and, to some degree, experience powerless emotions of happiness, embarrassment, surprise, sadness, fear, shame, and guilt more than men. Men are believed to express the powerful emotions of anger, contempt, and pride more than women.
- Strong prescriptive norms exist that specify the emotional reactions that are socially acceptable for men and women. These include the idea that males not cry and that females express positive emotions by smiling.
- Men and women may be motivated to conform to gender stereotypes because such behavior is socially approved, whereas stereotype-inconsistent behavior tends to be socially sanctioned.
- Studies of behavior confirm that to some degree there is correspondence between the stereotypes and the actual emotional behavior of men and women.
- Gender stereotypes contribute to these differences in emotions because they prescribe how and when it is appropriate for men and women to experience and express specific emotions. They create expectations about men's and women's emotional reactions, which may influence their emotional behavior, thereby generating self-fulfilling prophecies.
- Women are in some ways more emotionally competent than men. Except for the emotion of anger, they seem to send and read facial expressions of emotion with greater accuracy than men, are more aware of their emotions, and use a greater number of effective emotion regulation strategies.
- Gender stereotypes indirectly contribute to gender differences in emotions because they provide the basis for the socialization of "gender-appropriate" emotional behavior.
- Finally, gender differences in emotions are not invariant and universal, but are linked to men and women's social roles, to their relative status and power, to their socialization history, and to culture.

Learning Links

1. Learn about gender differences in emotion, offering experimental findings, and discussion of the socialization of emotion. https://www.youtube.com/watch?v=YagL2d4hS84
2. Hear an interview with Dr. Marianne LaFrance, an expert on the study of emotion and gender. https://www.youtube.com/watch?v=qxSR9U_LbSw
3. Read this *Psychology Today* article about men and women and their emotions. https://www.psychologytoday.com/blog/sexual-personalities/201504/are-women-more-emotional-men

References

Adams, S., Kuebli, J., Boyle, P. A., & Fivush, R. (1995). Gender differences in parent-child conversations about past emotions: A longitudinal investigation. *Sex Roles, 33*(5–6), 309–323. doi:10.1007/BF01954572.

Adler, P. A., Kless, S. J., & Adler, P. (1992). Socialization to gender roles: Popularity among elementary school boys and girls. *Sociology of Education, 65*(3), 169–187. doi:10.2307/2112807.

Baron-Cohen, S., & Wheelwright, S. (2004). The empathy quotient: An investigation of adults with asperger syndrome or high functioning autism, and normal sex differences. *Journal of Autism and Developmental Disorders, 34*(2), 163–175. doi:10.1023/B:JADD.0000022607.19833.00.

Barrett, L. F., & Bliss-Moreau, E. (2009). She's emotional. He's having a bad day: Attributional explanations for emotion stereotypes. *Emotion, 9*(5), 649. doi:10.1037/a0016821.

Barrett, L. F., Lane, R. D., Sechrest, L., & Schwartz, G. E. (2000). Sex differences in emotional awareness. *Personality and Social Psychology Bulletin, 26*(9), 1027–1035. doi:10.1177/01461672002611001.

Barrett, L. F., Robin, L., Pietromonaco, P. R., & Eyssell, K. M. (1998). Are women the 'more emotional' sex? Evidence from emotional experiences in social context. *Cognition and Emotion, 12*(4), 555–578. doi:10.1080/026999398379565.

Bem, S. L. (1979). Theory and measurement of androgyny: A reply to the Pedhazur-Tetenbaum and Locksley-Colten critiques. *Journal of Personality and Social Psychology, 37*(6), 1047–1054. doi:10.1037/0022–3514.37.6.1047.

Birnbaum, D. W., & Croll, W. L. (1984). The etiology of children's stereotypes about sex differences in emotionality. *Sex Roles, 10*(9–10), 677–691. doi:10.1007/BF00287379.

Birnbaum, D. W., Nosanchuk, T. A., & Croll, W. L. (1980). Children's stereotypes about sex differences in emotionality. *Sex Roles, 6*(3), 435–443. doi:10.1007/bf00287363.

Brackett, M. A., Rivers, S. E., Shiffman, S., Lerner, N., & Salovey, P. (2006). Relating emotional abilities to social functioning: A comparison of self-report and performance measures of emotional intelligence. *Journal of Personality and Social Psychology, 91*(4), 780–795. doi:10.1037/0022–3514.91.4.780.

Bradley, M. M., Codispoti, M., Sabatinelli, D., & Lang, P. J. (2001). Emotion and motivation II: Sex differences in picture processing. *Emotion, 1*(3), 300–319. doi:10.1037/1528–3542.1.3.300.

Brebner, J. (2003). Gender and emotions. *Personality and Individual Differences, 34*(3), 387–394. doi:10.1016/S0191–8869(02)00059–4.

Brechet, C. (2013). Children's gender stereotypes through drawings of emotional faces: Do boys draw angrier faces than girls? *Sex Roles, 68*(5–6), 378–389. doi:10.1007/s11199–012–0242–3.

Brescoll, V. L., & Uhlmann, E. L. (2008). Can an angry woman get ahead? Status conferral, gender, and expression of emotion in the workplace. *Psychological Science, 19*(3), 268–275. doi:10.1111/j.1467–9280.2008.02079.x.

Brody, L. R. (1997). Gender and emotion: Beyond stereotypes. *Journal of Social Issues, 53*(2), 369–393. doi:10.1111/0022–4537.00022.

Brody, L. R. (1999). *Gender, emotion, and the family*. Cambridge, MA: Harvard University Press.

Brody, L. R. (2000). The socialization of gender differences in emotional expression: Display rules, infant temperament, and differentiation. In A. H. Fischer (Ed.), *Gender and emotion: Social psychological perspectives* (pp. 24–47). New York: Cambridge University Press. doi:10.1017/CBO9780511628191.003.

Brody, L. R., & Hall, J. A. (2000). Gender, emotion, and expression. In M. Lewis & J. M. Haviland-Jones (Eds.), *Handbook of emotions: Part IV: Social/personality issues* (2nd ed., pp. 325– 414). New York: Guilford Press.

Brody, L. R., & Hall, J. A. (2008). Gender and emotion in context. In M. Lewis, J. M. Haviland-Jones & L. F. Barrett (Eds.), *Handbook of emotions* (3rd ed., pp. 395–408). New York: Guilford Press.

Brody, L. R., & Hall, J. A. (2010). Gender, emotion, and socialization. In J. C. Chrisler & D. R. McCreary (Eds.), *Handbook of gender research in psychology, Vol 1: Gender research in general and experimental psychology* (pp. 429–454). New York: Springer Science + Business Media. doi:10.1007/978–1–4419–1465–1_21.

Buck, R., Miller, R. E., & Caul, W. F. (1974). Sex, personality, and physiological variables in the communication of affect via facial expression. *Journal of Personality and Social Psychology, 30*(4), 587–596. doi:10.1037/h0037041.

Chaplin, T. M., Cole, P. M., & Zahn-Waxler, C. (2005). Parental socialization of emotion expression: Gender differences and relations to child adjustment. *Emotion, 5*(1), 80–88. doi:10.1037/1528–3542.5.1.80.

Coats, E. J., & Feldman, R. S. (1996). Gender differences in nonverbal correlates of social status. *Personality and Social Psychology Bulletin, 22*(10), 1014–1022. doi:10.1177/01461672962210004.

Cole, E. R. (2009). Intersectionality and research in psychology. *American Psychologist, 64*(3), 170–180. doi: 10.1037/a0014564.

Copeland, A. P., Hwang, M. S., & Brody, L. R. (1996). Asian-American adolescents: Caught between cultures. Poster presented at the Society for Research in Adolescence, Boston, MA.

Davis, M. A., LaRosa, P. A., & Foshee, D. P. (1992). Emotion work in supervisor-subordinate relations: Gender differences in the perception of angry displays. *Sex Roles, 26*(11–12), 513–531. doi:10.1007/BF00289872.

Doherty, R. W. (1997). The emotional contagion scale: A measure of individual differences. *Journal of Nonverbal Behavior*, *21*(2), 131–154. doi:10.1023/A:1024956003661.

Durik, A. M., Hyde, J. S., Marks, A. C., Roy, A. L., Anaya, D., & Schultz, G. (2006). Ethnicity and gender stereotypes of emotion. *Sex Roles*, *54*(7–8), 429–445. doi:10.1007/s11199–006–9020–4.

Eagly, A. H. (1987). Reporting sex differences. *American Psychologist*, *42*(7), 756–757. doi:10.1037/0003–066X.42.7.755.

Eagly, A. H., & Steffen, V. J. (1984). Gender stereotypes stem from the distribution of women and men into social roles. *Journal of Personality and Social Psychology*, *46*(4), 735–754. doi:10.1037/0022–3514.46.4.735.

Eagly, A. H., & Steffen, V. J. (1986). Gender and aggressive behavior: A meta-analytic review of the social psychological literature. *Psychological Bulletin*, *100*(3), 309–330. doi:10.1037/0033–2909.100.3.309.

Else-Quest, N. M., & Hyde, J. S. (2016). Intersectionality in Quantitative Psychological Research: I. Theoretical and Epistemological Issues. *Psychology of Women Quarterly*, *40*(2), 1–16. doi:10.1177/0361684316629797.

Else-Quest, N. M., Hyde, J. S., Goldsmith, H. H., & Van Hulle, C. A. (2006). Gender differences in temperament: A meta-analysis. *Psychological Bulletin*, *132*(1), 33–72. doi:10.1037/0033–2909.132.1.33.

Fabes, R. A., & Martin, C. L. (1991). Gender and age stereotypes of emotionality. *Personality and Social Psychology Bulletin*, *17*(5), 532–540. doi:10.1177/0146167291175008.

Feldman, J. F., Brody, N., & Miller, S. A. (1980). Sex differences in non-elicited neonatal behaviors. *Merrill-Palmer Quarterly*, *26*(1), 63–73.

Ferguson, T. J., & Crowley, S. L. (1997). Gender differences in the organization of guilt and shame. *Sex Roles*, *37*(1–2), 19–44. doi:10.1023/A:1025684502616.

Ferguson, T. J., Eyre, H. L., & Ashbaker, M. (2000). Unwanted identities: A key variable in shame–anger links and gender differences in shame. *Sex Roles*, *42*(3–4), 133–157. doi:10.1023/A:1007061505251.

Fischer, A. H. (1993). Sex differences in emotionality: Fact or stereotype? *Feminism & Psychology*, *3*(3), 303–318. doi:10.1177/0959353593033002.

Fischer, A. H., & Manstead, A. R. (2000). The relation between gender and emotion in different cultures. In A. H. Fischer (Ed.), *Gender and emotion: Social psychological perspectives* (pp. 71–94). New York: Cambridge University Press. doi:10.1017/CBO9780511628191.005.

Fischer, A. H., Rodriguez Mosquera, P. M., Van Vianen, A. E., & Manstead, A. S. (2004). Gender and culture differences in emotion. *Emotion*, *4*(1), 87–94. doi: 10.1037/1528-3542.4.1.87.

Fivush, R., & Wang, Q. (2005). Emotion talk in mother-child conversations of the shared past: The effects of culture, gender, and event valence. *Journal of Cognition and Development*, *6*(4), 489–506. doi:10.1207/s15327647jcd0604_3.

Frost, W. D., & Averill, J. R. (1982). Differences between men and women in the everyday experience of anger. In J. R. Averill (Ed.), *Anger and aggression* (pp. 281–316). New York: Springer-Verlag.

Fujita, F., Diener, E., & Sandvik, E. (1991). Gender differences in negative affect and well-being: The case for emotional intensity. *Journal of Personality and Social Psychology*, *61*(3), 427–434. doi:10.1037/0022–3514.61.3.427.

Graham, J. W., Gentry, K. W., & Green, J. (1981). The self-presentational nature of emotional expression: Some evidence. *Personality and Social Psychology Bulletin*, *7*(3), 467–474. doi:10.1177/014616728173016.

Gross, J. J., & John, O. P. (1995). Facets of emotional expressivity: Three self-report factors and their correlates. *Personality and Individual Differences*, *19*(4), 555–568. doi:10.1016/0191–8869(95)00055-B.

Grossman, M., & Wood, W. (1993). Sex differences in intensity of emotional experience: A social role interpretation. *Journal of Personality and Social Psychology*, *65*(5), 1010–1022. doi:10.1037/0022–3514.65.5.1010.

Hall, J. A. (1984). *Nonverbal sex differences: Communication accuracy and expressive style*. Baltimore, MD: Johns Hopkins University Press.

Hall, J. A., & Friedman, G. B. (1999). Status, gender, and nonverbal behavior: A study of structured interactions between employees of a company. *Personality and Social Psychology Bulletin*, *25*(9), 1082–1091. doi:10.1177/01461672992512002.

Hall, J. A., & Matsumoto, D. (2004). Gender differences in judgments of multiple emotions from facial expressions. *Emotion, 4*(2), 201–206. doi:10.1037/1528–3542.4.2.201.

Hampson, E., van Anders, S. M., & Mullin, L. I. (2006). A female advantage in the recognition of emotional facial expressions: Test of an evolutionary hypothesis. *Evolution and Human Behavior, 27*(6), 401–416. doi:10.1016/j.evolhumbehav.2006.05.002.

Hatfield, E., Cacioppo, J. T., & Rapson, R. L. (1994). *Emotional contagion.* Cambridge: Cambridge University Press.

Heilman, M. E. (2001). Description and prescription: How gender stereotypes prevent women's ascent up the organizational ladder. *Journal of Social Issues, 57*(4), 657–674. doi:10.1111/0022–4537.00234.

Hess, U., Adams, R. J., & Kleck, R. E. (2005). Who may frown and who should smile? Dominance, affiliation, and the display of happiness and anger. *Cognition and Emotion, 19*(4), 515–536. doi:10.1080/02699930441000364.

Hess, U., Senécal, S., Kirouac, G., Herrera, P., Philippot, P., & Kleck, R. E. (2000). Emotional expressivity in men and women: Stereotypes and self-perceptions. *Cognition and Emotion, 14*(5), 609–642. doi:10.1080/02699930050117648.

Hutson-Comeaux, S. L., & Kelly, J. R. (2002). Gender stereotypes of emotional reactions: How we judge an emotion as valid. *Sex Roles, 47*(1–2), 1–10. doi:10.1023/A:1020657301981.

Johnson, J. T., & Shulman, G. A. (1988). More alike than meets the eye: Perceived gender differences in subjective experience and its display. *Sex Roles, 19*(1–2), 67–79. doi:10.1007/BF00292465.

Kelly, J. R., & Hutson-Comeaux, S. L. (1999). Gender-emotion stereotypes are context specific. *Sex Roles, 40*(1–2), 107–120. doi:10.1023/A:1018834501996.

Kelly, J. R., & Hutson-Comeaux, S. L. (2000). The appropriateness of emotional expression in women and men: The double-bind of emotion. *Journal of Social Behavior and Personality, 15*(4), 515–528.

King, L. A., & Emmons, R. A. (1990). Conflict over emotional expression: Psychological and physical correlates. *Journal of Personality and Social Psychology, 58*(5), 864–877. doi:10.1037/0022–3514.58.5.864.

Kring, A. M. (2000). Gender and anger. In A. H. Fischer (Ed.), *Gender and emotion: Social psychological perspectives* (pp. 211–231). New York: Cambridge University Press. doi:10.1017/CBO9780511628191.011.

Kring, A. M., & Gordon, A. H. (1998). Sex differences in emotion: Expression, experience, and physiology. *Journal of Personality and Social Psychology, 74*(3), 686–703. doi:10.1037/0022–3514.74.3.686.

Kring, A. M., Smith, D. A., & Neale, J. M. (1994). Individual differences in dispositional expressiveness: Development and validation of the emotional expressivity scale. *Journal of Personality and Social Psychology, 66*(5), 934–949. doi:10.1037/0022–3514.66.5.934.

LaFrance, M., & Banaji, M. (1992). Toward a reconsideration of the gender–emotion relationship. In M. S. Clark (Ed.), *Emotion and social behavior* (pp. 178–201). Thousand Oaks, CA: Sage Publications.

LaFrance, M., & Hecht, M. A. (2000). Gender and smiling: A meta-analysis. In A. H. Fischer (Ed.), *Gender and emotion: Social psychological perspectives* (pp. 118–142). New York: Cambridge University Press. doi:10.1017/CBO9780511628191.007.

Lane, R. D., Sechrest, L., Riedel, R., Shapiro, D. E., & Kaszniak, A. W. (2000). Pervasive emotion recognition deficit common to alexithymia and the repressive coping style. *Psychosomatic Medicine, 62*(4), 492–501. doi:10.1097/00006842–200007000–00007.

Levenson, R. W., Carstensen, L. L., & Gottman, J. M. (1994). Influence of age and gender on affect, physiology, and their interrelations: A study of long-term marriages. *Journal of Personality and Social Psychology, 67*(1), 56–68. doi:10.1037/0022–3514.67.1.56.

Matsumoto, D., Takeuchi, S., Andayani, S., Kouznetsova, N., & Krupp, D. (1998). The contribution of individualism vs. collectivism to cross-national differences in display rules. *Asian Journal of Social Psychology, 1*(2), 147–165. doi:10.1111/1467–839X.00010.

Mayer, J. D., Salovey, P., & Caruso, D. R. (2004). Emotional intelligence: Theory, findings, and implications. *Psychological Inquiry, 15*(3), 197–215. doi:10.1207/s15327965pli1503_02.

Mignault, A., & Chaudhuri, A. (2003). The many faces of a neutral face: Head tilt and perception of dominance and emotion. *Journal of Nonverbal Behavior, 27*(2), 111–132. doi:10.1023/A:1023914509763.

Mirgain, S. A., & Cordova, J. V. (2007). Emotion skills and marital health: The association between observed and self-reported emotion skills, intimacy, and marital satisfaction. *Journal of Social and Clinical Psychology, 26*(9), 983–1009. doi:10.1521/jscp.2007.26.9.983.

Niedenthal, P. M., Augustinova, M., Rychlowska, M., Droit-Volet, S., Zinner, L., Knafo, A., & Brauer, M. (2012). Negative relations between pacifier use and emotional competence. *Basic and Applied Social Psychology*, *34*(5), 387–394. doi:10.1080/01973533.2012.712019.

Niedenthal, P. M., Mermillod, M., Maringer, M., & Hess, U. (2010). The simulation of smiles (SIMS) model: Embodied simulation and the meaning of facial expression. *Behavioral and Brain Sciences*, *33*(6), 417–433. doi:10.1017/S0140525X10000865.

Nolen-Hoeksema, S. (2004). Gender differences in risk factors and consequences for alcohol use and problems. *Clinical Psychology Review*, *24*(8), 981–1010. doi:10.1016/j.cpr.2004.08.003.

Nolen-Hoeksema, S., & Harrell, Z. A. (2002). Rumination, depression, and alcohol use: Tests of gender differences. *Journal of Cognitive Psychotherapy*, *16*(4), 391–403. doi:10.1891/jcop.16.4.391.52526.

Ontai, L. L., & Thompson, R. A. (2002). Patterns of attachment and maternal discourse effects on children's emotion understanding from 3 to 5 years of age. *Social Development*, *11*(4), 433–450. doi:10.1111/1467–9507.00209.

Park, C. L., & Levenson, M. R. (2002). Drinking to cope among college students: Prevalence, problems and coping processes. *Journal of Studies on Alcohol*, *63*(4), 486–497. doi:10.15288/jsa.2002.63.486.

Plant, E. A., Hyde, J. S., Keltner, D., & Devine, P. G. (2000). The gender stereotyping of emotions. *Psychology of Women Quarterly*, *24*(1), 81–92. doi:10.1111/j.1471–6402.2000.tb01024.x.

Plant, E. A., Kling, K. C., & Smith, G. L. (2004). The influence of gender and social role on the interpretation of facial expressions. *Sex Roles*, *51*(3–4), 187–196. doi:10.1023/B:SERS.0000037762.10349.13.

Robinson, M. D., & Johnson, J. T. (1997). Is it emotion or is it stress? Gender stereotypes and the perception of subjective experience. *Sex Roles*, *36*(3), 235–258. doi:10.1007/BF02766270.

Ross, C. E., & Mirowsky, J. (1984). Components of depressed mood in married men and women. The center for epidemiologic studies' depression scale. *American Journal of Epidemiology*, *119*(6), 997–1004.

Rotter, N. G., & Rotter, G. S. (1988). Sex differences in the encoding and decoding of negative facial emotions. *Journal of Nonverbal Behavior*, *12*(2), 139–148. doi:10.1007/BF00986931.

Rudman, L. A. (1998). Self-promotion as a risk factor for women: The costs and benefits of counterstereotypical impression management. *Journal of Personality and Social Psychology*, *74*(3), 629–645. doi:10.1037/0022–3514.74.3.629.

Rychlowska, M., Korb, S., Brauer, M., Droit-Volet, S., Augustinova, M., Zinner, L., & Niedenthal, P. M. (2014). Pacifiers disrupt adults' responses to infants' emotions. *Basic and Applied Social Psychology*, *36*(4), 299–308. doi:10.1080/01973533.2014.915217.

Salovey, P., & Mayer, J. D. (1990). Emotional intelligence. *Imagination, Cognition and Personality*, *9*(3), 185–211. doi:10.2190/DUGG-P24E-52WK-6CDG.

Salovey, P., Mayer, J. D., Caruso, D., & Lopes, P. N. (2003). Measuring emotional intelligence as a set of abilities with the Mayer-Salovey-Caruso emotional intelligence test. In S. J. Lopez & C. R. Snyder (Eds.), *Positive psychological assessment: A handbook of models and measures* (pp. 251–265). Washington, DC: American Psychological Association. doi:10.1037/10612–016.

Scholten, M. M., Aleman, A., Montagne, B., & Kahn, R. S. (2005). Schizophrenia and processing of facial emotions: Sex matters. *Schizophrenia Research*, *78*(1), 61–67. doi:10.1016/j.schres.2005.06.019.

Schulte-Rüther, M., Markowitsch, H. J., Shah, N. J., Fink, G. R., & Piefke, M. (2008). Gender differences in brain networks supporting empathy. *Neuroimage*, *42*(1), 393–403. doi:10.1016/j.neuroimage.2008.04.180.

Schwartz, G. E., Brown, S., & Ahern, G. L. (1980). Facial muscle patterning and subjective experience during affective imagery: Sex differences. *Psychophysiology*, *17*(1), 75–82. doi:10.1111/j.1469–8986.1980.tb02463.x.

Shields, S. A. (2002). *Speaking from the heart: Gender and the social meaning of emotion*. New York: Cambridge University Press.

Stapley, J. C., & Haviland, J. M. (1989). Beyond depression: Gender differences in normal adolescents' emotional experiences. *Sex Roles*, *20*(5–6), 295–308. doi:10.1007/BF00287726.

Stevens, J. S., & Hamann, S. (2012). Sex differences in brain activation to emotional stimuli: A meta-analysis of neuroimaging studies. *Neuropsychologia*, *50*(7), 1578–1593. doi:10.1016/j.neuropsychologia.2012.03.011.

Stoppard, J. M., & Gruchy, C. G. (1993). Gender, context, and expression of positive emotion. *Personality and Social Psychology Bulletin*, *19*(2), 143–150. doi:10.1177/0146167293192002.

Tamres, L. K., Janicki, D., & Helgeson, V. S. (2002). Sex differences in coping behavior: A meta-analytic review and an examination of relative coping. *Personality and Social Psychology Review*, 6(1), 2–30. doi:10.1207/S15327957PSPR0601_1.

Tangney, J. P. (1990). Assessing individual differences in proneness to shame and guilt: Development of the self-conscious affect and attribution inventory. *Journal of Personality and Social Psychology*, 59(1), 102–111. doi:10.1037/0022-3514.59.1.102.

Thayer, J. F., & Johnsen, B. H. (2000). Sex differences in judgement of facial affect: A multivariate analysis of recognition errors. *Scandinavian Journal of Psychology*, 41(3), 243–246. doi:10.1111/1467-9450.00193.

Timmers, M., Fischer, A. H., & Manstead, A. R. (1998). Gender differences in motives for regulating emotions. *Personality and Social Psychology Bulletin*, 24(9), 974–985. doi:10.1177/0146167298249005.

Timmers, M., Fischer, A. H., & Manstead, A. R. (2003). Ability versus vulnerability: Beliefs about men's and women's emotional behaviour. *Cognition & Emotion*, 17(1), 41–63. doi:10.1080/02699930302277.

Vassallo, S., Cooper, S. L., & Douglas, J. M. (2009). Visual scanning in the recognition of facial affect: Is there an observer sex difference? *Journal of Vision*, 9(3), 11–11. doi:10.1167/9.3.11.

Vingerhoets, A., & Scheirs, J. (2000). Sex differences in crying: Empirical findings and possible explanations. In A. H. Fischer (Ed.), *Gender and emotion: Social psychological perspectives* (pp. 143–165). New York: Cambridge University Press. doi:10.1017/CBO9780511628191.008.

Vingerhoets, A. J. J. M., & Becht, M. C. (1996). Adult crying inventory (ACI) (Unpublished questionnaire). Department of Psychology, Tilburg University, The Netherlands.

Wagner, H. L., Buck, R., & Winterbotham, M. (1993). Communication of specific emotions: Gender differences in sending accuracy and communication measures. *Journal of Nonverbal Behavior*, 17(1), 29–53. doi:10.1007/BF00987007.

Weinberg, M. K., Tronick, E. Z., Cohn, J. F., & Olson, K. L. (1999). Gender differences in emotional expressivity and self-regulation during early infancy. *Developmental Psychology*, 35(1), 175–188. doi:10.1037/0012-1649.35.1.175.

Zammuner, V. L. (2000). Men's and women's lay theories of emotion. In A. H. Fischer (Ed.), *Gender and emotion: Social psychological perspectives* (pp. 48–70). New York: Cambridge University Press. doi:10.1017/CBO9780511628191.004.

Zeman, J., Penza, S., Shipman, K., & Young, G. (1997). Preschoolers as functionalists: The impact of social context on emotion regulation. *Child Study Journal*, 27(1), 41–67.

12 Universals and Cultural Differences in Emotions

The authors of this book know a man who is Polish, grew to adolescence in Poland, and then lived in the United States for more than 50 years. Quite frequently, the man admitted, "I have lived here for many years, but I am still not completely comfortable with Americans' emotions. They smile all the time, and say that they are 'happy.' I hardly ever use this word." A Dutch friend says, "You know, the Americans and the British, when they do something wrong, they always say they are sorry. But they do not really feel sorry." Many Europeans and European Americans think that Asians are inscrutable, that they seem to mask their true feelings. And individuals from Mediterranean countries think that Scandinavians do not actually experience much emotion at all because they never seem to show emotion, an accusation to which a Swede might respond, "Yes, but still waters run deep." Meanwhile, a Finnish man once told one of us that Finns are generally suspicious of adults who do not control their expression of emotion, especially in public. Dramatic displays of emotion are seen as immature or slightly out of control.

What is going on here? These comments and beliefs seem to suggest that there is variation in the ways in which people across countries or continents feel, express, or label emotions. Are there cultural differences in the experience of emotion, or do the earlier comments merely reflect stereotypes and values that mask underlying similarity? This is a difficult question to answer because, as we have seen, emotions have many components. In this chapter we consider similarities in emotion processes that have been observed across the world. Then, we look at examples of variation. Finally, we introduce specific ways to define and compare cultures of the world. We derive hypotheses about possible cultural differences in emotion processes and review the scientific evidence for these predictions.

A Brief History of Cross-Cultural Studies of Emotion

Research on emotion began with the search for universal emotions (Mesquita, 2001; Mesquita & Haire, 2004). Scientists believed that if there were universal facial expressions, it would be evidence of evolved, total emotional states composed of all of the components, including bodily, facial, feeling, and cognitive components (Tomkins, 1962, 1963). As we saw in Chapter 4, there is evidence for universal facial expressions of emotion (Haidt & Keltner, 1999). The same is true of vocal affect. A number of studies have examined the universal recognition of emotion in the voice (e.g., Scherer, Banse, & Wallbott, 2001; Van Bezooijen, Otto, & Heenan, 1983), and the results show that the recognition of emotions, expressed in the same vocal stimuli, is above chance, suggesting a universality of vocal affect.

The initial quest for experimental evidence in favor of the existence of universal emotions limited the focus of research on emotion to similarities. More inadvertently, however, the approach tended to promote a certain inattention to ways in which differences could conceivably occur (Mesquita, 2001a; Mesquita & Haire, 2004). Recall from Chapter 1 that most appraisal theorists and psychological constructionists reject the claim made by evolutionary theory that the components of emotion are part of a single affect program. Rather, they believe that the components of emotion (e.g., physiology, facial expression, feelings) tend to co-occur but do not have to. Thus, some states of anger, *but not all*, involve high sympathetic nervous system activation, a furrowed brow, and the readiness to strike (Barrett, 2006; Lindquist, 2013; Moors, 2013; Scherer, 2009). The emerging consensus that the components of emotion are only loosely coupled allowed scientists to imagine that there could be some similarities but also some differences in people's emotions as a function of culture (Mesquita & Frijda, 1992; Mesquita, Frijda, & Scherer, 1997).

But who should differ (and be similar) and why? Asking the question in this way requires that the researcher adopt a theory of the possible ways groups of people in the world cluster together into groups, that is, to have a theory of culture and cultural groupings. Most recently, therefore, the study of emotion has been guided by theories of culture that were initially developed within the fields of anthropology and ethnography (Lutz, 1987, 1988; Shweder, 1993; 1994; Shweder & Haidt, 2000) and linguistics (Wierzbicka, 1986, 1992). The theories of cultural differences state that culture and emotion are interactive processes such that culture influences how emotions are expressed, managed, and understood; and emotions influence the development of cultural meanings and practices (Mesquita, 2003; Shweder, 1994, 2002; Solomon, 1995; see also Barrett, 2006).

Looking for Similarities

What do emotions look like in the body and face, and what evidence do we have that these appearances and their meanings are the same the world over? That's the question that drives much of the research on the universality of emotion.

Expression of Emotion in Movement and Music

Throughout human history we have expressed emotion in movement (such as dance) and in music. In fact, some scientists think that music and dance have evolved from the communication of emotion in animals (Snowdon, Zimmermann, & Altenmüller, 2015). If the expressions of emotion in movement and music are evolved, then they should be universal. Movement and music might also be fundamentally related or have similar properties. For example, you could imagine that anger is expressed in movement that is sudden, vigorous, and aggressive and that anger is expressed in music in sounds that are also sudden, vigorous, and aggressive.

The possibility that emotions are expressed similarly in movement and music was tested in research conducted by Sievers and colleagues (2013). The scientists developed a computer program that allowed an individual to direct the movement of an animated red ball or to produce music using the same platform. Specifically, participants in their study used five slider bars on a computer screen to animate the movements of a three-dimensional red ball until it seemed to express anger, joy, sadness, peacefulness, and fear. The ball was given two white "eyes" to anthropomorphize it, making it seem like a head. The slider bars varied the rate (speed) of movement, jitter (i.e., regularity of movement), visual roughness or smoothness of the ball, step size (i.e., the height bounced), and direction of the movement (see Figure 12.1). Other participants were invited to make music that expressed the same emotions, using sliders that varied the same factors, phrased in more musical terminology: rate (i.e., speed), regularity, dissonance of the sound, step size (i.e., amount of change), and direction (i.e., getting higher or lower).

Participants in the study were first recruited in the United States. Then, other participants were recruited in a remote tribal village of Cambodia. This way, the researchers could investigate two questions. One was whether movement and music are expressed in the same ways, with the same physical properties. And the other was whether people in the United States think that the same physical properties represent the same emotions in movement and music as tribal Cambodians. The results showed that the answer to both questions was yes. The features of movement and music were highly correlated. And the Americans and Cambodians represented emotions in movement and music in the same way. Figure 12.2 shows how similar animations of anger and of happiness were across the two cultures. You can see that anger movements were harsh (and they were also vigorous and chaotic) and happy ones were smooth (and also bouncy and predictable).

Figure 12.1 Participants in a study by Sievers et al. (2013) manipulated slider bars on a computer screen that corresponded to five dynamic features to create either animated movement or musical clips that expressed emotions named by the experimenters.

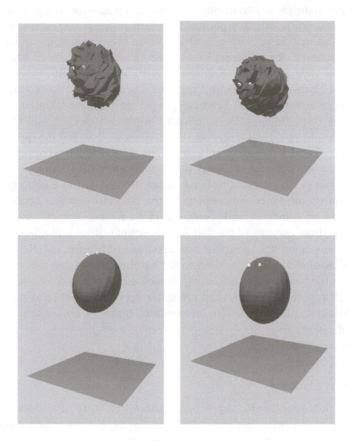

Figure 12.2 On top: United States angry animated change and movement on the left and Cambodian (Kreung) angry movement on the right. On the bottom: United States happy animated change and
movement on the left and Cambodian (Kreung) happy movement on the right.

If emotions are expressed similarly in movement and music and these similarities hold across
two very different cultures that have not interacted with each other, what about other aspects
of emotion such as facial expression and the feelings and underlying physiology of emotion?

Bodily Feelings of Emotion

What are the bodily states that correspond with the psychological states that accompany a given
emotion? Although researchers have not yet linked a specific pattern of physiology to every
emotion, they have discovered some physiological changes that characterize some emotions,
especially those of anger and fear. Do the same patterns characterize anger and fear across
culture?

Physiology

In Chapter 1 we introduced research on the physiology of emotion by Levenson, Ekman, and
Friesen (1990), which was conducted with the participation of American university students.
That study showed distinct patterns of autonomic nervous system reactivity in the participants

when they arranged their faces into displays of distinct facial expressions of emotion. When they smiled with joy, for instance, a particular pattern of heart rate, skin conductance, finger temperature, and muscle activity was observed. In order to test the universal nature of these autonomic patterns, the same study was conducted several years later in Indonesia, using Minangkabau men from West Sumatra as participants (Levenson et al., 1992). The experimenter-guided muscle contraction procedure was again used to produce recognizable facial expressions of emotion. Then, heart rate, finger temperature, skin conductance, finger pulse, transmission time, finger pulse amplitude, respiratory period, and respiratory depth were measured. The physiological responses of the Minangkabau and the (previously studied) Americans were similar; differences in only two of the physiological measures were observed. This suggests some cross-cultural similarity in the physiology of emotion.

Tsai and Levenson (1997) tested similarity of physiology during emotional states among East Asian and European American couples. In the laboratory, while hooked up to physiological monitoring equipment, couples engaged in a baseline, neutral discussion and then a discussion of the strongest area of conflict in their couple. Both self-report and physiological indicators of their emotions during the conversations were assessed. Results showed that although discussion of a conflict compared to the baseline discussion was much more emotional, as shown by the two types of indicators, physiological changes did not differ by national group. In fact, self-reports of emotion did not differ very much either. Another study using a controlled acoustic startle stimulus (in other words, blasts of noise) showed that Chinese Americans had the same level of physiological response as did Mexican Americans (Soto, Levenson, & Ebling, 2005).

SELF-REPORTED BODILY SENSATIONS

A number of researchers have also asked individuals to verbally describe the physiological changes that occur during emotional states. The question here is whether individuals *perceive* physiological changes during different emotions in the same way.

In a series of studies, Rimé, Philippot, and Cisamolo (1990) showed that people from the same country agree in their descriptions of bodily sensations of emotion. For instance, the researchers asked participants about the extent to which the following sensations characterized joy, anger, fear, and sadness: lump in throat, breathing problems, stomach sensations, feeling cold, feeling warm, feeling hot, heartbeat acceleration, muscle tension, muscle relaxation, and perspiration. The four emotions studied were associated with quite distinct, but also very consensual, patterns of peripheral bodily changes. More importantly for this chapter, the same distinct patterns of bodily experiences were also reported by individuals from Belgium, Bolivia, Indonesia, Italy, Mexico, and the United States (Breugelmans et al., 2005; Philippot & Rimé, 1997).

One criticism of these studies is that the features of emotions were described in language. The ways in which translations were conducted might have assured the detection of similarity rather than difference across cultures. Nummenmaa et al. (2014) therefore used a nonverbal approach. They created a computer-based, topographical self-report method called emBODY. In the procedure, participants from Finland, Sweden, and Taiwan were shown two silhouettes of bodies next to emotional words, stories, movies, or facial expressions. Then they had to color the bodily regions whose activity they felt to be increased (using warm colors) or decreased (using cool colors) during that state. The participants' responses could be averaged to make maps of bodily sensations associated with different emotions. Findings showed that the emotions were associated with clearly distinct bodily sensation maps that were consistent across European and East Asian participants (see Figure 12.3).

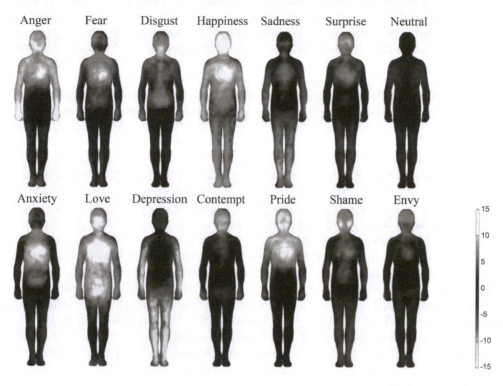

Figure 12.3 Bodily topography of basic (upper) and nonbasic (lower) emotions associated with words. The body maps show regions whose activation increased (warm colors) or decreased (cool colors) when feeling each emotion. From Nummenmaa et al. (2014).

Together with the studies of movement and music, research on underlying physiology reveals more similarity than difference for the processes of emotion that are somewhat automatic. What about the things that people can control, such as their expressions of emotion on the face and their interpretations of life events and experiences?

Looking for Difference

As we have already seen in Chapter 5, there is some agreement across cultures about the way that the face expresses anger, disgust, fear, happiness, sadness, and surprise (Ekman, 1972; Ekman & Friesen, 1971; Izard, 1971). However, there are also differences in the accuracy with which people across countries recognize these expressions and the ways in which they confuse the expressions, leading to lively debate as to whether facial expressions are universal (Gendron et al., 2014; Nelson & Russell, 2013). Whatever the outcome of the debate, it is undeniable that there are both similarities and differences in how emotions are expressed across cultures.

Emotional Expression Dialects

Research shows that individuals recognize emotional expressions displayed by members of their own national in-group more accurately than expressions displayed by people from other national groups. This "in-group advantage" was supported by a meta-analysis of the results of 87 studies involving 182 different samples of participants (Elfenbein & Ambady, 2002). It appeared, for example, that the Japanese could recognize their country-person's emotional expressions better than they recognized the expressions of other national groups.

The in-group advantage appeared to hold, moreover, independent of the emotional expression or of the experimental method used in the study. The meta-analysis also provided evidence of an in-group advantage in the recognition of emotion from other nonverbal signals of emotion including the voice and body language. Subsequent studies designed to test the implications of the meta-analysis found evidence in favor of an in-group advantage among American, Japanese, and Indian observers and expressers (Elfenbein et al., 2002) and among non-Asian American and Chinese observers who recognized Caucasian and Chinese expressions (Elfenbein & Ambady, 2003).

A **dialect theory** of facial expression is used to explain the in-group advantage (Elfenbein, 2013; Elfenbein & Ambady, 2003). Drawing a parallel with dialects in languages, this theory states that there is a universal, perhaps innate, language of emotion, which underlies the better-than-chance recognition of a set of facial expressions (and other nonverbal behavior) across national boundaries. But then, similar to variations in accent, grammar, and vocabulary within a language (for instance, the differences between American and British English), groups of people add "accents" and "vocabularies" of emotional expression that are unique to that group. These dialects are the result of learning (Leach, 1972). But they are not necessarily conscious and do not involve the regulation of emotion or emotional expression in accordance with social norms (Elfenbein & Ambady, 2003). So, the in-group advantage in the recognition of facial expression might occur because members of a given country are used to seeing a particular manifestation (the dialect) of an otherwise universal facial expression of emotion (Kang & Lau, 2013; Wickline, Bailey, & Nowicki, 2009; see Matsumoto, 2005 for criticisms of this view).

More direct evidence for the dialect theory comes from research that measures specific configurations of muscles movements, also called action units (see Chapter 2). For example, in one study, researchers identified action units that were similar, but also some that varied across facial expressions of emotions posed by French Canadian and Gabonese participants (Elfenbein et al., 2007). The results suggested that the typical expressions of sadness, happiness, and so forth looked quite similar but contained clear indications of dialects as well (see Figure 12.4).

DIALECT THEORY

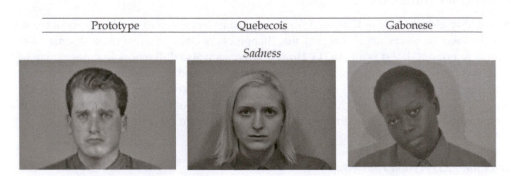

Figure 12.4 Sadness dialects from Quebec, Gabon, and a prototype derived in a North American (non-Quebecois sample, at left). Slightly different action units are present in the expressions. From Elfenbein et al. (2007).

The studies of the universality of emotional expression and of in-group dialects, when taken together, seem to reveal that there is a mix of similarity and difference in the ways in which emotions are reflected on the face across the world.

Expressiveness of Northerners and Southerners

When scientists study facial expression, they ask participants in their studies to make a face that corresponds to an emotion label such as "disgust." What about how much or how intensely people express their emotions? Does that also vary across the globe? Charles de Secondat Montesquieu published a treatise on human behavior in 1748 entitled *The Spirit of the Laws*. In that book, drawing on eighteenth-century beliefs about physiology, he argued that the warmer climate found in more southern countries (of the northern hemisphere) causes the skin to become more relaxed and the nerve endings to become more sensitive compared to colder climates that make the nerves of the skin less sensitive to all forms of stimulation. Because of these differences in the effect of climate, individuals in northern countries, he argued, were generally stolid and reserved in character, whereas those in southern countries were more social and emotional. Part of this view is communicated in the stereotype of Scandinavians as being unexpressive and of Italians as being very expressive. Is there any validity in this 270-year-old theory?

Pennebaker, Rimé, and Blankenship (1996) solicited participants from 26 countries and asked them whether individuals in the northern and southern regions of their country were emotionally expressive and whether they themselves were emotionally expressive. The results supported Montesquieu's hypothesis, particularly in Europe and Asia where the populations have been stable, without strong migration and immigration influences, for thousands of years. Participants thought that people who lived in the southern regions of their country were more expressive than those in the northern regions. Moreover, participants from southern regions also described themselves as more expressive than did the participants in the northern regions.

Irish versus Scandinavians also seem to embody the content of the southern and northern stereotypes, respectively, even though they are both geographically northern countries. Specifically, the Irish are oriented toward dramatic expressions of tragedy and the use of laughter and humor in the social sharing of the experiences of life (Greeley, 1979, 1981). Scandinavians have been characterized as a people who value the moderation of emotional expression and stoicism in the service of maintaining social order.

Tsai and Chentsova-Dutton (2003) conducted a study to test the validity of these descriptions of the Irish and Scandinavians in a controlled laboratory experiment. Irish American and Scandinavian American participants performed the **relived emotions task**, which is an effective elicitor of emotions (e.g., Levenson et al., 1991; Oliveau & Willmuth, 1979). In the task, participants were provided with a label for a target emotion, such as "happiness," and also a description of a situation in which the target emotion occurred, such as "a time when you did something or something happened that you wanted very much, so that you felt very good." Participants had to recall a time when they experienced the target emotion, focus on it, and relive it. When they were able to feel the emotion, they pressed a button to signal their success at the task. In all, the participants were exposed to five target emotions. As the participants relived the target emotions, their facial expressions were recorded by a hidden camera. Facial expressions were later coded with the use of the Facial Action Coding System (FACS; Ekman & Friesen, 1978). Irish Americans were more facially expressive than were Scandinavian Americans for all five emotions, except pride, and particularly for the emotions of happiness and love.

Later in the chapter, we'll examine how cultural rules and expectations might govern how transparent or visible emotions should be. But for now, we'll turn to differences in causes of emotional reactions.

Antecedent Events

What kinds of events spur specific emotions like happiness and sadness? In an enormous study of Americans, Europeans (from eight countries), and Japanese, Scherer and colleagues (1988) sought to identify the antecedent events for four emotions, including anger, sadness, happiness, and fear. Participants were asked to describe the situations in which the four emotions were experienced, and the nominated situations were later coded as falling into a number of possible categories or having specific themes. Although the researchers expected quite high similarity in the frequency with which different types of situations and themes were nominated across the national groups, this was not the case. Joy was associated with diverse events, especially for the Japanese. For instance, although cultural pleasures, births, and bodily pleasures were important for the Europeans and Americans, all were much less frequent antecedents of joy for the Japanese. In addition, achievements were antecedents of joy for Americans and Europeans far more than for the Japanese.

The antecedent events of sadness also varied. Death, for instance, was a much less common antecedent event for sadness for the Japanese than for the Americans and Europeans. Americans were more often saddened by separation and the Japanese more saddened by relationship problems, with the Europeans somewhere in between for both types of situations. More than the Americans and Europeans, the Japanese felt fear when confronting novel situations and in the context of relationships.

Finally, causes of anger were also quite varied. Americans and, to some degree, Europeans experienced most anger within close relationships, whereas Japanese experienced most anger in the context of strangers. Injustice also caused anger in Americans and Europeans significantly more often than in Japanese.

The differences in the antecedent events for emotion across countries are in and of themselves interesting. However, we cannot really know *why* these differences exist. Perhaps they exist because the same situations have very different meanings. In order to know if that is the case, it is therefore important to study the appraisals and the meanings of emotional situations.

Appraisals

There are two ways to think about how appraisals could vary across people in the world. One way is that different patterns of appraisals cause different emotions in different parts of the world. In fact, most appraisal theories of emotion, such as those reviewed in Chapter 1, started with the assumption that when any two people make the same appraisal of a situation, they will have the same emotional reaction to it. This has been called the **universal contingency hypothesis** (Ellsworth, 1994; Mesquita & Ellsworth, 2001).

The universal contingency hypothesis holds for most appraisal dimensions, but not for all (e.g., Frijda et al., 1995; Roseman et al., 1995; Scherer, 1997). For instance, Mauro, Sato, and Tucker (1992) investigated how appraisal dimensions were related to the experience of 14 different emotional states, using participants from the United States, Japan, the People's Republic of China, and Hong Kong. Mauro and colleagues predicted and found little variability in the extent to which pleasantness, certainty, and goal conduciveness were related to specific emotions across the participants from the different countries. The scientists anticipated this because (as we saw in Chapter 1) these appraisal dimensions are more primitive in that they occur earlier in the appraisal process and/or require fewer cognitive resources (Sander, Grandjean, & Scherer, 2005). There was significant variation, however, in the differentiation of specific emotions by the more cognitively demanding appraisal dimensions. Such appraisals included the extent to which the event could be controlled, responsibility, and anticipated effort. Those evaluations did not predict the same emotions across cultures.

This means that the full pattern of appraisal (across all dimensions) does not predict the same emotional experience across cultures.

A second hypothesis is that general classes of situations are not regularly appraised in the same ways across culture. Maybe just as individuals vary in how they appraise situations, there is also reliable cultural variation. There is ample evidence to support this hypothesis. For instance, Imada and Ellsworth (2011) examined how people from the Unites States and Japan appraised success and failure situations. They also asked their participants how they felt about the successes and failures. Results showed that Americans were more likely to take credit for success and blame their failures on others or the situation than were the Japanese. The American tendency to take credit for successes was further associated with more feelings of pride. Findings such as these demonstrate one reason why two national groups can have a hard time understanding each other's feelings (Roseman et al., 1995). In particular, they show that what looks like the same event is actually not met with the same emotional response for people all over the world.

Thus far, our review of differences in how people experience or express emotion has focused on studies that compare multiple countries. We now turn to comparisons of culture—a concept that has emerged relatively recently.

Culture and Cultural Difference

Culture is a set of explicit and implicit patterns of historically derived beliefs and their embodiment in institutions, practices, and artifacts (Kroeber & Kluckhohn, 1952; Matsumoto, 2007). It has evolved as a means to efficiently teach and perpetuate social rules and expectations, including what people should achieve in their lives, the ways that they relate to each other, and what they should emphasize and value (Kitayama, 2002; Shweder, 2003). For example, child-rearing practices tend to reflect what the culture values in an adult. The practices are designed to facilitate the attainment of valued skills and characteristics. Without the rules provided by culture, people probably would not live successfully in groups; social life would be chaos. Because emotions are basic motivators of social behavior, norms for the display and regulation of emotion are likely to be a very important part of culture (Matsumoto & Hwang, 2011). But how does one divide people of the world into different cultural groups? And which way to describe culture is the most useful for making predictions about cultural relativity of emotion? As we shall see, there is not one single way to describe culture, and the next section outlines different ways in which researchers have defined cultural groups.

Culture Constructs

In order to compare cultures, scientists first define clusters of values, beliefs, or environmental forces that are somehow related and shown to be fundamental (Matsumoto, 2003; Mesquita & Markus, 2004; Smith & Schwartz, 1999). In this way, they can then assign individuals and even countries into larger cultural groupings. These groupings might not be the same things as countries.

There are at least three general ways to sort people and countries into cultural groupings that relate to emotions. One is to sort them according to social-orientation expectations, or the ways in which people typically relate to each other and their groups. Another is to make groupings according to the life goals taught by basic religious orientations. A final is to assign individuals or countries to cultural groups based on their cultural homogeneity or heterogeneity.

Social-Orientation Expectations

In order to live together and prosper, all human societies come to some agreement on how to define the relationship between the individual and the groups to which they belong. An individual and a group might be you and your university, you and your country, or you and your family. Two ways of defining this relationship are called **individualism** versus **collectivism**.

Individualism and Collectivism

Cultures are classified by researchers as individualistic or collectivistic as a function of how the society defines the basic determinants and aims of their behaviors and their identities or self-concepts (Triandis, 1995). The definitions are summarized in Table 12.1. Self-concepts, or identities, in individualistic cultures have been characterized as independent: one views oneself as a unique person with characteristic traits that are separable from a group. In contrast, self-concepts in collectivistic cultures are said to be interdependent: one views one's identity as connected to one or two larger groups (initially a family and later perhaps a professional group) and inseparable from it (Markus & Kitayama, 2004; Mesquita & Markus, 2004). This may be particularly true for members of groups with strong hierarchies because in such groups most of the people do not hold a position of power (Yamaguchi, 1994). Importantly, independence versus interdependence does not refer to differences in desire for intimacy or caring for others, but the extent to which people feel like they are embedded in fields of relational force (Adams, Anderson, & Adonu, 2004).

Valued goals differ as well between the two types of cultures. In particular, individualistic cultures may foster the pursuit of personal goals over those of one's in-group, whereas collectivistic cultures may foster the pursuit of in-group goals (Yamaguchi, 1994). Relatedly, individualistic cultures are thought to encourage exchange relationships between individuals, whereas collectivistic cultures in theory promote communal relationships. Finally, in individualistic cultures, one's internal states such as personal attitudes and emotions are thought to be important causes of behavior. In contrast, norms are somewhat more significant causes of behavior in collectivistic cultures (Suh et al., 1998).

Research suggests that East Asian and some African countries endorse collectivistic values and North American countries endorse individualistic values. European countries have been described either as individualistic cultures or a mix of the two (Kitayama et al., 2009). Very likely the current concepts of individualism and collectivism are too simplistic and do not yet do an exhaustive job of describing the values of individuals all over the world (Vignoles et al. 2016).

Table 12.1 Summary of the basic determinants and aims of behaviors and identities or self-concepts in individualistic and collectivistic cultures

Concept	Individualism	Collectivism
Self	Independent (identity from individual traits)	Interdependent (identity from belonging)
Goal	Discover and express one's uniqueness	Maintain connections, fit in, perform role
What matters	Personal achievement and fulfillment; rights and liberties; self-esteem	Group goals and solidarity; social responsibilities and relationships; family duty
Coping method	Change reality	Accommodate to reality
Morality	Defined by individuals (self-based)	Defined by social networks (duty-based)
Relationships	Many, often temporary or casual; confrontation acceptable	Few, close and enduring; harmony valued
Attributing behavior	Behavior reflects one's personality and attitudes	Behavior reflects social norms and roles

Broad hypotheses involving cultural variation in emotion across individualistic versus collectivistic cultures have been tested. We examine first the role of context in interpreting facial expression of emotion and the rules for the regulation of emotion.

When people feel embedded in a social field—intrinsically related to others in their group—they tend to perceive the world in a slightly different way than those who feel like a separate person, separable from their group (Uchida et al., 2009). Research has shown that individuals in collectivist cultures perceive information in a more holistic way than do those in individualistic cultures (Oyserman & Lee, 2007; see Chapter 3 for a reminder of what it means to process information holistically, in that case due to positive affect). This is not because they are happier, but presumably because they are encouraged by cultural imperatives to pay attention to and integrate larger chunks of social information (e.g., the circumstances in which an action is occurring) and not just individual details (e.g., one action produced by one person; Miyamoto & Wilken, 2013; Nisbett et al., 2001). Relating this to emotion, studies suggest that individuals from collectivistic cultures are influenced by the emotional tone of a surrounding context in judging the emotion expression on a single person's face somewhat more than those from individualistic cultures (Matsumoto, Hwang, & Yamada, 2012). For example, Ito, Masuda, and Li (2013) showed East Asian and European Canadian participants images in which a target person, who was expressing sadness or happiness, was surrounded by other individuals who either expressed the same emotion or a different one as shown in Figure 12.5.

Participants had to judge the intensity of sadness or happiness felt by the central figure. As expected, East Asians were more influenced than European Canadians by the emotions expressed by the crowds surrounding the central figure. So, for example, if the central figure was expressing sadness, East Asian participants rated the central figure as sadder if the surrounding crowd was also expressing that emotion. This finding and other similar ones (e.g., Masuda et al., 2008) have been interpreted to mean that individuals in collectivistic cultures take the emotional information from members of a social group into account when assessing the meaning of a facial expression of any given individual more than do those from individualistic cultures. The latter might be more likely to see an experience of emotion in one individual as separate from the experiences of the group.

Members of individualistic cultures, as noted, think of emotions as personal reactions to an object or an event. Emotional expression is a display of individual reaction and preference. However, members of collectivistic cultures more often worry that individual expression of emotion will negatively influence social relations (Kim & Sherman, 2007; Matsumoto, Yoo, & Fontaine, 2008). Too much anger might disrupt the overall harmony of the group. Too much happiness may be seen as a sign of gloating (Miyamoto & Ma, 2011). Too much of almost any emotion (with some exceptions) might draw unacceptable attention to oneself and one's own needs. Thus, in general, the value for collectivistic cultures is to suppress displays of emotion. **Display rules** are "what people learn, probably quite early in their lives, about the need to manage the appearance of particular emotions in particular situations" (Ekman & Friesen, 1975, p. 137). By the time children are three years old, their caretakers have begun to teach display rules quite explicitly (Miller & Sperry, 1987). Probably the first study to demonstrate the existence of cultural differences in display rules involved the participation of Japanese and American individuals who were

Figure 12.5 Example facial expression stimuli used in Ito, Masuda, and Li (2013). In the top image the central figure is expressing the same emotion as the others, and in the bottom image he is expressing a different emotion.

exposed to a stress-inducing film (Ekman, 1973; Friesen, 1972). When the participants watched the film alone, they all showed evidence of facial disgust, fear, and distress, and differences were not detected. When the participants then watched the films in the presence of a higher-status experimenter, American participants continued to express the negative emotions of disgust, fear, and distress, whereas the Japanese tended to mask their negative feelings with smiles.

More specific cultural analyses of display rules have also been advanced (e.g., Matsumoto, 1990; Matsumoto et al., 1998). Matsumoto (1990) proposed that East Asian and North American display rules for in-group and out-group settings should differ. Specifically, he suggested that the Japanese should possess display rules according to which the expression of negative emotions to the out-group is permissible because it emphasizes the in-group–out-group boundary and enhances in-group identity and solidarity. That is, an us–them distinction is clear if we act differently around them than we do around our own. At the same time, the Japanese should not condone expression of negative emotions to the in-group, because this would disrupt group harmony. The Americans, he proposed, should condone just the opposite set of rules. Specifically, for Americans, it should be fine to express negative emotions to the in-group because in that context one can demonstrate one's individuality. By the same token, displaying negative emotions to the out-group would not be condoned because one might become a member of that group in the future.

In the study, Japanese and American participants were exposed to pictures of faces expressing anger, disgust, fear, happiness, sadness, and surprise. They rated the extent to which it was "appropriate" to display these expressions to different groups, some of which were in-groups and others of which were out-groups. Some support for the hypotheses was observed. Specifically, Americans thought that it was more appropriate to express disgust and sadness to the in-group and rated happiness as more appropriate to express in public than did the Japanese. At the same time, the Japanese thought that it was more appropriate to express anger to the out-group than did the Americans.

Differences in overall display rules for emotion have wide-ranging consequences. Chapter 9 identified some psychological, biological, and health costs of suppressing the expression of emotions (e.g., Gross & John, 2003). In particular, as we saw, suppression is linked to poorer memory, lower likeability within one's social group, less social support, and increased physiological arousal (Gross, 2008; Richards & Gross, 1999; Srivastava et al., 2009). Perhaps unsurprisingly, however, the same costs of suppressing bodily displays of emotion are not seen to the same extent in individuals from collectivist cultures (Soto et al., 2011). This means that suppressing emotions is not necessarily inherently unhealthy, but that suppressing is unhealthy when emotional expression is valued and expected.

Cultures of Honor

Another kind of social-orientation value concerns the value of honor. **Honor** refers to an individual's self-respect or sense of self-esteem as determined by his own reputation or status and by the reputation of his own group, especially family. In so-called cultures of honor, family members are supposed to uphold the reputation of the family, especially through their public behavior and avoidance of humiliation (Miller, 1993). Mediterranean and South American countries have been described as honor cultures (Pitt-Rivers, 1965), as have the cultures of the American South and the American West (Cohen, 1998; Nisbett, 1993). The value of honor in such cultures is not trivial, but is a fundamental one that influences much social behavior and social organization (Boiger et al., 2014).

Developmental Detail

Children Learn Emotional "Fit" to Their Culture

Emotional expression and regulation are two parts of the experience of emotion that are highly susceptible to cultural influence. It makes sense that parents would exert considerable effort to teach children display rules and strategies that promote a successful fit in their cultural community (Harkness & Super, 1996). In a series of questionnaire studies, Keller and Otto (2009) measured parents' beliefs about the expression and regulation of emotions in their infants. In particular, these scientists wanted to compare the socialization of emotion practices in an urban, middle-class Western community and an agricultural non-Western community. To represent the latter type of community, Keller and Otta interviewed Nso farmers in the African country of Cameroon. The Nso were compared to a sample of middle-class parents from cities in Germany.

The Nso can be described as a community of people who prioritize social relatedness, whereas the Western urbanites prioritize personal autonomy (Keller, 2003). Indeed, results of an initial questionnaire study revealed that the German mothers prioritized autonomous socialization goals and that Nso mothers prioritized social relatedness goals. (Note, though, that both autonomy and relatedness are basic human needs that need to be met in any type of community.) Consistent with these goals, Keller and Otto expected that Nso parents would strive not to teach the expression of emotion, but rather control over emotional expression in their infants. In the German urban environment, they expected that the expression of positive emotionality would be particularly encouraged because positive emotions signal and advance autonomy. They were right! The results of a second questionnaire study showed that Nso mothers believed that infants should learn to control the expression of their emotions during the first three years of life, whereas German mothers did not hold this socialization goal.

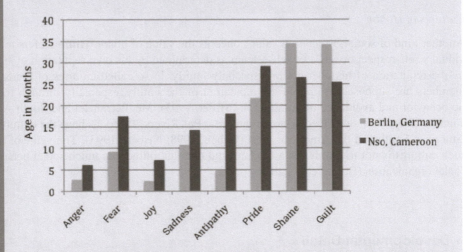

Age at which Nso and German mothers thought expression of specific emotions was appropriate. From Keller and Otto (2009).

Nso and German mothers were also interviewed about the age at which they thought it was acceptable to express specific emotions. As can be seen in the figure, consistent with their socialization goals, the Nso mothers thought that the expression of specific emotions should emerge later than the German mothers. The exceptions were expression of shame and guilt. As we learned in Chapter 6, these expressions let everyone else know that you want to be accepted back into the group, so they serve well the goal of social relatedness.

Researchers have investigated a number of specific proposed differences in the experience of emotion in cultures of honor compared mostly to northern European (as represented both in Europe and in the American North) cultures, in which honor is not an inherent value (e.g., Cohen et al., 1996; Fischer, Manstead, & Rodriguez Mosquera, 2000; Rodriguez Mosquera, Manstead, & Fischer, 2002). One such hypothesis is that anger and violence as responses to insults to honor are both more often felt and more often expressed by individuals in honor cultures (Cohen & Nisbett, 1994; Cohen et al., 1996).

Support for this hypothesis comes from a series of three studies by Cohen and colleagues (1996). The researchers invited male university students who had grown up in the American South or the American North into the laboratory. In the context of completing some questionnaires, the experimenters made the participants believe they had inconvenienced another person, who was actually a confederate of the experimenter, by making him move aside to let them walk down a hallway. When obliged to let the participant pass by a second time, the confederate bumped into the participant and called him an "asshole." Other confederates of the experimenter sitting in the hallway discreetly observed and noted the behavior of the participant as a function of the insult. In addition, some hormonal measures were taken under the guise of a concern with physiological correlates of general performance. Specifically, the stress hormone cortisol was measured to assess the degree of anger or upset, and testosterone was measured to assess the participants' physiological readiness for aggression (levels of both were measured simply by obtaining a saliva sample). Among other things, compared with Northerners, who were relatively impervious to the insult, Southerners were more likely to engage in aggressive and dominant behaviors (as observed by the confederates), were made more upset by the insult (as indicated by a rise in cortisol levels), and were more physiologically readied for aggression (as indicated by a rise in testosterone levels). Anger has also been reported to be elicited by insults to honor more in Spain (an honor culture) than in the Netherlands (Fischer et al., 1999; Rodriguez Mosquera et al., 2002).

Religious Values: Dialetical vs. Optimizing Doctrines of Positive Emotions

Dominant religious doctrines provide cultural rules for the experience of emotion (e.g., Bagozzi, Wong, & Yi, 1999; Leu, Mesquita, & Ellsworth, 2005; Peng & Nisbett, 1999, 2000). The religions of Daoism, Buddhism, and Confucianism are the major religions in East Asia. They teach a **dialectical** understanding of the experience of positive and negative emotions. In a dialectical doctrine, good feelings and experiences are fundamentally linked to bad feelings and bad experiences (Ji, Nisbett, & Peng, 2001). Daoism, for example, teaches that "happiness is unhappiness." In a related way, Buddhism and Confucianism view striving for happiness specifically as inappropriate. In Buddhism, such a pursuit interferes with an individual's ability to resist succumbing to desire; such resistance is taught as the way to overcome basic human suffering. In Confucianism, the pursuit of happiness can disrupt group harmony because it can elicit jealousy in others (Edwards, 1996) or threaten social order through its emphasis on individualism (Heine et al., 1999). As a result of these religious beliefs, the East Asian rules for emotion involve striving for a balance between positive and negative feelings (Leu et al., 2005). This relationship or balance is represented by the yin and yang symbol, which is explained in Figure 12.6.

Western religious traditions teach a different set of beliefs about emotion. Early Christianity prescribed negative experience as the way to show one's religious virtue. Thus, in pre-Reformation and early Reformation cultures, being virtuous involved physical and emotional suffering. Over the nineteenth century and the modernization of Western society, because of its relation to passivity (or sloth), sadness slowly lost its religious punch. In its place, especially in North America, cheerfulness came to signify virtue because of its link to personal resourcefulness and agency (Kotchemidova, 2005). Happiness in post-Enlightenment

Figure 12.6 An explanation of how the yin and the yang symbol represents Eastern religious beliefs about the close relationship between happiness and unhappiness. Those states are thought to be different components of the same experience.

religious traditions became a valued endpoint, in contrast with the East Asian model. In the West we therefore are said to have an **optimizing** view of positive emotion (Leu et al., 2005), in the sense that we strive to maximize positive emotions and minimize negative ones.

The results of studies of positive and negative emotion in East Asia compared to North America document people's dialectical versus optimizing beliefs about emotion. Across both cultures, positive emotions are generally more desirable and socially appropriate than negative emotions. However, this difference is greater in Western cultures than East Asian ones, and negative emotions are more undesirable in Western cultures than in East Asian cultures (Eid & Diener, 2001). Furthermore, when asked to describe happiness, Americans mention positive features of happiness, such as the fact that it feels pleasurable. In contrast, East Asians are more likely to also mention negative features of happiness, such as the fact that it can be fleeting or have negative social repercussions (e.g., eliciting envy in others; Uchida & Kitayama, 2009).

Another hypothesis that can be derived from the dialectical versus optimizing view of emotion is that East Asians ought to report feeling more moderate positive and negative feelings, and to more often feel both in a given situation, whereas Westerners should report feeling more positive feelings and only positive or negative feelings—but not often both—in any given situation. Kitayama and colleagues found support for this prediction (Kitayama, Markus, & Kurokawa, 2000). In related work, Mesquita and Karasawa (2002) showed that on self-reports with scales ranging from very pleasant to very unpleasant, East Asian participants tended to use the midpoint of the scale when reporting their feelings. Americans tended to report high pleasant feelings more often using the extreme positive end of the scale. Studies of emotion regulation also indicate that Westerners are less likely to try to dampen their positive emotions and are more likely to savor them than East Asians (Miyamoto & Ma, 2011), thereby likely contributing to Westerners' experiencing more positive feelings than East Asians.

In addition, positive and negative emotions are negatively correlated in the reports of emotional experience of Westerners but not of East Asians (Perunovic, Heller, & Rafaeli, 2007; Schimmack, Oishi, & Diener, 2002; Shiota et al., 2010). The stronger negative correlation in the former cultures means that the experience of positive emotion implied the absence of negative emotions.

Of course, some people actually live a life that is called bicultural in the sense that they speak multiple languages and engage in the practices of more than one culture in their daily lives. This is true of many individuals in Canada and the United States. In an online diary study of bicultural individuals, Perunovic, Heller, and Rafaeli (2007) showed that when East Asian Canadian biculturals were identifying with their East Asian culture or were interacting in their Asian language, their reports of positive and negative emotions were not strongly correlated. However, when they were identifying with Western culture and were interacting speaking a non-Asian language, their positive and negative emotions were negatively correlated. These findings suggest that bicultural individuals may fluidly adopt the emotional experiences that are consistently recognized and associated with the culture that they are currently operating in. This result is depicted in Figure 12.7.

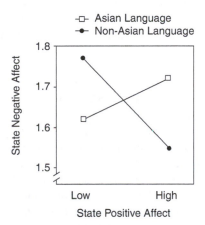

Figure 12.7 The with-in person associations between self-reports of positive affect and negative affect as a function of language of interaction by Asian Canadian participants in a study by Perunovic, Heller, and Rafaeli (2007).

Affect Valuation Theory

Not only can our religious-based cultural beliefs influence how we experience emotion, but they can also influence which kinds of emotional experiences we value. The **Affect Valuation Theory** proposes that ideal affect ("what is the right way to feel?") is distinct from actual feelings ("how am I feeling?") and that we strive for ideal affect over actual affect. Thus, the dialectical view teaches East Asians to seek specific kinds of low-arousal positive emotion (i.e., calm feelings), whereas Westerners' optimizing view teaches them to seek more activated types of positive feelings (i.e., aroused happiness or excitement; Tsai, Miao, & Seppala, 2007).

These teachings can be seen in analysis of the content of children's books (Tsai et al., 2007) and in several other studies. In one such study, participants who endorsed a dialectical view of ideal affect tended to prefer physicians who also seemed to try to promote low-arousal pleasant states in their patients, whereas participants who endorsed a more optimizing view tended to prefer physicians who promoted the attainment of activated positive emotions. Frequency of participants' actual emotional states did not predict their preferences in physicians. So, it seems that people choose physicians based on whether the affective states a physician wants to achieve matches how people ideally want to feel (Sims et al., 2014). Differences in ideal affect influence people's consumer preferences as well. For example, people with optimizing beliefs tend to prefer exciting (vs. calming) consumer products such as music and teas (Mogilner, Aaker, & Kamvar, 2012; Tsai, Chim, & Sims, 2015).

Social-Ecological Factors: Historical Homogeneity–Heterogeneity

Like religion, social-ecological aspects of the environment can also produce cultures of emotion. A country or region's history of migration and immigration is one of those factors. Some countries and regions of the world—including most of the countries of Asia and Europe—are populated by descendants of generations of the inhabitants of the same country or region. Other countries and regions—including most of North and South America and some of Africa and the Middle East—are populated by descendants of people who migrated to these regions from many other countries over the centuries. Imagine what it would be like if your neighbors or the proprietors of the stores you frequented spoke a language different from yours and came from a country where the norms for emotion experience and expression were different from yours, too. Probably, over time, you and your neighbors would start to develop a culture of emotional transparency. In the absence of shared language and culture of emotion, you would favor using clear and perhaps even exaggerated expressions of emotion in order to communicate desires and intentions.

This is the hypothesis that Rychlowska and others tested in research involving reports of display rules from different countries (Rychlowska et al., 2015). That study showed that **historical heterogeneity**—defined as the number of source countries that have contributed to a given country's present-day population over the last 500 years (Putterman & Weil, 2010)—is positively correlated with the display rules for emotional expressivity. In other words, in countries where people from many national backgrounds and emotion practices have lived over many centuries, transparent expression of emotional states is favored to a greater degree than in countries in which the population has remained homogeneous over many centuries. The migration history of the country was a better predictor of display rules than many other aspects of a country's culture, such as individualism-collectivism or present-day cultural diversity (see Figure 12.8).

The differences also go beyond self-reported display rules. In another study, Wood, Rychlowska, and Niedenthal (2016) re-analyzed data from 90 existing studies that examined the accuracy of recognition of emotional expression cross-culturally. These studies involved people from 76 different cultures making judgments about the emotion expressions produced by expressers from many other cultures. Results of the reanalysis showed that compared to homogeneous cultures, individuals from heterogeneous cultures made facial expressions that were more easily recognized by people from all over the world. This was true even when controlling for the perceiver and expresser cultures' individualism–collectivism. Thus, when people from diverse backgrounds co-exist over centuries (not right away), a culture of emotional transparency can develop. This is seen both in reports of display rules and in the ease of recognizing facial expressions of people from historically heterogeneous cultures.

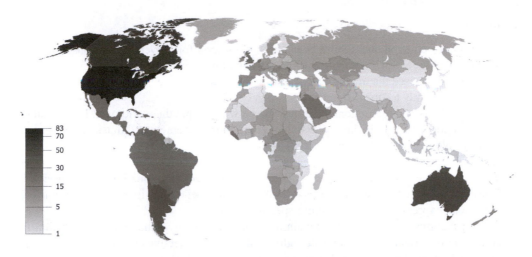

Figure 12.8 Map of historical heterogeneity. Darker countries are more heterogeneous, meaning their present-day populations originate from a greater number of source countries (values on the legend refer to number of source countries). Map generated at http://gunn.co.nz/map and based on data from World Migration Matrix (www.econ.brown.edu/fac/louis_putterman/world%20migration%20matrix.htm).

Summary

- The study of emotion and culture began with the search for universal emotions and later addressed cultural variation in the different components of emotion. Researchers have recently emphasized the importance of testing hypotheses derived from theories of culture rather than merely testing differences between countries.

- Certain aspects of our emotional lives are shared with people the world over. In particular, there is some similarity in the expression of emotion in movement and music, as well as in the physiological component of emotion.

- At the same time, other aspects of emotional experience differ widely. Variation in how some appraisals are related to the experience of discrete emotions has been observed. Cross-national studies show differences in how emotion-eliciting situations are appraised. And facial expressions contain culture-specific dialects.

- Several theories of culture help explain and generate new hypotheses about variation in emotional experience. These include individualism and collectivism, and also cultures of honor, which are both ways to describe social orientations.

- Features of dominant religions and socioecological factors are also specifically related to how emotions are understood and regulated, as well as how clearly they are expressed, respectively.

Learning Links

1. Read about how the interpretation of emojis varies across culture. http://www.npr.org/sections/thetwo-way/2016/04/12/473965971/lost-in-translation-study-finds-interpretation-of-emojis-can-vary-widely
2. Explore an interactive web application that tracks and visually represents the emotional content of tweets across the globe. http://wefeel.csiro.au/#/
3. Read a discussion of smiles and culture. https://www.translatemedia.com/us/blog-us/the-meaning-of-a-smile-in-different-cultures/

References

Adams, G., Anderson, S. L., & Adonu, J. K. (2004). The cultural grounding of closeness and intimacy. In D. Mashek & A. Aron (Eds.), *The handbook of closeness and intimacy* (pp. 321–339). Mahwah, NJ: Lawrence Erlbaum Associates.

Bagozzi, R. P., Wong, N., & Yi, Y. (1999). The role of culture and gender in the relationship between positive and negative affect. *Cognition & Emotion, 13*(6), 641–672. doi:10.1080/026999399379023.

Barrett, L. F. (2006). Are emotions natural kinds? *Perspectives on Psychological Science, 1*(1), 28–58. doi:10.1111/j.1745–6916.2006.00003.x.

Boiger, M., Güngör, D., Karasawa, M., & Mesquita, B. (2014). Defending honour, keeping face: Interpersonal affordances of anger and shame in Turkey and Japan. *Cognition and Emotion, 29(7)*, 1255–1269. doi:10.1080/02699931.2014.881324.

Cohen, D. (1998). Culture, social organization, and patterns of violence. *Journal of Personality and Social Psychology, 75*(2), 408. doi:10.1037/0022–3514.75.2.408.

Cohen, D., & Nisbett, R. E. (1994). Self-protection and the culture of honor: Explaining southern violence. *Personality and Social Psychology Bulletin, 20*(5), 551–567. doi:10.1177/0146167294205012.

Cohen, D., Nisbett, R. E., Bowdle, B. F., & Schwarz, N. (1996). Insult, aggression, and the southern culture of honor: An "experimental ethnography." *Journal of Personality and Social Psychology, 70*(5), 945. doi:10.1037/0022–3514.70.5.945.

Edwards, P. (1996). Honour, shame, humiliation and modern Japan. In O. Leaman (Ed.), *Friendship East and West: Philosophical perspectives* (pp. 32–55). New York: Curzon.

Eid, M., & Diener, E. (2001). Norms for experiencing emotions in different cultures: Inter-and intranational differences. *Journal of Personality and Social Psychology*, *81*(5), 869. doi:10.1037/0022–3514.81.5.869.

Ekman, P. (1972). Universal and cultural differences in facial expression of emotion. In J. R. Cole (Ed.), *Nebraska symposium on motivation, 1971* (pp. 207–283). Lincoln: Nebraska University Press.

Ekman, P. (1973). Cross-cultural studies of facial expressions. In P. Ekman (Ed.), *Darwin and facial expression: A century of research in review* (pp. 169–229). Cambridge, MA: Malor Books.

Ekman, P., & Friesen, W. V. (1971). Constants across cultures in the face and emotion. *Journal of Personality and Social Psychology*, *17*(2), 124. doi:10.1037/h0030377.

Ekman, P., & Friesen, W. V. (1975). *Unmasking the face: A guide to recognizing the emotions from facial cues*. Englewood Cliffs, NJ: Prentice Hall.

Ekman, P., & Friesen, W. V. (1978). *The facial action coding system (FACS): A technique for the measurement of facial movement*. Palo Alto, CA: Consulting Psychologists' Press.

Elfenbein, H. A., & Ambady, N. (2002). On the universality and cultural specificity of emotion recognition: A meta-analysis. *Psychological Bulletin*, *128*(2), 203. doi:10.1037/0033–2909.128.2.203.

Elfenbein, H. A., & Ambady, N. (2003). When familiarity breeds accuracy: Cultural exposure and facial emotion recognition. *Journal of Personality and Social Psychology*, *85*(2), 276. doi:10.1037/0022–3514.85.2.276.

Elfenbein, H. A., Beaupré, M., Lévesque, M., & Hess, U. (2007). Toward a dialect theory: Cultural differences in the expression and recognition of posed facial expressions. *Emotion*, *7*(1), 131–146. doi:10.1037/1528–3542.7.1.131.

Elfenbein, H. A., Mandal, M. K., Ambady, N., Harizuka, S., & Kumar, S. (2002). Cross-cultural patterns in emotion recognition: Highlighting design and analytical techniques. *Emotion*, *2*(1), 75. doi:10.1037/1528–3542.2.1.75.

Friesen, W. V. (1972). Cultural differences in facial expressions in a social situation: An experimental test of the concept of display rules. (Unpublished doctoral dissertation). University of California, San Francisco, CA.

Frijda, N. H. (1986). *The emotions*. Cambridge: Cambridge University Press.

Frijda, N. H., Markam, S., Sato, K., & Wiers, R. (1995). Emotions and emotion words. In J. Russell, J. Fernandez-Dols, A. Manstead & J. C. Wellenkamp (Eds.), *Everyday conceptions of emotion* (pp. 121–143). Dordrecht, The Netherlands: Kluwer Academic Publishers. doi:10.1007/978–94–015–8484–5_7.

Gendron, M., Roberson, D., van der Vyver, J. M., & Barrett, L. F. (2014). Perceptions of emotion from facial expressions are not culturally universal: Evidence from a remote culture. *Emotion*, *14*(2), 251. doi:10.1037/a0036052.

Greeley, A. M. (1979). The American Irish: A report from Great Ireland. *International Journal of Comparative Sociology*, *20*(1–2), 67–81. doi:10.1177/002071527902000105.

Greeley, A. M. (1981). *The Irish-Americans*. New York: Harper & Row.

Gross, J. J. (2008). Emotion regulation. In M. Lewis, J. M. Haviland-Jones & L. F. Barrett (Eds.), *Handbook of emotions* (pp. 497–512). New York: Guilford Press.

Gross, J. J., & John, O. P. (2003). Individual differences in two emotion regulation processes: Implications for affect, relationships, and well-being. *Journal of Personality and Social Psychology*, *85*(2), 348. doi:10.1037/0022–3514.85.2.348.

Haidt, J., & Keltner, D. (1999). Culture and facial expression: Open-ended methods find more expressions and a gradient of recognition. *Cognition & Emotion*, *13*(3), 225–266. doi:10.1080/026999399379267.

Harkness, S., & Super, C. M. (Eds.). (1996). *Parents' cultural belief systems: Their origins, expressions, and consequences*. New York: Guilford Press.

Heine, S. J., Lehman, D. R., Markus, H. R., & Kitayama, S. (1999). Is there a universal need for positive self-regard? *Psychological Review*, *106*(4), 766–794.

Imada, T., & Ellsworth, P. C. (2011). Proud Americans and lucky Japanese: Cultural differences in appraisal and corresponding emotion. *Emotion*, *11*(2), 329–345. doi:10.1037/a0022855.

Ito, K., Masuda, T., & Li, L. M. W. (2013). Agency and facial emotion judgment in context. *Personality and Social Psychology Bulletin*, *39*(6), 763–776. doi:10.1177/0146167213481387.

Izard, C. E. (1971). *The face of emotion*. New York: Appleton-Century- Crofts.

Ji, L. J., Nisbett, R. E., & Su, Y. (2001). Culture, change, and prediction. *Psychological Science*, *12*(6), 450–456. doi:10.1111/1467-9280.00384.

Kang, S.-M., & Lau, A. S. (2013). Revisiting the out-group advantage in emotion recognition in a multi-cultural society: Further evidence for the in-group advantage. *Emotion, 13*(2), 203–215. doi:10.1037/a0030013.

Keller, H. (2003). Socialization for competence: Cultural models of infancy. *Human Development, 46*(5), 288–311. doi:10.1159/000071937.

Keller, H., & Otto, H. (2009). The cultural socialization of emotion regulation during infancy. *Journal of Cross-Cultural Psychology, 40*(6), 996–1011. doi:10.1177/0022022109348576.

Kim, H. S., & Sherman, D. K. (2007). " Express yourself": Culture and the effect of self-expression on choice. *Journal of Personality and Social Psychology, 92*(1), 1. doi:10.1037/0022–3514.92.1.1.

Kitayama, S. (2002). Culture and basic psychological processes—toward a system view of culture: Comment on Oyserman et al.(2002). *Psychological Bulletin, 128*(1), 89–96.

Kitayama, S., Markus, H. R., & Kurokawa, M. (2000). Culture, emotion, and well-being: Good feelings in Japan and the United States. *Cognition & Emotion, 14*(1), 93–124. doi:10.1080/026999300379003.

Kitayama, S., Park, H., Sevincer, A. T., Karasawa, M., & Uskul, A. K. (2009). A cultural task analysis of implicit independence: Comparing North America, Western Europe, and East Asia. *Journal of Personality and Social Psychology, 97*(2), 236. doi:10.1037/a0015999.

Kotchemidova, C. (2005). From good cheer to" drive-by smiling": A social history of cheerfulness. *Journal of Social History, 39*(1), 5–37. doi:10.1353/jsh.2005.0108.

Kroeber, A. L., & Kluckhohn, C. (1952). Culture: A critical review of concepts and definitions. *Papers. Peabody Museum of Archaeology & Ethnology, Harvard University.*

Leach, E. (1972). The influence of cultural context on non-verbal communication in man. In R. Hinde (Ed.), *Non-verbal communication* (pp. 315–349). London: Cambridge University Press.

Levenson, R. W., Carstensen, L. L., Friesen, W. V., & Ekman, P. (1991). Emotion, physiology, and expression in old age. *Psychology and Aging, 6*(1), 28. doi:10.1037/0882–7974.6.1.28.

Levenson, R. W., Ekman, P., & Friesen, W. V. (1990). Voluntary facial action generates emotion-specific autonomic nervous system activity. *Psychophysiology, 27*(4), 363–384. doi:10.1111/j.1469–8986.1990.tb02330.x.

Levenson, R. W., Ekman, P., Heider, K., & Friesen, W. V. (1992). Emotion and autonomic nervous system activity in the Minangkabau of West Sumatra. *Journal of Personality and Social Psychology, 62*(6), 972. doi:10.1037/0022–3514.62.6.972.

Lindquist, K. A. (2013). Emotions emerge from more basic psychological ingredients: A modern psychological constructionist model. *Emotion Review,5*(4), 356–368. doi:10.1177/1754073913489750.

Lutz, C. (1987). Goals, events, and understanding in Ifaluk emotion theory. In N. Quinn & D. Holland (Eds.), *Cultural models in language and thought* (pp. 290–312). Cambridge: Cambridge University Press.

Lutz, C. (1988). *Unnatural emotions: Everyday sentiments on a Micronesian atoll and their challenge to western theory*. Chicago, IL: University of Chicago Press.

Markus, H. R., & Kitayama, S. (1994). A collective fear of the collective: Implications for selves and theories of selves. *Personality and Social Psychology Bulletin, 20*(5), 568–579. doi:10.1177/0146167294205013.

Masuda, T., Ellsworth, P. C., Mesquita, B., Leu, J., Tanida, S., & Van de Veerdonk, E. (2008). Placing the face in context: Cultural differences in the perception of facial emotion. *Journal of Personality and Social Psychology, 94*(3), 365. doi:10.1037/0022–3514.94.3.365.

Matsumoto, D. (1990). Cultural similarities and differences in display rules. *Motivation and Emotion, 14*(3), 195–214. doi:10.1007/bf00995569.

Matsumoto, D. (2003). The discrepancy between consensual-level culture and individual-level culture. *Culture & Psychology, 9*(1), 89–95. doi:10.1177/1354067x03009001006.

Matsumoto, D. (2005). Apples and oranges: Methodological requirements for testing a possible ingroup advantage in emotion judgments from facial expressions. In U. Hess & P. Philippot (Eds.), *Group dynamics and emotional expression* (pp. 140–181). New York, NY: Cambridge University Press.

Matsumoto, D. (2007). Culture, context, and behavior. *Journal of Personality, 75*(6), 1285–1320. doi:10.1111/j.1467–6494.2007.00476.x.

Matsumoto, D., & Hwang, H. S. (2011). Evidence for training the ability to read microexpressions of emotion. *Motivation and Emotion, 35*(2), 181–191. doi:10.1007/s11031–011–9212–2.

Matsumoto, D., Hwang, H. S., & Yamada, H. (2012). Cultural differences in the relative contributions of face and context to judgments of emotion. *Journal of Cross-Cultural Psychology, 43*, 198–218. doi:10.1177/0022022110387426.

Matsumoto, D., Takeuchi, S., Andayani, S., Kouznetsova, N., & Krupp, D. (1998). The contribution of individualism vs. collectivism to cross-national differences in display rules. *Asian Journal of Social Psychology, 1*(2), 147–165. doi:10.1111/1467–839x.00010.

Matsumoto, D., Yoo, S. H., & Fontaine, J. (2008). Mapping expressive differences around the world: The relationship between emotional display rules and individualism versus collectivism. *Journal of Cross-Cultural Psychology, 39*(1), 55–74. doi:10.1177/0022022107311854.

Mauro, R., Sato, K., & Tucker, J. (1992). The role of appraisal in human emotions: A cross-cultural study. *Journal of Personality and Social Psychology, 62*(2), 301. doi:10.1037/0022–3514.62.2.301.

Mesquita, B. (2001). Emotions in collectivist and individualist contexts. *Journal of Personality and Social Psychology, 80*, 68–74. doi:10.1037/0022–3514.80.1.68.

Mesquita, B. (2003). Emotions as dynamic cultural phenomena. In R. Davidson, H. Goldsmith & K. R. Scherer (Eds.), *The handbook of the affective sciences* (pp. 871–890). New York: Oxford University Press.

Mesquita, B., & Ellsworth, P. (2001). The role of culture in appraisal. In K. R. Scherer & A. Schorr (Eds.), *Appraisal processes in emotion: Theory, methods, research* (pp. 233–248). New York: Oxford University Press.

Mesquita, B., & Frijda, N. H. (1992). Cultural variations in emotions: A review. *Psychological Bulletin, 112*(2). 179–204. doi:10.1037/0033–2909.112.2.179.

Mesquita, B., Frijda, N. H., & Scherer, K. R. (1997). Culture and emotion. In J. W. Berry, P. R. Dasen & T. S. Saraswathi (Eds.), *Handbook of cross-cultural psychology: Vol. 2. Basic processes and human development* (pp. 255–297). Boston, MA: Allyn & Bacon.

Mesquita, B., & Haire, A. (2004). Emotion and culture. *Encyclopedia of Applied Psychology, 1*, 731–737. doi:10.1016/b0–12–657410–3/00393–7.

Mesquita, B., & Karasawa, M. (2002). Different emotional lives. *Cognition & Emotion, 16*(1), 127–141. doi:10.1080/0269993014000176.

Mesquita, B., & Markus, H. R. (2004, April). Culture and emotion. In A. Manstead, N. Frijda, & A. Fischer (Eds.), *Feelings and emotions: The Amsterdam symposium* (p. 341). Cambridge: Cambridge University Press. doi:10.1017/cbo9780511806582.020.

Miller, P., & Sperry, L. L. (1987). The socialization of anger and aggression. *Merrill-Palmer Quarterly, 1982*, 1–31.

Miller, W. I. (1993). *Humiliation and other essays on honor, social discomfort, and violence*. Ithaca, NY: Cornell University Press.

Mitchell, G., Tetlock, P. E., Mellers, B. A., & Ordonez, L. D. (1993). Judgments of social justice: Compromises between equality and efficiency. *Journal of Personality and Social Psychology, 65*(4), 629–639. doi:10.1037/0022-3514.65.4.629.

Miyamoto, Y., & Ma, X. (2011). Dampening or savoring positive emotions: A dialectical cultural script guides emotion regulation. *Emotion, 11*(6), 1346. doi:10.1037/a0025135.

Miyamoto, Y., & Wilken, B. (2013). Cultural differences and their mechanisms. In D. Reisberg (Ed.), *Oxford handbook of cognitive psychology* (pp. 970–985). Oxford: Oxford University Press.

Mogilner, C., Aaker, J., & Kamvar, S. D. (2012). How happiness affects choice. *Journal of Consumer Research, 39*(2), 429–443. doi:10.1086/663774.

Montesquieu, C. de (1989). *The spirit of the laws*. Cambridge: Cambridge University Press. [Original work published in 1748].

Moors, A. (2013). On the causal role of appraisal in emotion. *Emotion Review, 5*(2), 132–140. doi:10.1177/1754073912463601.

Nelson, N. L., & Russell, J. A. (2013). Universality revisited. *Emotion Review, 5*(1), 8–15. doi:10.1177/1754073912457227.

Nisbett, R. E. (1993). Violence and US regional culture. *American Psychologist, 48*(4), 441. doi:10.1037/0003–066x.48.4.441.

Nisbett, R. E., Peng, K., Choi, I., & Norenzayan, A. (2001). Culture and systems of thought: Holistic versus analytic cognition. *Psychological Review*, 108(2), 291–310. doi:10.1037/0033–295x.108.2.291.

Nummenmaa, L., Glerean, E., Hari, R., & Hietanen, J. K. (2014). Bodily maps of emotions. *Proceedings of the National Academy of Sciences*, 111(2), 646–651. doi:10.1073/pnas.1321664111.

Oliveau, D., & Willmuth, R. (1979). Facial muscle electromyography in depressed and nondepressed hospitalized subjects: A partial replication. *The American Journal of Psychiatry, 136*, 548–550.

Oyserman, D., & Lee, S. W. S. (2007). Priming "culture". In S. Kitayama & D. Cohn, *Handbook of cultural psychology*, (pp. 255–279). New York, NY: Guilford Press.

Peng, K., & Nisbett, R. E. (1999). Culture, dialectics, and reasoning about contradiction. *American Psychologist, 54*(9), 741. doi:10.1037/0003–066x.54.9.741.

Peng, K., & Nisbett, R. (2000). Dialectical responses to questions about dialectical thinking. *American Psychologist, 55*(9), 1067–1068. doi:10.1037/0003–066x.55.9.1067.

Pennebaker, J. W., Rimé, B., & Blankenship, V. E. (1996). Stereotypes of emotional expressiveness of northerners and southerners: A cross-cultural test of Montesquieu's hypotheses. *Journal of Personality and Social Psychology, 70*(2), 372. doi:10.1037//0022–3514.70.2.372.

Perunovic, W. Q. E., Heller, D., & Rafaeli, E. (2007). Within-person changes in the structure of emotion the role of cultural identification and language. *Psychological Science, 18*(7), 607–613. doi:10.1111/j.1467–9280.2007.01947.x.

Philippot, P., & Rimé, B. (1997). The perception of bodily sensations during emotion: A cross-cultural perspective. *Polish Psychological Bulletin, 28*, 175–188.

Pitt-Rivers, J. (1965). Honor and social status. In J. G. Peristiany (Ed.), *Honor and shame: The value of Mediterranean society* (pp. 18–77). London: Weidenfeld & Nicolson.

Putterman, L., & Weil, D. N. (2010). Post-1500 Population Flows and the Long-Run Determinants of Economic Growth and Inequality. *The Quarterly Journal of Economics, 125*(4), 1627–1682. doi:10.3386/w14448.

Richards, J. M., & Gross, J. J. (1999). Composure at any cost? The cognitive consequences of emotion suppression. *Personality and Social Psychology Bulletin, 25*(8), 1033–1044. doi:10.1177/01461672992511010.

Rimé, B., Philippot, P., & Cisamolo, D. (1990). Social schemata of peripheral changes in emotion. *Journal of Personality and Social Psychology, 59*(1), 38–49. doi:10.1037/0022–3514.59.1.38.

Rodriguez Mosquera, P. M., Manstead, A. S., & Fischer, A. H. (2002). The role of honour concerns in emotional reactions to offences. *Cognition & Emotion,16*(1), 143–163. doi:10.1080/02699930143000167.

Roseman, I. J., Dhawan, N., Rettek, S. I., Naidu, R. K., & Thapa, K. (1995). Cultural differences and cross-cultural similarities in appraisals and emotional responses. *Journal of Cross-Cultural Psychology, 26*(1), 23–48. doi:10.1177/0022022195261003.

Rychlowska, M., Miyamoto, Y., Matsumoto, D., Hess, U., Gilboa-Schechtman, E., Kamble, S., . . . Niedenthal, P. M. (2015). Heterogeneity of long-history migration explains cultural differences in reports of emotional expressivity and the functions of smiles. *Proceedings of the National Academy of Sciences, 112*(19), E2429–E2436. doi:10.1073/pnas.1413661112.

Sander, D., Grandjean, D., & Scherer, K. R. (2005). A systems approach to appraisal mechanisms in emotion. *Neural Networks, 18*(4), 317–352. doi:10.1016/j.neunet.2005.03.001.

Scherer, K. R. (1997). The role of culture in emotion-antecedent appraisal. *Journal of Personality and Social Psychology, 73*(5), 902. doi:10.1037/0022–3514.73.5.902.

Scherer, K. R. (2009). The dynamic architecture of emotion: Evidence for the component process model. *Cognition and Emotion, 23*(7), 1307–1351. doi:10.1080/02699930902928969.

Scherer, K. R., Banse, R., & Wallbott, H. G. (2001). Emotion inferences from vocal expression correlate across languages and cultures. *Journal of Cross-Cultural Psychology, 32*(1), 76–92. doi:10.1177/0022022101032001009.

Scherer, K. R., Matsumoto, D., Wallbott, H. G., & Kudoh, T. (1988). Emotional experience in cultural context: A comparison between Europe, Japan, and the USA. In K. R. Scherer (Ed.), *Facets of emotion: Recent research* (pp. 5–30). Hillsdale, NJ: Erlbaum.

Schimmack, U., Oishi, S., & Diener, E. (2002). Cultural influences on the relation between pleasant emotions and unpleasant emotions: Asian dialectic philosophies or individualism-collectivism? *Cognition & Emotion, 16*(6), 705–719. doi:10.1080/02699930143000590.

Shiota, M. N., Campos, B., Gonzaga, G. C., Keltner, D., & Peng, K. (2010). I love you but . . . : Cultural differences in complexity of emotional experience during interaction with a romantic partner. *Cognition and Emotion, 24*(5), 786–799. doi:10.1080/02699930902990480.

Shweder, R. A. (1993). The cultural psychology of the emotions. In M. Lewis & J. M. Haviland (Eds.), *Handbook of emotions* (pp. 417–443). New York: Guilford Press.

Shweder, R. A. (1994). "You're not sick, you're just in love": Emotion as an interpretive system. In P. Ekman & R. Davidson (Eds.), *The nature of emotions: Fundamental questions* (pp. 32–44). New York: Oxford University Press.

Shweder, R. A. (2002). The nature of morality: The category of bad acts. *Medical Ethics, 9*(1), 6–7.

Shweder, R. A. (2003). Toward a deep cultural psychology of shame. *Social Research, 70*: 1401–1422.

Shweder, R. A., & Haidt, J. (2000). The cultural psychology of the emotions: Ancient and new. In M. Lewis & J. Haviland (Ed.), *Handbook of emotions* (2nd ed., pp. 397–414). New York: Guilford.

Sievers, B., Polansky, L., Casey, M., & Wheatley, T. (2013). Music and movement share a dynamic structure that supports universal expressions of emotion. *Proceedings of the National Academy of Sciences, 110*(1), 70–75. doi:10.1073/pnas.1209023110.

Sims, T., Tsai, J. L., Koopmann-Holm, B., Thomas, E. A., & Goldstein, M. K. (2014). Choosing a physician depends on how you want to feel: The role of ideal affect in health-related decision making. *Emotion, 14*(1), 187. doi:10.1037/a0034372.

Smith, P. B., & Schwartz, S. H. (1999). Values. In M. H. Segall & C. Kagitcibasi (Eds.), *Handbook of cross-cultural psychology* (Vol. 3, pp. 77–118). Boston, MA: Allyn & Bacon.

Snowdon, C. T., Zimmermann, E., & Altenmüller, E. (2015). Music evolution and neuroscience. *Progress in Brain Research, 217*, 17–34. doi:10.1016/bs.pbr.2014.11.019.

Solomon, R. C. (1995). *A passion for justice: Emotions and the origins of the social contract.* Lanham, MD: Rowman & Littlefield.

Soto, J. A., Levenson, R. W., & Ebling, R. (2005). Cultures of moderation and expression: Emotional experience, behavior, and physiology in Chinese Americans and Mexican Americans. *Emotion, 5*(2), 154–165. doi: 10.1037/1528-3542.5.2.154.

Soto, J. A., Perez, C. R., Kim, Y. H., Lee, E. A., & Minnick, M. R. (2011). Is expressive suppression always associated with poorer psychological functioning? A cross-cultural comparison between European Americans and Hong Kong Chinese. *Emotion, 11*(6), 1450. doi:10.1037/a0023340.

Srivastava, S., Tamir, M., McGonigal, K. M., John, O. P., & Gross, J. J. (2009). The social costs of emotional suppression: A prospective study of the transition to college. *Journal of Personality and Social Psychology, 96*(4), 883. doi:10.1037/a0014755.

Suh, E., Diener, E., Oishi, S., & Triandis, H. C. (1998). The shifting basis of life satisfaction judgments across cultures: Emotions versus norms. *Journal of Personality and Social Psychology, 74*(2), 482. doi:10.1037/0022–3514.74.2.482.

Tomkins, S. S. (1962). *Affect, imagery, consciousness: Vol. 1: The positive effects.* New York: Springer-Verlag.

Triandis, H. C. (1995). *Individualism & collectivism.* Boulder, CO: Westview Press.

Tsai, J. L., & Chentsova-Dutton, U. (2003). Variation among European Americans in emotional facial expression. *Journal of Cross-Cultural Psychology, 34*(6), 650–657. doi:10.1177/0022022103256846.

Tsai, J. L., Chim, L., & Sims, T. (2015). Consumer behavior, culture, and emotion. In S. Ng & A. Lee (Eds.), *Handbook of culture and consumer behavior* (p. 68–98). New York, NY: Oxford University Press. doi:10.1093/acprof:oso/9780199388516.003.0004.

Tsai, J. L., Levenson, R. W., & McCoy, K. (2006). Cultural and temperamental variation in emotional response. *Emotion, 6*(3), 484. doi:10.1037/1528–3542.6.3.484.

Tsai, J. L., Louie, J. Y., Chen, E. E., & Uchida, Y. (2007). Learning what feelings to desire: Socialization of ideal affect through children's storybooks. *Personality and Social Psychology Bulletin, 33*(1), 17–30. doi:10.1177/0146167206292749.

Tsai, J. L., Miao, F. F., & Seppala, E. (2007). Good feelings in Christianity and Buddhism: Religious differences in ideal affect. *Personality and Social Psychology Bulletin, 33*(3), 409–421. doi:10.1177/0146167206296107.

Uchida, Y., & Kitayama, S. (2009). Happiness and unhappiness in east and west: Themes and variations. *Emotion, 9*(4), 441. doi:10.1037/a0015634.

Uchida, Y., Townsend, S. S., Markus, H. R., & Bergsieker, H. B. (2009). Emotions as within or between people? Cultural variation in lay theories of emotion expression and inference. *Personality and Social Psychology Bulletin, 35*(11), 1427–1439. doi:10.1177/0146167209347322.

Van Bezooijen, R., Otto, S. A., & Heenan, T. A. (1983). Recognition of vocal expressions of emotion: A three-nation study to identify universal characteristics. *Journal of Cross-Cultural Psychology*, 14(4), 387–406. doi:10.1177/0022002183014004001.

Vignoles, V. L., Owe, E., Becker, M., Smith, P. B., Easterbrook, M. J., Brown, R., . . . & Lay, S. (2016). Beyond the 'East–West' Dichotomy: Global Variation in Cultural Models of Selfhood. Journal of Experimental Psychology: General, 1145, 966–1000.

Wickline, V. B., Bailey, W., & Nowicki, S. (2009). Cultural in-group advantage: Emotion recognition in African American and European American faces and voices. *The Journal of Genetic Psychology*, *170*(1), 5–30. doi:10.3200/gntp.170.1.5–30.

Wierzbicka, A. (1986). Italien reduplication: Cross-cultural pragmatics and illocutionary semantics. *Linguistics, 24*(2). doi:10.1515/ling.1986.24.2.287.

Wierzbicka, A. (1992). Talking about emotions: Semantics, culture, and cognition. *PCEM*, 6(3), 285–319. doi:10.1080/02699939208411073.

Wood, A., Rychlowska, M., & Niedenthal, P. (2016). Heterogeneity of long-history migration predicts emotion recognition accuracy. *Emotion, 16*(4), 413–420. doi: 10.1037/emo0000137.

Yamaguchi, S. (1994). Collectivism among the Japanese: A perspective from the self. In U. Kim, H. C. Triandis, C. Kagitcibasi, S. C. Choi & G. Yoon (Eds.), *Individualism and collectivism* (pp. 175–188). Newbury Park, CA: Sage.

Index